Mothers at Work: Effects on Children's Well-being

This important book examines the effects of the mother's employment on family life and children's well-being. It starts with a thorough review of previous research on this topic and then reports the results of a study designed to answer the key questions that emerge. The study focuses on 369 families with an elementary school child, living in an industrialized city in the Midwest. They include both one-parent and two-parent families, African Americans and Whites, and a broad range of economic circumstances. Extensive data have been obtained from mothers, fathers, children, teachers, classroom peers, and school records. The analysis reveals how the mother's employment status affects the father's role, the mother's sense of well-being, and child-rearing patterns and how these, in turn, affect the child.

Mothers at Work provides an intimate picture of urban life and how families cope with mothers' employment. It will be valuable reading for social workers, therapists, policy makers, and scholars in child development and women's studies.

Lois W. Hoffman is Professor Emerita of Psychology at University of Michigan, Ann Arbor. She is author of *Working Mothers, The Employed Mother in America,* and the textbook *Developmental Psychology Today.*

Lise M. Youngblade is Instructor and Research Associate in the Department of Psychology, University of Colorado at Colorado Springs.

Cambridge Studies in Social and Emotional Development

Mothers at Work

Effects on Children's Well-being

LOIS W. HOFFMAN

LISE M. YOUNGBLADE

with

Rebekah Levine Coley
Allison Sidle Fuligni
Donna Dumm Kovacs

CAMBRIDGE
UNIVERSITY PRESS

PUBLISHED BY THE PRESS SYNDICATE OF THE UNIVERSITY OF CAMBRIDGE
The Pitt Building, Trumpington Street, Cambridge, United Kingdom

CAMBRIDGE UNIVERSITY PRESS
The Edinburgh Building, Cambridge CB2 2RU, UK   http://www.cup.cam.ac.uk
40 West 20th Street, New York, NY 10011-4211, USA   http://www.cup.org
10 Stamford Road, Oakleigh, Melbourne 3166, Australia

First published 1999

Printed in the United States of America

Typeface Times Roman 10.25/13 pt   *System* QuarkXPress™   [HT]

A catalog record for this book is available from the British Library

Library of Congress Cataloging-in-Publication Data is available

ISBN 0 521 57289 4 hardback
ISBN 0 521 66896 4 paperback

This book is dedicated with love to our children and grandchildren:

Elena Julia Levine Coley
Maya Louise Levine Coley
Eric Karl Diehl
Christopher Walter Diehl
Benjamin Dean Fuligni
Gabriel Luke Fuligni
Jill Adrienne Hoffman
Sarah Leila Ahmed
Amy Gabrielle Kilroy
Nicole Erin Kilroy
Allison Leigh Kilroy

Contents

Preface

Few would challenge the statement that one of the major social changes in the United States is the increased employment of mothers. For mothers with children under age eighteen, the United States has gone from less than 30 percent in the labor force in 1960 to less than 30 percent *not* in the labor force today. Yet, despite the fact that there have been numerous studies of the effects of mothers working over the years, we still know very little about how a mother's employment status affects her family, her children, and her own well-being. The prevailing view that mothers' employment is a social problem has been challenged in recent publications, but few empirical studies have really examined how being a mother with a paid job or one who is a full-time homemaker affects family life and children's development. That is the focus of this book.

In this book, we first review the previous literature and then present a study designed to trace the impact of the mother's employment status on three aspects of family life – the father's role, the mother's well-being, and the parents' childrearing orientations – and how these, in turn, affect children. The study focuses on 369 families with a child in the third or fourth grades of the public schools in an industrialized city in the Midwest. They represent a broad socioeconomic range and include both one-parent and two-parent families, African Americans and Whites. Extensive data have been obtained from mothers, fathers, children, teachers, classroom peers, and school records. Throughout the book, attention is given to how socioeconomic conditions, the mother's marital status, ethnicity, and the child's gender affect these patterns.

This study was a group endeavor. Although the basic plan and design was set by the senior author, the research involved a considerable number of others, primarily graduate and undergraduate students at the University of Michigan.

xi

Two former graduate students, Rebekah Levine Coley and Allison Sidle Fuligni, were partners in this project from the beginning. The original plan was to include only two-parent families because of the particular interest in the father's role, but Dr. Coley was particularly interested in single-mother families, and it was her influence that led to their inclusion, thus enormously enriching the research. She modified the mother interview for single mothers, recruited other graduate students to take part in interviewing the children, and played a major role throughout the study. Allison Sidle Fuligni directed the field operation, supervised the coding, and was a major force in keeping the whole project moving and organized. The third core member of the team was Donna Dumm Kovacs, who brought her expertise to the data processing. All three traveled daily to the study site to collect classroom data and interview the children individually. Each had her own area of interest and completed her doctoral dissertation with data from the project, but it seemed appropriate that they should also be part of this book, which reports the major results of our investigation. Thus, each took part in writing specific chapters, and their contributions are noted there.

Lise Youngblade joined the project at a later point. She took charge of the statistical analyses and became a co-author. Drs. Hoffman and Youngblade planned the book together. Although each took responsibility for specific chapters, both contributed to all of the chapters.

In addition to the core group, several of the Michigan Developmental Psychology graduate students joined us in our trips to the study site to obtain classroom data and interview the children in the study individually. These included John Coley, Gil Diesendruck, Karen Fingerman, Michelle Hollander, John Seale, and Marianne Taylor. The coding of the children's stories of their After School Day was carried out by Rebekah Levine Coley, John Coley, Tamara Halle, and Marianne Taylor. Marianne Taylor also helped develop the measure of children's gender-role attitudes. Kate Wadsworth joined the project after the data were collected but was an intrinsic part of the group contributing statistical and computer assistance.

Undergraduates who participated in either the data collection or coding included Juan Casas, Shari Cook, Joanna Fischer, Elisa Golden, Jeff Haessler, Bryan Husk, Heather Lackey, Deanna Nagels, Mary Rubio, Lucinda Steenberger, Rachel Story, Kelly Taylor, and Jason Wanacek. We particularly want to thank Mary Jo Beck, who helped in many ways – as financial accountant, secretary, collector of teacher ratings, and all-around trouble shooter.

We are deeply grateful to the Office of Administration of the Public Schools in the city where the study took place, the principals of the participating schools, and the teachers for their cooperation with this project. The success of this study, however, is due mainly to the children and parents who so openly shared their feelings and experiences with us. Finally, we want to thank the William T. Grant Foundation, which funded the project from its inception to its completion and came through when events took some unexpected turns.

1   Introduction and Review of the Literature

Introduction

This book examines the effects of the mother's employment on family life and children's well-being. It starts with a review of the previous research and then reports the results of a study designed to answer the questions that emerge. The study focuses on 369 families with a child in the third or fourth grades of the public schools in an industrialized city in the Midwest. They represent a broad socioeconomic range and include both one-parent and two-parent families, African Americans and Whites. Extensive data have been obtained from mothers, fathers, children, teachers, classroom peers, and school records. The guiding hypothesis that emerges from the review of previous research is that maternal employment has few, if any, direct effects on the child; it operates mainly through the effect on the family. Three aspects of family life seem particularly important in mediating child effects: the role of the father, the mother's sense of well-being, and the parents' childrearing attitudes and behaviors. The data analyses reported here trace each of these links and reveal how the mother's employment affects family life and, by that route, affects child outcomes.

The book is divided into three parts. The first includes a review of the previous research and a description of the study. The second reports the results of the analyses that examine how the mother's employment status affects the father's role in the family, the mother's sense of well-being, and childrearing patterns. The third section deals with the effects on the child and how these are mediated or moderated by the effects on the three dimensions of family life. Throughout the book, attention is given to how socioeconomic conditions, the mother's marital status, ethnicity, and the child's gender affect these patterns. We start in this chapter with a review of the literature that served as background to our study.

Review of Previous Research

Any review of the research on the effects of maternal employment in the United States must first place the pattern in its social context. Currently, most mothers in the United States are employed. Not only is this true for mothers of school-aged children, as it has been for two decades, but it is also true for mothers of infants less than one year old (U.S. Bureau of the Census, 1997). The pace with which maternal employment rates have increased to this point, however, is so rapid that many people fail to realize its prevalence. Furthermore, attempts to understand its effects often ignore the fact that this change is part of a whole complex of social changes. Both employed mothers and homemakers today live in a very different environment than their counterparts forty or even twenty years ago.

There are few social changes that are so easy to document as the increased employment of mothers in the United States. The steady rise in maternal employment rates over the years is clearly illustrated in Table 1.1. The pattern, rare in 1940, had become modal by 1977. By 1996, 70 percent of the mothers with children under eighteen were in the labor force.

Maternal employment rates still differ by age of the youngest child, but this difference has diminished as the greatest recent increases have occurred among married mothers of infants and preschoolers. The rate of employment for married mothers of infants one or under almost doubled between 1975 and 1995, from 30.8 percent to 59 percent (Table 1.2). As Table 1.3 shows, in 1960 18.6 percent of all married mothers of preschoolers were employed, but by 1996, that rate had jumped to 62.7 percent.

Table 1.3 also indicates another change over the years. Whereas in 1960, employed mothers were more likely to be from single-parent families, this

Table 1.1. *Labor Force Participation Rates of Mothers with Children under 18, 1940 and 1946–1996*

Year	Percent in Labor Force
1940	8.6%
1946	18.2%
1956	27.5%
1966	35.8%
1976	48.8%
1986	62.5%
1996	70.0%

Table 1.2. *Labor Force Participation Rates for Wives, Husband Present, by Age of Youngest Child, 1975–1995 (in percent)*

Age of Youngest Child	1975	1985	1995
1 year or younger	30.8	49.4	59.0
2 years	37.1	54.0	66.7
3 years	41.2	55.1	65.5
4 years	41.2	59.7	67.7
5 years	44.4	62.1	69.6
6 to 13 years	51.8	68.2	74.9
14 to 17 years	53.5	67.0	79.6

difference has now vanished. For single mothers who have been married, the current employment rates are just slightly higher than those of married mothers, while both groups show higher rates than never-married mothers. The statistics in these three tables document a major social change in the United States.

It is reasonable to assume that a mother's employment status affects the child's development – that the accommodation to the dual demands of employment and parenting influences the family structure, functioning, interaction patterns, and childrearing orientations, which, in turn, have significance for child outcomes. Yet, in fact, we know amazingly little about what the differences are between these families and how such differences affect children.

Table 1.3. *Labor Force Participation Rates for Mothers by Marital Status and Age of Youngest Child, 1960–1996 (in percent)*

Year	Married		Widowed, Divorced, Separated		Never Married	
	6 to 17 years	Under 6 years	6 to 17 years	Under 6 years	6 to 17 years	Under 6 years
1960	39.0	18.6	65.9	40.5	NA	NA
1970	49.2	30.3	66.9	52.2	NA	NA
1980	61.7	45.1	74.6	60.3	67.6	44.1
1990	73.6	58.9	79.7	63.6	69.7	48.7
1996	76.7	62.7	80.6	69.2	71.8	55.1

NA, not available.

There are two major reasons for this lack of knowledge. First, much of the research in this area fails to take account of the social changes that have occurred. Maternal employment research is often built on data collected in the 1950s, as though family life had remained unchanged. However, as maternal employment patterns have changed over the years, so, too, have other aspects of society and particularly the family. Family size in America has decreased, the management of a household has become more efficient, marital stability has declined, notions of what a person should expect from life have changed, women's roles have been reconceptualized, childrearing orientations are different, and the adult roles for which children are being socialized are not the same as they once were. The selective factors that determine which women will seek employment and which will not have been altered; what was once the deviant choice is now the modal choice. It is not only the employed mother today who must justify her role and cope with possible guilt and anxiety about how this affects her children, but also the full-time homemaker who feels a need to explain her decision and to defend her failure to contribute economically to the family and to conform to the new image of women (Hoffman, 1984b, 1989).

Second, in all of the research during the last forty years, it has been clear that the mother's employment status is not so robust a variable that the simple comparison of the children of employed and nonemployed mothers will reveal consistent differences (Hoffman, 1961, 1974, 1979, 1989). For one thing, relationships had to be examined with attention to other variables that moderated effects; particularly important were social class, the mother's marital status, whether the employment was full- or part-time, the parents' attitudes, and the child's gender. In addition, the research needed to examine the relationships between the mother's employment status and the more proximal variables that mediated the effects on the child. It needed to consider, for example, how maternal employment affected the child's experience in the family and how these experiences, in turn, influenced child outcomes. Unfortunately, few studies have sought indirect effects through linkages, and fewer still have adopted a mediation model in studying the effects of employment on children.

This review begins with a summary of the research that has examined the direct relationship between the mother's employment status and child outcomes and then concentrates on the three variables that have emerged as most likely to be mediators of child outcomes: the father's role, the mother's state of well being, and parent–child interaction patterns. A final section describes the efforts to examine socioeconomic, marital status, and ethnic differences in maternal employment effects. Studies of the effects of day care, other forms of nonmaternal care, and after-school care will be reviewed in Chapter 11.

Differences Between Children of Employed and Nonemployed Mothers

Most of the studies that have compared the children of employed and nonemployed mothers on child outcome measures (e.g., indices of cognitive and socioemotional development) have failed to find significant differences (Heynes, 1982; Zaslow, 1987). The research that has shown reasonably consistent differences has examined the relationships within subgroups based on social class and gender. Patterns that have been revealed over the years include the following:

1. Daughters of employed mothers have been found to have higher academic achievement, greater career success, more nontraditional career choices, and greater occupational commitment (Alessandri, 1992; Eccles & Hoffman, 1984; Hoffman, 1979, 1980).

2. Studies of children in poverty, in both two-parent and single-mother families, found higher cognitive scores and higher scores on socioemotional indices for children with employed mothers (Cherry & Eaton, 1977; Heynes, 1978; Kreisberg, 1970; Vandell & Ramanan, 1992).

3. A few studies have found that sons of employed mothers in the middle class showed lower school performance and lower IQ scores during the grade school years. Although two recent studies did not replicate this finding (Gottfried, Gottfried & Bathurst, 1988; Stevenson, 1982), a third did (Desai, Chase-Lansdale, & Michael, 1989).

4. Some nonacademic differences between characteristics of children with employed and nonemployed mothers have also been found, but with less consistency. Daughters of employed mothers have been found to be more independent, particularly in interaction with their peers in a school setting (Hoffman, 1974, 1979; Schachter, 1981; Siegel, Stolz, Hitchcock, & Adamson, 1963), and to score higher on socioemotional adjustment measures (Alessandri, 1992; Gold & Andres, 1978a). Results for sons have been quite mixed and vary with social class, preschool experience, and age at testing (Zaslow, 1987).

5. Sons and daughters of employed mothers have less traditional sex-role ideologies (Hoffman, 1979, 1989).

The Father's Role

In addition, several studies have found relationships between the mother's employment status and family patterns that, in turn, have been related to children's sex-role attitudes, academic performance, and social competence. Of particular note is the father's participation in household tasks and child care. Fathers play a more active role when the mother is employed (Gottfried, Gottfried, & Bathurst, 1988; Gottfried, Bathurst, & Gottfried, 1994; Hoffman, 1983, 1986; Pleck, 1983). Three possible consequences of this increased participation of fathers have been suggested:

1. It mitigates the mother's potential overload from the dual role.
2. A less traditional model of adult roles is presented.
3. It enhances the child's cognitive development.

Relief for the Mother. There is some support for the first suggested consequence: In a national sample study, Kessler and McRae (1982) found that among currently married mothers, the higher morale of employed mothers commonly reported in the research holds only when their husbands help with child care.

Less Gender Role Traditionalism. There is also evidence for the second possible consequence. The increased participation of fathers associated with the mother's employment has been found to extend across the traditional division of labor. For example, Baruch and Barnett (1987) found that in single-wage families, more active fathers participate by spending more time with their children, but are not as likely to take part in child care and household tasks. In dual-wage families, on the other hand, a merging of roles is more common. Research has shown that fathers in dual-wage families participate more in family tasks traditionally carried out by mothers (Hoffman, 1983, 1986; Pleck, 1983). This effect is more pronounced when the mother is employed full-time, when there is more than one child, and when there are no older children in the family, particularly no older daughters. Furthermore, some studies indicate that the effect is more pronounced when the mother's income approaches the father's (Model, 1981; Scanzoni, 1978). The fact that the husbands of employed mothers are more active in household tasks and child care also appears to be a causal relationship, and not merely a selective factor, because the relationship holds even when sex-role ideology is controlled (Crouter & Huston, 1985; Hoffman, 1986), and it is frequently reported by parents as an effect of employment (Gottfried,

Gottfried, & Bathurst, 1988; Hoffman, 1983). Because father involvement has increased generally in recent years (Bond, Galinsky, & Swansberg, 1998; Hill & Stafford, 1980; Pleck, 1983), it has been suggested that there also has been an increased responsiveness by fathers to their wives' employment (Lamb, 1981).

The effects of maternal employment on the traditional division of labor in the family are important in several respects. In particular, it is likely that this is one of the routes by which maternal employment operates to diminish sex-role traditionalism. The employment of a mother calls for some accommodation by the father. Although the response has been modest, there has been some, and this, in turn, diminishes traditionalistic attitudes in families (Baruch & Barnett, 1986b). Data have shown that the relationship between the father's participation and children's diminished sex-role traditionalism is significantly stronger in the employed-mother families than in the families with nonemployed mothers (Baruch & Barnett, 1986b). This difference may reflect the nature of the father's participation: in the employed-mother family there is more of a merging of roles between the parents, while in the nonemployed-mother family, the involved father spends more time with the children but the traditional sex-based division of labor is maintained (Baruch & Barnett, 1987; Crouter, Perry-Jenkins, Huston, & McHale, 1987). The repeated finding that the children of employed mothers hold less stereotyped attitudes about sex roles than do the children of nonemployed mothers may be at least partly explained by the intermediating effect on the parental division of labor. The children's nonstereotyped attitudes might be because of the parents' attitudes but also because they observe their parents' less traditional roles.

Cognitive Enhancement. The third hypothesis is that fathers' involvement with children *enhances* the child's cognitive abilities and that by this route employed mothers' children are more advantaged than the children of full-time homemakers (Hoffman, 1980; Gold & Andres, 1978a; Gottfried, Gottfried, & Bathurst, 1988). There are two forms of this idea.

One of these is specific for daughters: that is, father participation may decrease gender-role stereotyping, and this may have positive effects on daughters' achievement motivation and behavior. Since daughters of employed mothers are often found to have higher cognitive scores as children and to show higher achievement patterns as adults, this is a viable hypothesis, but the actual chain of connection – from maternal employment, to father participation, to decreased traditionalism, to daughters' higher achievement – has not previously been empirically examined.

The other hypothesis is that father–child interaction is particularly cognitively stimulating, especially with respect to competence in math. This hypothesis derives from earlier research that compared achievement test scores of children in single-mother families and two-parent families and found such advantages for the latter group. This body of work has been criticized and the suggestion has been made that it is not the presence of the father but the financial advantage of a father that accounts for the difference (Barber & Eccles, 1992; Herzog & Sudia, 1973). Nevertheless, Gottfried, Gottfried, and Bathurst (1988) found that higher involvement of fathers was associated with children's higher cognitive scores within a primarily two-parent sample with social class controlled.

Such results, however, do not mean that father involvement per se has a special advantage. They might mean that the benefits for children stem from having an additional adult of either gender involved – that it is augmented parenting that is advantageous. This possibility receives some support from the research of Dornbusch and his colleagues (1985), which indicated that some of the problems associated with single-mother status are mitigated by the presence of an additional adult of either gender. It is possible that father involvement in employed-mother families compensates for lesser interaction with employed mothers, but does not provide an overall enhancement of the child's environment. As yet, no study has actually demonstrated special benefits of fathers' involvement with children. Neither are there any data showing that the father's involvement mediates cognitive or achievement outcomes in employed-mother families – either compensation or enhancement (Gold & Andres, 1978a; Gottfried, Gottfried, & Bathurst, 1988).

In summary, then, the data show that the father's role in the family is affected by the mother's employment status. They also show that his role has significance for child outcomes. More attention needs to be given, however, to how different aspects of the father's participation in household tasks and child care affect children. Such research should separately examine families with employed mothers and those with full-time housewives. The separate examination is particularly important because data suggest that the nature and effects of father participation are different in the employed-mother family than in the nonemployed-mother family (Barnett & Baruch, 1987; Crouter & Crowley, 1990; Crouter, Perry-Jenkins, Huston, & McHale, 1987). For example, Crouter and her colleagues (1987) found that the increased involvement of fathers associated with mothers' employment includes functional rather than fun activities. A fuller understanding of these issues could shed light on the higher achievement patterns so often

found for daughters of employed mothers: the diminished sex-role traditionalism in dual-wage families could be the important link. Further, either
the greater interaction between fathers and children or specific patterns of
interaction could be involved in the link between the mother's employment
status and children's cognitive abilities.

The Marital Relationship. A research issue that has been considered is
whether the mother's employment status affects the marital relationship.
Further, the possibility has been raised that the father's participation in
household tasks and child care may moderate such effects (Hoffman, 1989).

Most studies investigating the effects of maternal employment on marital satisfaction find no difference (Smith, 1985; Warr & Perry, 1982). When
differences are found, a negative correlation between maternal employment
and marital satisfaction occurs more often when there is sex-role traditionalism, resentment of the employment by either parent, a lower-class
sample, or the father is the reporter. A positive relationship is more likely to
be found when the sample is educated or middle class, the mother wants to
work, the work is part-time, or the mother is the reporter (Hoffman, 1986).
In several studies of highly educated *dual-career* couples, both parents
report that the mother's career has enhanced their marriage, despite the
inconveniences it has caused (Emmons et al., 1987; Gilbert, 1985). It is
interesting also to note that for employed women, the impact of marital
stress seems to be less pervasive (Weinraub, Jaeger, & Hoffman, 1988), and
work provides a buffer against debilitating anxiety (Cleary & Mechanic,
1983; Hetherington, 1979; Stewart & Malley, 1987; Stewart & Salt, 1981).

Consistent with the idea that the nature and significance of the father's
participation in child care may be different in single-wage and dual-wage
families, however, high father participation has been found to be related to
fathers' marital dissatisfaction in dual-wage families and not in single-wage
(Baruch & Barnett, 1987; Crouter et al., 1987). The reason for the different relationships to marital satisfaction is not clear, but there are at least
two possible explanations. One is that because the father's participation in
child care in the dual-wage family may not be intrinsically motivated, he
may resent it. There is evidence that fathers in dual-wage families often
complain about their wives' availability for child care and indicate concern
that their own careers may be suffering because of the family demands on
their time (Baruch & Barnett, 1986a, 1987; Emmons et al., 1987; Gilbert,
1985). Another possible explanation has to do with the nature of the
father's involvement. As already noted, in single-wage families, the active
fathers participate by spending time with their children, but not by carrying

out the child care and household tasks, as active fathers do in dual-wage families. This pattern of participation may not only be more pleasurable, but it may also avoid the conflicts that can emerge when both parents are involved in the same activities (Hoffman, 1983). Little attention has been paid to the role of marital satisfaction as a possible link between a mother's employment status and child outcomes, but it may be an important one, both in terms of the direct effect of the marriage relationship on children and through its effects on the mother's morale.

The Mother's Sense of Well-being

Another aspect of family life that is often seen as linking the mother's employment status to effects on the child is the mother's sense of well-being, and numerous studies have compared employed mothers to full-time homemakers on various indices of mental health and life satisfaction. Most of this research has found a higher level of satisfaction among the employed. These results have been found for professional women (Birnbaum, 1975) and for blue-collar workers (Ferree, 1976), in national samples (Kessler & McRae, 1982; Veroff, Douvan, & Kukla, 1981) and in more homogeneous ones (Gold & Andres, 1978a, 1978b). In addition, employed mothers have been found to score lower on psychosomatic symptoms, measures of depression, and various stress indicators (Burke & Weir, 1976; Kessler & McRae, 1982; McLoyd, Jayaratne, Ceballo, & Borquez, 1994). Furthermore, employment has been shown to be a source of psychological support in times of family difficulties (Cleary & Mechanic, 1983; Hetherington, 1979; Stewart & Malley, 1987; Stewart & Salt, 1981). Nevertheless, these relationships can be affected by the mother's attitude toward the job (Gove & Zeiss, 1987; Baruch & Barnett, 1987; Staines, Pleck, Shepard, & O'Conner, 1978), by the stability of child-care arrangements (Goldberg & Easterbrooks, 1988), and, as already noted, by the father's participation in child care (Kessler & McRae, 1982).

Although the bulk of the research on employment status and mothers' mental health has found higher morale among employed mothers, some investigators found no significant differences (Baruch & Barnett, 1986c; Radloff, 1980; Repetti & Crosby, 1984; Ross, Mirowsky, & Huber, 1983). However, despite an extensive search, we found no study that showed the mental health of full-time homemakers to be higher than that of employed women, and this same conclusion is reported in other reviews (Repetti, Mathews, & Waldron, 1989; Warr & Parry, 1982b). Because most of this research has been conducted with middle-class samples, it has sometimes been suggested that the absence of negative mental health effects of employment is a result peculiar to the middle class. In fact, however, the mental health advantage of employment is more consistently found in working class or poverty samples (Ferree, 1976; Warr & Parry, 1982a; McLoyd, Jayaratne, Ceballo, & Borquez, 1994), an observation also made by Warr and Parry (1982b).

This social-class difference may seem surprising since the jobs available to middle-class women are generally considered more attractive (Menaghan & Parcel, 1990). Furthermore, recent research has shown positive effects on mothers and children associated with the job characteristics of complexity, autonomy, and challenge (Greenberger, O'Neil, & Nagel, 1994; Menaghan & Parcel, 1995), and middle-class jobs are more likely to offer these qualities than are working-class jobs. It may be, however, that for working-class women, the satisfactions from employment are not from the job per se but from the increased social support and stimulation provided by co-workers, the marked advantages that their wages bring to their families, and the greater sense of control they feel over their lives. This hypothesis is supported by several studies of working-class mothers (Ferree, 1976; Rosen, 1987).

It is also possible that the alternative role of full-time homemaker is a less attractive one in the lower class than in the middle class, so the advantage of employment for working-class mothers comes primarily from higher levels of depression among the working-class homemakers. In other words, the morale advantage of employment in the lower class may be relative to the particularly unhappy state of the homemakers in that class. In addition, as noted above, several studies have shown that employment can serve as a buffer against stress and depression both of which are more prevalent in lower socioeconomic circumstances. This social class difference is important because previous research has also shown more consistent advantages of maternal employment for children in the working class than in the middle class (Desai, Chase-Lansdale, & Michael, 1988; Gold & Andres, 1978b, 1978c; Hoffman, 1979; Zaslow, 1987). It is possible that the greater advantage of maternal employment for working-class children is mediated by its more positive effect on the mother's sense of well-being.

A large body of research demonstrates a positive relationship between maternal mental health and both more effective parenting and children's cognitive and emotional adjustment (Yarrow, 1979; Downey & Coyne, 1990; Rutter, 1990; Lyons-Ruth, 1995). However, although previous research has demonstrated a relationship between the mother's employment status and her mental health, and other research has demonstrated a relationship between maternal mental health and both parenting and child outcomes, no previous study has examined the possibility that the mother's mental health or well-being mediates the relationship between employment status and either parenting styles or child outcomes. In one recent investigation, all three levels were examined: employment status, maternal depressed mood, and parenting styles. McLoyd, Jayaratne, Ceballo, and Borquez (1994), in a study of lower-class, single, African-American mothers of adolescents, found that full-time homemakers were more depressed than employed mothers, and also that depression was significantly related to both a negative perception of the maternal role and to the use of power-assertive discipline. However, no test was made to see if depression carried the relationship between the mother's employment status and her parenting style.

There is another body of research that is related to the issue of the mother's morale as the link between employment status and child outcomes. This focuses on the mother's satisfaction with her employment status. Several investigators have found that the mother's satisfaction with her role as a full-time homemaker or as an employed mother, a pattern called *congruence,* is associated with low scores on measures of depression (Hock & DeMeis, 1990; Ross, Mirowsky, & Huber, 1983), the quality of the mother–child relationship (Hock, 1980; Schubert, Bradley-Johnson, & Nuttal, 1980; Stuckey et al., 1982), and children's higher scores on cognitive and mental health indices (Farel, 1980; Guidubaldi & Nastasi, 1987). However, this research is confounded by the fact that the mother's role satisfaction can be a function, or expression, of her happier state, her attitude toward her child, or the child's level of functioning. The predictor and the outcome may not be independent. Furthermore, in several of these studies, closer examination of the data indicates that the relationship is carried by the dissatisfied homemakers (Dienstag, 1986; Farel, 1980; Hock & DeMeis, 1990; Ross, Mirowsky, & Huber, 1983). It might be that the mother who is home full-time with her children and indicates a preference for employment is expressing dissatisfaction with her mother role, while the employed mother's dissatisfaction may indicate a preference for more time with her children. The consequences for mother–child interaction might then be different in each case.

Thus, although the empirical work to date suggests that a mother's employment status may affect family life and child outcomes through its effect on the mother's well-being, this has not been directly examined. Further, there is a need to more thoroughly assay the mother's sense of well-being and role satisfaction by tying it to other aspects of the family environment in order to disentangle the cause-and-effect aspect of the relationships. There is also a need to identify what conditions influence when employment has a positive effect on the mother's mental health, why such effects occur, and when such effects carry over to the child's well-being. Finally, the existing research, particularly the findings on maternal employment effects on mothers' morale, reveals a need to understand more fully how social context variables such as social class, ethnicity, and marital status affect these patterns.

Childrearing Patterns

Although several hypotheses in the literature suggest that a mother's employment status affects her children through its effects on childrearing practices, few studies have attempted to trace this linkage. Sometimes the researcher only examines the relationship between employment status and parenting attitudes or behavior. More often, however, the relationship between employment and child outcomes is examined and the childrearing orientation is simply inferred. But even in studies that have looked at both parenting and child outcomes, tests were not conducted to see if the outcomes were carried by the parenting effects. This research will be reviewed here, organized under three headings. The first examines mother–child interaction and concentrates on studies of infants and toddlers. The second concerns the dimensions of autonomy-granting, monitoring, encouragement of independence, and stress on achievement goals. The third describes research investigating how the gender of the child moderates the relationship between the mother's employment status and parent–child interaction.

Mother–Infant Interaction. Whereas most of the research discussed thus far has been conducted with school-aged children, the research that has looked directly at parent–child interaction has been conducted primarily with infants and preschoolers. For infants and young children, valid outcome measures are difficult to obtain and so parent–child interaction is studied instead (Hoffman, 1984a; 1989). These studies have looked at the quantity and quality of the mother–child interaction, the home environment as measured by the HOME (Caldwell & Bradley, 1987) or the Family Environment Scale (Moos & Moos, 1981), and the parent–child attachment relationship. In general, findings indicate that full-time employed mothers spend less time with their infants and preschoolers than do part-time and nonemployed mothers, but this effect diminishes with maternal education. Differences also diminish with the age of the child (Duckett & Richards,

1989; Hill & Stafford, 1980). In addition, the effect is also less when the nature of the interaction is considered. Data indicate that employed mothers tend to compensate for their absence in the proportion of direct interaction and in the amount of time with the child during nonwork hours and on weekends (Easterbrooks & Goldberg, 1985; Hoffman, 1984a). Several studies that used behavioral observations of mother–infant interaction showed that employed mothers were more highly interactive with their infants, particularly with respect to verbal stimulation (Hoffman, 1984a; Pedersen, Cain, Zaslow, & Anderson, 1982; Schubert, Bradley-Johnson, & Nuttal, 1980); one study, however, found the opposite – the full-time home-makers were the more interactive (Zaslow, Pederson, Suwalsky, Cain, & Fivel, 1985). In a study of toddlers, no difference was found in the mother's behavioral sensitivity in a problem-solving situation (Goldberg & Easterbrooks, 1988).

Three studies that compared the quality of the home environment using the HOME index (Caldwell & Bradley, 1987), a measure that includes ratings of mother–child interaction, found no differences between the families with employed and nonemployed mothers (Gottfried, Gottfried, & Bathurst, 1988; Mackinnon, Brody, & Stoneman, 1982; Owen & Cox, 1988). The study by Gottfried, Gottfried, and Bathurst (1988), a longitudinal investigation that examined the home environment from infancy through age 7, and in a later publication through age 12 (Gottfried, Bathurst, & Gottfried, 1994), also found no differences on the Family Environment Scale.

A particularly active area of maternal employment research since 1980 has involved the comparison of dual-wage and single-wage families with respect to mother–infant attachment.[1] In most of these studies, no significant differences were found (Chase-Lansdale & Owen, 1987; Easterbrooks & Goldberg, 1988; Hock, 1980; Owen & Cox, 1988; Schwartz, 1983; Vaughn, Gove, & Egelund, 1980). However, in the research of Barglow, Vaughn, and Molitor (1987) and Belsky & Rovine (1988), the number of insecure attachments was statistically higher, although the majority of mother–infant attachments in the full-time employed-mother group was secure. Furthermore, in reviews that have combined subjects across studies (Belsky, 1988; Clarke-Stewart, 1989), full-time employed mothers were more likely than part-time employed and nonemployed mothers to have insecurely attached infants.

The results showing an association between early maternal employment and mother–infant attachment have received a great deal of attention in the media. However, the measure of attachment used in that research is the Strange Situation measure (Ainsworth, Blehar, Waters, & Wall, 1978). This measure has proven useful over the years in predicting subsequent child-hood behavior, but its validity had not been established for employed-mother families (Clarke-Stewart, 1989; Hoffman, 1989). In fact, in a follow-up of an earlier study, Vaughn, Deane, and Waters (1985) found that the measure did not predict later socioemotional competence for the early-employment group, even though it predicted well for the full-time home-maker group.

The measure is a laboratory measure and it assumes that the situation of entering an unfamiliar room, meeting a new adult, and experiencing two brief separations from the mother produces anxiety and activates attach-ment behavior. However, if such experiences are familiar to the child, as they are likely to be if the mother is employed, the child might not be anx-ious, and thus the behavior might not be a basis on which to judge the attachment relationship. In the studies that found more insecure attachment for the children with full-time employed mothers, the type of insecure attachment found was the *avoidant* pattern. The avoidant infant is one who seems to be independent, which might be a defense against anxiety, as it has been shown to be in earlier research (Sroufe & Waters, 1977). On the other hand, independence might be an appropriate behavior if the child is not anxious in the situation. Thus, distinguishing between avoidant insecu-rity and lack of anxiety can be difficult.

The most recent and most extensive investigation of these issues is an ongoing study of the effects of nonmaternal care in early childhood con-ducted by the National Institute of Child Health and Development. This is a collaborative effort involving multiple sites and a large team of prominent researchers. Data have been presented supporting the validity of the Strange Situation *as used in this study.* In this study, the amount of the non-maternal care (whether the infant received more than thirty hours a week or less than ten) was not related to the security of the attachment, nor was the child's age at onset of the mother's employment (NICHD Early Child Care Research Network, 1997b). The high quality of this investigation, and the fact that the consortium of investigators included researchers from both sides of this highly politicized issue, may have led to more precise coding operations, which eliminated the uncertainties sometimes involved in dif-ferentiating independence from insecure-avoidant attachment.

It should be added that a few studies have looked at maternal employ-ment during the early years in relation to child outcome measures obtained later. These investigations have been conducted with large longitudinal data sets that require complex analyses differentiating early from concurrent employment and exercising multiple controls (McCartney & Rosenthal,

1991; Heynes and Catsambis, 1986; Vandell & Ramanan, 1991). Because of these complications, the results of these efforts have been disappointing and, in several cases, different research teams have reported contradictory results with the same data set. For example, Belsky and Eggebeen (1991) and McCartney and Rosenthal (1991) analyzed the same data with different results; as did Milne, Myers, Rosenthal, and Ginsberg (1986) and Heynes and Catsambis (1986); and also Desai, Chase-Lansdale, and Michael (1989) and Baydar and Brooks-Gunn (1991). The difficulties of identifying long-term effects of early maternal employment are discussed more fully in previous reviews (e.g., Hoffman, 1984a).

Independence, Autonomy-Granting, and Achievement. A number of researchers have suggested, in post hoc discussions or theoretical papers, that the childrearing dimension that includes encouragement of independence, maturity demands, and autonomy-granting is the link between the mother's employment status and observed child outcomes (Bronfenbrenner & Crouter, 1982; Hoffman, 1979; Moore, 1975). This dimension can encompass the extremes of overprotection, on the one hand, and neglect, on the other. It is believed that employed mothers encourage independence in their children more than nonemployed. The encouragement of independence is consistent with the situational demands of the dual role, because it enables the family to function more effectively in the mother's absence (Hoffman, 1961, 1974, 1979, 1989). It has also been hypothesized that the child's growing independence may be threatening to the full-time home-maker who feels a need to justify her role choice by demonstrating the importance of her full-time presence in the home (Birnbaum, 1975; Hoffman, 1979).

This difference in childrearing orientations has been invoked as the explanation for the observation that daughters of employed mothers show more independence and higher professional achievements than daughters of nonemployed mothers. The latter, it is suggested, often receive too little encouragement of independence, a pattern noted to characterize traditional childrearing and one that is seen as detrimental to top academic and profes-sional achievement in females (Hoffman, 1972, 1977).

This same dimension has also been invoked to explain the pattern of lower school grades and I.Q. scores that has sometimes been found for mid-dle-class sons of employed mothers during the elementary school years and younger. Alternative hypotheses have been proposed to explain this pattern: (1) these results might reflect too much encouragement of dependency by full-time homemakers, which results in overconformity and better performance in grade school, where conformity is an academic asset for boys; or (2) employed mothers might grant sons too much autonomy, resulting in underconformity or too much peer influence. That is, because sons traditionally are granted more autonomy than daughters, an increment might be excessive. Furthermore, the impact of greater peer influence for boys is seen as more likely to be counter to adult standards (Bronfenbrenner & Crouter, 1982; Hoffman, 1979, 1980; Moore, 1975).

These hypotheses are predicated on the belief that employed mothers emphasize independence training and grant their children more autonomy than do nonemployed mothers. The data behind this assumed difference in childrearing, however, are far from solid. Most of the evidence comes from early research conducted in the 1950s and 1960s. Thus, Yarrow and her colleagues (1962) found, in a comparison of employed and nonemployed mothers of elementary-school children, that employed mothers who had not attended college were more likely to stress independence training and to assign their children more household responsibilities than their nonemployed counterparts, but they did not find differences among the college-educated mothers. Burchinal (1963) also found a greater stress on independence on the part of employed mothers across a sample of high-school aged children. McCord, McCord, and Thurber (1963) reported less overprotection by employed mothers and more encouragement of independence in a study of lower-income boys, but only for families identified as stable. Birnbaum's (1975) study of professionally employed mothers also suggests that they placed a higher value on independence for their children than did the comparison group of educated mothers who were full-time homemakers.

Only a few of the more recent studies have examined differences in parental attitudes toward independence or relevant childrearing patterns. Goldberg and Easterbrooks (1988) contrasted employed and nonemployed mothers of toddlers with respect to attitudes toward their child's independence and found no differences, while Gold and Andres (1978c) found that full-time employed mothers of preschool boys reported less overprotection, but there was no difference for mothers of daughters. New support for the idea that employed mothers encourage independence in their daughters, however, is provided in a recent study conducted with a sample of low-income, single-mother families with a child between ten and twelve years old (Alessandri, 1992). In this study, daughters of full-time employed mothers reported a greater emphasis on independence and achievement in their families, indicated higher scholastic competence, and showed higher academic performance in schools.

The greater emphasis on achievement by employed mothers was also found in the longitudinal research of Gottfried, Gottfried, and Bathurst (1988). This study was based on a middle-class sample of two-parent families. For both boys and girls, at ages five and seven, both contemporaneous and earlier maternal employment predicted to higher educational aspirations for children, more out-of-school lessons, and less TV-viewing by both mothers and children. Employed mothers were also more involved in discussing school activities with their children. Although these parental behaviors themselves predicted to a variety of measures of the children's academic competence, there was no direct relationship between the mother's employment status and the indices of child competence.

Recent studies (Bartko & McHale, 1991; Medrich, Roizen, Rubin & Buckley, 1982) have reconfirmed the greater participation of school-age children in household tasks and self-care (e.g., cleaning their own room) when mothers are employed, a finding that has remained fairly solid over the years. This pattern has been seen as promoting responsibility and maturity in children (Bartko & McHale, 1991; Elder, 1974).

On the other hand, the widely believed idea that employed mothers' children are less well monitored has received little support, either in the past (Hoffman, 1974) or in recent research. Crouter, MacDermid, McHale, and Perry-Jenkins (1990), in a study of nine- to twelve-year-old children from small towns and rural areas, found no effects of the mother's employment status or child gender on parental monitoring. They did find, however, that unmonitored boys, but not girls, had lower school grades and felt less competent academically. In addition, they found more conduct problems among less well-monitored boys in the dual-wage families than for such boys in single-wage families or for girls, suggesting that the consequences of inadequate supervision might be more serious for sons of employed mothers even though the degree of supervision was not less. The results suggesting more negative consequences of insufficient monitoring of boys than girls are consistent with hypotheses proposed by Bronfenbrenner and Crouter (1982) and Hoffman (1979) discussed earlier.

Thus, a limited body of data has documented differences between employed-mother families and nonemployed-mother families in their behavior and expectations regarding their children's independence and achievement, and there is some evidence that these childrearing patterns are related to child outcomes, or that employment status itself is related to relevant child outcomes. However, as yet there are no studies that have tapped all three levels and shown that these childrearing patterns actually mediate a relationship between employment and child outcomes.

Behavior and Attitudes of Parents and Gender of Child. The hypotheses about how child autonomy and independence training might mediate a relationship between mothers' employment and child outcomes were geared toward explaining previous research results that suggested positive outcomes of maternal employment for girls but sometimes negative outcomes for boys. Other hypotheses have also been proposed to explain this pattern. One, discussed earlier, is that traditional gender-role attitudes are dysfunctional to girls' independence, achievement, and self-esteem, and if mothers' employment operates to diminish these attitudes, their daughters will benefit. Another is a modeling hypothesis: the employed mother is more of a model of independence and achievement than the full-time homemaker; and there is evidence that daughters of employed mothers, from preschool through adulthood, are more likely to hold a concept of the female role that includes less restrictions and more independence, to incorporate these aspects of the female role into their self-concept, and to name their mother as the person they most admire (Hoffman, 1974; Miller, 1975).

Still another hypothesis has emerged from the research. Recent research with younger children has revealed additional advantages for daughters in the employed-mother family. In two studies, parents were found to engage in more positive interactions with daughters when the mother was employed, and in more positive interactions with sons when the mothers were not employed (Stuckey, McGhee, & Bell, 1982; Zaslow, Pederson, Suwalsky, & Rabinovich, 1983). Furthermore, in an interview study with mothers of three-year-olds, full-time employed mothers who had more than a high school education described their daughters but not their sons in the most positive terms; the opposite pattern was found for the nonemployed mothers (Bronfenbrenner, Alvarez, & Henderson, 1984). Two later studies failed to replicate this pattern (Greenberger & O'Neil, 1992; Zaslow et al., 1985.) However, in a study of school-aged children, Crouter and Crowley (1990) found that fathers in dual-wage families spent about the same amount of time in dyadic interactions with sons and daughters (about one hour per week), but fathers in single-wage families spent more time with sons (ninety minutes per week compared with thirty for daughters).

Several post hoc explanations have been offered to explain these differences in effects of maternal employment status on parents' attitudes and behavior toward daughters and sons. First, the traditional pattern is for parents to favor boys and to interact more with sons than with daughters (Block, 1983). Thus, the findings for families with nonemployed mothers are simply replications of previous results from studies where the mother's employment status was not considered. Because families with employed mothers are less likely to hold traditional sex-role attitudes, the prevalent son preference might be diminished. It is also possible that when mothers are employed, the traditional pattern of higher father-son interaction is pre-empted by the need for supplementary child care created by the mother's job demands. An additional explanation has to do with possible differences in stimulus qualities of male and female children. Data on sex differences suggest that boys are more active and less compliant than girls (Block, 1983). In the employed mother home, this may provide an inconvenience because of the potential stress of the dual roles, making sons more of a strain than daughters. Furthermore, since day-care experience is more common for employed-mother's children and has been noted to increase the activity level and noncompliance of children (Clarke-Stewart, 1989), this effect might be exacerbated (Hoffman, 1989).

Although these differences in parent–child interaction and parental attitudes toward sons and daughters are not firmly established, they do suggest another route by which the mother's employment status could affect gender differences in child outcomes.

The Social Context

An issue that has not been adequately addressed in the research on maternal employment is: To what extent are the effects of the mother's employment status affected by the larger social context? Is the impact of a mother's employment status different in different socioeconomic settings? Are the effects different in one-parent than in two-parent families? Does ethnicity moderate the effects?

Social Class. We have already indicated that some effects are more solidly established for one social class than another. For example, the positive effects of employment on the mother's sense of well-being have been found more consistently in the lower- than in the middle-class. In addition, the finding that the children of employed mothers show cognitive and mental health advantages is a more reliable one in poverty samples. However, while social-class differences in effects have been given more attention than the other social-context variables, drawing firm conclusions about the moderating influence of social class is limited because these results are primarily generalizations across different studies. With a few exceptions (e.g., Desai, Chase-Lansdale, & Michael, 1989; Gold & Andres, 1978b), most of the research in this field has been conducted with samples that are homogeneous with respect to socioeconomic status, and class contrasts are based

on the different patterns of results in different studies that have used different measures and different analysis strategies. More solid conclusions
about how a mother's employment might affect one class differently than
another require comparisons within a single study or across studies with
comparable measures and procedures.

The research on mothers' employment status, in general, has not given
sufficient attention to the process by which effects occur, but this is particularly apparent in contrasting social class patterns. For example, several
hypotheses have been proposed for why maternal employment might show
more consistent positive effects for children in the lower class, but none has
been put to an empirical test. Some of these hypotheses are as follows:

1. Nonmaternal care is likely to be lower relative to the care the
   middle-class mother would provide, but higher than the care the
   lower-class mother would provide, because of the educational
   discrepancies of mothers in the two social classes (Desai et al.,
   1989).
2. In the lower class, where economic circumstances would seem
   to call for the mother's employment, the full-time homemakers
   may be under more stress than the employed mothers, and this
   stress keeps them out of employment. Thus, the positive effects
   are not from employment per se but from pre-employment conditions (Hoffman, 1984c).
3. The mother's wages have a larger effect on the family's standard of living in the lower class than the middle class
   (Hoffman, 1984c).
4. Full-time homemakers in the lower class, and particularly in
   poverty conditions, may be highly stressed and emotionally
   depressed. Employment can be a buffer to this stress, making
   the mother a more effective parent.

Whether one of these hypotheses, or all of them, explain the particular
advantage maternal employment seems to have in lower-class families has
not yet been empirically established.

Marital Status. It is also possible that the mother's employment status has a
different impact in one-parent than in two-parent families, but a distinction
here is not yet clear. Research on the effects of maternal employment on children in single-mother families has been scarce, and with only a few exceptions (Duckett & Richards, 1989; Richards & Duckett, 1991; Weinraub &
Wolf, 1983), this work has been conducted with lower class or poverty

samples. This concentration on lower-income populations probably reflects the social concern for children being reared by single-mothers in poverty. However, it may also reflect sample availability: First, a popular data set has been the National Longitudinal Survey of Youth, which represents lower-income families more than middle-income, particularly when families with children are selected (Baker & Mott, 1989). It also includes a sizable group of single mothers. This data set has been the source for several recent maternal employment studies. Second, there is a scarcity of nonemployed single mothers in the middle class. In 1994, 91 percent of the college-educated single mothers of children over age five were in the labor force (U.S. Bureau of the Census, 1995). As these demographics indicate, it is difficult to obtain an adequate sample of single full-time homemakers for contrast in the middle class. To further complicate matters, most of the research on single mothers in poverty has been conducted with all-African-American samples (Cherry & Eaton, 1977; McLoyd et al., 1994; Woods, 1972), or predominantly African American samples (Heynes, 1978; Kriesberg, 1970; Vandell & Ramanen, 1992). Thus, the moderating roles of poverty, marital status, and ethnicity are difficult to untangle.

Two studies conducted in the 1970s examined the effects of maternal employment in low-income families with attention to the mother's marital status. Kreisberg (1970) found that maternal employment was related to higher school grades only in one-parent families. The other study, by Cherry and Eaton (1977), is often cited in reviews as a study with contrasting results that found positive effects of employment on children's cognitive performance only for two-parent families (e.g., Heynes, 1982; McLoyd, 1993). Actually, however, in the Cherry and Eaton study, when statistical comparisons were made among the four marital/maternal-employment types, they found the highest scores on the cognitive measure, a language development test, were obtained by the children of the single-employed mothers, second by the married employed, third by the single-nonemployed, and fourth by the married-nonemployed – a pattern reported as statistically significant (Cherry and Eaton, 1977, p. 163); the scores were higher in both groups with employed mothers. However, in an analysis that tested the significance of the employment differences separately for each marital status group, the employment advantage was significant only for the children with married mothers.

Only a few other studies have considered the issue of whether effects were the same or different in the two family forms. However, three studies that used the National Longitudinal Survey of Youth data set, already described, also considered marital status, and none found that it moderated the relationship between maternal employment and child outcomes (D'Amico, Haurin, & Mott, 1983; McCartney & Rosenthal, 1991; Vandell & Ramanan, 1992).

An additional analysis of the NLYS data set (Vandell & Ramanan, 1991) selected a particularly economically disadvantaged segment to examine the effects of after-school care. The children who returned home to mother care were predominantly the children of full-time homemakers. In comparison with "latchkey" children and those in other-adult care, the children in mother care had lower cognitive scores and more socioemotional problems. They were also more likely to be living below the poverty line and their homes had poorer emotional environments as measured by that component of the HOME index. It is interesting to note, however, that in two-parent families the negative child outcomes associated with mother care were totally mediated by these two variables, but in one-parent families the negative effects of mother care persisted even when they were controlled. The interpretation of this difference in results for the two family forms is unclear, but it suggests additional factors are involved for the one-parent families.

Two recent investigations of maternal employment status, already discussed, provide data on both child outcomes and family interaction in samples that included only lower-class, single-mother families (Alessandri, 1992; McLoyd, Jayaratne, Ceballo, & Borquez, 1994). The study by Alessandri was discussed as providing support for the hypothesis that employed mothers encourage independence and achievement in their daughters. In addition, both sons and daughters of employed mothers indicated higher self-esteem and their self-perceptions showed more congruence with their mothers' views. They also reported more family cohesion and a higher degree of household organization than did the children of full-time homemakers, a finding reminiscent of results obtained by Woods (1972) twenty years earlier with a similar sample. Within this low-income sample, there were no effects of income, the mother's educational level, or ethnicity.

The research of McLoyd and her colleagues was undertaken as a study of job loss with a focus on effects on maternal mental health. Past work interruption, however, was not related to depressive symptomotology, whereas current employment status was. Therefore, the analysis was conducted with the latter variable. As already indicated, higher levels of depression were found among the full-time homemakers, and depression was related to the mother's negative perception of the maternal role and to the use of power-assertive discipline. In addition, homemakers' children reported more negative relations with the mother, perceived more economic hardships, and had higher general anxiety scores. There was no direct relationship, however, between employment status and discipline, and, although homemakers had lower incomes and indicated more financial strain, indicating financial strain did not mediate the relationship between employment status and maternal depression. Both Alessandri and McLoyd and her colleagues have provided valuable data on the effects of maternal employment in poor, one-parent families; whether these effects would also be found for comparable two-parent families, however, is unknown.

As already noted, scarcer than studies of lower-class single mothers are studies of middle-class single mothers. An extensive search produced only two relevant investigations that did not use exclusively or predominantly lower income families.

Duckett and Richards (1989; Richards & Duckett, 1991), with a large sample of working- and middle-class children in fifth through ninth grades, found that in single-mother families, full-time employment was linked to the child's enhanced daily affect and self-esteem, but there was no relationship in two-parent families. In addition, children of full-time employed single mothers reported higher affect when with their mothers, though no such difference was found for the children in two-parent families. In this analysis, socioeconomic variables were controlled but no effort was made to see if effects differed in each class. The results were interpreted in terms of greater mental health advantages of employment for single women, but maternal mental health was not examined directly.

The other study was a carefully executed investigation of middle-class mothers of toddlers (Weinraub & Wolf, 1983). The study was limited by the small sample – a matched sample of fourteen single and fourteen married mothers – but, among its strengths, was the fact that the mother-child interaction was assessed by behavioral observations in a structured laboratory task. The only maternal employment effect that emerged that was moderated by marital status was that employment increased the exercise of maturity demands and control over the child for single mothers, but decreased them for married mothers. This was interpreted as reflecting guilt about employment on the part of married mothers, which led them to avoid exerting controls and demands on their children. Single mothers, on the other hand, saw their employment as necessary and therefore used a pattern that was more consonant with their work needs.

On the whole, however, the existing data do not indicate any clear pattern of differences between the effects of maternal employment in single- or married-mother families. If there is any pattern discernable, it might be that advantages of employment are more often found in single-mother families. Even if this is true, however, the reasons for it are not. Does it reflect the particularly disadvantaged and depressed state of the single homemakers? To what extent might these "effects" reflect pre-existing selective factors? That is, are the single mothers who are not in the labor force unable to work because of extra family burdens, poor mental or physical health, lack of education and job training? If employment is having a positive effect, is it carried by financial or psychological advantages?

Ethnicity. Most of the research on maternal employment has been conducted with convenience samples, without regard to ethnicity. Most often, these samples are primarily European Americans but may include other ethnicities present in the population. Sometime there are a sufficient number of African Americans that ethnicity is examined as a possible moderating variable or analyzed separately (e.g., Alessandri, 1992; Parcel & Menaghan, 1994), and some studies, all of them conducted with low-income families, have included only African-American families (Cherry & Eaton, 1977; McLoyd et al., 1994; Woods, 1972). A few studies have examined maternal employment effects in all-Hispanic samples (Valdez & Coltrane, 1993; Holtzman & Gilbert, 1987), but few other ethnic groups have been selected for separate consideration.

Hypotheses have been proposed to explain why the implications of maternal employment for families and children might be different for African Americans than for other groups (Heynes, 1982; McLoyd, 1993; Woods, 1972). These often start with the longer history of maternal employment in African-American families. Because of this, it is suggested that social patterns and family interactions have accommodated to maternal employment and it is more socially accepted, and even expected. Further, because of economic insecurity and the paucity of employment opportunities for African-American men, the mother's employment is a major contribution toward greater economic stability. African-American husbands are more likely to approve of their wives' working and extended family help is more readily available (McLoyd, 1993). The expectation drawn from these considerations is that maternal employment will have more positive effects among African Americans.

There is no real evidence at present, however, that ethnicity does make a difference in the sequelae of maternal employment, apart from socioeconomic effects. It is true that most of the research on families in poverty are based on African-American families and have found positive effects; however, where moderating effects of ethnicity were examined, none was found (Alessandri, 1992; Parcel & Menaghan, 1994).

One analysis that would seem to support the idea that maternal employment effects are more benign for African Americans is a controversial one by Milne, Myers, Rosenthal and Ginsberg (1986). These investigators analyzed a large, combined data set and found that maternal employment had a positive effect on the achievement of elementary-school children from one-parent families, but only if they were African American. Heynes and Catsambis (1986) reanalyzed the White, two-parent subsample where negative effects of employment had been reported and found very different results. They did not reanalyze the data for single-parent families, but it is possible that these data are also vulnerable to reinterpretation.

Thus, the question of whether maternal employment effects are influenced by ethnicity has not yet been answered, and attempts to answer will have to grapple with the complicated interrelationships that prevail in this country among ethnicity, poverty, and marital status.

Conclusions

The existing data reviewed here suggest that mothers' employment may have effects, both positive and negative, on the child's social and academic competence, but these effects are not direct ones. They are carried by the effects on the family environment. Three aspects of the family environment have been highlighted here: the father's role, the mother's sense of well-being, and parental orientations toward independence and autonomy. Some of the routes by which each of these might carry effects from the mother's employment status to child outcomes have been suggested in this review, with the available evidence presented.

First, if fathers in employed-mother families engage in more child care and household tasks, as most studies have found, gender-role traditionalism may be decreased for both parents and children, and this may operate to increase the independence and achievement of daughters. In addition, some data suggest that increased interaction with fathers may be beneficial for the cognitive competence of both sons and daughters (Gottfried, Gottfried, & Bathurst, 1988), but it is not clear whether the father in the employed-mother family simply compensates for the mother's lesser availability or actually enhances the overall level of attention children receive. The significance of the father's role as the link between employment status and child outcomes needs to be more fully examined and attention needs to be given to gender-role attitudes as part of this linkage.

Second, existing data indicate that, on the whole, maternal employment is likely to have positive effects on maternal mental health, with more consistent evidence for the lower than for the middle class. Other variables have also been shown to modify the mental health advantage of employment, and one study found that the father's help with child care was a necessary condition (Kessler & McRae, 1982). Since maternal well-being has been found to relate to parenting, it has been suggested that maternal employment can benefit children through the higher morale of employed mothers and the positive effects of morale on parenting. The full sequence of this chain, however, has not been investigated.

Third, a persistent hypothesis is that employed mothers encourage independence, grant autonomy, and assign responsibilities more than nonemployed. It has been suggested that this has positive consequences for daughters but, at least for independence and autonomy-granting, possible negative consequences for sons. The actual evidence for the association of these different childrearing styles with maternal employment, however, is sparse – most of it obtained thirty years ago. And there is no evidence for the full causal chain.

This review has also indicated the importance of considering how the social context interacts with these processes. The need to attend to factors such as class, marital status, and ethnicity in addressing the effects of maternal employment has long been noted, but discovering and understanding discrepancies in results in different contexts has been slowed by the reliance on homogeneous samples and the failure to consider why relationships exist. If full-time, lower-class, single homemakers are depressed, for example, is it finances, loneliness, a sense of powerlessness? Is the lack of employment a cause, an effect, or both?

It is clear that there are major gaps in our knowledge about the effects of the mother's employment status on family life and children. The more recent studies, except for some of the infancy research, have moved from a focus on child outcomes to an involvement in understanding the process by which effects take place (e.g., Crouter et al., 1987; Gottfried, Gottfried, & Bathurst, 1988), and they have provided important new leads. But many of the basic questions remain. In an effort to answer these, we launched the current investigation.

We concluded from our review of the maternal employment literature that there were five major questions that needed answers:

1. How does the role of the father mediate effects of the mother's employment status on the child?
2. How does the mother's sense of well-being mediate effects of the mother's employment on the child?

3. How do parenting styles in general, and orientations toward independence, autonomy and maturity, in particular, mediate effects of the mother's employment status on the child?
4. How does the age of the child when the mother first enters the labor force affect the child's development?
5. How do the nonmaternal care arrangements of employed and nonemployed mothers affect the outcomes for children?

The first three questions are the major focus of this study. In addition, however, data were obtained pertaining to the fourth question and these are presented in Chapter 7 along with outcome results for mothers' current employment status. The fifth question is the focus of the large, ongoing, multi-site NICHD investigation and was therefore not central in ours. However, Chapter 11 provides a review of the literature on nonmaternal care from infancy through the school years and presents data from the current study on patterns and effects of monitoring and after-school care.

Notes

1. Most of the attachment research has focused on whether or not the mother was employed during the first year, but some studies have contrasted returns to work during the first and second halves of the first year. Among the latter, some are guided by the hypothesis that a return to work during the first six months is more harmful than a return later in the first year; others are guided by the hypothesis that a return during the second six months is more harmful. Hypotheses that view the first six months as harmful focus on the mother's attachment to the child; those that view a return during the latter part of the first year as harmful focus on the child's attachment. According to Ainsworth and her colleagues (1978) and Yarrow (1964), nonmaternal care initiated prior to six months of age may be less stressful than care initiated later because it is only later in the year that the child is cognitively able to form an attachment, and a change during the period when the attachment is forming is particularly stressful.

2   Methodology*

To answer the questions that emerged from the review of the previous research in Chapter 1, a study was designed that would obtain a vast amount of data on a moderate-sized sample of families. We needed measures of parent–child interaction, childrearing attitudes and behaviors, the father's role in the family, the marital relationship, parents' gender-role attitudes, the mother's sense of well-being, demographic variables, and the mother's employment history. In addition, the study required measures of the child's attitudes, self-concepts, and perceptions of their families, as well as independent measures of the child's social and academic competence. Thus, we obtained an extensive data set from multiple sources.

In this chapter, we describe the basic design and methodology of this research. The details of the statistical analyses and descriptions of specific measures are taken up in individual chapters.

The chapter begins with an explanation for our choice of the study's location and our decision about the age of the children who would be the focus of this investigation. We then go on to describe the site and the sample. The sample description is complicated because, although data are obtained for 675 children, the basic sample consists of the 553 children for whom we had the necessary demographic data. For most of the analyses, however, we use only the 369 families for whom we obtained the full set of data. Following the description of the sample selection process, we explain the data collection procedures and the major measures used in the study.

Selecting the Sample and the Site

The first two decisions made were the age of the children who were to be the focus of the study and the research site. Third-grade children were cho-

---

* This chapter was written by Lois W. Hoffman and Allison Sidle Fuligni.

sen so that the target child would be part of the cohort of children for whom a sizable number of mothers returned to employment within a year of their birth. This was so that there would be enough children whose mothers returned during their first year to enable us to contrast them on child outcomes with those who returned later, thus addressing the fourth question listed in the preceding chapter. Third-grade children were also chosen to have a sample for whom the selective factors that affect employment status would be the same as the current ones. Data obtained from older children or data obtained from longitudinal data sets are dealing with different selective factors because mothers who entered the labor force during the child's infancy were a more unusual group even fifteen years ago. Third-graders are also young enough that their mothers would be able to accurately report their employment history since the child's birth. On the other hand, third-graders are old enough that the children themselves can be interviewed, achievement test scores are adequately reliable, and teacher and peer ratings can be used effectively to tap the child's school behavior patterns.

To obtain an adequate size sample of third-graders, we had to recruit through schools, and we wanted to conduct the study within a single school system. This was partly for efficiency, since obtaining the cooperation of a school system can be quite time-consuming, but it was also to maintain as much uniformity as possible across schools with respect to procedures and academic tests available. In addition, it was important that the school system encompass an ethnically and socioeconomically diverse population, because examining whether effects of maternal employment differed across groups was an important part of our quest. We, therefore, sought a large school system that served a diverse population.

Because the focus of the study was stable employment status, and not involuntary work disruption, we did not want a city with a high unemployment rate. Further, we needed a location near enough to our university base to enable student-interviewers to travel to and from the site in one day. We found the perfect place.

Site

The site of this research was an industrialized midwestern city with a heterogeneous population of 333,000. It is a stable community in several respects. Although it is not immune to the increase in unemployment rates that characterized many large midwestern cities, it has a more diversified economy, and thus escaped the sharp shifts and high unemployment rates shown by the nearby automobile-dominated cities in the 1980s and early in

1990. The population has also been relatively stable, and many families have lived in the area for generations. It is primarily a blue-collar city, but the economic range is from poverty to upper-middle class. More than 20 percent of the population are African American. Other ethnic groups are present but in smaller proportions, including Polish Americans, Arab Americans, and Mexican Americans.

Sample

The city school administration in granting permission for the study gave as a requirement that the collection of data from the children be completed by May 1. The collection of data could not begin before the preceding November, so a decision was made to include both third- and fourth-grade children. This made it possible to obtain an adequate size sample from a smaller number of schools. Because each additional school required meetings with the administrative staff and teachers, letters and forms sent to parents, and special scheduling and space arrangements, fewer schools was an important efficiency and made it possible to meet the May 1 deadline. Eight elementary schools (twenty-seven classrooms) were involved in the project.

Parental permission for the child's participation was obtained at two different points. The first was prior to the administration of any measures and sought permission for the child's participation in that part of the study which involved the administration of questionnaires in the classroom. Each school principal mailed a letter to the parents describing the study and the classroom measures and procedures. The phone numbers of the principal and the research staff were provided, and parents were invited to call if they had any questions. Parents were asked to inform the school either by phone or by returning a form enclosed with the letter if they did not want their child to participate. Three parents asked that their child be excluded; one child declined to participate. The classroom measures were administered to 675 children.

On the day of the administration of the classroom measures, each child was sent home with a letter describing the study more fully and requesting permission for the child's participation in the second phase of the study, which involved individual interviews with each child. Mothers were also asked if they would be willing to be interviewed in their homes. The permission form also requested information about the mother's employment status currently and for the previous three years, her occupation, her marital status, the child's father's occupation, the gender and age of the other children in the family and whether they were full siblings, half siblings, stepsiblings or foster children. A gift of $50 was offered to mothers who completed an interview, and children were given an inexpensive but attractive gift for returning the permission form to the teacher, regardless of whether the parent agreed to any further participation.

We obtained a high rate of permission for children to participate further in the study (83 percent). In most cases, failure to obtain permission was because the form was not returned, and this was largely affected by the teacher's enthusiasm for the study. In each school, many teachers were very excited about being part of this research, reminded the children daily about their forms, and succeeded in getting 100 percent of the forms in their classrooms back. Where teachers were less involved, or even annoyed, the rate was as low as 68 percent. We were also aided by the enthusiasm of the children. They had enjoyed the classroom administration. Our research staff, except for the principal investigator, were all student volunteers. They loved the experience and the children enjoyed the interaction. But perhaps the *coup de grâce* was the fact that the University of Michigan was having a very successful year in athletics. We were celebrities because we knew the Fabulous Five (our winning basketball team) and Desmond Howard, our Heisman trophy winner. Sports are big in the Midwest.

Although attrition from self-selection was minimal, we did not include all of the children for whom we had permission in the study. Of the 558 children for whom we had parental permission, only 485 were given full interviews and included in the sample. Reasons for exclusion included the following: the current mother had not reared the child during the early years (e.g., foster mothers, stepmothers, grandmothers); the mother did not speak English; the family had recently immigrated to the United States; the child was new to the school; the child moved out of the school district before the interview was scheduled; the child was absent on the days the interviews were conducted in the school; the interviews could not be completed before the May deadline.

The sample of 485 children included twenty pairs of siblings; thus, only 465 families were represented. For the analyses in this book, one sibling was randomly excluded. This sample was made up of 288 children from two-parent families (62 percent) and 177 children from one-parent families (38 percent). The ethnic makeup of this group was 73 percent White and 24 percent African American. Ten Hispanic children (.02 percent) were also included. Occupational levels for the parents in this sample are indicated in Table 2.1.

Seventy-three percent of the mothers volunteered to be interviewed (80 percent of the White mothers and 64 percent of the African-American mothers). The same criteria for exclusion were used in selecting the mothers

Table 2.1. *Occupations of Mothers and Fathers in One- and Two-Parent Families, for Families with Permission to Interview Children, Families with Interviewed Children, and Families with Interviewed Parents and Children*

Sample	Occupation					
	Unskilled	Semi-Skilled Blue	Skilled Blue	Sales and Clerical	Semi-Professional	Professional
Permission to Interview Child						
Married fathers	29	65	79	16	66	41
Married mothers	28	24	14	50	53	29
Single mothers	24	23	10	31	23	5
Child Interviewed						
Married fathers	27	63	76	16	64	37
Married mothers	26	23	14	47	51	29
Single mothers	17	17	10	22	19	5
Family Interviewed						
Married fathers	18	59	70	15	52	36
Married mothers	25	20	13	37	45	29
Single mothers	15	12	7	18	18	5

Note. Cases excluded from table are missing data for occupation and/or are not currently employed.

who would be interviewed as were used in selecting the children. Six mothers who initially volunteered to be interviewed either refused when they were contacted or failed to keep four scheduled appointments with the interviewer. Five mothers moved out of the geographical area before they could be interviewed, but for the most part, moves within the general area were traced.

Altogether, 369 mothers were interviewed – 256 married mothers and 113 single mothers. The ethnic distribution across the two groups was skewed, with African-American mothers more likely to be single. Of the married mothers, 218 were White or Hispanic and 38 were African American, whereas the single mothers included 60 White and 53 African-American women. In addition, employment status varied by ethnicity. African-American mothers had a lower employment rate, especially among the unmarried mothers (see Table 2.2).

At the time of the home interview with the 256 married mothers, questionnaires were left for the fathers. Fathers were provided with stamped envelopes in which to return completed questionnaires, and they were informed that an additional $10 would be paid for their participation. The response rate for fathers was 83 percent ($n = 212$), with 181 White fathers and 31 African-American fathers responding.

Thus, the data reported in this volume were obtained from samples that vary in size depending on the particular measures being discussed. The largest sample is the group of children who provided classroom data. Some publications from this data set have used the full sample (Kovacs, Parker, & Hoffman, 1996; Kovacs, 1996); however, all analyses in this volume require data on the mother's employment status and parents' occupations. Therefore, the largest sample used here is 553, the number of completed permission forms that were returned. Figure 2.1 provides a schematic view of the sample sizes.

Table 2.2. *Marital Status, Ethnicity, and Employment Status of Interviewed Mothers*

	Employed	Not Employed	Total
Married			
White	149	69	218
African American	21	17	38
Single			
White	48	12	60
African American	28	25	53
			369

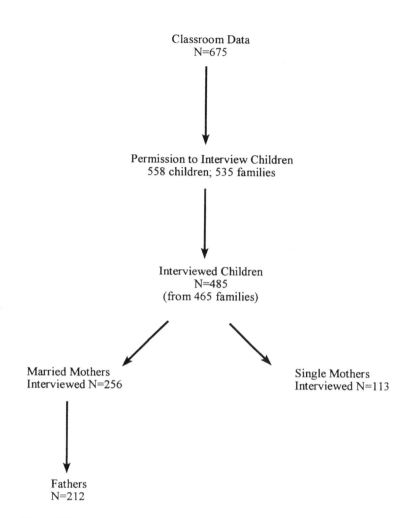

Figure 2.1. Schematic diagram of sample sizes.

Procedures

Classroom Procedures

Data collection began in November after classrooms had settled into their routines and the children had an opportunity to know one another. The classroom data were collected in a single one-hour session. At the beginning of the session, the research staff introduced themselves and briefly described the project. Children were assured that their participation was voluntary, that they could decline to participate at any point, and that all responses would be confidential. After this introduction, the children were administered the sociometric measures of peer acceptance, friendship choices, and behavioral reputation of their classmates; the Harter Perceived Competence Scale (1982); the Nowicki and Strickland Children's Locus of Control Scale (1973); and a measure of sex-role stereotypes.

For each instrument, one member of the research staff read the directions and each item on the questionnaire, while the children filled in their answers on prepared forms. Four other staff members roamed the classroom to help children who had questions or seemed to be having difficulty. In almost all cases, the teacher left the classroom. Some, however, preferred to remain but did not participate in the data collection process. When all the data were collected, the children were given the permission letters for their parents and shown the prize they would receive when the form was returned. Teachers were given the Teacher-Child Rating Scale (Hightower et al., 1986) forms with instructions for completion. These were to be completed by the end of the school year and teachers were given $50 for their time. In order to complete all of the classrooms in a school in one day, two research teams were often used to obtain the data from two classrooms simultaneously. Most of the research staff were graduate students in developmental psychology, but some were undergraduate students majoring in psychology.

Children's Interviews

Children for whom parental permission was received were interviewed individually at the school during the regular school day. They were first asked to describe the composition of their families and then to provide a narration of everything they had done from the end of school on the previous day until their arrival at school on the day of the interview. This account was guided by the interviewer using a focused interview format. It included information about who was with the child during each activity described and the nature of the interaction. This report and all other child interview data were recorded by the student interviewer. Following the narration, the child answered specific questions about family roles.

The questionnaire about family roles, called the *Day at Home,* was modeled after an earlier one developed by Herbst (1952). It consisted of two parts: Part I included questions about who performs various household tasks and child-care activities and Part II included questions about the child's affective relationships (e.g., Who gives you hugs and kisses?). The final measure administered asked the child about his or her hopes and expectations for the future (job aspirations, going to college) and who he or she would like to be like as an adult. The interview lasted about thirty minutes. For the children and the interviewers, this was the high point of the study. The children loved the attention and the interviewers were thrilled and enlightened by the opportunity to interact with this diverse group of children who told their stories openly, without guile (the charm of this age group). At the conclusion, the child was given another small gift and returned to the classroom.

Mothers' Interviews

The interviewing of mothers began after the child interviewing was completed. These interviews were conducted by a team of middle-aged women trained by staff from the University of Michigan's Institute for Social Research. Interviewers were matched to respondents by ethnicity. Because of concern that the families' work and child-care arrangements could change during the summer months, all interviews were completed before the end of the school year. These interviews were conducted in the home and lasted about two hours.

The interviews included detailed descriptions of household composition, the mother's marital history, and employment and child-care arrangements since the target child's birth; various measures of childrearing attitudes and practices; measures of gender-role attitudes and the division of labor between the husband and wife; measures of the mother's well being; the Locke-Wallace Measures of gender-role Marital Happiness (1959); and additional questions about demographic characteristics. Interviews for single mothers were virtually identical to those for married mothers, but included additional questions about social support; they did not include the measure of the division of labor between the spouses nor the measure of marital happiness.

Fathers' Questionnaires

The fathers' questionnaire, left with the married mothers at the conclusion of the interview, included the same measures administered to the mothers for the division of labor, gender-role attitudes, and goals held for the target child. It also included an eighteen-item questionnaire asking how many times in the previous week the father had engaged in various activities with the child. (Mothers had answered a parallel measure about their own interactions with the child.) Also included was a brief measure of marital happiness.

Additional Sources of Data

The schools provided achievement test scores from the Metropolitan Achievement Test for all of the children in the study. In addition, for each child whose mother was interviewed, the only group for whom we had addresses, crime ratings of the child's neighborhood were obtained from police records.

Measures

This extensive set of data from the target children, peers, mothers, fathers, teachers, school records, and police files yielded a great many measures. Many different concepts were operationalized, and there were multiple measures of the more important variables. In some cases, the same or similar measures were obtained from different sources. For example, matched measures of the father's role were obtained from mothers, fathers, and children. Similar aspects of the child outcome variables came from teachers, achievement test scores, peers, and the children themselves. In other cases, different aspects of a variable came from the same source. Mothers' interviews, for example, were used to tap many different aspects of their child-rearing attitudes and behavior.

Because of the extensive number of measures used in this research, many of which are specific to individual chapters, we will not describe the full set here. Instead, measures will be described in the individual chapters where they are employed. In this chapter, we will take up only a limited set of major measures that have significance for several of the individual analyses reported in subsequent chapters. First, we will describe two complex instruments, included in the mother's interview, which are designed to tap her discipline or control styles. These measures are used in four of the later chapters. Second, the basic demographic concepts that are germane to every chapter will be explained: the mother's employment status, marital status, and socioeconomic status. Finally, a description of the child outcome measures, used in five of the twelve chapters, will be presented.

Measures of Discipline and Control Styles

Two important measures in this study are the Behavior-based Discipline measure and the Parental Control measure. The first is an original instrument based on the work of M. Hoffman (1988) and modeled after a comparable measure used by L. Hoffman (1961; Hoffman & Lippitt, 1960); the second is a modification of Greenberger's (1988) Parental Control measure and is influenced by the work of Baumrind (1967).

Behavior-based Discipline. In the first, ten scenarios were presented that described common situations where the child's desired behavior was in conflict with the mother's (e.g., the child wanted to continue watching television and the mother wanted him or her to stop; the mother wanted the child to go to bed, but the child did not want to go; the child "talked back" to the mother). The mother was asked to think about the last time this occurred with the target child and to report what she did by selecting responses from a checklist of eight to thirteen possible actions. The checklist included typical examples of discipline patterns that represented power assertion, power assertion but with a softening "cushion," love withdrawal, induction (reasoning or providing an explanation), bribery, and giving in to the child's wishes. The mother, with the interviewer's guidance, selected the response that best described what she did, as well as any others that fit. A final question asked what the mother usually did in most discipline situations and provided a list of seventeen possible responses. Scores were computed to tap the extent to which each mother relied on power assertion, physical punishment, love withdrawal, induction, or permissiveness. By tying the report to a specific episode, the response was more objective and behaviorally based. In the cognitive process of recall, the need to give a socially correct response was diminished.

Parental Control. The Parental Control measure consisted of a set of thirty-eight statements such as, "When I make a rule, I just *make* it: I don't go into explanations"; "When my child has done something really wrong, I show my disappointment by spanking him/her"; and "Before punishing my child, I always listen to the child's side of the story." Mothers indicated their agreement with each statement on a six-point scale, and scores for the different styles were computed across items. The two measures, Behavior-based Discipline and Parental Control, yielded comparable concepts, but differed in the extent to which they were tied to attitudes or behavior.

Demographic Measures

Mother's Employment Status. Securing information about whether a mother is employed is relatively easy; operationally defining it for research is more complicated. In most research, the measure is simply whether she is or is not currently employed. However, several studies have shown that recent employment or sporadic employment is quite different in its effects on children from steady employment or employment after the early months of adjustment (Moorehouse, 1991; Thompson, 1981). Similarly, unemployment that is temporary or results from job loss is quite different from *nonemployment,* or being a full-time homemaker. In this study, we were not interested in job loss or in the disequilibrium that accompanies job shifts, but in examining how families and children are affected by having a mother who is employed rather than a mother who is a full-time homemaker. Thus, for most of the analyses in this book we selected families where the mother had been either employed or a full-time homemaker for the three previous years. This reduced the sample size, but it seemed a purer measure. If the mother's employment status was ambiguous (e.g., she worked in the home or less than ten hours a week), the family was also excluded from the sample.

The employment group was subdivided into part-time and full-time, depending on whether they worked thirty-five or more hours. All analyses were first run with the three distinctions (full-time, part-time, and nonemployed), but in this sample differences were usually slight or nonexistent for the two employment groups and they were combined in most analyses. This is different from some of the previous research and may reflect the age of the children and the fact that this is the 1990's. Much of the work showing the advantage of part-time employment over the other two has come from studies of infants or young children or from the research of the 1960s and 1970s (Bronfenbrenner, Alvarez, & Henderson, 1984; Bronfenbrenner & Crouter, 1982; Greenberger & O'Neil, 1992; Hoffman, 1984a). In those cases where the full-time/part-time distinction did make a difference, however, this is reported.

Marital Status. The family was considered a two-parent family if the mother had a male partner who had lived in the house for more than a year and was considered part of the conjugal family. Where the term *married mothers* is used, it includes all mothers who fit this pattern, whether or not the couple were legally married.

Socioeconomic Status. Two measures of socioeconomic status were used. For the sample of interviewed mothers, Hollingshead's (1970) Four-factor Index of Social Status was used. This measure involves coding the educational level obtained by each parent on a seven-point scale and each parent's occupational level on a nine-point scale. These scores are then weighted and combined, resulting in a family social status score ranging from 8 to 66.

This measure was used because it considers the mother's employment and marital status. If the mother is employed, her education and occupation were averaged along with the father's; if she is a full-time homemaker, only the father's information is used. In single-mother families, the score uses only the mother's education and occupation if the father is not providing child support, but considers the father's if he is. These scores can be used as a continuum or divided into a dichotomous variable. In most cases here, it was used as a dichotomous variable with scores of 38 or above defining the middle class (professional and white-collar) and those with less than 38 defining the lower, or blue-collar, class, as suggested by Hollingshead.

A second measure was used for all the children whose parents had returned a completed permission form. Since the form included information about parents' occupation but not education, a social status measure was developed from the occupational information alone. We followed the general procedures recommended by Hollingshed for the Four-factor Index using the mother's occupation for single mothers and weighting the status of the mother's occupation for dual-wage families. For most analyses, these were divided, as with the Four-factor Index, into two groups – a white-collar group and a blue-collar group. This dichotomous classification was compared with the dichotomous classification yielded by the Four-factor Index for all families that had both scores. Of the 363 families who did, only 5 families had been assigned a different status. These divergent cases were examined, and in each instance they involved two-parent families where the mother's occupational level was notably higher than the father's and required advanced education. In most cases the mother was a public school teacher and the father was a semi-skilled worker; all were African American. In the Four-factor Index, the mother's educational level had moved the score to the middle-class group. Each was recoded to correspond to the middle-class classification assigned by the Hollingshead scoring. Because some of the chapters (e.g., Chapter 7) use a lower cut-off to approximate a poverty group for some analyses, we also compared the two sets of scores for this division. There were no discrepancies in classification here.

Child Outcome Measures

The child outcome measures came from four different sources: peers, teachers, school records, and the target child.

Peer Ratings. Five peer rating measures were used. The first was a measure of *likability* or acceptance that used a sociometric procedure in which the children in the classroom were given a list of all their classmates' names and asked to rate how much they liked each child on a five-point scale, from "like a lot" to "dislike a lot." Two scores were computed for each child: the average rating received from peers of the same sex and the average rating received from the opposite sex. Higher scores indicated the child was liked more.

A peer nomination behavioral assessment format was used for the other four measures (Hymel & Rubin, 1985). Children were given a list of all their classmates' names and asked to nominate who was characterized by the following behaviors:

- Who says mean things to other kids?
- Who hits or shoves other kids?
- Who helps others a lot?
- Who is shy and quiet?

They could nominate more than one person. Each child's score was based on the percentage of children who nominated him or her for that particular behavior.

Teacher Ratings. All children in the classrooms were rated by the teachers using the Teacher–Child Rating Scale (T-CRS), a widely used instrument developed by Hightower and his colleagues (1986). Items on this scale tap children's behavioral problems and social and academic competence. For behavioral problems, teachers rate each item using a scale from 1 ("not a problem") to 5 ("very serious problem"). For competence items, teachers rate each item using a scale ranging from 1 ("not at all") to 5 ("very well").

The thirty-eight T-CRS items form seven subscales:

1. Acting out behavior (e.g., overly aggressive, disruptive in class)
2. Shyness and anxiety (e.g., shy, withdrawn, anxious)
3. Learning problems (e.g., poorly motivated, underachieving, has difficulty learning)
4. Frustration tolerance (e.g., accepts things not going his or her way, tolerates frustration, accepts imposed limits)
5. Positive assertiveness (e.g., defends own views, comfortable as a leader, participates in class discussion, questions rules that seem unfair or unclear)
6. Task orientation (e.g., functions well even with distractions, works well without adult support, completes work)
7. Peer social skills (e.g., is friendly toward peers, makes friends easily, is well-liked by classmates)

Higher scores on the first three scales indicate greater difficulty; higher scores on the last four indicate greater competence. The reliability for each of the seven scales was as follows: acting out, alpha = .94; shyness-anxiety, alpha = .85; learning skills, alpha = .95; frustration tolerance, alpha = .92; positive assertiveness, alpha = .90; task orientation, alpha = .94; peer social skills, alpha = .95.

School Records. The school district provided Metropolitan Achievement Test scores in mathematics, language, and reading for all participants in the study. These standardized tests were administered in the spring of the same academic year that the rest of the data were collected. Raw test scores were transformed using national norming tables, and normal-curve-equivalent scores ranging from 1 to 99 for each of the tests were used in the study.

Children's Reports. Three of the outcome measures were based on children's reports. These tapped self-perceptions of social and academic competence, *locus of control* (the extent to which the child feels he or she can have an influence on personal events and outcomes), and the child's gender-role stereotypes. All three instruments were administered in the classroom.

Children's self-concepts were measured by the Harter Perceived Competence Scale for children (Harter, 1982, 1983). This consists of thirty-six contrasting statements such as: "Some kids have a lot of friends," and "Other kids don't have many friends." The children are asked to indicate on a form which "kids" they are like and then to indicate if that is "really true for me" or "just sort of true." Scores of 1 to 4 are given for the response to each item. The measure yields six subscores tapping the child's self-perceptions of (1) scholastic competence (alpha = .72), (2) social acceptance (alpha = .70), (3) athletic competence (alpha = .74), (4) physical appearance (alpha = .75), (5) behavioral conduct (alpha = .74), and (6) global self-worth (alpha = .73).

The Nowicki and Strickland (1973) measure of Locus of Control was administered to the children. This scale taps the extent to which the child feels in control of his or her life (internal locus of control), as opposed to feeling that control is in the hands of others or depends on luck (external locus of control). This eighteen-item measure yields a composite score with high scores indicating external locus of control and low scores indicating internal locus of control. It includes items such as, "Do you usually feel that it is almost useless to try in school because most other children are just plain smarter than you are?"; "Are you the kind of person who believes that planning ahead makes things turn out better?": and "Do you believe that when bad things are going to happen they just are going to happen no matter what you try to do to stop them?" Each item is answered "yes" or "no" with one point given for an answer indicating an external orientation. Although the reliability for this scale was not high (alpha = .60), its extensive previous use has provided considerable construct validity (Kliewer 1991; Kliewer & Sandler, 1992; Nowicki & Barnes, 1973; Nowicki & Strickland, 1973).

The children's gender-role stereotypes were measured by an instrument developed for this study. It was based on a measure used by Miller-Rosenwasser (Miller, 1975) for kindergarten children and later adapted for older children by Signorella & Liben (1985). Our version consisted of a list of thirty-one adult activities that were presented to the child. The child was asked to indicate if this was something only men could do, something only women could do, or something both could do. Some of the items were stereotypically male (e.g., build a house); some were stereotypically female (e.g., bake cupcakes); and some were neutral (e.g., go to the beach).

Only the twenty-five gender-typed activities were scored. Each answer that indicated that only men could do the male activities or only women could do the female activities was scored 0; each answer that indicated both or the counter-stereotyped choice was scored 1. Scores were summed to yield three scores: a score for the activities stereotyped as male, a score for the activities stereotyped as female, and a total score consisting of the sum of the two. Inter-item reliabilities were alpha = .83, .84, and .90, respectively. A higher score indicates a less stereotyped view.

Summary

This chapter presented the basic design of the study, including the rationale behind the site chosen and the age of the children selected for study; descriptions of the site, the sample, and methods of data collection; and explications of some of the major variables that are used in several of the chapters. The sample description is a complicated one. Although data were collected for 675 children, the basic sample is the 558 children for whom we had the necessary demographic data. Most of the analyses in this volume, however, use measures obtained from the personal interviews with mothers in their homes, and here the sample drops to 369 families. For this group, a wide range of measures was obtained from multiple sources. This is a study with a modest sample size but a very rich array of data, as subsequent chapters will show.

3   Children's Daily Family Lives:
The After School Day Interview*

The sample of families used in this study has been described in the previous chapter using traditional demographic categories such as race, marital status, and social class. It is clear from these numbers that we studied a heterogeneous population, but such statistics tend to blur the distinctions between individual families, leaving the reader with the impression that all "single, employed mother" or "married, father employed/mother homemaker" families are somehow the same. Indeed, the goal of research often seems to be to make generalizations about categories. What is obscured in research, mass media coverage, and in many people's minds is the wide variation that occurs within any category. What is also obscured is the wide variety of family forms, adaptations, and routine behavior patterns that children experience – even in Middle America.

The other chapters in this book conform to the standard social science research procedures. Here, however, we want to tap into the more qualitative data that were obtained to provide a fuller picture than that offered by statistical analysis. A particular strength of this project was the vast array of data on each family. These data came from multiple reporters and a variety of measures, ranging from objective, standardized instruments to open-ended questions that elicited free personal responses. A particularly unique measure was the children's interview, in which children gave detailed descriptions of daily family life. These interviews, called the After School Day, were described in Chapter 2. They were coded to yield specific measures: for example, indices to tap the degree of supervision and monitoring the child receives, the self-sufficiency and independence of the child in the family, and the quality of the parent–child relationship. But they also provide a window through which to glimpse the wide range of family patterns that American children experience.

* This chapter was written by Allison Sidle Fuligni and Lois W. Hoffman.

The sample used in this chapter consists of the 465 families with children who were interviewed, one-on-one, by the student interviewers. As outlined in Chapter 2, the children were first asked to describe the composition of their families and households. If a child indicated that a parent, usually the father, was not part of the household, the child was asked if he or she had contact with that parent. In the After School Day portion that followed, the children were asked to talk about everything they had done from the end of school on the previous day until they arrived at school on the morning of the interview. All interviews were conducted on a day following a school day. Although the children were encouraged to simply tell their stories, interviewers used standard questions to probe on topics such as who else was present, whether they were interacting with the child, where the activity took place, and how long it lasted. Attention was given to supervision, how much time the child spent alone, whether the child ate the evening meal with the whole family and whether the meal was at a table or in front of the television set, bedtime hours and rituals, breakfast patterns, and the extent to which the child was self-sufficient in areas like dressing, bathing, and getting ready for school. The children were asked if the day they described was typical; if it was not, they were asked to describe their usual day. These scenarios revealed wide diversity that our demographic labels did not capture. They also revealed that, for this age child, patterns that would seem unusual to many adults were viewed as a normal part of family life to the child who lived them. Following the narration, children were administered a structured questionnaire about family roles (the Day at Home measure, described in Chapter 2) and a brief questionnaire about their future hopes and aspirations. Except for the Day at Home answers, which followed a format, children's responses were recorded verbatim by the interviewer. These responses provide the substance of this chapter.

This chapter is devoted to providing some examples of the things we learned about children's family lives from our interviews with them. The children spoke frankly about the composition of their families, their childcare situations, and family routines and interactions. Examples of the variations in children's experiences in these areas are included here. Some numbers are reported to describe the experiences and daily lives of the children in our sample, such as the number of children living with extended family members or going home after school to an empty house. However, the bulk of the chapter will provide brief anecdotes taken from the interviews, as examples of the wide range of experiences of these children. Pseudonyms are used in place of real names, but as much as possible these children's stories are presented in their own words, giving them a chance to speak for themselves.

The materials presented are organized around four general themes. First, we take up the question of what constitutes a family. It is a cliché to say that a family is not limited to the model presented by the television program *Leave it to Beaver,* with two married parents and their biological children. Not even television today conforms to that image. But the complexities of what constitutes a family are still unresolved, and from the child's view, the family members may include more variations than commonly realized. We begin with who lives in the household. Then we consider the functional and emotional relationships with friends and kin who do not share the child's home, but may play a significant part in the child's life.

Second, because this is a book about maternal employment, we give examples of some of the different ways that children are cared for while their parents work. This discussion overlaps with the first because household members and extended family relationships play an important role in children's after-school care.

Third, we describe some of the variations in family routines, and we use the children's descriptions of their family life to show that knowing the demographic classification of a family does not communicate the quality of the child's life. As our fourth and final theme, we relate the children's reports of some of the difficulties they encounter because of poverty or overcrowding.

It is important to keep in mind, in reading these descriptions, that although we have selected some of the more interesting revelations, this is not a poverty sample. Only about 20% of our sample would be classified as living in poverty. The children attend the public schools of an industrialized city in Middle America where unemployment rates are moderate to low; it is primarily a middle- and working-class population.

Who Is in the Child's Family?

National statistics show that the American family does not consist only of two parents and their offspring. In 1996, 68 percent of the children in the United States were living with two parents, although they were not necessarily the original ones. Another 25 percent were living with single mothers in households that may include other persons. Four percent lived with single fathers and 4 percent lived with neither parent (U.S. Bureau of the Census, 1997). Furthermore, previous ethnographic work has also indicated that extended family ties are often so strong that the nuclear family is almost absorbed within it (Stack 1974). The children's interviews clearly indicate that households of both one-parent and two-parent families include more complex patterns than the common notion of a conjugal family suggests. They also show that close family ties are not confined to the household. They include grandparents, aunts, uncles, cousins, and friends. And they also include nonresident fathers, even when the fathers have never been married to the child's mother.

The Composition of the Household

The previous chapter distinguished two marital status categories: one-parent and two-parent. Actually, the households in which these children live range from living with a single mother who is the only adult in the home to households in which the target child is the only child in a houseful of adults. Some *single* mothers are the sole adult in the household, but many live with their own parents, brothers, sisters, nieces, nephews, or friends. Married mothers include those who are married to the child's biological father as well as those who are married to a man other than the child's father. Even those families that are intact with respect to the target child in the study may be more accurately considered *blended families* because other children in the family may be from a previous union.

The distribution of these various household patterns for the sample of interviewed children is presented in Table 3.1. It is important to note, however, that this sample had already been prescreened. If the permission form included information indicating that the child was not living with his or her mother, through birth or legal adoption, the full personal interview was not conducted (see Chapter 1). In several cases, however, this fact only emerged during the interview, so a small number of children living with single fathers or neither parent was inadvertently interviewed.

Table 3.1 shows that 55 percent of the sample lives with both their mother and father, while 12 percent live with one parent and one stepparent. Eleven children (2.4 percent) reported living with neither parent. If both one-parent and two-parent families are included, there are grandparents present in 9.8 percent of the households, and aunts, uncles, and/or cousins live in the homes of 9.2 percent. Nonrelated adults (including romantic partners of the parents) live in 6 percent of the households. Two adults are present in the majority of families (72%), and 10 percent of the households include three or more adults.

The children's descriptions of their households revealed not only a wide variation in the adult membership, but also variety among the children pre-

Table 3.1. *Adults Living in Child's Household*

	N	Percent
Child lives with both original parents; Household includes only conjugal unit	237	51.6
Child lives with both original parents; Household includes adults outside conjugal unit	15	3.3
Child lives with original parent and stepparent	57	12.4
Child lives with single mother and no other adult	75	16.3
Child lives with single mother and adult relative(s)[a]	33	7.2
Child lives with single mother and nonfamily adult woman[a]	2	.4
Child lives with single mother and nonfamily adult man[a]	23	5.0
Child lives with single father	9	2.0
Child lives with neither parent	11	2.4

[a] These categories are nonexclusive. Total N for sample reported here is 459; in 6 cases this information was not ascertained.

sent. This included various sibling relationships (such as stepsiblings and half siblings) and the presence of children who were not siblings but cousins, children of the mothers' friends, or foster children. In addition, the descriptions indicated that full siblings did not always live in the same household. Many children described large numbers of siblings, and then reported that, for various reasons, they did not live with any of them. This chapter presents a number of examples of the family diversity encountered, including many variations on extended family living arrangements.

The size of a child's household will play an important role in that child's daily experiences, and an important factor is the number of adults relative to children in the home. We encountered family size variation ranging from two to sixteen household members. Both extremes were households of single mothers. Although all two-person households in the sample consisted of the child and her mother, most of the very large households included a single mother and maternal kin. For example, Shantal, a nine-year-old, reported living with her mother, three younger sisters, a younger brother, her grandmother, an uncle, two aunts, and six cousins. This household of sixteen individuals ranged in age from one year (Shantal's baby brother) to the grandmother, and included two teenagers (the uncle was sixteen and one of the cousins was fourteen).

Shantal's household was large, with four adults, two teenagers, and ten young children. In contrast, ten-year-old Kelly was the only child in a five-person household consisting of herself and her single mother, two grandparents, and an uncle. Similarly, Fran lived with her two adoptive parents and four adopted siblings who were all in their thirties. However, Fran did enjoy the company of a seven-year-old niece also living in the home and attending the same school. Another household in which the adults outnumbered the children was the multigenerational home of nine-year-old Christopher, who lived with his mother, his mother's boyfriend, his grandmother, great-grandmother, and two younger siblings.

These patterns of extended kin living together were most common with single mothers. Often single mothers lived with their own parents and siblings (the target children's grandparents, aunts, and uncles). These usually involved cases where the grandparents were providing support by incorporating the family into their household. Ten-year-old Abby, for example, lived with her mother, two single uncles, and her grandfather in the grandfather's house. Nine-year-old Gabe and his single mother also lived in the mother's nuclear family home with Gabe's grandmother, grandfather, and two uncles.

Single mothers were not the only ones who lived with their parents, although in the two-parent families it was more often this family unit who was aiding a grandparent by having him or her live with them. This was clear in Maureen's family, which consisted of her mother, father, older sister, and grandmother. However, it was not always apparent which family was providing assistance, or whether it was a reciprocal arrangement. For instance, Janet was an eight-year-old girl living with her two parents, two older brothers, grandfather, aunt, and uncle. In this case, Janet's parents might have invited the grandfather, aunt, and uncle into their home, or the mother and father might be living in the original home of the grandfather, along with his other adult children.

Extended family living arrangements also included family members within the same generation sharing a household, without the grandparent generation living there. This was the case for Travis, who lived with his single mother, brother (age twenty-two), and two aunts. In this case, the three sisters live together, along with the two widely spaced sons of one of the sisters.

Many of the children in our sample told us that their mothers were teenagers when they were born. Others had older siblings who were teen parents themselves. Patterns of teen parenting thus affected the household composition of several children in our sample – in some cases the single mothers living with their own parents were our target child's sisters. For example, Ellis was ten years old and the youngest of nine children. He lived with his mother, father, sister, and his sister's daughter (Ellis's niece). His other brothers and sisters are "all grown and moved out," he said. As a slightly different twist, Peggy lived with her mother and father, older sister, younger sister, cousin, and her cousin's young daughter. Other evidence of early sexual activity of the siblings comes in the family description given by nine-year-old Marcus. He lived in a two-parent family with his twenty-year-old brother. His two other brothers, ages eighteen and fifteen, each live with their girlfriends.

Some children live in blended households that are not made up of extended kin. For example, David, a third-grade boy, lives with his single mother and another single mother with her son, who is a year younger than David. Both of the mothers have boyfriends who often sleep in the home as well. David has two younger sisters; one lives with his "ex-stepfather" and one lives with his father. David had not seen his father in six months at the time of his interview.

Of course, a number of children did live with single mothers and no other adult. Some of these families consisted of a number of siblings from the same father who was no longer in the household due to separation or divorce, while other single mothers had never been married. Some of the single mothers had children from a number of different men. For instance, Julia was a vivacious eight-year-old girl, blonde, blue-eyed, and very comfortable with the interviewer. Her mother lived alone with four children; she had never been married. In Julia's description of her family it was clear that each of the four children had a different father. Furthermore, in the description she gave of the previous day, it became apparent that all four fathers were actively involved with the family. She said, for example, "My big sister's daddy took us to McDonald's for dinner."

When the Day at Home measure was administered, Julia, like all the children, answered each question descriptively and then the interviewer and the child together filled out the answer form. When the interviewer asked "Who buys big new things for the family?" Julia replied: "Well, my daddy bought us a Nintendo set. My big brother's daddy bought Mom our new refrigerator. My little brother's dad has been out of work lately so he can't buy much now. My sister's daddy bought us a TV last year for Christmas." To "Who goes on picnics with you in the summertime?" the reply was "My daddy doesn't like picnics, but he takes us bowling. Last summer, my little brother's dad took us to Cedar Point and we had a picnic there." When asked who she wanted to be like when she was grown, Julia replied unhesitatingly, "Oh, like my Mama – because she has a wonderful job. She's a beautician, and that's what I want to be when I'm grown. And she's pretty and nice."

Households Without Parents

The examples of household compositions given thus far all include the child and a parent. Although they were later deleted from the data analyses, we also interviewed children who did not live with either parent, but maintained some parental contact. Parents who may be unable to care for their children for a number of reasons, such as being quite young themselves, having addiction problems, or being incarcerated or otherwise involved in the legal system, may find relatives with whom their children can live. In many of these cases, children lived with cousins, and not with their own siblings, as these siblings were distributed among other families. For example, one ten-year-old girl, Bernice, lived with her aunt and uncle and their seven children (Bernice's cousins), who ranged in age from six to nineteen years. Bernice said she visits her mother every weekend, and sees her father every Sunday in church.

Tanya is a ten-year-old third-grade girl who described her four younger brothers and a younger sister (ages nine, eight, six, five, and four years), but lives with her single grandmother and only one of her brothers. Another of Tanya's brothers lives across the street with her aunt and cousin. Tanya said she sees her father "sometimes on weekends," but has only seen her mother twice. Tiffany, who is in the same third-grade class with Tanya, has a similar living arrangement. She stays with her aunt (a single mother) and two cousins. Although she reported having four siblings, only one was mentioned in her description of daily life – a brother who lives in a foster home, but with whom Tiffany walks home from school. Although Tiffany did not volunteer the reason that she does not live with her parents or other siblings, she did say that she sees both parents about twice a week and talks with them frequently on the phone.

Another third-grade girl, Tanisha, told us that she lived with her grandparents because her mother was fifteen and ran away from home when Tanisha was born. She lives with her grandmother, grandfather, uncles, and aunts. She indicated she had two older and three younger "step" siblings, and three younger "real" siblings. None of the siblings live in the house with Tanisha, but she said they visit sometimes. She sees her father almost every day when he picks up her stepsister at school, and sometimes he brings Tanisha home after school. Tanisha sees her mother occasionally on weekends, but she said "sometimes I don't like to see her."

Samantha, a third-grader, explained that she lives with her grandmother and grandfather during the week "because it's closer to school," and she spends the weekends at her mother's house. At the grandparents' house, she lives with her two grandparents, her ten-year-old sister, and a nine-year-old cousin. On the weekends, Samantha lives with her mother, stepfather, sister, and a five-year-old half brother. Another half brother, three years old, lives with "his own mom." Samantha's biological father is incarcerated, and she visits him monthly.

Eight-year-old Dawn also had different living situations during the week than on weekends. She spent weekdays living with her grandmother, grandfather, their thirteen-year-old daughter (Dawn's aunt), and three cousins aged five and under whose own mother lived in Tennessee. On the weekends, Dawn lived with her mother and father, a seventeen-year-old brother, and a three-year-old brother. Her father also had children aged thirteen and nine who lived with their own mother.[1]

Another third-grade girl, Angelique, told of having a twin sister and a younger sister, an older half brother, and two older stepsisters. She lives with her aunt, uncle, and twenty-three-year-old cousin. Her father died before she was born, and she sees her mother every other weekend. This living arrangement, according to Angelique, was only for the duration of the school year, and in the summer she expected to live with her mother again. She said she had had to move in with her aunt and uncle because her mother "liked to stay up late" and couldn't get Angelique to school on time. Other adult contacts she mentioned were a stepfather she sees "sometimes" and her "stepdad's other girlfriend" who gave her a ride home from school.

Ann was tall, slim, and very serious, and seemed overly mature for her nine years. She lived with her grandparents, and repeated often that this was a great privilege, for her siblings were living with her mother and "the man she lives with." In her description of the previous day, it seemed to be an advantageous arrangement for her grandparents too, because it was she who made breakfast for all three, washed the dishes, cleaned the house, and helped prepare the evening meal. When asked who she wanted to be like when grown, she chose a classmate – "because she is popular; everyone likes her." The follow-up question was "Would you like to be like your mother?" Her reply was "Oh no. She lives with that terrible man. He's really mean."

Extended Family Ties Outside the Home

The previous examples of living arrangements that include extended family members as part of the child's household illustrate the importance of relatives in the daily lives of these urban, Midwestern children. These ties are not confined to the household but extend to the broader neighborhood, and sometimes even to other geographical areas. Within the city, neighbor-hoods are often defined by ethnicity. There are sections where African Americans, Arab Americans, or Mexican Americans predominate, and rela-tives often live close to each other. Thus, one child described his "after-school day" by reporting that he returned home but his mother was not there, so he went to his aunt's house. Asked how far that was, he said "next door," and added that his grandmother lived across the street. Thus, there are ethnic pockets where extended kin live in close proximity. Since the population is a stable one, families may have lived in the same neighbor-hood for generations and immigrants to the city – from other countries or from southern states – often seek housing near kin.

Having extended family nearby is advantageous for many families, who rely on their kin for help in the day-to-day tasks of caring for children. Many of the children we interviewed mentioned grandparents, aunts, and uncles who provide transportation, care after school, and meals for them on typical days. For instance, Ian lives with his mother, father, and two younger brothers in part of his grandmother's house. He told the inter-viewer that "Grandma gave us the upper level of the house and half of the basement." The grandmother lives on the lower floor, but cooks meals for the entire family. On the night of his interview, "Grandma cooked beef stew, and we ate it in the kitchen at our table. Grandma ate it, too, but she eats downstairs at her table."

Nine-year-old Amber also lives in a two-parent family that receives reg-ular assistance from extended family. On the day Amber described in her interview, her grandfather picked her up from school and took her to her private violin lesson, while her mother took her younger children to Amber's grandmother's house to be cared for there. Amber's grandfather also drives her to school every morning.

Lauren, a seven-year-old girl living with her mother, mother's boyfriend, and one-year-old sister, told how her family uses the proximity of other family members to provide fall-back child care. On the afternoon she described in her interview, Lauren walked home from school and, finding no one at home, went next door to her thirteen-year-old cousin's house. She immediately called her grandmother, to let her know she was at the cousin's, although her aunt and aunt's boyfriend were also there. Lauren's mother works until 5 P.M. every day, but Lauren always goes straight home after school to see if her mother's boyfriend is home. If no one is there, she goes to the cousin's house and calls her grandmother to check in.

One example of the elaborate assistance provided by extended kin was provided in the story told by nine-year-old Zeke. Zeke lives with his mother, stepfather, two brothers, and a sister. The children receive care from their grandmother when the parents are working. After school, Zeke and his brother walked to their grandmother's house, where they are regularly cared for, along with several cousins. Soon, Zeke's mother picked him and his brother up and took them home. In Zeke's case, the mother spends the rest of the afternoon and the evening with her children; however, other cousins stay at the grandmother's house later, until their mothers get off work. Some of the cousins eat dinner there, and are often joined by their mothers, who stay on for dinner before returning home with their children. One cousin is picked up late in the evening, after he is put to bed at the grandmother's house. Although Zeke and his brother spend only a short period of time at their grandmother's after school, she also cares for them before school. In the morning, Zeke's mother wakes him up at 5 A.M.. He and his brother dress and are then taken to their grandmother's house, where they go back to sleep. Then at 8 A.M., Zeke's grandmother awakens the children, and Zeke, his brother, and another cousin eat breakfast and walk to school together.

The Nonresident Father and Other Males

Those children who did not live with their biological fathers were asked how often they see their fathers. Some had never seen their fathers, and others had seen their fathers only a handful of times in their lives. Overall, 33 percent of the children who did not live with their biological fathers see them once a week or more; 20 percent see their father's every other weekend; 11 percent see them more than once a year, but not more than once a month; and 36 percent see them once a year or less (including 13 percent who said they "never" see their fathers).

The children's descriptions of their relationships with their nonresidential fathers varied enormously, from warm and close to nonexistent. The following stories show not only the variety of family situations, but also the openness of children of this age and their acceptance of the patterns they experience, even when these patterns might seem unusual to others whose environmental backgrounds are quite different.

The story of Julia presented earlier is a rich example of the involvement of nonresidential fathers: all four fathers had contact with the children in the household, and seemed to provide assistance when possible. Another example of involvement by nonresidential fathers was provided by eight-year-old Grant, who lives with his mother and stepfather and has no siblings. He visits his "real" father every other weekend, and has regular contact with him during the week. On the afternoon he described in his interview, Grant was driven by his stepfather to his father's shop. Then Grant's father took him to his karate class. After karate, father and son used the father's truck for snowball target practice for a while before Grant's father took him home.

Ten-year-old Matthew lives with a single mother and both an older and younger brother, but reported seeing his father "lots." On the day of his interview, Matthew walked home from school, and his mother and younger brother were home when he got there. He watched television by himself while his brother was in his room playing and his mother was cleaning. Then his father picked him up and took him shopping and to his Cub Scouts meeting. Matthew's father is the leader of the Scout troop. After the meeting, his father dropped him back at home, and Matthew ate pizza in front of the television with his mother.

Occasionally, children told us why they do not see their fathers. Brad, an attractive, poised, eight-year-old, when asked if he saw his nonresidential father, replied: "No, not since the fire." "The fire?" the interviewer probed. "Yeah, when I was about three, I was visiting my dad and – my dad's into drugs. And there was this other family that were selling drugs, too, and they were mad at my dad and they burned the house down. I was in it and my mom was so mad she won't let me go back there anymore, so I haven't seen him since I was real little." Another eight-year-old boy, Jaymar, told the interviewer, "I used to see my dad, but not anymore. He didn't help my mom out with me and so she took him to court, but he didn't show up for the court date. So I haven't seen him in a few months."

In addition to, or instead of, maintaining contact with biological fathers, some children remain close to other members of the father's family. For instance, Shantal, the girl described in the sixteen person household, told us that her father's sister comes for her every day to take her to school. Although Shantal did not have contact with her father, she does not lack older males in her life. These include her sixteen-year-old uncle who supervises the children's outdoor play, her fourteen-year-old cousin Troy who is responsible for waking the children in the morning, her "Granny's boyfriend" who had made dinner that night, and her mother's boyfriend, who brought McDonald's food for breakfast.

Eight-year-old Paul lives with his single mother and twelve-year-old half sister. He last saw his own father when he was three, but he maintains an active relationship with his older sister's father, whom he calls "my dad." This man picks Paul up from school three days a week, and then goes to the junior high to retrieve the older child. Paul also described an "uncle Billy," who was at their house on the day he described, first sleeping upstairs, then going out to get milk for the family.

This pattern of the mother's current or past romantic partner as a presence in the child's life was a common one. Nine-year-old Kendall, a third-grader, lives with his mother, an older sister, and his mother's boyfriend, Todd. He visits his father every other weekend and "some weeknights." On the day of his interview, Kendall walked home from school with some friends, and Todd was home when he got there. Kendall watched cartoons on television alone for two hours, while Todd "was downstairs." After watching TV, Kendall called his father: "I told him what I got on my report card, and he was happy. Then we talked about whether he's gonna move away." They talked for about "five or ten minutes," and Kendall said that he calls his father every day. Then Kendall and Todd ate dinner together. His mother had cooked the meal, but Todd warmed it up. After dinner, Kendall went to the drug store with Todd, and they came home and had ice cream. Kendall got sick and vomited, and Todd took care of him. Kendall's mother was home by 10 P.M.. She told him it was time to go to bed. In the morning, it was his mother who prepared his breakfast and took him to school, while Todd was sleeping. On Wednesdays, Kendall goes to church after school with his aunt and cousin, but most days, it is Todd who is home when Kendall gets there.

Carrie was a soft-spoken nine-year-old who lived with her single mother and her aunt. She told the interviewer: "I never met my daddy. But my mom's old boyfriend lived with us from when I was only two months old until I was seven. And his three kids lived with us, too. Since he moved out, I still see him once every week."

These descriptions provide examples of some of the diverse family structures in which the children lived. Although the majority of the children lived in nuclear families with one or two parents and all their siblings, there were wide variations. Children lived with stepparents, friends and romantic partners of their parents, and extended kin. The other children in their homes included full siblings, stepsiblings, and halfsiblings, as well as cousins, young aunts or uncles, foster children, or children of parents' friends. In addition, there might be full siblings or parents who live in different households. But if it was clear that the household itself was not confined to the parents and their offspring, it was equally clear that the "family" was not confined to those who lived in the household. The children sought and received support from neighbors, kin, and family friends.

Who Cares for the Children While Parents Work?

Both mothers and children provided information about nonmaternal care. Here we draw only on our interviews with the children, and focus on how parental work patterns affect their daily experiences and routines. Children whose parents are at work during the nonschool hours experience a wide range of care and supervision arrangements. In Chapter 11, the issue of *latchkey* children, the term used to describe children who return home to an empty house, is taken up. As noted there and in Chapter 6, this pattern may occur because of the mother's employment but it is not exclusive to that group.

The children who were interviewed ranged from seven to ten years of age, and there was much variation in the extent to which they were under adult supervision before and after school. Most of these children (74%) reported that they went straight home after school. For those children who do not go home after school, there are a variety of other arrangements, presented in Table 3.2. Close to 5 percent go to the home of a relative after school, and 4 percent go to the home of a babysitter. A significant number of children attend after-school programs or other formal activities after school (such as roller-skating or bowling). Several children described being picked up from school by their mothers or another relative and then taken on various errands before stopping for a fast-food supper and going home for the night.

Of those children who went home after school, 73 percent had one or both of their parents there when they arrived home. An additional 8 percent were cared for by another adult relative, and 2 percent had an unrelated adult caregiver (babysitter) in their home. Twelve percent of the children were cared for at home after school by an older sibling. Only two of the children reported having a babysitter under fifteen years of age, and one child said she herself was the caregiver for her younger sibling. Seventeen children (5%) said that no one was at home when they got there, but three of these indicated that they were home alone for only ten or fifteen minutes.

A common kind of after-school care was the after-school supervision programs provided by the school or other community agencies. Melanie described an afternoon similar to many other children's: "After school, I went outside and found Miss Marcie, and we walked down to Rainbow Center." Many children, like Melanie, were picked up outside of school by a child-care worker who walked the children to a nearby child-care center. Other children were picked up by a van that drove them to the YMCA or roller-skating rink or other activity. One school had a YMCA-sponsored

Table 3.2. *Where Children Go After School*

Location	N	Percent
Home	344	74.0
Formal after-school activity (e.g., scouts, sports practice)	30	6.5
Home of a relative	23	4.9
After-school supervision program	21	4.5
Home of a regular babysitter	19	4.1
Errands with parent	14	3.0
Friend's house, with adult supervision	8	1.7
Other location, without adult supervision (including friend's house, mall, etc.)	3	.6
Errands with relative	3	.6

after-school program on-site – children went to the school auditorium and gym where they were supervised, given a snack, and could work on home-work or participate in group activities. Some children took French classes after school before joining the other children in this Y-program. Melanie described her afternoon at the center: "We went out in the playground and played, then we went into the field and played snowballs for a while. After we were finished, we went back inside and ate our snack and made Valentines pictures. Then I sat down and did my homework until my dad picked me up at five o'clock." At this particular center, there are about twenty five children, ranging in age from five to eleven years.

Another source of child-care assistance is other parents who live nearby. Nine-year-old Stacey, who lives alone with her single working mother, explained the arrangement her mother has with a neighbor: "Every day after school I always go to my neighbor's house. She takes care of her baby at home, so I walk her other little boy home from school. I play games there and watch TV, then I go home at about 4:15 because my mom doesn't mind if I'm home alone for 15 minutes – she gets home at 4:30."

As Stacey's story reminds us, while some parents rely on other families to provide care for their children, others are the ones who provide the care. Some do both. Nine-year-old Billy lives with his two parents and younger brother, in a household very affected by parental work schedules. After school, he is brought home by the mother of a friend, and he stays home with his mother and brother for about an hour. His father is still at work. Then at 4 P.M. Billy's mother drives him and his brother to their grand-mother's home before going to work. He and his brother are cared for in the evening by this grandmother two nights a week, and his other grandmother one night a week. The other nights, his mother is off work, so they are at home. Billy's mother picks up the boys at around 9 P.M.. Their father does not come home until "ten or eleven or twelve. Poor guy," said Billy, "he should deserve a break." In the morning, Billy's mother cares for several neighbor children while their mother goes to work. The children eat breakfast at their house, and she drives them all to school.

Grandparents and other extended family members often provide child-care assistance to parents. The story of Zeke and his cousins at their grandmother's house was one example. Another is the after-school care of nine-year-old Mason, who is the oldest of four children of two working parents. When he arrives home from school, his mother and siblings are there, but his mother leaves for work at 5 P.M. Mason's grandmother arrives at the house before his mother leaves for work, and she watches the four children, cooks supper, and puts the children to bed. Mason's father comes home from work at 10 P.M., after the children are asleep, and his mother comes home at 1 A.M..

No Adult at Home After School.

The children who return to a house without adults may be a preselected group – a group, that is, whose parents know that they can handle it (Coley & Hoffman 1996). Ten-year-old Darnell, for example, on the day described in the interview, returned to an empty house with his three younger sisters, who ranged in age from five to eight. Although they were alone until 8:30 in the evening, they followed standard routines. The children first did their chores, then watched cartoons on television, and then played hide and seek together. Darnell prepared a microwave meal for himself and his sisters, which they ate together at the dining-room table. After dinner, the children took baths and watched television until their mother returned from work at 8:30. This was unusual in Darnell's family because his stepfather, who is usually home after school, was out of town on business.

For Drew, a nine-year-old, and his older brother, twelve, returning home to an empty house is standard. The boys live with their mother and stepfather, both of whom are employed. On the day he described, the boys made their own supper and ate it together at the kitchen table. The dishes were left for a parent to clean up later. Their mother works until midnight as a nurse, and their stepfather gets home between 6 and 8 P.M.. The boys usually wait until the stepfather comes home before having dinner, but on this night, he was picking them up to take them to a baseball game, so they ate ahead of time.

Eight-year-old Greta has two working parents, a nine-year-old brother, and younger brothers aged two and four. She and her older brother take the bus home from school and arrive home to an empty house. (The two younger boys are at a babysitter's during the day.) Greta and her brother call their mother at work when they get home, and spend the afternoon similarly to Darnell and his sisters: watching cartoons, doing homework, and playing video games. Both parents come home at 5 P.M.. On the day described, Greta went with her mother at that time to pick up her little brothers and to be dropped off at her Brownie meeting. Greta admitted that "sometimes I get scared when I am at home without my parents and only my brother is taking care of me."

Ted, the oldest of four brothers in a two-parent family, seemed particularly responsible for his age. Ted walked home from school with friends and arrived, as usual, at an empty house. He immediately did his homework, then watched TV until his mother arrived home. His mother picked up the three younger boys from a babysitter's house, and arrived home about 45 minutes after Ted. It is a household rule that Ted cannot go outside until his mother is home, and as soon as she arrived, he went out to play. Ted's father returned from work just before supper. In the morning, the family is up early; the alarm goes off at 5:15 A.M. Ted gets himself dressed and, on the morning described, "helped to iron his mother's clothes for work." By 7 A.M. Ted's father was already gone. His mother left for work later, taking Ted's brothers to the babysitter's on her way. Ted stayed home alone, made and ate his breakfast, then walked to school with a friend. Before leaving for school, Ted always calls his mother at work to tell her he is on his way.

Claire, a fourth grader, and her fourteen-year-old sister also seem capable of being home without an adult, although they might benefit from more interaction with an adult. Claire is a crossing guard after school. When she is done, she goes home, and she and her sister are alone there until their mother returns from work at 5 P.M. Their mother, who is single, works in their apartment building, cleaning apartments, and she leaves a note telling the girls where she is that day so they can call her to check in when they arrive home. Television is the main activity, and on the day Claire described, three other girls came over and watched TV while Claire's mother was at work. After dinner, Claire helped her mother select clothes to wear when she went out with a friend. After the mother's departure, the girls were alone again. They decided on their own when to go to bed. The older sister went to bed at 8:30; Claire at 9:30. Claire commented to the interviewer: "It doesn't bother me that mom's not home, as long as I know the door is bolted and locked."

In all of these cases, the children are required to remain in the house and there is telephone contact with the parents or other adults. This was the common pattern, but it was not always the case. Neither was it always the case that the older child seemed to be a responsible caretaker for younger ones. When Gregory returned home from school, his fourteen-year-old brother was there, but he left the house shortly afterward. Gregory did some homework but then left to go to the park to "shoot baskets." He hoped to join other boys who might be there, but found none. After more than an hour, he returned home. His brother arrived later and the two boys ate TV dinners together. Then the brother left again. Gregory also went out briefly to see if other neighborhood boys were around. Since they weren't, he returned home and watched TV. At about 9 P.M., his brother returned, and shortly after that their mother came home from work. Gregory watched television with his mother until 10:30 and then went to bed.

No Adult at Home at Other Times

Studies of *latchkey* children usually focus on who is home after school, but exclusive focus on that period would underestimate the extent to which children are left without adult caretakers. Sometimes parents are home after school, but have to leave for work early in the morning before the child can depart for school. Work hours often include Saturdays. And sometimes parents work late shifts, or double shifts.

As an example, Katlyn, a nine-year-old, lives with her mother, her seven-year-old brother, and their baby sister. Their mother, a beautician, is there both before school and after. In the course of the narrative, however, Katlyn mentioned that her mother works half-days on Saturday. During this time, the three children are left alone. Katlyn and her brother are responsible for caring for the baby.

Evan's mother, a divorced UPS employee, works from 10 P.M. until 3 A.M. Thus, she is home when Evan comes home from school, is there for dinner and his bedtime (10 P.M. on the night he described in the interview), and she is there to see him off to school in the morning. But our interview of Evan revealed that when Evan got in bed, his mother came in to say "goodbye" rather than "goodnight." She was off to work, leaving Evan and his thirteen-year-old sister to sleep alone in the house. Evan's grandmother lives in the apartment downstairs, and although she stays in her own home, Evan said she is available to "answer our door if anyone comes."

Some parents have work schedules that seem especially challenging for themselves and their families. For example, Loretta's mother works two eight-hour shifts on many days. Loretta, a fourth-grade girl, walks home after school with her ten-year-old stepsister, and they are home alone until 5 P.M. When they get home, they call Loretta's aunt to check in – this aunt takes care of Loretta's baby sister during the day. When Loretta's mother came home on the day of this interview, they went to pick up the baby sister at her aunt's, then returned home. At some point, the mother went to sleep, and Loretta said, "I had to wake her up so I could eat some dinner." The rest of the evening, the children occupied themselves while the mother slept. Loretta is responsible for waking her mother up for her 11 P.M. shift at work, and the children are left sleeping alone in the house until midnight, when Loretta's stepfather returns from work.

Variations in Work Patterns

As in the situations for Evan and Loretta, parents' work hours are not always the conventional ones. Sometimes variant work schedules seem to make childcare issues more complicated, sometimes easier. In several of our dual-wage families, both parents worked night shifts and needed, therefore, to find other hours to sleep. Thus, the children described being home with sleeping parents after school or in the mornings. For example, third-grader Alexis lives with her two working parents, a twelve-year-old sister, and a five-year-old brother. These children were not left unattended, but the parents' work patterns did affect family routines and parent–child interaction. When Alexis arrived home from school on the afternoon she described, her sister was home, and her father was home but sleeping. Soon, Alexis's mother came home, and by suppertime, the whole family was awake and ate at the same time, although the parents ate in front of the television while the children ate in the kitchen. During the meal, the babysitter arrived, and first Alexis's mother and then her father left for work. The babysitter helped get the children into bed and stayed as the children slept. In the morning, Alexis washed and dressed as her mother, who had returned home at some point during the early morning, slept. Her father came home from work in time to make breakfast for the children, and to see them off to school. The typical pattern in this family is that the father is sleeping in the afternoon when the children come home from school, and the mother is sleeping in the morning as the children wake up and get ready for school.

Nicholas is the youngest of four boys living with their working mother and stepfather. His stepfather works from 3 P.M. to 12 A.M., and his mother works from 4 P.M. to 11 P.M. every day. Nicholas and his brothers come straight home after school, where they immediately eat supper with their mother. A babysitter then comes to the house to care for the boys and put them to bed. In the morning, the boys get themselves up, dressed, and fed, and then they walk to school together while their parents sleep.

By contrast, some jobs provide more flexibility than others in the ways that child care is handled. Tracy, a third-grader, described her time after school at the restaurant where her father works: Her mother picked her and her brother up from school and dropped them off at the restaurant, and the children stayed in a back room. The children worked on homework and then played tag in the restaurant after the customers had left. At around 4:30 the children went home and spent the evening with their father, who cooked dinner and talked with the children about what happened that day at school. Tracy's mother came home at 8:30 P.M., and was there to say good-night to Tracy when she got in bed at 9:00. In the morning, it was her mother who was there to wake the children and help get them off to school, while her father was already gone for the day. These parents have arranged their work schedules so that one of them is always responsible for the children: On Tuesdays and Thursdays, the children spend the afternoon with their father at his place of work and the evenings at home with him, on Mondays their father is home with them after school, and on Wednesdays and Fridays their mother picks them up and cares for them at home.

Lily is a nine-year-old with two working parents and three sisters, whose father's job also provided some flexibility. Lily's father is a firefighter, which means that he works one full day and then has two days off. On the day of her interview, her father was home, and he cared for the girls and drove Lily to her cheerleading practice. Lily's mother came home at 6:30, but it was her father who made supper and put the girls to bed. On days when her father is working, the girls are home alone after school, with the two older girls (aged fourteen and twelve) in charge; they call their mother at work to check in.

Thus, even for families with school-aged children, work presents a challenge to parents in their efforts to provide adequate care and supervision. The community in this study probably provided more support than many others. The schools were open to children before classroom teaching began in the morning and provided supervision and breakfast. Several schools provided on-site supervision after school, and there were various school-related and community-sponsored after-school programs as well. Nevertheless, the coordination of work schedules with family life and children's needs requires ingenuity and support networks. Clearly it is a challenge for parents to find ways to work and provide for the financial well-being of their families, while also ensuring adequate supervision and sufficient opportunities to be with their children. The children's stories of their "after-school day" attest to the variety of adaptations that have been made.

Variations Within Categories

The presentation by the media in America, even when tolerant of the new family styles, still suggests an inherent deficiency in the single-mother family and the employed-mother family. Part of this imagery is based on a stereotype of the two-parent, full-time homemaker family that is not borne out in our children's stories. Does the child in the "model" family come down to a hot breakfast prepared by his or her mother? Does the entire family gather around the dining room table, Norman Rockwell style, for the evening meal? Does the child whose mother is a full-time homemaker get the benefit of her time and attention? Is the family with the two original parents always a warm and interactive one for the child? In this section we present the children's scenarios to show the wide variations that exist within social categories. We start, however, with the children's reports about some standard family routines.

Routines

Table 3.3 shows the distribution of children's meal-time routines, including who prepares breakfast and supper and who eats the evening meal together. Eighty-five percent of the children had breakfast at home before school (44% fixed it themselves; 41% had it fixed for them by a parent or someone else in the household). An additional 8 percent of the children ate breakfast at school (provided free or at reduced-cost to low-income children), and 1 percent (5 children) ate breakfast at a fast-food restaurant before school. Another 5 percent (24 children) did not eat any breakfast on the day of their interview.

Most children reported that supper was prepared for them by a parent or other adult (85% with twelve of these children assisting in the meal preparation). Nine children (2%) prepared their own evening meal, and seven (1.6%) had supper prepared by an older sibling. Supper was prepared outside the home (at a restaurant or take-out establishment) for fifty-one children (11%), and two children said they did not have any supper on the night described in the interview. However, a fuller picture of these children's family lives is given when we consider not only who prepared the meal, but

Table 3.3. *Meal-time Routines*

	N	Percent
Who Makes Breakfast?		
Child	199	43.9
Parent	153	33.8
Child eats breakfast at school	38	8.4
Someone else at home	34	7.5
Child did not eat breakfast	24	5.3
Child eats fast food	5	1.1
Who Makes Supper?		
Parent	319	71.4
Other adult	47	10.5
Child and parent(s)	12	2.7
Child (with or without siblings)	9	2.0
Older sibling	7	1.6
None of the above (child ate at a restaurant or take-out)	51	11.4
Child did not eat supper	2	.4
Who Eats Supper with Child?		
Whole family	272	60.2
Sibling(s) but not parents	44	9.7
Mother, but not father	38	8.4
Father, but not mother	23	5.1
Child eats alone	23	5.1
Extended family members, but not parents	21	4.6
Child and parents, but not sibling(s)	11	2.4
Family members each eat separately	10	2.2
Child ate at a friend's house	6	1.3
Sitter or other adult	4	.9

who ate it together. In 60 percent of the households, all family members ate together, and in the rest, family members ate either singly or in different combinations. Five percent of the children ate completely alone, and 10 percent ate with their siblings but not their parents. Often, some family members would eat together while others ate in different rooms of the house – usually to watch television.

Although all children's reports were about a day preceding a school day, bedtime practices varied widely. The most common bedtime was between 8 and 9 P.M. (47% of the children interviewed), and a fair proportion (33%) went to bed after 9 but before 10 P.M. Fourteen percent of the children went to bed at 10 P.M. or later, and the remaining 6 percent went to bed at 8 P.M.

or earlier. The children were asked whether anyone came in to say good-night to them after they were in bed, and while most children had at least one parent or other adult say goodnight to them, 21 percent reported that no one came in to say goodnight.

Interactions

As the children described their after-school day, wide variations were apparent in the quality of their lives. A particular contrast was the extent to which the child moved into a highly interactive environment or an isolated one.

The children's narratives were coded to indicate how much time the child spent during the hours after school without interacting with others, regard-less of whether there was an adult or anyone else present. Twenty-three per-cent of the children spent no significant amount of time without interaction; 16% spent two or more hours without interactions. The majority of children (61%) described spending a moderate amount of time – typically less than two hours a day – without interacting with others. This was related neither to employment status nor marital status, and unexpectedly, the child with the lowest level of interactions with others lived in an intact family with his original parents, and his mother was a full-time homemaker.

Brandon was a sober nine-year-old child. He had no siblings. His mother was always home when he returned from school. When he arrived home on the day he described, he went straight to his bedroom where he first com-pleted his homework and then played Nintendo until his mother brought supper to him on a tray. In response to the interviewer's probes, he reported that his mother was home but "downstairs" during the entire time except for delivering his meal. He did not mention his father but he explained, when asked, that his father came home at 5:30. After his supper, Brandon turned to television; at 7:30 he prepared himself for bed, and at 8:00 his mother came up to tell him it was time to turn the television off. Again, the inter-viewer asked about the parents' activities and Brandon reported that they stayed downstairs and talked and ate supper together. Asked if that was a typical day, he said yes, except that bedtime was later on Friday and Saturday nights, and that sometimes on Saturdays his parents went out and a sitter came to the house.

A similar story of isolation within the home was told by Amanda. Amanda is ten and lives with her mother, stepfather, and fifteen-year-old brother. Both parents work. On the day she described, she stayed after school an extra hour for "singing practice." Her mother picked her and a friend up at school and dropped both off at a skating rink. They were picked up at 6 P.M. by the friend's father. Amanda ate dinner with her parents when she arrived home, but for the rest of the evening, she entertained herself. She played by herself outside in the snow after the meal and then came inside and watched television alone for an hour and a half. During this time, her brother was in his room watching his TV, and her mother and stepfather were in their room watching their TV. Amanda commented that her brother "hardly ever comes out of his room." At 10 P.M. Amanda decided to go to bed, and she took a shower, picked out her clothes for the next day, and went to bed without saying goodnight to anyone. Amanda's alarm clock woke her at 6:30 the next morning. Both her mother and stepfather had already left for work. Her brother was home until he had to leave for school at 7:10. She watched TV until 7:30, made herself breakfast, then walked to a friend's house. The friend's mother drove them to school. Amanda said this represented a pretty typical day – she usually goes straight home, either after school or singing practice, and her brother is usually the only one home. She has no contact with her parents until they come home from work – her mother at 4:30, and her stepfather at 6:00. She does not see her original father on a regular basis, and had last seen him six months prior to her interview.

Eight-year-old Timothy provides another example of a child who seems to be alone at home, even when others are there. Timothy lives with his single mother and twenty-year-old sister. His mother does not work but his sister does. After school on the day he described, he walked home and began his homework as soon as he arrived. His mother was at home, but he did not mention any interactions with her. After finishing his homework, he watched cartoons on TV while his mother took a bath. Timothy's sister was at work all afternoon and evening. His mother prepared spaghetti for dinner, and she ate in the living room while Timothy ate in the kitchen. Each of them watched television as they ate. After supper, his mother dressed to go out to a movie. This night, however, was a special one for Timothy because it was a night to spend with his Big Brother (a community volunteer from the Big Brothers program). His Big Brother picked him up just before the mother left, and he spent the evening at his "brother's" house. "We got to play pool, and also a game called Life. Then we watched wrestling on TV. It was really fun, and I got to stay there until 10:30, even though I usually go to bed at 9:30."

In marked contrast to the descriptions given by Brandon, Amanda, and Timothy are those provided by Erin, Myesha, Hank, and Kevin. Erin is a third-grade girl who lives in a dual-wage family, with her original parents and six-year-old sister. Erin's mother gets out of work at 3:00, the same time that school is over, so it was 3:30 before the girls could be picked up from school. They worked on their homework in the school's supervised reading room until their mother arrived. Once home, Erin spent about ten minutes finishing her homework then watched a children's television program with her mother and sister. Next, the girls played school in their room for about half an hour, and then they helped their mother prepare supper. The entire family sat at the table together for the meal, and they talked about what the mother and father had done at work that day and what the girls had done at school. Erin reported that she enjoyed the meal. Afterward, she helped her mother with the dishes, and the whole family watched the evening news together on television. Next, the whole family went together to the grocery store, and the sisters played outside briefly after returning home. Finally, the girls came in, got ready for bed, and watched television briefly before going to bed at 8:45. Both parents came in to kiss the girls goodnight.

Myesha is another example of a child whose family life is interactive. Like Timothy, Myesha lives in a single-mother family. Her mother is employed, and she has two younger sisters. She returns from school to an empty house where she is responsible for her school-aged sister. Like some of the examples in the previous section, ten-year-old Myesha seems to be able to handle this responsibility. However, her situation seems different from some in the previous section, such as Claire, because Myesha's day includes considerably more parent–child interaction. On the day of her interview, Myesha walked home with her sister and a friend. As soon as she and her sister were in their house, she called her youngest sister's babysitter to tell her they were okay, and then the two older sisters played "beauticians." After about half an hour, she offered to help her sister with homework, but there had been none assigned. So, her sister "got out markers and paper and drew while I did my homework. I saved a couple of problems for when my mom got home. Then I made a frame for my sister's picture with popsicle sticks and plastic – I learned how to do it at camp. Then we straightened up our room, and Mom came home at five o'clock. She picks up my little sister on the way home. I showed my mom the problems that I needed help on, and after she helped me, we all watched TV." After two television programs, "Mom asked what we wanted for dinner." Myesha said she enjoyed eating at the dining-room table with her two sisters and mother, and talking about her sister's day at school. The girls helped clean up after dinner, and then the three girls and their mother played "Charades." The younger girls went to bed as Myesha and her mother did some housecleaning. At around 8:30, Myesha decided to get ready for bed. She then wrote in her diary for ten minutes, and her mother came in and kissed her goodnight at 9:00. In the morning, Myesha's mother woke the girls, helped them pick their clothes and do their hair. Then their mother left for work taking the youngest child to the sitter on the way. The two older sisters ate breakfast and then walked to school. Myesha said this was a pretty typical day: she always goes straight home after school, and "if I'm lucky, Mom's there. But usually, it's no one. Mom gets home at six at the latest."

Hank, a nine-year-old boy with three older siblings and a younger brother, lives with their single mother. He also described a family life with supportive interaction. After school on the day he described, he took the bus home. His nonemployed mother was home with his sister and younger brother. Hank changed his clothes, and went to "basketball practice" with some other boys in the neighborhood. After practice, his mother spent an hour with him, helping him with his homework. Next, his mother prepared supper while Hank and his younger brother set the dinner table. The whole family ate together in the dining room. The dinner ritual included family prayers, and after dinner, they all watched television together. At nine o'clock, Hank's mother sent him upstairs to shower and get ready for bed, then she came in to "tuck him in." "First, she sat on my bed and we talked a little about school, and about not doing drugs and other stuff. Then she gave me a kiss and said goodnight." In the morning, Hank's oldest brother wakes him up at 7 A.M., and his next oldest brother picks out Hank's clothes. Their mother makes breakfast, and he eats with his mother and one brother before taking the bus to school.

Kevin's family consists of his two parents, a younger brother, and a preschool sister. As he described his after-school day, it got off to a bad start. Normally, Kevin walks home from school with his younger brother, but on this day, he walked home with a friend while his brother walked to a friend's house. Kevin found no one was home when he arrived and, worse, the door was locked and he had no key. "I waited on the back porch until my mom and sister came home. I was in a bad mood then because my mom didn't tell me she was going to get a haircut and wasn't going to be home," he said. Once in the house (the wait was about 15 minutes), Kevin did his homework and watched television alone until his father and brother came home. Then the whole family went to the YMCA: Kevin and his brother had basketball practice, his mother took an aerobics class, his father worked out with a friend, and his little sister was in the YMCA babysitting center. After their workout, the family came home, and ate a meal, prepared by Kevin's mother, together in the dining room. Kevin explained: "We don't watch TV during dinner. We talked about school and sports, and ate really good spaghetti and garlic bread." After dinner, the family watched television together and talked about the shows. Kevin decided at 9:30 to go to bed, and both parents came in to say goodnight.

These seven narratives are meant to illustrate that the quality of the child's experience is not determined by employment status, or marital status, or even socioeconomic status, for the contrasting sets presented provide examples from each category. In later chapters, particularly Chapter 6, we will see whether categories such as dual-wage versus single-wage show statistically significant differences in parent/child interaction patterns. But it is important to realize that even when they do (and they often do not) we are only demonstrating a central tendency, and within each group there is wide variation.

Poverty and Stress

Even the children who lived in the particularly impoverished inner-city section of the community or in "the Projects" did not talk about their poverty nor describe themselves as poor, but their stories often revealed very crowded households and limited facilities. For example, Debra lived with five brothers, a younger sister, and both parents, but in addition, the house was often filled with various friends of her parents. When she arrived home from school, she watched television until "dinner" was served. It consisted of various members of the family eating different things in the living room while watching television. Since Debra's mother had made eggs, Debra made a sandwich with them for her meal. She then did some chores. After watching television again, Debra "went into my mom's room and lay on her waterbed with her. Then my mom's friend came in and asked her to go with him to get a steak, and she said yes. So we went to get a steak: me, my mom, my mom's two friends, and her friend's baby and daughter. It was fun. She gave me some of her steak and I had some fries. After we were back home, my mom was in the kitchen talking to her friend and smoking a cigarette. I tried to sit with them, but my dad grabbed my arm and said not to go in there. He didn't want no kids in there." It was after 10 P.M. when Debra went to her room. She sleeps on a mattress on the floor "because my mom gave my bunk bed to my niece, and she needs her check to get me a new one."

Debra was not the only child who mentioned a shortage of sleeping space or beds. Some children slept with their mothers or grandmothers. Nine-year-old Emily lives with her mother, stepfather, grandmother, and younger brother and sister. Describing her bedtime, she said, "My daddy told me it was time at eight o'clock, so I went upstairs. I sleep on the floor because we don't have enough beds." Logan, an eight-year-old, reported that his bed was broken so he couldn't sleep in it, but his dad was going to fix it.

Broken furniture and appliances were mentioned in other stories. Stephanie, for example, lives with her mother, her mother's boyfriend, Max, and her younger brother. On the day described, Max picked the children up at the babysitter where they went after school, and the three went to buy fish for dinner. When Stephanie's mother came home from work, she and Max made supper together. The whole family ate dinner at the same time, but "Max had to eat in the living room because one of our chairs is broken." Nor was that all that was broken: "After dinner we all went over to my mom's friend's house to take showers because the water heater at our house is broken." But back at home, promptly at 9 P.M., the children said goodnight to Max and went up to bed. When Stephanie and her brother were in bed, their mother came in to "pray with us and give us kisses."

For older children, the lack of privacy and opportunity to do homework, study, or read might have been more manifest, but for these elementary school children, the repeated theme was lack of sleep. Nicole's description of her after-school day focuses on this. Nicole is an eight-year-old who lives with her two parents and three older siblings. In addition, the family had just taken in two foster children. After school on the day described, Nicole's mother picked her up at school and drove her home. When they arrived, her father and brother were there but her father was asleep. "My dad is always home when I get home, but he's always sleeping because he likes to stay up late." Nicole was tired and wanted to take a nap. "I went to my room and got my sheet. I lay down and slept for a few minutes, but my brother was talking too loud and it woke me up. I tried to get back to sleep but the other kids were home and the television was on, so I got up and watched with them." Nicole's family, both parents and the six children, watched television all evening. Supper was eaten in front of the set. After supper, Nicole "just tried to go back to sleep in front of the TV. But everybody was screaming and laughing, so I couldn't. I just stayed there 'til about ten and then went to bed." The rest of the family remained in front of the TV.

Ten o'clock was not late for many of these children. Tanisha, for example, who lives with her grandparents, aunts, and uncles, reported that on the night before her interview she went to bed at 10 or 11 P.M. "That's when I go to bed on school nights, but sometimes I go late, like at three. My granddad, grandma, uncles, or aunties tell me to go to bed then. But I can watch TV in my room. Last night, after I went to bed I watched TV and played with my Barbies in bed." Asked whether anyone came in to say goodnight, she replied "No, never. But sometimes my grandma sleeps with me in my bed when she wants to get away from my granddad."

Danger

Although children's experience with violence in their neighborhoods was not an explicit focus of the interview, some comments reflected the fact that some of the children live in neighborhoods where violence is a real concern. Some children were not allowed to play outside without adult supervision. Others were not allowed to walk to school, even when they lived close enough to make this feasible. Brad, the boy whose father's house had been burned down by drug dealers, said he takes the bus to school but not home: "My mother doesn't want me taking the bus home 'cause she heard about a man who killed four black boys going home by themselves." Eight-year-old Eliza, a third-grader who lives alone with her mother, told of a dinner conversation about the dangers of the neighborhood. She and her mother were having supper with her grandparents who lived close by. "We all were at the kitchen table and we talked about someone who kidnapped people. Grandma said I'd better be careful."

Leanne lives with her two parents and five brothers and sisters ranging in age from five to fifteen years. Comments during her interview reflect how neighborhood violence affects her family's routines. She explained that after school she walked home, and played video games with her dad until her older brother came home. "My brother's school is further so he goes first to my auntie's house after school. Then my auntie calls my mom to tell her he's safe." In describing bed time, Leanne said, "I took a bath with my older sister, and then mommy and daddy came in to say goodnight. They gave each of us a kiss on the forehead, and made sure all the doors and windows were locked up tight."

Angelique, who was described earlier living with her aunt, uncle, and adult cousin during the school year, described her fears. She stayed at school for tutoring until 4 P.M., then came home and worked on homework and an art project by herself. There was little interaction with the three adults, although all were at home. Her aunt fixed supper, and Angelique ate alone in the kitchen, while her uncle ate in the dining room. She said that during supper, "I was scared, 'cause the kitchen's in the basement and I hear noises." After supper, Angelique colored with her markers, then took a bath and got herself ready for bed. Her aunt went to work, but her uncle was home. Angelique watched TV in her bedroom with her twelve-year-old brother who had come over to visit. Although she usually goes to sleep at 9 P.M., on this night she didn't go to sleep until 11 or 12 P.M. "I couldn't go to sleep without my aunt," she explained. "I was scared of noises."

Had the interview focused more on fears or even on violence witnessed, more of such materials would probably have been elicited, for some of the neighborhoods included in our sample had very high crime rates. In fact, two of the local interviewers hired to conduct mothers' interviews in their homes refused to go into the Projects alone. But in these open-ended descriptions of the children's day, these themes were not prominent. Most of the schools were homogeneous with respect to socioeconomic status, and thus, what might seem unusual to someone from a different background may seem commonplace to children of this age whose interactions are confined to their neighborhood and families. We didn't ask if they passed drug dealers on their way to school, so if they did, they didn't think it was interesting enough to mention.

Conclusion

The sample used in this study is a diverse one in that it represents a wide socioeconomic range and different ethnic groups. In this chapter, we have emphasized individual family diversity. There are differences in what constitutes a family, individual variations in how families handle the interface between work patterns and home life, variations in household routines, and differences between families in degrees of intimacy and levels of interactions. And while there may be more commonality within groups of families that have similar economic circumstances, or employment patterns, or marital status, there are also wide variations within these categories.

To show this, we have relied heavily on the children's stories of "what they did yesterday from the time they got out of school until they arrived at school this morning." The children enjoyed telling their stories. Most children were not only excited to participate in the study because the interview provided a break from their normal school-day routine; they liked having someone ask them about their lives and their families. The children told us of their lives very matter-of-factly, seeming to have no sense that their lives were unusual, or might seem so to the interviewers. Although our sample of children was socioeconomically diverse, the children tended to be living in neighborhoods and attending schools mostly with other children like themselves, so they were unlikely to think that their situations were anything other than "normal." In this chapter we have presented the stories of some of these children to add to the stories that are told by the statistical analyses in the chapters that follow. These simple stories of single days in these children's lives speak to a different aspect of their family life experiences.

Notes

1. More than one child we interviewed described siblings on their fathers' side in such a way as to suggest that the father had children with more than one woman during the same general time period. One example is "Dolisha," who lived with her mother and natural father, her grandfather, a sixteen-year-old-brother, and a seven-year-old sister. However, Dolisha listed several other siblings with ages both older and younger, and said, "My dad has nine kids, but I don't know the ninth one. My other brothers and sisters live with their mamas."

4   The Husband–Wife Relationship

We begin our analysis by examining the relationship between the mother's employment status and the role of the father in the family. This has been a topic of continuing interest in itself since the 1950s (Blood, 1963; Nye & Hoffman, 1963), and, in addition, consequences of maternal employment for children are often seen as operating through the effects on the father's role (see Chapter 1). The relationships to be examined here are illustrated in Figure 4.1. We will first take up the relationships between the mother's employment status and various aspects of the father's role in the family, particularly with respect to the division of household tasks and childrearing functions. Second, we will examine the relationships between maternal employment and the parents' gender-role attitudes. Third, we turn to the links between the father's role and the gender-role attitudes, and explore the possibility that the father's role mediates a maternal employment/gender-role attitude connection. Finally, we consider the complex relationships among maternal employment, father's role, and the marital satisfaction of each parent.

Sample

Because the focus here is on the role of the father in the household, the analysis in this chapter includes only two-parent families. A family was defined as two-parent if the mother had a male partner who had resided in the home for more than one year, and was considered part of the conjugal family by the mother. We also include only families where the mothers have had a stable employment status for the past three years.

Measures

Division of Roles: Who Does It More?

During the home interview with mothers a forty-eight-item list of household tasks and child-care activities was presented. The mothers were asked

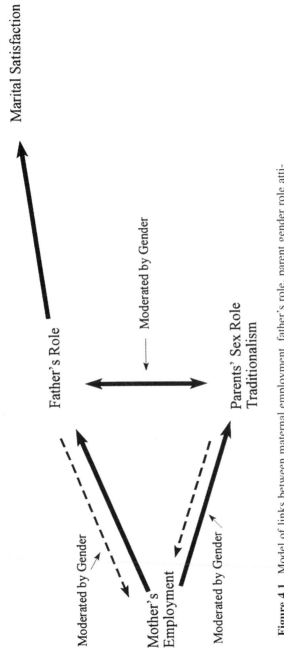

Figure 4.1. Model of links between maternal employment, father's role, parent gender role attitudes, and marital satisfaction.

to indicate for each if that was an activity that was done by the mother only, the mother mostly but the father ("husband" or "male partner") sometimes, both equally, the father mostly but the mother sometimes, by the father only, or by neither. Each item was scored on a five-point scale: 4 = mother, not father; 3 = mother mostly, but father sometimes; 2 = both equally or neither does it; 1 = father mostly but mother sometimes; 0 = father, not mother. Seven composite variables were made by grouping the items in the following manner:

1. *Traditional female tasks* was a sum of ten household tasks that have been traditionally assigned to women (e.g., cleans and dusts, cooks the evening meal, does the laundry)
2. *Child-care tasks* included seven items (e.g., takes care of the children, gets the children to eat the foods they should, gets the children to go to bed)
3. *Functional interactions* included four interactive activities with the child that were primarily functional (e.g., takes them shopping, takes them to the doctor)
4. *Financial tasks* included three items having to do with money (e.g., buys big new things for the family; pays the monthly bills)
5. *Play* covered eight items (e.g., plays games in the house with the children, plays outside with the children, roughhouses with the children)
6. *School/educational* included six school-related and teaching activities (e.g., helps the children with school work, reads to them or listens to them read)
7. *Nurturance* covered five affectionate and nurturant behaviors (e.g., expresses affection to the children, takes care of them when they're sick, praises them)

For each of these composites, higher scores indicate that the mother performs the activity relatively more than the father and lower scores indicate that the father performs the activity relatively more than the mother.

The primary measure used in this analysis is based on the mother's reports. However, the same instrument was completed by fathers in self-administered questionnaires, and a child's version was administered during a personal interview conducted in the school. The measure administered to the children used a different format and includes an additional scale tapping discipline roles. This instrument is described later. There was substantial agreement among reporters. The correlations between the parents' reports ranged from .79 for traditional female tasks to .53 for child care; in all cases the correlations were statistically significant with $p < .001$. Parent–child agreement was similar but lower; for example, mother–child agreement on traditional female tasks was .50 ($p < .001$) and for child care was .23 ($p < .01$).

Father–Child Interactions with Target Child

The self-administered questionnaire for fathers included a list of eighteen activities with a request to indicate how often they had done each with the target child during the previous seven days. Possible answers to be checked were: not at all, once, twice, three or four times, more than four, or "not at all this past week, but we usually do." Composite scores were constructed by combining similar items. Each item was scored on a six-point scale with 0 for not at all and 5 for more than four times. If the father checked the last, indicating "not this week but usually," the item was given the modal score for the composite.

There were five composites: *Fun* activities consisted of five items (e.g., played a game in the house, played outside, went somewhere just for fun – like movies or a park). *Talk* included two items, "talked about what happened at school" and "had a talk about other things." *Affectionate* had four items (e.g., "Showed affection – hugged or kissed", "Helped with something he/she wanted help with," "Went for a walk together"). *Educational* consisted of five items (e.g., read a book together, helped with homework). *Total* was the sum of all eighteen items. In each case, a high score indicates higher reported interaction by the father.

Although there is overlap in the content of the Division of Role measures and the Father–Child Interactions with the Target Child, the measures are different in two respects. First, the Division of Role measures tap the role of the father relative to the mother while Father–Child Interaction taps how active the father actually is. Thus, a father might be more affectionate to the child than the mother is, as indicated in the Division of Roles measure, Nurturance, but still not obtain a high score on the Affectionate index of the Father–Child Interactions measure if the overall expression of parental affection is low. Second, the Division of Roles measures family roles, while the Father–Child Interactions with Target Child measures dyadic interaction with the specific child in the study. Thus, the former asks, "Who plays games in the house with the children?" but the latter asks, "How often over the last seven days did you play games with (specific child)?"

Fathers' Roles as Perceived by Children

In a personal interview, children were asked a series of "Who does it?" questions that were matched in content to the parents' measures. This instrument, called the Day at Home, was modeled after a form originally developed by Herbst (1952) and modified in subsequent research (Hoffman & Lippitt, 1960; Goodnow, 1988). Our version consisted of forty-eight items. The child was asked, for example, "Who gets breakfast in your family?" and then was asked to indicate the person or persons who did it most of the time, others who often did it, those who did it occasionally, and those who never did it. A list of all of the members of the child's household was provided for each item, and the child, with the help of the interviewer, marked with circles, underlines, and cross-outs the role of each member of the household. The child could also mark "nobody" if no one did the activity. This instrument was divided into two sections. One dealt with family roles and the other with interactions with the child (e.g., "Who cleans and dusts?" versus "Who praises you and says you were good?").

A number of different scales were constructed from this measure. In this chapter, six scales measure the role of the father relative to the mother's role (i.e., which parent does the activity relatively more often than the other?). The children's responses were scored just as described for the "Division of roles/Who does it more?" scales. The six composite variables include:

1. *Traditional female tasks,* based on the sum of the scores of seven questions about household tasks traditionally assigned to women that were also part of the parent measure
2. *Child-care tasks,* which included six of the items in the parents' child-care scale
3. *Financial tasks,* consisting of the same three items used in the parents' scale
4. *Teaching and school-related tasks,* which includes six items (e.g., talks about school, helps with school work, explains things)
5. *Nurturance,* based on six items, including those in the parents' measure
6. *Discipline,* which consists of five items (Who says they'll punish you if you don't behave?; Who punishes you?; Who hits you?; Who says no?; Who gets angry?).

The second section of the children's Day at Home questionnaire was used to construct indices of the extent to which the father interacted with the target child. Each question was scored on a three-point scale from 0 to 2 – 2 if the father was circled as most active, 1 if he was underlined, and 0 if the activity was rarely or never done by the father. Scales were formed by summing the scores for each item in the scale. Five scales, comparable to those derived from the fathers' questionnaires, were used in the analyses presented in this chapter. They are as follows: *Fun* includes five items ("Who takes you to fun places?"; "Who plays with you?". "Who is fun to be with?"; "Who watches television with you?"). *Educational* consists of five items covering who "teaches you," "talks to you about school," "explains things," "answers your questions," and "reads to you." *Talk* includes three items (e.g., "just talking," "listens to you"). *Affectionate* has six items (e.g., "smiles at you a lot," "gives you hugs and kisses," and "Who do you go to when you are sad?"). Finally *Total Positive* is a summary measure including sixteen items concerning expressions of positive affect. A high score indicates high father–child interaction.

Parental Gender-role Attitudes

Two measures of gender-stereotypes about family roles were developed for this study, one having to do with stereotypes about the division of roles and power between husbands and wives and the other having to do with attitudes toward differences in how sons and daughter should be reared. Both measures consisted of statements to which the respondent indicated if he or she strongly agreed, agreed, disagreed, or strongly disagreed.

The scale called *Gender-based Attitudes toward Marital Roles* consisted of six statements, such as, "Men should make the really important decisions in the family" and "A man should help in the house, but housework and child care should mainly be a woman's job." The measure was developed from a larger set of items administered to both mothers and fathers in this study. The factor analysis that led to its development and data supporting its construct validity and reliability (alpha = .83 for mothers; .85 for fathers) are reported in Hoffman and Kloska (1995).

The scale called *Gender-based Attitudes toward Child Rearing* consisted of seven statements such as, "It is more important to raise a son to be strong and independent than to raise a daughter that way," and "It's important to raise a son so he will be able to hold down a good job when he's grown, but that's not so major with a daughter." This measure was also administered to both parents and is discussed in Hoffman and Kloska (1995). The alphas are .85 for mothers and .77 for fathers.

Marital Satisfaction

During the home interview, mothers were asked to respond to the Locke–Wallace measure of marital satisfaction (1959). The score is a weighted sum of responses to a series of sixteen questions about marital satisfaction. The range of scores is 2 to 158, with higher scores indicating higher marital satisfaction. As part of the father's questionnaire, fathers responded to a single item that asked the respondent to check the answer that "best describes the degree of happiness, everything considered, of your present marriage." Fathers answered on a seven-point scale (1 = very unhappy; 4 = as happy as most; 7 = perfectly happy).

Maternal Employment and the Father's Role in the Family

In order to test the relationship between maternal employment and variables reflective of the father's role, 3 (maternal employment) by 2 (social class) analysis of variance tests (ANOVAs) were run on the "Who Does it More" scales for married mothers. Recall that these are mother reports of who performs various household functions, and that higher scores indicate that the mother performs the activity relatively more often than the father, lower scores indicate that the father performs the activity relatively more often than the mother. These analyses are in Table 4.1A.

As can be seen in the table, several main effects for employment emerged. Fathers performed more Traditional Female tasks, more Child-Care tasks, and more Functional-interactive child care in employed-mother households. In addition, mothers played a more active role in Financial activities when employed. There was only one main effect for social class, in that mothers were more nurturant than fathers in working-class homes compared to middle-class homes. None of the employment effects, however, were qualified by social class, since there were no significant interactions.

Analyses examining the effects of maternal employment and social class on fathers' reports of father–child activities are reported in Table 4.1B. Only one significant main effect for maternal employment emerged: fathers talk more with their children in homemaker families than in families where the mother is employed. In addition, there is a trend relationship between class and Fun, such that working-class fathers report more Fun activities with their children than middle-class fathers, and there is also a significant interaction effect: middle-class fathers whose wives are employed full-time report the lowest frequency of fun activities with their children.

Table 4.1. *Analysis of Variance (ANOVA); Effects of Maternal Employment and Social Class on Father's Role*

	Means					F-Values		
	ME			SC		ME	SC	ME × SC
	NE	PT	FT	WC	MC	ME	SC	ME × SC
A. Relative Participation of Parents in Tasks[a]						(2,192)	(1,192)	(2,192)
Trad. female	32.79	31.49	26.96	30.58	29.31	20.75***	.61	.95
Child care	19.93	18.29	16.95	18.57	17.84	13.02***	.60	.98
Financial	5.33	6.69	6.53	6.20	6.25	5.41**	.13	.04
Play	15.67	16.13	15.42	15.94	15.46	.67	.91	1.48
School/educational	14.50	14.73	14.19	14.76	14.12	.51	2.18	.44
Nurturance	11.33	11.45	11.15	11.57	11.02	.35	3.77*	.70
Functional	11.52	11.96	10.76	11.16	11.47	4.99**	1.35	.75
B. Frequency of Father–Child Interaction[b]						(2,161)	(1,161)	(2,161)
Fun	12.32	11.71	11.18	12.24	11.08	1.01	3.36#	3.23*c
Talk	8.24	7.24	7.88	7.70	7.93	3.85*	1.07	1.38
Educational	14.64	13.58	14.75	14.58	14.23	1.42	.37	.90
Affectionate	11.90	10.87	11.68	11.61	11.45	1.81	.07	.90
Total	53.76	50.04	52.62	53.65	50.88	1.38	2.59	2.21

Notes. ME = maternal employment; SC = social class; NE = nonemployed; PT = employed part-time; FT = employed full-time; WC = working class; MC = middle class.

[a] Higher scores indicate that mother performs the activity *relatively* more often than father does; lower scores indicate that father performs the activity *relatively* more often than mother does.

[b] Higher scores indicate greater frequency of activity.

[c] Means: WC/NE = 12.10; WC/PT = 11.82; WC/FT = 12.68; MC/NE = 12.68; MC/PT = 11.61; MC/FT = 10.07.

# $p < .10$; * $p < .05$; ** $p < .01$; *** $p < .001$.

Discussion of the Maternal Employment/Father Role Link

These results are interesting in that they are consistent with previous findings, but they are more explicit because of (1) the breakdown in the kinds of activities, (2) the differentiation of the father's role in relation to the mother's from the actual frequency of father–child interaction, and (3) the consideration of social class differences. Thus, the finding that fathers are relatively more active in traditional "female" tasks and child-care activities when mothers are employed is consistent with previous research conducted since the 1950s (Hoffman, 1989; Hoffman & Nye, 1974; Nye & Hoffman, 1963). So is the finding that employed mothers play a relatively more active financial role (Blood, 1963).

However, only one previous study has differentiated child-care tasks from leisure/fun activities (Crouter, Perry-Jenkins, Huston, & McHale, 1987). In their longitudinal research on families living in a primarily rural environment, Crouter and her colleagues found, like the present analysis, that fathers in employed-mother families were more active in routine child-care activities, but they were not more involved with their children in what these investigators called *leisure activities,* which correspond closely to what we have called *play* and *fun.* Our findings expand this to show that maternal employment is also not related to fathers' involvement in school-related or educational activities, nor to nurturance or affection. These data also show that this pattern prevails whether the father's participation is relative to his wife or simply in contrast to other fathers. And it is interesting that *talk* shows the opposite pattern: fathers whose wives are homemakers report more talking with their children.

Because the Crouter sample was smaller and more homogeneous than the sample discussed in this book, it was not possible to analyze the data for interactions with social class. Thus, the current finding that it is in the middle-class families with full-time employed mothers that fathers report the *fewest* fun interactions is a new one. Crouter et al. (1987) do provide data supporting the idea that fathers' work-related available time affects their one-on-one leisure activities with children, and it is likely that middle-class fathers' jobs are more intrusive into family time (Hoffman, 1986). This possibility is consistent with the few main effects of class shown in Table 4.1. In combination with full-time maternal employment, which pulls fathers into household tasks traditionally assigned to women and child care tasks, the work demands of middle-class jobs may leave little time for fathers to simply play with their children.

Gender Differences

As noted in Chapter 1, Crouter and her colleagues also found gender differences: Fathers in single-wage families spent more time in dyadic relationships with sons than with daughters, but fathers in dual-earner families spent equal amounts of time with daughters as with sons. The data in Table 4.1 were therefore examined to see if the child's gender modified the results reported there. Child gender was included as a factor in the ANOVAs. There was only one significant maternal employment by gender interaction.

Although fathers in dual-wage families showed higher relative participation in traditional female tasks and this was not affected by whether they had sons or daughters, fathers in single-wage families were more active if they had sons than if they had daughters. A similar pattern was found for child care but only at the trend level ($p < .10$). In other words, when mothers were employed, fathers were more active in child care whether they had sons or daughters, and the gender of the child did not make a difference, but in homemaker families, the father's child-care participation was lower if the child was a daughter. There were no maternal employment by child gender interactions for the father–child dyadic interaction variables, however.

Analyses with Child Reports

These same analyses were repeated using the children's reports. The results were basically the same. Fathers in dual-wage families were seen as significantly more active in traditional female tasks and less active in financial tasks. For child-care, the direction was the same as with the mother's reports, but it was just short of significance. The child reports did not include a separate measure of functional tasks. However, the measure of negative discipline, only obtained from children, indicated that fathers in dual-wage families were the major disciplinarians, but mothers were the major disciplinarians in the single-wage family ($F [2,191] = 2.68; p < .10$). Of the five father interaction variables examined – fun, talk, educational, nurturance, and total – none showed main effects of maternal employment. There was, however, an interesting main effect of gender for the variable Fun: sons reported more Fun interactions with fathers than daughters did, but separate examination of the data for the different maternal employment groups showed that this gender difference was carried by the homemaker families. If mothers were employed full-time, the fathers' Fun interactions were the same for daughters as for sons. As in Crouter's data, the effect of maternal employment was to eliminate the fathers' "son-preference" in interaction patterns.[1]

Maternal Employment and Parents' Gender-role Attitudes

In this section we consider the links between maternal employment and parents' gender-based attitudes toward marital roles and childrearing. Analyses examining the effects of maternal employment and social class on parents' gender-role traditionalism are reported in Table 4.2.

Again 3 (maternal employment) by 2 (social class) ANOVAs were run for both mothers' and fathers' gender-based attitudes toward marital roles and childrearing practices. As seen in Table 4.2, employed mothers and

Table 4.2. *Effects of Maternal Employment and Social Class on Parental Gender Role Attitudes*

	Means					F-Values		
	ME			SC		ME	SC	ME × SC
	NE	PT	FT	WC	MC			
Mother						(2,193)	(1,193)	(2,193)
Marital roles	17.10	18.18	19.74	17.43	19.58	12.60***	22.49***	.50
Child rearing	23.00	23.55	24.15	22.60	24.62	1.77	27.14***	.61
Father						(2,161)	(1,161)	(2,161)
Marital roles	16.52	17.87	18.61	17.13	18.43	4.25*	3.55#	.87
Child rearing	22.52	23.44	23.43	22.82	23.50	1.32	1.48	.83

Notes. Higher scores on parental attitude variables represent less stereotyped views. ME = maternal employment; SC = Social class; NE = nonemployed; PT = employed part-time; FT = employed full-time; WC = working class; MC = middle class.

# $p < .10$; * $p < .05$; ** $p < .01$; *** $p < .001$.

their husbands report less stereotyped attitudes toward marital roles than do full-time homemakers and their husbands; the least stereotyped attitudes are reported when the mother is employed full-time. The mother's employment status, however, is not significantly related to gender stereotyping about childrearing. In terms of social class, mothers in middle-class homes indicate less traditional attitudes toward both marital roles and childrearing; for middle-class fathers, there is only a trend ($p < .10$) toward less traditional attitudes toward marital roles. Social class, however, does not modify the relationships between employment and gender-role attitudes. In a separate analysis, these results were examined for moderating effects of child's gender, but there were none.

Father's Role and Parents' Gender-Role Attitudes

Having examined the relationships between maternal employment status and both the father's role in the family and parents' gender-role attitudes, we now consider the connections between the father's role and the parents' attitudes. Table 4.3 presents partial correlations (controlling for social class) between the gender-based attitudes of the parents and the mothers' reports of fathers' participation in household tasks, as well as the fathers' reports of their interactions with the target child.

Table 4.3. *Correlations Between Father's Role Variables and Parents' Gender Role Attitudes, Controlling for Social Class*

	Child-Rearing Attitudes[a]		Marital Role Attitudes	
	Mother	Father	Mother	Father
A. Relative Participation of Parents in Tasks[b]				
Trad. female	−.20**	−.13#	−.31***	−.29***
Child care	−.12#	−.21**	−.13#	−.26***
Financial	.05	.11	.06	.23**
Play	.03	.02	.05	−.05
School/educational	−.06	−.18*	−.01	−.20**
Nurturance	.00	−.16*	.01	−.16*
Functional	−.08	−.12	−.15*	−.25***
B. Frequency of Father–Child Interaction[c]				
Fun	.06	.13#	.04	.24***
Talk	−.03	.19*	−.02	.20**
Educational	.06	.19*	.10	.32***
Affectionate	.05	.22**	.04	.30***
Total	.06	.19**	.03	.28***

[a] Higher scores indicate less stereotyped attitudes.
[b] Higher scores indicate that mother performs the activity *relatively* more often than father does; lower scores indicate that father performs the activity *relatively* more often than mother does.
[c] Higher scores indicate greater frequency of the activity.
# $p < .10$; * $p < .05$; ** $p < .01$; *** $p < .001$.

As seen in the table, in families where the father is more active in Traditional Female tasks and Child Care, both mothers and fathers report less stereotyped attitudes toward both marital roles and childrearing, although for mothers, the child-care relationships were only marginally significant ($p < .10$). In families where mothers have a relatively more active role in financial tasks (the less traditional pattern), fathers also report less stereotyped attitudes toward marital roles. Where fathers are more active in school-related and nurturing tasks with the children, fathers report less stereotyped attitudes about marital roles and childrearing. Finally, when fathers participate more actively in Functional tasks with children, both parents report less stereotyped attitudes toward marital roles.

Fathers' reports of the frequency of father–child interactions were related to fathers', but not mothers', reports of gender-role attitudes in the family. For the total index as well as each of the subparts, the more interactions the father reported, the less stereotyped were his attitudes toward marital roles. The same pattern held for childrearing attitudes: the more interactions, the less likely were the fathers to hold different standards and goals for male and female children. We examined the data to see if the gender of the target child with whom these interactions occurred affected the father's gender-based stereotypes about rearing children. The only case where the child's gender made a difference was for Talk, where the relationship was significant only if the interaction was with a daughter.

Children's Reports

The data were also examined to see how the children's reports of father–child interaction related to the fathers' Gender-based Attitudes toward Childrearing. The correlations comparable to the ones presented for parents in Table 4.3B, showed no significant relationships. However, when they were examined separately by gender and employment status, an interesting pattern emerged. These data are presented in Table 4.4. In employed-mother families, girls who perceive high interaction with their fathers have fathers who are equalitarian in their childrearing attitudes. Except for Fun, all the interaction variables attain at least a trend level of significance. For girls in homemaker families, all the father-interaction variables are in the opposite direction. For Fun, this is a significant relationship; the more gender-stereotyped the father, the more the daughter reports having playful interactions with him. For boys, there are no significant relationships in either group. For contrast, the comparable analyses using fathers' reports are also included in the table. Although the gender difference is not apparent with father reports, these also show the heavier concentration of significant relationships for employed-mother families.

Discussion of the Links among Maternal Employment, Father's Role, and Gender-based Attitudes toward Childrearing

Two different gender-role attitude measures have been used in these analyses – one to tap parental attitudes toward marital roles and the other to tap the extent to which parents hold different goals and standards for sons than for daughters. Although there is a vast literature examining the former, there has been almost no attention given to gender stereotypes about rearing children (Hoffman & Kloska, 1995). Yet attitudes about whether education and job competence are important for daughters as well as sons, and attitudes about whether independence is an appropriate goal for daughters

Table 4.4. *Correlations Between Father–Child Interaction (Child's and Father's Report) and Fathers' Gender-based Attitudes toward Child Rearing, Separately by Gender for Families with Employed Mothers and Families with Nonemployed Mothers*

	Families with Employed Mothers		Families with Nonemployed Mothers	
	Boys	Girls	Boys	Girl
Child's Report[a]				
Fun	−.20	.20	.04	−.42*
Talk	−.16	.22[#]	−.14	−.20
Educational	.01	.26*	.02	−.30
Affectionate	−.08	.26*	−.22	−.06
Total	−.10	.27*	−.12	−.28
Father's Report[b]				
Fun	.20	−.03	.08	.36[#]
Talk	.26[#]	.39**	−.07	.07
Educational	.35**	.19	−.05	.14
Affectionate	.31*	.13	.09	.40[#]
Total	.29*	.11	.10	.24

Notes. Higher scores on fathers' attitudes represent less stereotyped views.

[a] Higher scores indicate the father is relatively more active.

[b] Higher scores indicate greater frequency of the activity by father.

[#] $p < .10$; * $p < .05$; ** $p < .01$.

as well as sons, would seem to be key in affecting daughters' academic achievement, occupational goals, and coping styles. And, although no previous research has examined the relationship between the mother's employment status and such parental attitudes, it seems reasonable that the experience of being an employed wife, or having one, would move parental attitudes in a less gender-stereotyped direction.

In fact, however, a relationship between maternal employment and gender-based attitudes toward childrearing is not found in this analysis. The mother's employment status was significantly related to gender stereotypes about marital roles, but not to gender stereotypes about childrearing (Table 4.2). The data do show, however, that the father's relative participation in child care, school/education, and nurturance, as well as his absolute level of interaction with the child in educational activities, talking, affectionate activities, and total positive, are all significantly related to his childrearing attitudes (Table 4.3). That is, fathers who are more involved in child care, and who report higher levels of interaction with their child, are less likely to indicate that their goals and standards would be different for sons than for daughters. Only one of these variables, Child Care, shows the expected significant relationship to the mother's employment (Table 4.1). Thus, only for Child Care can we speak of a chain effect of maternal employment on gender stereotypes about childrearing. However, none of the father's role variables can be said to *mediate* a relationship between maternal employment and childrearing attitudes, since there is no such relationship to mediate.

The data in Table 4.4, however, suggest that the relationships between the father's interaction and his childrearing attitudes are somewhat stronger in the dual-wage families; they suggest that maternal employment serves as a moderator. This table is also interesting in that different relationships emerge when the reporter of the interaction is the child rather than the father. In interpreting these reporter differences, it is important to keep in mind the differences in the measures. Although the content of the items is similar for both sets of reporters, the father's measure was a count of how often such interactions had occurred during the previous week, while the children were reporting on who is the person who does these things generally. Thus, the children may be reporting on the overall quality of the relationship, whereas fathers are noting their occurrence. For these interaction items also, in contrast to the reports of which parent performs certain tasks, there is more opportunity for the child's interpretation of the emotional quality to affect his or her answers. A child might, for example, experience a father as nurturant because of his general style and communication of love, even though the child might not be able to recount specific interactions to document that.

The differences in the reports of fathers and children are interesting in a number of ways. For one thing, the pattern of the children's reports suggest that it is the daughters of employed mothers who show the most consistency between high interaction levels and nonstereotyped attitudes. This is the pattern that one might expect. In employed-mother families, positive interactions with daughters would be expected to diminish stereotypes about matters such as the lesser importance of jobs, education, and independence for girls. Her mother works, so the expectation that she will also work should be greater. In addition, in the measure of gender attitudes toward childrearing, the nonstereotyped response is more favorable to girls; thus, positive interaction with a *daughter* would be more likely to move the father in a nonstereotyped direction. These issues will be taken up again in Chapter 8, where we examine the relationships between father–child interaction and child outcomes.

The Links among Maternal Employment, Father's Role, and Gender-based Attitudes toward Marital Roles: Mediational Analyses and Discussion

In contrast to the results found for attitudes toward childrearing, parents' gender-based attitudes toward marital roles were significantly related to employment status; the most traditional views were endorsed by both mothers and fathers in the full-time homemaker families and the least traditional in the full-time employed-mother families (Table 4.2). In addition, analyses indicated that in employed-mother families, fathers take on a larger share of the tasks traditionally assigned to women, as well as a larger share of both direct child-care tasks and the functional interactions with children (e.g., taking them shopping).

There are two major hypotheses to explain these results. One is that the father's increased role in tasks and child care is a functional response to the demands of the dual-wage family and the parents' attitudes accommodate to the new reality of their roles. The other is that parents' attitudes change in response to the mother's employment and this, in turn, facilitates a move toward less traditional family roles.

To test these empirically, mediational analyses were undertaken. The first addresses the question: Do these shifts in the father's role mediate the relationship between maternal employment and less traditional parental attitudes toward marital roles? Regression techniques were used and Baron and Kenny's (1986) criteria for determining whether variables functioned as mediators were followed. According to these criteria, a variable is said to function as a mediator when the following four conditions are met:

1. A significant relation exists between the predictor (maternal employment) and criterion (marital-role attitudes) variables.
2. A significant relation exists between the predictor and mediator (e.g., traditional female tasks) variables.
3. There is a significant relation between the mediator and criterion variables, when the mediator and predictor variables are entered simultaneously into the analysis.
4. When the mediator and predictor variables are entered simultaneously, the previously significant relationship between the predictor and criterion variables is reduced to zero (as in the case of total mediation) or is attenuated (as in the case of partial mediation).

Specifically, we infer that a mediation occurs by examining whether the predictor's beta value is attenuated when the criterion is regressed onto the predictor and the hypothesized mediator simultaneously, as compared to when the criterion is regressed onto the predictor alone. The significance of beta attenuation (i.e., mediational influence) is tested using the procedure developed by Sobel (1982) and described by Baron and Kenny (1986).[2] In the following analyses, employed and nonemployed mothers are contrasted, and social class is controlled in each equation.

In terms of the question at hand, we first regressed mothers' and fathers' reports of attitudes toward marital roles on maternal employment. These relationships are depicted in Figure 4.2. As seen in Figure 4.2, maternal employment significantly predicted the marital-role attitudes of both mothers ($F[2,195] = 23.49$, $p < .0001$; Figure 4.2[A.1]) and fathers ($F[2,164] = 8.81$, $p < .0001$; Figure 4.2[B.1]).

The second step was to consider the relation between each of the three mediators (Traditional Female tasks, Child Care, Functional-interactive) and maternal employment. Functional-interactive was not significantly related to maternal employment, and therefore cannot function as a mediator. Traditional Female tasks was significantly related to maternal employment in the model predicting mothers' attitudes ($F[2,195] = 10.45$, $p < .001$; Figure 4.2[A.2]) and in the model predicting fathers' attitudes ($F[2,164] = 9.99$, $p < .001$; Figure 4.2[B.2]). Maternal employment also predicted Child Care tasks in the mothers' model ($F[2,195] = 11.11$, $p < .001$; Figure 4.2[A.3]) as well as in the fathers' model ($F[2,164] = 9.03$, $p < .001$; Figure 4.2[B.3]).

The third step involved regressing mothers' and fathers' attitudes on both maternal employment and the mediators. As seen in Figure 4.2(A.2), Traditional Female tasks partially mediated the relationship between employment and mothers' attitudes ($F[3,194] = 20.50$, $p < .0001$). This is because (1) Traditional Female tasks was a significant predictor of mothers' attitudes when entered with maternal employment and (2) the relationship between maternal employment and mothers' attitudes was attenuated, but not reduced to zero. Sobel's (1982) test was performed to test the degree of attenuation. Sobel's t-ratio was 2.70 ($p < .01$), which indicates the attenuation was significant. Child Care tasks, on the other hand, did not mediate the association between maternal employment and mothers' attitudes because Child Care was a nonsignificant predictor of mothers' marital-role attitudes when entered into the regression with maternal employment (Figure 4.2[A.3]).

In terms of predicting fathers' marital-role attitudes, both Traditional Female tasks and Child Care mediated the link between employment and

A. Predicting Mothers' Attitudes Toward Marital Roles

1. Direct Relationship:

Maternal Employment $\xrightarrow{.23***}$ Mother's Attitudes

2. Mediated Relationship: Traditional Female Tasks

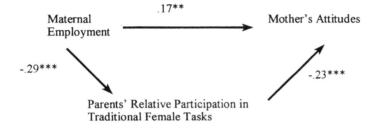

3. Mediated Relationship: Child Care

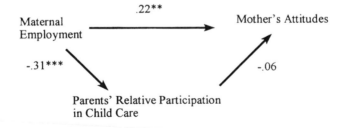

Figure 4.2. Mediation of the link between maternal employment and parents' attitudes toward marital roles by father's role. ** $p < .01$. *** $p < .001$. (*Figure continues.*)

B. Predicting Fathers' Attitudes Toward Marital Roles

1. Direct Relationship:

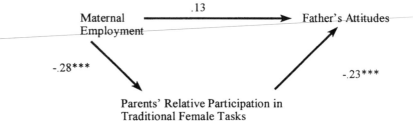

2. Mediated Relationship: Traditional Female Tasks

3. Mediated Relationship: Child Care

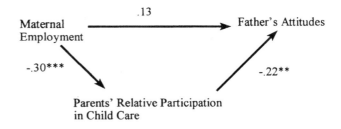

Figure 4.2 *(continued)*

attitudes. This is because the relationship between the mediators and fathers' attitudes was significant when entered with maternal employment (Traditional Female tasks: $F[3,163] = 9.27$, $p < .0001$; child care: $F[3,163] = 8.78$, $p < .001$) and because, in both cases, the relationship between maternal employment and fathers' attitudes was reduced to zero with the introduction of the mediator (Figure 4.2[B.2 and B.3]).

These results support the hypothesis that the father's role mediates the relationship between the mother's employment status and parental gender-based attitudes toward marital roles. However, it is also possible that the second hypothesis is true – that gender-role attitudes are also directly affected by the mother's employment status, and that this less traditional viewpoint, in turn, affects role behavior. To test this possibility, the same test for mediational effects was conducted to see if gender attitudes toward marital roles mediated the relationship between the mother's employment status and the father's role. Again, the mediation hypothesis was supported.

Thus, there is evidence both that because the mother is employed, husbands take on more responsibilities in tasks and child care and that this, in turn, leads to less traditional views of marital roles, and also that the mother's employment directly affects role attitudes and thus increases the father's task and child-care participation. In short, the analyses suggest that there is an interaction between the attitudes and the roles, such that each is affected by the mother's employment status and each also affects the other. But the relationship is probably even more complex than these statistical tests reveal. Less traditionalism and higher participation of the father in household tasks and child care can also operate as determinants of employment; they reduce the barriers to the mother's employment and they facilitate it. They may exist prior to employment; they may both be increased as effects; and each can augment the other. It is likely that all these processes occur – that there are interactive effects. Nevertheless, the two mediational analyses do add support to the previous evidence that the mother's employment plays an *active* role affecting both marital-role behavior and marital-role attitudes.

Maternal Employment, Father's Role, and Marital Satisfaction

We turn now to consideration of the affective side of the marital relationship, first examining whether the mother's employment status is related to marital satisfaction and then examining the relationships between the father's role and marital satisfaction for single-wage and dual-wage families.

Maternal Employment and Marital Satisfaction

In Chapter 1, the review of previous research indicated that most studies examining marital satisfaction found no relationship between the mother's employment status and the marital satisfaction of either partner. When a difference was found, a positive relationship was more likely if the sample was middle-class or educated, the work was part-time, or the mother was the reporter. A negative relationship was more likely if the sample was lower-class, the father was the reporter, or the parents held traditionalistic gender-role attitudes.

A 3 (maternal employment) by 2 (social class) ANOVA was run to see if the mother's marital happiness, as measured by the Locke-Wallace scale, was related to her employment status. It was not. The results showed that mothers in the middle class were significantly more satisfied with their marriage than were mothers in the lower class, but social class did not modify the null results for employment status. The father's marital satisfaction was measured by a single item, but here too, maternal employment status showed no effects. Fathers' marital satisfaction was also unrelated to social class, and there were no interaction effects. Furthermore, there were no statistically significant differences between part-time employment and either of the other two groups. For both mothers and fathers, the means for part-time employed and full-time employed were similar.

Father's Role and Marital Satisfaction

We turn now to the relationship between the father's role in the family and marital satisfaction. It was reported in Chapter 1 that previous research had found that the father's increased involvement in child care was related to his marital dissatisfaction but only in dual-wage, not single-wage families (Baruch & Barnett, 1987; Crouter et al., 1987). Two hypotheses had been suggested as possible interpretations of these results (Hoffman, 1989). One was that the father's involvement in child care was likely to be intrinsically motivated in single-wage families and thus more pleasurable than in dual-wage families, where the father's involvement was required because of the mother's job demands. The other was that the nature of the father's involvement might differ in the two kinds of families: the suggestion was that, as we have found here, the involvement of fathers in dual-wage families was more likely to be in direct caretaking and household tasks than in leisure-time interactions with children. Possibly the former, but not the latter, was associated with fathers' marital dissatisfaction.

To explore these issues, correlations were run between the different aspects of the father's role and measures of the marital happiness of each parent, separately for the two employment groups. These results are reported in Table 4.5.

Table 4.5. *Correlation Between Father's Role and Parents' Marital Satisfaction, Controlling for Social Class, and Separately by Employment Category (Nonemployed vs. Employed)*

	Mother's Marital Satisfaction		Father's Marital Satisfaction	
	Nonemployed	Employed	Nonemployed	Employed
A. Relative Participation of Parents in Tasks[a]				
Traditional female	−.13	−.28***	−.17	.01
Child care	−.23#	−.36***	−.04	−.14
Financial	.03	−.18#	.12	−.10
Play	−.43***	−.41***	−.06	−.16#
School educational	−.16	−.36***	−.28*	−.12
Nurturance	−.39**	−.49***	−.40**	−.21*
Functional	−.02	−.44***	.26#	−.20*
B. Frequency of Father–Child Interaction[b]				
Fun	.10	.16	.00	.11
Talk	.12	.26**	.12	.28**
Educational	.00	.19*	−.02	.15#
Affectionate	.06	.18#	.02	.09
Total	.11	.25**	.04	.19*

[a] Higher scores indicate that mother performs the activity relatively more often than father does.
[b] Higher scores indicate greater frequency of activity.
# $p < .10$; * $p < .05$; ** $p < .01$; *** $p < .001$.

There is no evidence here that fathers' participation in child care, or any other kind of parent–child interaction, is associated with marital dissatisfaction for fathers in dual-wage families. The two measures of fathers' role in child care that were found here to be related to mothers' employment are Child Care and Functional Tasks (see Table 4.1A). The variable, Child Care, is the one most like those used in previous research that taps standard, routine child care. Table 4.5A shows that there is no significant relationship between Child Care and marital satisfaction for either group of fathers, and the direction of the relationship for dual-wage fathers is opposite to the expectation; that is, it shows a nonsignificant relationship between high father participation and father's high marital satisfaction. For Functional Tasks, the other variable that showed dual-wage fathers to be more active, we also find that high participation by the dual-wage fathers is associated with higher marital satisfaction, and this relationship is statistically significant. The relationship for single-wage fathers is in the opposite direction and at the trend level of significance. Thus, the suggesstion from the previous research that high father participation is associated with marital dissatisfaction for dual-wage fathers receives no support in these data. In addition, the hypothesis that the kind of father participation that is more common in dual-wage than single-wage families leads to fathers' marital dissatisfaction is also not confirmed, at least not for the dual-wage fathers.

The relative participation of fathers vis-à-vis mothers in Table 4.5A shows that the more fathers with employed wives take part in nurturance and functional interactions with children, the more likely they are to indicate satisfaction with their marriage. At the trend level, the same pattern is found for Play. In no case does the opposite direction occur for the dual-wage fathers. The frequency of fathers' activities with children (Table 4.5B) shows the same pattern. For both Talk and Total, the relationships are significant; for Education, the relationship is at the trend level. If there is a difference between the fathers in dual-wage and single-wage families, it is only that there are fewer significant correlations for the single-wage fathers, and the only relationship showing father involvement associated with marital dissatisfaction occurs in the homemaker families (Functional Tasks, $p < .10$).

Looking at the mother's marital satisfaction, we find that father participation is strongly related to marital happiness for the employed mothers. For employed mothers, the only relationship that does not reach at least a trend level of significance is for the frequency of father's Fun activities in Table 4.5B.

Among the homemakers, higher relative participation of fathers in Play, Nurturance, and, at the trend level, Child Care is associated with marital satisfaction (Table 4.5A). None of the measures of the reported frequency of father–child interaction (Table 4.5B) shows an association for the homemakers.

In a final effort to explore the relationship between fathers' participation and marital satisfaction, the sample of fathers was divided into two groups based on their scores on the Gender Attitudes toward Marital Roles Scale. Scores were split at the median to establish a group that endorsed the traditional gender-role stereotypes and a group that rejected them. Each group was then subdivided into an employed-mother group and a homemaker-mother group, yielding two concordant groups – nontraditional fathers in dual-wage families and traditional fathers in single-wage families – and two discordant groups – traditional fathers in dual-wage families and nontraditional fathers in single-wage families. For each group, correlations were computed between their marital satisfaction scores and their participation scores for Traditional Female Tasks and Child Care. These are the dimensions of the father's role most often used in previous research, and they showed no significant relationship to fathers' marital satisfaction in Table 4.5A.

In the analysis of the concordant and discordant groups, none of the father participation/marital satisfaction correlations were statistically significant. One, however, showed a relationship at the trend level ($p < .10$): for fathers in dual-wage families who endorsed a gender-stereotyped view of marital roles (discordant), high participation in Child Care was associated with marital dissatisfaction.

Summary of the Analyses of Maternal Employment, Father's Role, and Marital Satisfaction.

The analysis of the relationship between mothers' employment status and parents' marital satisfaction was consistent with most of the previous research; there was no significant relationship between employment status and the marital satisfaction of either parent. Although middle-class mothers showed higher marital satisfaction than lower class, socioeconomic status did not modify these results.

In general, higher involvement of fathers with their children was associated with higher marital satisfaction, but there were some variations in patterns, with more significant outcomes in the dual-wage families. Thus, for employed mothers, the participation of fathers in routine child care and almost all of the other child-relevant activities was associated with higher marital satisfaction. For this group also, higher participation in Traditional Female tasks was associated with higher marital satisfaction. It is noteworthy that, for the employed mothers, all of the father participation variables that were found to be higher for dual-wage families (Table 4.1) were also associated with marital satisfaction. An implication of this is that although there was no direct link between maternal employment and marital satisfaction, there may be an indirect link through the father role variables. Such a link might also operate for the dual-wage fathers through Functional Tasks, because that variable was related to both the mother's employment status and to the marital satisfaction scores of dual-wage fathers. In addition, for both parents in the dual-wage families, more frequent father–child activities (Table 4.5B) were associated with marital satisfaction scores at significant or trend levels for Talk, Educational, and Total Positive; none of the activity measures approached significance for either parent in the single-wage family.

Despite the previous findings reported by Baruch and Barnett (1987) and by Crouter and her associates (1987) of an association between dual-wage fathers' involvement in child care and their marital dissatisfaction, we found no evidence for this – with one possible exception: a trend-level relationship was found between high participation in child care and marital dissatisfaction for dual-wage fathers who held a gender-stereotyped view of marital roles. Our failure to replicate the earlier finding may reflect changes in attitudes over the years. There has been a shift in attitudes over the last decade away from the idea that parenting is primarily a mother's job. In addition, the sample in the Crouter study was a rural one, in contrast to our urban sample. Thus, this earlier research may have included a higher percentage of dual-wage fathers who held gender-stereotyped attitudes toward women's roles. This explanation is consistent with the trend level result we found for our dual-wage fathers who held traditional views.

Chapter Summary

The analyses described in this chapter show that fathers in dual-wage families play a greater role than fathers in single-wage families in traditional female tasks, routine child care, and functional-interactive child care tasks and a lesser role in financial tasks. They do not, however, play a greater role nor report more interactions with the target child for sheer play and fun activities, educational activities, nurturant or affectionate, and they report *less* talking with the child. The data also indicated that middle-class fathers in employed-mother homes report the lowest frequency of playing with their children. There was one significant employment by gender interaction: fathers in single-wage families participated less in traditional female tasks if the child in the study was a daughter but the gender of the child did not affect the participation of dual-wage fathers. A similar pattern emerged when children's reports of fathers' roles were used for "fun" activities: single-wage fathers played more with sons, but the dual-wage fathers' interactions were not affected by gender. All of these findings are consistent with previous data, but they extend them because of the wider and more differentiated coverage of the father's role in parenting.

Both the employed mothers and their husbands indicated less gender-role traditionalism in their attitudes toward marital roles, but maternal employment status did not affect gender-based stereotypes about childrearing. Both the marital-role attitudes and childrearing attitudes of the fathers, however, were related to the fathers' higher involvement in female-traditional tasks, child care, and most of the other indices of the fathers' involvement in tasks and interactions with the child. For mothers, only the fathers' participation in "female" tasks was significantly related to both attitude measures; in addition, father participation in functional tasks was also related to their marital-role attitudes.

The relationship between father–child interaction and gender-based childrearing attitudes was also examined separately for each employment-status group. This analysis revealed that the relationships between high interaction and the absence of gender-differentiated attitudes was stronger when the mother was employed. In addition, an identical analysis using the child's report of interaction with the father showed that only for daughters of employed mothers was the link between fathers' high interaction and less gender-stereotyping manifest.

To explore the links among the mother's employment, the father's role, and attitudes toward the marital relationship, two mediational analyses were conducted, one to see if the father's role mediated the employment/attitude relationship and the other to see if attitudes mediated the employment/role relationship. Both paths were supported. The results are consistent with the view that the mother's employment status directly affects both the father's role and marital role attitudes, although each also affects the other.

The final analyses examined the relationships among the mother's employment status, the father's role, and parents' marital satisfaction. There was no significant relationship between employment status and marital satisfaction, but, in general, higher involvement of fathers with their children was associated with higher marital satisfaction. This was most marked for the marital satisfaction of employed mothers.

The results reported here sharpen and extend our understanding of the differences in fathers' roles in families where mothers are in the labor force from those where the mother is a full-time homemaker. The major focus of this study, however, is the child. It is for that reason that we have tried to delineate specific child-relevant dimensions of the father's role. It is also for that reason that we have employed a measure that taps gender-based attitudes toward childrearing.

Chapter 1 listed three different routes by which the father's role might affect children:

1. The father's increased participation in tasks and child care may mitigate the overload of the dual-role strain for the mothers, thus lessening stress and increasing her marital satisfaction.
2. To the extent that maternal employment functions to move parental roles and attitudes in a less traditional direction, the behavior, achievement patterns, and self-concepts of daughters will be affected.

3. Increased interaction with fathers may have benefits for children, particularly in the cognitive area, either because it augments the amount of adult–child contact or because it compensates for less interaction with the employed mother, or because there are specific benefits for children from interaction with fathers – possibly depending on the domains involved.

In subsequent chapters, the results presented here will be examined further to explore the links to child outcomes. In Chapters 5 and 9, the first route will be considered–how the father's role affects the mother's well-being and how this, in turn, affects the child. In Chapter 8, we will examine how the father's role and parents' gender-based attitudes relate to children's gender-role attitudes and academic competence.

Notes

1. Means for full-time employed: sons, 4.52; daughters, 4.25; for part-time: sons, 4.43; daughters, 3.70; for homemakers: sons, 4.56; daughters, 3.34.
2. Sobel (1982) provides a formula for calculating the standard error for the indirect effect of the predictor variable on the criterion variable via the mediating variable. This serves as the denominator in a t ratio of the indirect effect to its standard error. The t ratio is based on the following formula:

$$\frac{bc}{\sqrt{(c^2 S_b{}^2 + b^2 S_c{}^2 + S_b{}^2 S_c{}^2)}}$$

where b represents the relationship between the predictor and the proposed mediator; S_b is the standard error for b; c represents the relationship between the mediator and the criterion; and S_c the standard error for c. The numerator represents the indirect effect of the predictor variable on the criterion variable via the mediator variable, while the denominator represents the standard error of the indirect effect. A t ratio of 1.96 or larger indicates a significant indirect effect ($p < .05$) and implies a significant reduction in the relation between the predictor and criterion variable due to the introduction of the mediator.

5   The Mother's Well-being

In this chapter we consider the link between maternal employment and the mother's mental health and well-being. A considerable amount of research has investigated the effects of mothers' employment status on their emotional state and mental health. The review of this literature in Chapter 1 suggests a higher level of satisfaction among the employed, particularly in the working class. This class distinction is important because previous research has also shown more consistent advantages of maternal employment for children in the working class than in the middle class (see Chapter 1). Previous publications (Hoffman, 1989) have suggested that one of the routes by which maternal employment affects child outcomes is through the mother's morale or mental health. Therefore, showing that the positive effect of employment on the mother's mental health is more pronounced in the working class, and that mental health mediates the relationship between employment status and parenting styles, would provide some insight into the particular advantage maternal employment offers in working-class families.

In this chapter, we begin our investigation of the role of mental health in linking maternal employment and child outcomes by focusing on the relations between maternal employment and the mother's well-being. Specifically, in this chapter we examine (a) the relationship between the mother's employment status and indices of maternal mental health and (b) whether these patterns prevail across social class. Because the previous literature is more consistent for working-class samples, the hypothesis predicting direction is specific to that group. The same empirical test conducted for the working-class group will be conducted separately for the middle-class group, but direction is not predicted for the latter. Previous data, however, suggest that full-time homemakers in the working class will indicate higher levels of depressive mood and lower levels of morale than will employed mothers.

In addition to examining the associations between maternal employment and the mother's well-being and how the pattern varies by social class, moderators and mediators of the employment/mental health link will also be considered. Seven variables will be examined as possible moderators of the relationship between employment and mental health, and three variables will be examined as possible mediators of this relationship.

The variables that previous research suggests may moderate the relationship between employment status and morale include the father's help in household tasks and child-care tasks, the presence of a preschool child, the number of children, the mother's marital status, ethnicity, and child-related social support (Kessler & McRae, 1982; Rosenfeld, 1989). The father's help and social support are seen as increasing the advantage of employment for the mother's emotional state; more children and the presence of a preschooler are seen as decreasing it. In addition, single-mother status has been suggested as a variable that could increase the advantage of employment because of the social and economic benefits of the job, or of decreasing the advantage because of the greater stress of the dual role without a marital partner (Hoffman, 1959). Thus, marital status will also be considered for moderating effects. Finally, some researchers have suggested that because of the longer history of maternal employment as a normative pattern in African-American families, it may be less stressful (McLoyd, 1993). We, therefore, examined the data to see whether ethnicity moderated the relations between maternal employment and the mother's well-being.

The three variables that will be examined as possible mediators of the employment/mental health relationship are feelings of loneliness, sense of personal control, and feelings of financial strain. Research by Ferree (1976) and Rosen (1987) suggests that loneliness and sense of personal control may be partial mediators for working class women – with loneliness and a lower sense of control carrying the depression and lower morale of homemakers. Researchers have also suggested that financial strain may be a mediator of depression and morale, particularly for working-class, single mothers; however, both Waldron and Jacobs (1989) and McLoyd and her colleagues (McLoyd, Jayaratne, Ceballo, & Borquez, 1994) failed to find evidence for that hypothesis.

Sample

For our analyses of the mother's well-being we selected only those interviewed mothers who had either been employed or nonemployed for the preceding three consecutive years, 280 in all. A cutoff score of 37 on the

Hollingshead Four-factor Index (Hollingshead, 1970) was used to create the working-class sample, which primarily includes blue-collar occupations. Scores of 38 and above defined the middle-class sample (white-collar and professional).

The working-class sample was comprised of 150 mothers, 54 of whom were single and 96 of whom were married. Sixty mothers were nonemployed and 90 were employed. Forty-nine of the mothers were African American and 101 were White.

The middle-class group had 27 single mothers and 103 married mothers. Because there were no middle-class, single, nonemployed mothers, causing empty cells in the analyses to follow, the final middle-class sample contains only married mothers.[1] Of these 103 married, middle-class mothers, 23 were nonemployed and 80 were employed; 96 were White and 7 were African American.

Measures

Demographic Information

Information about the mother's marital status, employment status and the number of children in the family was provided by the mother on each child's permission form and in the home interview. The mother's marital status was also cross-checked with information provided by children and teachers. As indicated in Chapter 2, if the mother had a male partner who had resided in the home for more than a year, and was considered part of the conjugal family by the mother, the family was coded as two-parent. Maternal employment status was coded from two items on the permission forms: mother's current employment status and mother's employment status over the past three years. The items were used to create a single, trichotomous variable tapping commitment to employment: no employment for the past three years, part-time employment for the past three years, and full-time employment for the past three years. Preliminary analyses for this chapter suggested no differences between part-time and full-time employment, but rather, between employment and nonemployment. Thus, for the purposes of this chapter, the full-time and part-time employed groups are collapsed and contrasted to the nonemployed group.

The number of children, as well as the presence of a preschooler, was based on the mother's report. All children who were permanent members of the household were considered siblings, including adopted children and children from a previous marriage of either spouse. Foster children were not included as siblings, nor were nonresident stepchildren. Presence of a preschooler was coded "yes" when at least one of the siblings was five years of age or younger, and coded "no" when there were no children under five years of age. Number of children was recoded into a dichotomous variable (1 to 2 children versus 3 or more).

Indices of Maternal Depressive Mood and Morale

The current frequency of mothers' depressive symptoms was assessed using the Center for Epidemiologic Studies Depression Scale (CES-D; Radloff, 1977). In contrast to other depression scales – for example, the Beck Depression Inventory (Beck & Beck, 1972) – the CES-D focuses on milder depressive symptoms, with an emphasis on depressed mood or affect. Participants are asked to indicate how frequently they experienced the listed symptoms within the past week. Each frequency level is translated into a numerical score ranging from 0 (rarely or none of the time) to 3 (most or all of the time). Answers are summed into a total score, with higher scores indicating a higher frequency of depressive symptomatology (alpha = .89). The psychometric properties of the CES-D are well established and have been reported by Radloff (1977).[2]

A measure of maternal morale or current satisfaction with life was also constructed. Morale is a three-point variable based on the mother's answers to two items asking (1) if she is satisfied with how her life is going these days and (2) if this is a particulary happy time in her life. If the mother was satisfied and happy, morale was scored as a *2;* if the mother was satisfied and not happy or not satisfied and happy, morale was scored as a *1;* and if the mother was not satisfied and not happy, morale was scored as a *0.*

The Father's Help

Married mothers were asked to indicate whether they or their husbands typically perform a series of ten traditionally female household chores and seven child-care chores. The household chores included getting breakfast, cleaning and dusting, cooking the evening meal, doing the dishes, setting the table, making the beds, buying the groceries, doing the family laundry, washing the kitchen floor, and vacuuming. The child-care chores included taking care of the children; taking the children to the doctor; and getting the children to eat the foods they should, to help around the house, to go to bed, to go to school, and to behave at the table.

Mothers' answers for each chore were scored on a five-point scale: 4 = mother, not father; 3 = mother mostly, but father sometimes; 2 = both equally or neither does it; 1 = father mostly, but mother sometimes; 0 = father, not mother. The scores for each household chore were summed to create a composite index of who performs traditionally female chores in the household. Likewise, the scores for each child-care chore were summed to create a composite index of who performs the child-care chores in the household.

Higher scores indicate that the mother performs the activity *relatively* more often than the father does, whereas lower scores indicate that the mother performs the activity *relatively* less often. For the analyses to follow, a median split was created on each of these two variables to represent mothers who received less help from their husbands and mothers who received more help from their husbands.

Nonparental Child-Related Social Support

A measure of nonparental child-related support was created from the mother's responses to eight items. Specifically, mothers were asked if someone besides themselves or their husbands (if married) helped their children with school work, took care of the children, gave the children spending money, got the children to behave, drove the children to places they needed to go, took the children on outings, played with the children and talked to the children. For each item, mothers, received a 1 for listing someone. Thus, scores could range from 0 to 8, with higher scores indicating more support. For the purposes of the moderation analyses, this variable was recoded into a dichotomous variable (1 = less support, 2 = more support), based on a median split.

Loneliness and Financial Worries

Following the format of the CES-D, we created two additional items that tapped, first, mothers' feelings of loneliness ("I felt a need to have someone to talk to about my problems") and, second, mothers' financial worries ("I was worried about money") during the past week. Mothers responded to these two questions using the same four-point response scale as for the CES-D.

Maternal Locus of Control

The mother's locus of control was assessed by her responses to four items rated on a four-point scale (1 = strongly agree; 4 = strongly disagree). The items were "Many times you feel that you have little influence over the things that happen to you"; "Getting ahead in life is mostly a matter of luck"; "If a person plans ahead, things are pretty likely to work out"; and "It is not always wise to plan too far ahead because many things turn out to be a matter of good or bad luck anyway." Items were recoded so that a higher score indicated a more internalizing locus of control, whereas a lower score indicated a more externalizing locus of control. A total score was created by summing the four items (alpha = .61). This measure was developed by the Institute for Social Research at the University of Michigan and has been used extensively in national survey studies (Robinson & Shaver, 1973).

Maternal Employment and Mental Health and Well-being

Our first analysis concerns differences in depressive mood and morale between employed and nonemployed mothers in the working class and in the middle class. To examine these differences, a series of one-way Analyses of Variance (ANOVAs) were run contrasting employed and nonemployed mothers, separately by social class. Table 5.1 presents these analyses. As can be seen in the table, nonemployed mothers in the working class were significantly more depressed and had significantly lower morale than employed mothers in the working class. In the married, middle-class sample, however, no statistically significant differences emerged between employed and non-employed mothers on either of the mental health variables.

These results show that, in the lower socioeconomic groups, as predicted, employment holds a positive mental health advantage. In the middle class, there was no significant relationship between employment status and depressive mood or morale. Thus, these results provide an important step in the attempt to understand why maternal employment has been found to be related to positive child outcomes more consistently in the working class than in the middle class (Chapter 1). It is in the working class, not the middle class, that maternal employment was found to be associated with emotional well-being.

Moderators of the Employment/Morale Link

A series of potential moderators of the links between employment and the mother's well-being are considered next. These variables include the father's help in household tasks and child-care tasks, the presence of a preschool child, the number of children in the family, the mother's marital

Table 5.1. *One-way ANOVAs for the Effect of Maternal Employment (Nonemployed vs. Employed) on Maternal Morale Measures*

	Means		
	Nonemployed	Employed	$F(1,148)$
A. Working Class			
Depression	14.98	10.20	11.14***
Morale	1.32	1.60	4.79*
n	60	90	
B. Married, Middle Class			
Depression	6.04	8.23	1.56
Morale	1.78	1.68	.66
n	23	80	

# *p* < .10; * *p* < .05; *** *p* < .001.

status, ethnicity, and nonparental child-related social support. To test the role of each moderator, we employed ANOVA techniques and followed Baron and Kenny's (1986) criterion for determining whether a variable plays a moderator role in the model. We conclude that a variable functions as a moderator if the analysis reveals a significant interaction term, regardless of whether any significant main effects also occur.

Specifically, we ran a series of two-factor ANOVAs, separately by social class, including maternal employment and each of the moderators as the two factors in the model. These analyses are presented in Table 5.2. (Analyses for the working class are in Part A and, for the middle class, in Part B).

Working-class Patterns

We first considered the role of the father. A significant main effect occurred indicating that mothers had higher morale when their husbands did more child-care tasks ($M = 1.79$) than when their husbands did fewer child-care tasks ($M = 1.39$). However, there was no evidence that the father's help with child care or with household tasks moderated the link between maternal employment and morale.

In families where there was a preschooler, mothers reported higher morale ($M = 1.50$) than in families where there was no preschooler ($M = 1.11$). However, presence of a preschooler did not modify the link between maternal employment and any of the maternal mood variables. As seen in the table neither did the number of children.

Table 5.2. *ANOVAS of the Moderators of the Employment/Well-being Link: Means and F-Values*

A. Working Class

1. Father's help with household chores

	Nonemployed		Employed		ME	HH	ME × HH
	More Help	Less Help	More Help	Less Help	(1,92)	(1,92)	(1,92)
Depression	14.10	13.60	8.06	10.21	5.42*	.51	.46
Morale	1.60	1.48	1.72	1.45	.02	2.02	.20

2. Father's help with child-care chores

	Nonemployed		Employed		ME	CC	ME × CC
	More Help	Less Help	More Help	Less Help	(1,92)	(1,92)	(1,92)
Depression	11.00	14.84	8.19	10.07	4.79*	1.94	.40
Morale	1.70	1.44	1.81	1.23	.02	6.95**	.40

3. Presence of a preschooler

	Nonemployed		Employed		ME	PP	ME × PP
	Pres.	No Pres.	Pres.	No Pres.	(1,145)	(1,145)	(1,145)
Depression	16.07	14.06	10.21	10.19	11.20***	.34	.45
Morale	1.11	1.50	1.52	1.75	6.84**	5.58*	.37

4. Number of children

	Nonemployed		Employed		ME	NC	ME × NC
	1–2	3+	1–2	3+	(1,145)	(1,145)	(1,145)
Depression	13.19	15.97	10.89	9.51	10.61***	.02	1.96
Morale	1.24	1.37	1.56	1.64	5.17*	.68	.02

5. Marital status

	Nonemployed		Employed		ME	MS	ME × MS
	Married	Single	Married	Single	(1,145)	(1,145)	(1,145)
Depression	13.74	16.79	.08	12.55	9.84**	5.04*	.02
Morale	1.51	1.04	1.59	1.62	4.35*	1.98	3.73#

6. Ethnicity

	Nonemployed		Employed		ME	ETH	ME × ETH
	White	Afr. Amer.	White	Afr. Amer.	(1,144)	(1,144)	(1,144)
Depression	13.60	16.61	10.06	10.67	8.57**	1.24	.59
Morale	1.30	1.32	1.52	1.86	6.52***	.87	1.32

7. Nonparental child-related support

	Nonemployed		Employed		ME	CS	ME × CS
	Less Supp.	More Supp.	Less Supp.	More Supp.	(1,145)	(1,145)	(1,145)
Depression	12.02	18.25	11.32	9.42	12.09***	.96	8.17**
Morale	1.45	1.18	1.59	1.60	5.14*	.69	1.22

(continued)

Table 5.2 *(continued)*

B. Married Middle Class

1. Father's help with household chores

	Nonemployed		Employed		ME	HH	ME × HH
	More Help	Less Help	More Help	Less Help	(1,98)	(1,98)	(1,98)
Depression	10.00	5.21	7.33	9.36	1.89	.44	2.42
Morale	2.00	1.74	1.72	1.61	1.38	1.28	.07

2. Father's help with child-care chores

	Nonemployed		Employed		ME	CC	ME × CC
	More Help	Less Help	More Help	Less Help	(1,98)	(1,98)	(1,98)
Depression	10.20	4.89	8.89	7.24	1.01	.49	.57
Morale	2.00	1.72	1.69	1.65	1.01	.49	.57

3. Presence of a preschooler

	Nonemployed		Employed		ME	PP	ME × PP
	Pres.	No Pres.	Pres.	No Pres.	(1,98)	(1,98)	(1,98)
Depression	4.25	8.00	10.50	7.13	2.05	1.15	4.16*
Morale	1.58	2.00	1.46	1.78	1.83	9.34**	.15

4. Number of children

	Nonemployed		Employed		ME	NC	ME × NC
	1–2	3+	1–2	3+	(1,98)	(1,98)	(1,98)
Depression	9.38	4.27	7.55	9.72	1.68	.10	3.98*
Morale	1.88	1.73	1.78	1.44	2.39	6.59**	.54

5. Child-related support

	Nonemployed		Employed		ME	CS	ME × CS
	Less Supp.	More Supp.	Less Supp.	More Supp.	(1,98)	(1,98)	(1,98)
Depression	6.11	5.80	5.60	9.80	.19	5.08*	1.26
Morale	1.72	2.00	1.77	1.62	.31	.39	1.88

Notes. HH, household chores; CC, child-care chores; PP, presence of preschooler; NC, number of children; MS, marital status; ETH, ethnicity; SE, social-emotional support; CS, child-related support; ME, maternal employment.

= $p < .10$; * = $p < .05$; ** = $p < .01$; *** = $p < .001$.

In terms of marital status, single mothers ($M = 14.48$) were more depressed than married mothers ($M = 10.78$). There was also a trend for marital status to modify the link between maternal employment and morale, with nonemployed single mothers reporting lower morale than nonemployed married, employed single, or employed married mothers. However, even though nonemployed single mothers evinced more depression than nonemployed married mothers, employed single mothers, or employed married mothers, marital status did not significantly modify the link between maternal employment and depressive mood.

We next examined whether African-American mothers differed from White mothers in terms of the way maternal employment affected their mood. There were no main effects for ethnicity. In addition, ethnicity did not moderate the effect of employment on mother's well-being.

Finally, we examined the role social support plays in modifying the effects of maternal employment on mother's mood. Nonparental child-related support significantly moderated the links between maternal employment and depression. Employed mothers who received less child-related support were more depressed than employed women who received more child-related support. The pattern for nonemployed women, however, was inverse: full-time homemakers who received more child-related support reported higher levels of depressive mood than homemakers who received less child-related support. When this analysis was run separately for married and single mothers, the finding held for single mothers only. Note that the mean CES-D score for homemakers who received more support is 18.25 (for single mothers in this group the mean was 19.24). In general, a cutoff of 16 is used to indicate more severe pathology (Radloff, 1977), so the level of depressive mood for this group of mothers is cause for concern. This finding raises the possibility that for a subset of women, those whose lives are most stressed and who are at a higher level of dysfunction, the direction of causality is reversed, and depression may be a factor that keeps these women out of the work force.

Summary and Discussion of Working-class Patterns

The results of this study indicate that, for working-class families, maternal employment is associated with lower depression and higher morale. Further, out of seven potential moderators, we found that only social support significantly moderated this link, with a trend-level moderating relationship for marital status. At the trend level, nonemployed single mothers had the lowest morale. As might be expected, employed women who received less child-related support were more depressed than employed women who received more child-related support. Nonemployed women, on the other hand, who received more child-related support were more depressed than nonemployed women who received less child-related support, a pattern that may reflect the response of others to special stress. Even when moderated, however, the basic employment findings remain the same – employed mothers are less depressed and have higher morale than full-time homemakers.

As in most contemporaneous research designs, however, a question can be raised about the direction of causality. Is the working-class home-maker's depression influenced by her lack of employment, or is the depression antecedent to her employment status? Is it the depression that keeps her out of the labor force? Are there selective factors that keep the women from employment which also increase their depression? Two pre-vious studies (Kessler, Turner, & House, 1989; Verbugge, 1987) have investigated this issue and both have provided support for the hypothesis that employment status plays the causal role. This study also provides data relevant to this issue. For example, although both number of children and the presence of a preschooler are possible selective factors that affect the mother's employment status, neither is related to depression in the work-ing class, and they do not moderate the relationship between employment and depression.

Another possible selection factor, however, has been proposed as a pos-sible explanation for previous findings that employed mothers in the work-ing class have children who show higher adjustment and academic scores. It has been suggested that working-class full-time homemakers may be kept out of the labor force because of the presence of a handicapped or chronically-ill child (Hoffman, 1979, 1984). Such a selection factor would be a deterrent to employment and would increase the mother's stress. To test this possibility a post-hoc analysis was conducted for the working-class single mothers, the only group for whom the necessary data were available. The presence of a handicapped or chronically ill child was not significantly related to the mother's employment status and there were no significant interactions when this variable was added as a factor in any of the ANOVAs. Thus, there was no indication that the effect of employment on maternal well-being scores was carried by this variable.

Finally, however, our data indicate that for a subset of single nonem-ployed women in the working class, the direction of causality may be reversed. That is, these women may be so stressed that they are unable to work. If this is the case, then efforts to move these women into the labor force, without also providing adequate mental health services, could exacerbate an already difficult situation (Hoffman, 1986).

Married, Middle-class Patterns

We repeated the moderation analyses in the middle class. Five moderators were examined: the father's help in household tasks and in child-care tasks, the presence of a preschool child, the number of children, and nonparental child-related social support.[3]

In terms of the father's help, the analyses revealed that neither help with household chores nor father's help with child care moderated the relation between maternal employment and maternal well-being.

The presence of a preschooler in the family had a direct impact on the mother's morale. Mothers with a preschooler reported lower morale ($M = 1.50$) than mothers with older children ($M = 1.82$). The presence of a preschooler also moderated the effect of maternal employment on the mother's depression. Employed mothers with a preschooler and nonemployed mothers with no preschooler reported higher levels of depressed mood than either employed mothers with no preschooler or nonemployed mothers with a preschooler.

Likewise, the number of children had a direct impact on the mother's morale. Mothers with one or two children reported higher morale ($M = 1.79$) than mothers with three or more children ($M = 1.55$). The number of children in the family also modified the effect of maternal employment on the mother's depression. Employed mothers with three or more children and nonemployed mothers with one or two children were more depressed than either employed mothers with one or two children or nonemployed mothers with three or more children.

Finally, in terms of support, mothers who received more nonparental child-related support were more depressed ($M = 9.44$) than mothers who received less nonparental child-related support ($M = 5.79$). However, the child-related support the mother received did not moderate the impact of employment on her well-being.

Summary and Discussion of Middle-class Patterns

For the middle-class, all-married sample, the father's household help and child-care help, the number of children, the presence of a preschooler, and child-related social support were examined as possible moderators. The number of children and the presence of a preschooler were found to moderate the relationship between employment and well-being in the middle class. Employed mothers with a preschooler or with three or more children, as well as nonemployed mothers with no preschoolers or less than three children, were more depressed than their counterparts. The moderating roles of number and age of children on maternal mental health in the middle class supports previous speculations in the literature (Hoffman, 1979; Birnbaum, 1975) that the role of the full-time housewife in the middle class is less fulfilling when there are no more than two children and they are both in school. Similarly, the reversed effect of number and age of children for employed mothers is consistent with the view that the benefits of employment are diminished when childrearing responsibilities are excessive (Hoffman, 1989).

Mediators of the Maternal Employment/Morale Link: Working Class

To further understand the relationship between the mother's employment status and her emotional well-being, analyses were conducted to identify variables that mediated this connection. Since mediation analysis involves identifying variables that link two other significantly related variables, this was only examined within the working class. This is because there were no significant associations between maternal employment and maternal well-being in the married, middle-class sample.

Three mediation variables have been proposed in the literature, particularly for the working class: financial concerns, loneliness, and sense of control (Hoffman, 1986; Ferree, 1976; Rosen, 1987). The relation between maternal employment, the mother's well-being, and these three potential mediators is depicted in Figure 5.1.

To test the model in Figure 5.1 we used regression techniques and followed Baron and Kenny's (1986) criteria for determining whether variables functioned as mediators (see Chapter 4).

Regressions of the two maternal well-being variables on maternal employment revealed that employment was a significant predictor of both depressive mood and morale. Regressions of the three mediating variables – loneliness, locus of control, and financial worries – on maternal employment showed that maternal employment was a nonsignificant predictor of financial worries, and only a marginally significant predictor of loneliness, and thus these two variables cannot function as mediators.

Figures 5.2 and 5.3 depict the results of the mediation analyses. As seen in Figure 5.2A, a significant direct relation between maternal employment and depressive mood exists ($F[1,145] = 10.95$, $p < .001$), satisfying Baron and

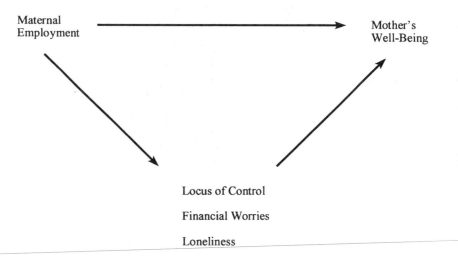

Figure 5.1. Mediated model of the effect of maternal employment on maternal well-being.

Kenny's (1986) first criteria. A significant relation between maternal employment and maternal locus of control also exists ($F[1,145] = 13.10$, $p < .001$; see Figure 5.2B), satisfying the second criterion. When depressive mood was regressed simultaneously on both employment and locus of control, locus of control emerged as a significant predictor, satisfying the third criterion, and the relationship between employment and depression was attenuated, satisfying the fourth criterion ($F[2,144] = 9.11$, $p < 002$; see Figure 5.2B). However, the attenuation was not complete, suggesting locus of control functions as a partial mediator. Sobel's (1982) test was performed to test the degree of attenuation. Sobel's t-ratio was 2.78 ($p < .01$), indicating a significant indirect path from maternal employment to depression through maternal locus of control. This indicates that the partial mediation is significant.

To test the second mediational model, three similar equations to those already described were tested. As seen in Figure 5.3A, a significant direct relation exists between maternal employment and the mother's morale ($F[1,145] = 4.79$, $p < .05$). In addition, there is a significant relation between maternal employment and maternal locus of control ($F[1,145] = 13.10$, $p < .001$). When morale is regressed on both locus of control and maternal employment, locus of control shows a marginally significant relation to morale and the previously significant relation between maternal employment and morale is reduced to zero, suggesting complete mediation ($F[2,144] = 3.65$, $p < .05$).

A. Direct Relationship

B. Mediated Relation

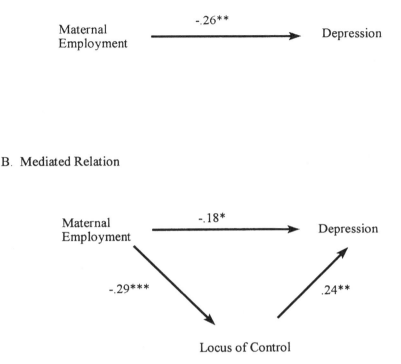

Figure 5.2. Mediation of the link between maternal employment and depression. * $p < .05$; ** $p < .01$; *** $p < .001$.

Previous researchers had suggested that because a mother's employment has a more profound effect on the family's economic circumstances in the working class than in the middle class, it might be the difference in the feeling of financial strain between the working-class employed mothers and full-time homemakers that carries the difference in their mental well-being. Our results, however, indicated that it was not financial worries per se that mediated the employment/mood connection, but rather, it was the feeling of having no personal control by the full-time homemakers that linked employment status to depressive mood and morale.

The measure of financial concerns was based on a single item, and thus its failure to show mediation could be because of that limitation. However, our result is bolstered by the fact that both McLoyd and her colleagues (1994) and Waldron and Jacobs (1989) also found that financial concerns

A. Direct Relationship

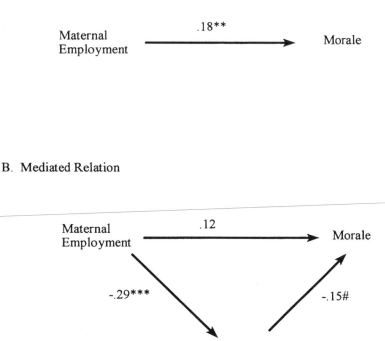

B. Mediated Relation

Figure 5.3. Mediation of the link between maternal employment and the mother's morale. [#] $p < .10$; [**] $p < .01$; [***] $p < .001$.

did not account for the higher depression scores of working-class home-makers. These results are also consistent with previous research by Ferree (1976) and Rosen (1987), which suggested that the principal psychological value of employment for blue-collar mothers lies in the sense of competence and personal control gained through the significance of their monetary contribution to the family's standard of living and in the companionship and social support of their co-workers.

Summary

In this chapter, we investigated the link between maternal employment and maternal well-being, and whether these patterns held across social class.

We also explored several moderators and mediators of this link. Our analyses indicated that, in the working class, employment holds a positive mental health advantage. That is, employed mothers are less depressed and have higher morale than nonemployed mothers. Employment is unrelated to the mother's well-being in the middle class.

Our analysis of potential moderators of this link showed that, in the working class, this link is marginally moderated by the mother's marital status, and is significantly moderated by the social support she receives. In the middle class, the presence of a preschooler and the number of children in the family serve to modify the effect of employment on the mother's mental health.

Mediators of the association between employment and maternal well-being were considered only in the working class, as there was no relation in the middle class between employment and mental health. These analyses revealed that the link between employment and depression and morale are partially explained by the mother's locus of control or sense of effectiveness.

Notes

1. This is not a peculiarity of the sample but reflects national employment patterns. Ninety-three percent of the middle-class mothers in the sample have at least some college; more than half graduated college. National statistics for 1995 show that only 15 percent of the single mothers with school-aged children and at least some college were not in the labor force and only 9 percent of those who graduated college (U.S. Bureau of the Census, 1996).

2. Inadvertently, one item was left off the interview packet. Thus, the measure administered in this study included nineteen items. The alpha coefficient reported in the current study matches that originally reported by Radloff (1977), and is similar to other reports in the literature using the twenty items. To determine how this deleted item ("I enjoyed life") affected total scores, we obtained the mean for a comparable item ("I was happy"). The mean was .3, so total scores are only modestly lowered by this deletion.

3. Marital status was not explored, because this sample contains only married women. And, it was not reasonable to examine ethnicity in these analyses because there are only seven African-American women in the married, middle-class sample.

6   Childrearing*

In this chapter we consider whether there are differences in childrearing styles between employed mothers and full-time homemakers. It was pointed out in Chapter 1 that there has been very little research directly examining the relationship between the mother's employment status and parenting behavior or orientations. Most of what have been proposed as differences have been inferred from outcomes, not examined empirically. Here we try to identify childrearing orientations that are associated with the mother's employment status. In Chapter 10, we will consider how such differences may affect the child.

The childrearing orientations to be examined are organized into three general categories. First we will focus on methods of discipline and control. Although these are not the variables typically examined in research on maternal employment effects, they have been the focus of research on children's competence, aggressiveness, and moral development (Baumrind, 1967; Dornbusch & Gray, 1988; M. Hoffman, 1988). Second, we look for differences between employment groups in attitudes and behaviors relevant to their children's independence, maturity, and achievement. As noted in Chapter 1, previous research has suggested that employed mothers encourage independence, maturity, and achievement in their children more than do full-time homemakers, particularly for daughters (Alessandri, 1992; Bartko & McHale, 1991; Gottfried, Gottfried, & Bathurst, 1988; Hoffman, 1989). Third, we examine differences in the amount of interaction and affection: Is it true that the mother's employment diminishes the quantity and quality of interaction for school-age children as those opposed to mothers' employment have argued?

* This chapter was written by Donna Dumm Kovacs and Lois W. Hoffman.

Method

Sample

As in Chapters 4 and 5, only mothers who had a stable history of employment over the preceding three years were included. Because there were so few single, middle-class, homemaker mothers, single middle-class mothers were excluded from the analyses.

Most of the measures of parenting styles were obtained from the mother interviews. For measures drawn from mother interviews, the sample size was 199 married mothers; 96 were working-class and 103 were middle-class. There were 54 single working-class mothers. In a few cases, the measures were obtained from the children themselves. For measures obtained from children, the sample size was 226 for children with married mothers and 63 for children with single mothers.

Measures

Discipline and Parental Control. Measures of discipline and parental control were designed to assess the overall styles of discipline used by the mother. Two separate instruments were used: behavior-based discipline and parental control. Both measures are described in Chapter 2.

From the discipline measure, four scales were used:

1. *Induction,* or the use of explanation and reason, such as explaining why the child should stop watching television (scale range: 0–12)
2. *Power assertion,* or the use of parental power, such as turning off the television or loudly telling the child what to do (range: 0–13)
3. *Strong power assertion,* a subset of power assertion responses, including hitting the child or threatening to hit the child (range: 0–13)
4. *Permissive action,* or letting the child do what he or she wanted, such as wanting the child to stop watching television but letting the child continue to watch it (range: 0–22)

For all scales, higher scores indicate that the mother uses the discipline style more.

From the parental control measure, eight scales and subscales were used:

1. *Permissiveness* (ten items, including, "I have no particular rules about bedtime – I leave it up to my child"; and "If you give children love, the rest will take care of itself")

2. *Authoritarian* (eleven items, including, "When my child has done something really wrong, I show my disappointment by spanking him (or her)," and "It is very important for a child to be obedient")

3. Obedience and respect, a subset of authoritarian (seven items, including, "It is very important for children to respect authority")

4. *Physical punishment,* a subset of authoritarian (two items, including, "It's impossible to bring up a child properly without occasionally hitting or spanking them")

5. *Hostile* (three items: "When I give my child responsibility for tasks around the house, I expect him (or her) to carry them out without my guidance or company", "When my child asks questions, I try to answer with a simple yes or no rather than going into a full explanation"; and "I don't give my child a lot of praise when he (or she) does something well, so as not to spoil him (or her)"

6. *Authoritative* (eleven items, including, "Third- or fourth-grade children should be allowed to take part in family decisions"; and, "If I enforce a rule or say no to the child, I think it's important to explain the reason")

7. *Child influence,* a subset of authoritative (four items, including, "Before punishing my child, I always listen to his/her side of the story")

8. *Child thinking for self,* a subset of authoritative (two items, including, "A child in the third or fourth grade should be encouraged to think for himself")

For each parental control scale, higher scores indicate greater endorsement for that particular method of parental control.

Independence, Achievement, and Maturity Demands. In order to assess parental emphasis on independence and achievement, as well as other goals, two types of measures were employed: a goals questionnaire and a questionnaire about school achievement. In addition, three different types of variables were used to assess maturity demands and autonomy granting:

parental expectations, child involvement in household tasks, and parental monitoring.

In order to measure the emphasis that mothers placed on the goals of achievement and independence, as well as on other goals, mothers were asked a series of questions, beginning with "How important is it to you that your child…?" Examples of questions include, "How important is it to you that your child be obedient?" and "How important is it to you that your child be kind?" Each item was rated on a five-point scale, ranging from "not really important" (1) to "perhaps the most important thing" (5). In addition to the rating-scale items, mothers were asked four close-ended questions about goals for their child. For example, one of the four close-ended questions was, "What is the most important quality you would like to see in your child?" Possible responses for this particular item were: "to be popular"; "to do well in school"; "to be independent"; "to be kind to others"; "to be strong and athletic"; and "to be obedient." Responses were scored to reflect the relative importance the mother assigned to various childrearing goals.

Scales for the goals items were constructed by combining items from the five-point rating scale measure with items from the set of four closed-ended questions. Four scales were compiled for both boys and girls, as follows:

1. *Independence* (combines two close-ended items, plus three rating-scale items; includes qualities such as "independent" and "think for self")
2. *Achievement* (combines two close-ended items, plus four rating-scale items; includes qualities such as "do well in school" and "be intelligent")
3. *Obedience* (combines one close-ended item, plus one rating-scale item; includes qualities such as "obedient")
4. *Kind and good* (combines three close-ended items, plus four rating-scale items; includes qualities such as "be kind" and "show concern for others")

A fifth scale, for the goal of femininity, was constructed only for girls, and combined the scores for four of the rating-scale items, including "be feminine" and "be sweet." Scale ranges are as follows: independence: 3–23; achievement: 4–28; obedience: 1–9; kind and good: 4–32; femininity: 4–20. For all scales, higher scores indicate that a greater value is placed on that particular goal.

In addition to the goals items, mothers were asked about their expectations for their children's education. The measure of educational expectations is the response to one eight-point item, which asked, "How much education do you think your child will get?" Responses on this item range from some high school but not graduate (1) to professional or graduate school (8); higher scores indicate higher expectations.

To assess maturity demands, mothers were asked a series of questions regarding their expectations for when, or at what age, their child should be able to do certain things by himself or herself. Examples of these questions include, "At what age would you expect your child to choose what clothes to wear to school each day?"; "At what age would you expect your child to help with the house cleaning?"; and "At what age would you expect your child to travel on a city bus by himself (or herself)?" Mothers responded to each item by giving an age in years. For each item, age-appropriate norms were then established. Mothers' individual responses to each item were coded using a six-point scale, reflecting whether their particular response was very early, a little early, on time, a little late, very late, or never. A composite score for maturity expectations was then formed by summing the scores for twenty-one expectations items. The scale range is 21 to 126, with lower scores indicating that the mother's maturity expectations are early, and higher scores indicating that the mother's maturity expectations are late.

To assess child involvement in household tasks, mothers were asked whether children helped with the following chores: doing dishes, helping with cooking, preparing meals by himself (or herself), cleaning and dusting, vacuuming, and washing floors. For each item, possible responses were "regularly," "sometimes," or "never." Subjects received two points for each response of "regularly" and one point for each response of "sometimes." Scores were summed across the six items, with a scale range of 0–12; higher scores indicate that the child does more chores.

Parental supervision and monitoring was assessed by a categorical variable. A single (composite) monitoring score was derived from two independent measures of monitoring: a child-report measure and a mother-report measure. Both mothers and children were asked a series of questions regarding what happens at the end of the school day, such as who is at home after school, and what the child does after school. Based on responses to these questions, three categories were formed: (1) regularly supervised; (2) unsupervised but monitored; and (3) unsupervised and unmonitored. For a fuller description of this measure of monitoring, see Chapter 11.

Interaction and Affection. Four types of interaction and affection variables were created, including both mother-report and child-report variables. Measures of interaction and affection included mother's report of mother–child interactions; mother's report of displays of affection; mother's report of parental commitment; and child's report of mother–child interactions.

For the mother's report of mother–child interactions, mothers were given a list of eighteen activities, and were asked to indicate how often they had done each activity with their child in the past week. Responses were scored on a five-point scale, ranging from "not at all" (1) to "more than 4 times" (5). A sixth response alternative, "not this past week but we usually do," received the score (1–5) that was equal to the mode for that particular item. The eighteen activities were combined to form five scales:

1. *Fun activities* (eight items, including "played a game together" and "visited relatives")
2. *Talk* (two items: "talked about what happened at school" and "talked about other things")
3. *Educational activities* (five items, including "read a book together" and "helped with homework")
4. *Nurturance* (four items, including "showed affection – hugged or kissed" and "helped with something he (or she) wanted help with")
5. Total positive interactions, the sum of all eighteen items

For each of the six scales, higher scores indicate more mother–child interaction.

A measure of the mother's display of overt affection was made by combining three items that directly asked mothers about overt affectionate displays. One of the three items ("How often in the last week did you and your child show affection – hugged or kissed?") was taken from the mother-report of mother–child interactions. The remaining two items ("I show my child love, but I don't go in for a lot of hugging or kissing" and "I don't give my child a lot of praise when he (or she) does something well, so as not to spoil him (or her)" were included in the questionnaire about parental control. Both items from the parental control measure were reverse-coded; and the standardized scores for the three items were summed. Higher scores indicate more mother–child displays of affection.

The mother's commitment to parenting was assessed by a twenty-two-item measure, an age-appropriate adaptation of a measure developed by Greenberger (1988) designed to tap the centrality of parenting to the self – that is, its salience in relation to other activities (Greenberger & Goldberg, 1989). Mothers were presented with a series of statements about being a parent and were asked to indicate how much they agreed with each statement, using a six-point scale, ranging from agree very strongly (1) to disagree very strongly (6). Examples of items include: "Being a parent is important to me, but isn't central in how I define myself"; "Children are very demanding and I often wish I had more time for other things"; and "I probably talk too much about my children" (reverse-scored). Scores for the twenty-two items were summed to form the parental commitment scale. Higher scores indicate more commitment to parenting.

Children's reports were also used to assess mother–child interaction. Child-report indices of mother–child interaction were compiled from the Day at Home, which is described in Chapter 4. These child-report indices indicate the extent to which the mother interacted with the children. Each question was scored on a three-point scale, with two points if the mother was circled (as doing the activity most often); one point if the mother was underlined (as doing the activity sometimes); or no points if the mother was not selected (i.e., she rarely or never did the activity). Six child-report indices were compiled:

1. *Fun activities* (four items, including, "Who takes you to fun places?" and "Who watches television with you?")
2. *Talk* (three items, including, "Who listens to you?" and "Who answers your questions?")
3. *Educational interactions* (five items, including, "Who teaches you?" and "Who talks to you about school?")
4. *Nurturance* (six items, including, "Who gives you hugs and kisses?" and "Who do you go to when you're sad?")
5. *Total positive interactions* (a summary of sixteen items measuring positive affect, including, "Who smiles a lot?"; "Who explains things to you?"; and "Who plays with you?")
6. *Negative-affect interactions* (five items, including "Who says no?" and "Who gets angry?")

For each scale, higher scores indicate more mother involvement. It should be noted that for these particular scales, the scores of married mothers and single mothers are not necessarily comparable, because children with married mothers had the opportunity to select the residential father, also, for each activity.

Analysis Plan

Analyses were conducted separately for married mothers and single, working-class mothers. For both married and single mothers, each of the parenting variables (with one exception, monitoring) in the three broad categories of discipline and parental control; independence, achievement, and maturity; and interaction and affection was used as the dependent variable in a separate ANOVA. For married mothers, a series of 2 (child gender) by 2 (social class) by 2 (maternal employment) ANOVAs were performed. For single mothers, a series of 2 (child gender) by 2 (maternal employment) ANOVAs were performed. The association between monitoring (a categorical variable) and maternal employment was assessed via chi-square tests. Interpretation of significant and trend-level interaction effects obtained in the ANOVAs was aided by a series of post-hoc analyses.

Results

Links Between Maternal Employment and Discipline and Parental Control

Married Mothers. Table 6.1 presents the results of the 2 (child gender) by 2 (social class) by 2 (maternal employment) ANOVAs for the discipline and parental control dependent variables, for married mothers. Means on each dependent variable for each employment group are also included in Table 6.1. Means on the dependent variables are listed for working-class boys, working-class girls, middle-class boys, and middle-class girls, for both employed and nonemployed mothers, in Table 6.2.

Discipline (Married Mothers). As shown in Table 6.1, for the group of married mothers, there were no significant main effects of maternal employment, and trend-level effects for maternal employment were found for only two of the scenario-based discipline measures: power assertion and strong power assertion. There was a tendency ($p < .10$) for employed mothers to use more power assertion than nonemployed mothers, but this is carried by the middle class, particularly the middle-class daughters (see means in Table 6.2). Post-hoc ANOVAs indicate a significant main effect of maternal employment in predicting the use of power assertion in the middle class ($F(1,100) = 7.37, p < 01$), but not in the working class ($F(1,93) = .00$, n.s.).

Additionally, there was a tendency for middle-class, employed mothers to use more strong power assertion with daughters. However, examination of the means in Table 6.2 suggests that this effect is carried by less gender differentiation for the employed mothers. The middle-class homemakers use relatively high levels of strong power assertion with sons but almost none with daughters, whereas, for employed mothers, scores for sons and daughters are close to equal. This interpretation was supported by a series

Table 6.1. *Effects of Child Gender, Social Class, and Maternal Employment on Discipline and Parental Control Measures, for Married Mothers*

	Means		F-Values from ANOVAs						
	EMP	NE	G	SC	ME	G×SC	G×ME	SC×ME	G×SC×ME[a]
Discipline									
Induction	4.94	4.71	1.49	2.74#	.11	1.43	1.51	.68	2.65
Power assertion	6.50	5.97	.21	.96	2.80#	.08	1.02	2.97#b	2.24
Strong power assertion	.30	.30	.15	1.40	.01	1.03	.08	.02	3.34#
Permissive action	1.65	1.67	5.43*	1.78	.17	1.07	.15	1.15	.08
Parental Control									
Permissive	14.31	16.14	2.39	1.56	6.07*	.92	.07	1.56	.18
Authoritarian	24.91	29.83	2.71	10.36**	19.62***	4.98*	.40	.03	10.10**
Obedience and respect	17.35	20.83	3.32#	5.16*	22.92***	9.94**	.21	.03	5.81*
Physical punishment	3.82	4.76	.52	9.04**	4.45*	.24	.21	.37	11.16***
Hostile	5.10	5.81	1.64	3.84#	3.88*	4.68*	1.78	1.12	1.03
Authoritative	42.80	42.33	.04	8.68**	.11	.14	2.07	1.75	2.30
Child influence	14.11	14.02	1.92	4.26*	.01	.85	.25	3.57#	4.42*
Child thinking for self	8.40	8.21	1.36	3.85#	.65	.99	1.06	.18	.10

Notes. EMP = employed; NE = nonemployed; G = child gender; SC = social class; ME = maternal employment.

[a]Means for G × SC × ME interactions are listed in Table 6.2.

[b]Means: Working class EMP = 6.46; Working class NE = 6.51; Middle class EMP = 6.54; Middle class NE = 5.13.

# *p* < .10; * *p* < .05; ** *p* < .01; *** *p* < .001.

Table 6.2. *Means on Discipline and Parental Control Measures for Employed versus Nonemployed Married Mothers, for Working-class Boys, Working-class Girls, Middle-class Boys, and Middle-class Girls*

| | Working Class | | | | Middle Class | | | |
| | Boys | | Girls | | Boys | | Girls | |
	EMP	NE	EMP	NE	EMP	NE	EMP	NE
Discipline								
Induction	4.32	4.95	5.03	3.38	5.67	5.50	4.70	5.07
Power assertion	6.61	6.55	6.30	6.46	6.28	6.12	6.75	4.60
Strong power assertion	.33	.24	.37	.54	.23	.50	.28	.07
Permissive action	1.26	1.00	1.87	1.92	1.58	2.00	1.82	2.27
Parental Control								
Permissive	13.58	16.23	15.37	17.85	14.08	14.25	14.30	15.53
Authoritarian	29.48	30.77	23.60	31.85	22.72	30.62	24.39	26.27
Obedience and respect	20.26	21.82	15.97	21.08	15.97	20.88	17.36	19.13
Physical punishment	4.77	4.68	3.87	6.31	3.36	5.50	3.48	3.13
Hostile	5.68	5.86	4.97	6.62	4.42	4.62	5.34	5.67
Authoritative	42.06	40.95	42.37	41.38	43.86	42.38	42.75	45.13
Child influence	13.48	13.32	14.47	13.38	14.42	14.00	14.07	15.60
Child thinking for self	8.48	8.09	8.03	7.92	8.61	8.25	8.43	8.60

Notes. EMP = employed; NE = nonemployed.

of post-hoc *t*-tests. Differences in mothers' use of strong power assertion with sons versus daughters was not significant for working-class employed mothers ($t(58) = -.17$, n.s.), working-class homemaker mothers ($t(32) = -1.45$, n.s.), or middle-class employed mothers ($t(76) = -.39$, n.s.). However, middle-class homemakers used significantly more strong power assertion with sons than with daughters ($t(20) = 2.53, p < .05$).

Control (Married Mothers). As shown in Table 6.1, the full-time homemakers indicate that they are more permissive than employed mothers. Inspection of the means in Table 6.2, however, shows this effect is primarily in the working class. The homemakers also indicate that they are more authoritarian, and this difference is especially true for middle-class mothers of boys and for working-class mothers of girls (as shown in Table 6.2). When post-hoc *t*-tests were performed, maternal employment was a significant predictor of authoritarian control for middle-class mothers of boys ($t(42) = -2.97$, $p < .01$) and for working-class mothers of girls ($t(41) = -4.42$, $p < .001$), but not for middle-class mothers of girls ($t(57) = -1.03$, n.s.), or for working-class mothers of boys $t(51) = -.73$, n.s.). The direction of the differences, however, was the same across groups.

When the subcomponents of authoritarian behavior were examined, differences between maternal employment groups were also evident. Full-time homemakers require more obedience and respect from their children. Again, differences between employed and nonemployed mothers were strongest for middle-class mothers of boys ($t(42) = -2.44$, $p < .05$) and working-class mothers of girls ($t(41) = -3.84$, $p < .001$). Differences were not as strong for middle-class mothers of girls ($t(57) = -1.50$, n.s.) or working-class mothers of boys ($t(51) = -1.46$, n.s.), as indicated by post-hoc *t*-tests. There was also a main effect of employment status for physical punishment. The full-time homemakers report a higher use of physical punishment and, again, this difference is strongest for middle-class mothers of boys ($t(42) = -2.51, p < .05$) and for working-class mothers of girls ($t(41) = -3.53, p < .001$). This difference in the use of physical punishment by employed versus nonemployed mothers was not found for middle-class mothers of girls ($t(57) = .48$, n.s.) or for working-class mothers of boys ($t(51) = .14$, n.s.), as indicated by post-hoc *t*-tests (see means in Table 6.2). Nonemployed mothers also report more use of a style of control that seems hostile.

There were no main effects of employment status for married mothers for authoritative control, but differences between maternal employment groups were found for one of the two subcomponents of the authoritative style, as shown in Table 6.1. Specifically, the three-way interaction of child

Table 6.3. *Effects of Child Gender and Maternal Employment on Discipline and Parental Control Measures, for Single, Working-class Mothers*

	Means		F-Values from ANOVAs		
	EMP	NE	G	ME	G × ME
Discipline					
Induction	4.66	3.44	5.08*	3.64#	.11
Power assertion	7.38	7.00	2.74	.26	.59
Strong power assertion	.86	1.68	.01	3.87#	1.07
Permissive action	1.86	.88	1.50	6.24*	.08
Parental Control					
Permissive	18.45	17.24	3.14#	.37	.18
Authoritarian	30.14	34.68	2.20	7.76**	.37
Obedience and respect	20.10	23.36	.00	11.04**	1.14
Physical punishment	4.93	5.40	1.13	.58	.04
Hostile	6.45	6.52	7.47**	.16	.03
Authoritative	42.79	38.40	1.50	10.74**	.87
Child influence	14.45	12.84	.18	5.36*	.04
Child thinking for self	8.55	7.56	.10	12.42***	1.51

Notes. EMP = employed; NE = nonemployed; G = child gender; ME = maternal employment.
# $p < .10$; * $p < .05$; ** $p < .01$; *** $p < .001$.

gender, social class, and maternal employment was significant in predicting the mother's encouragement of child influence. For middle-class mothers of girls, full-time homemaker mothers allow child influence more than employed mothers do ($t(57) = -2.68$, $p < .01$); but for working-class mothers of girls, the pattern tends to be reversed, with employed mothers allowing more child influence ($t(41) = 1.90$, $p < .10$). Differences in allowing child influence by employed versus nonemployed mothers were not significant for either working-class ($t(51) = .23$, n.s.) or middle-class ($t(42) = .54$, n.s.) mothers of boys, when post-hoc t-tests were performed (see means in Table 6.2).

Single Mothers. Table 6.3 presents the results of the 2 (child gender) by 2 (maternal employment) ANOVAs for the discipline and parental control dependent variables, for single working-class mothers. For each dependent variable, means for each employment group are also included in Table 6.3.

Discipline (Single Mothers). As shown in Table 6.3, the measure based on behavior scenarios showed a trend-level effect ($p < .10$) suggesting a higher use of induction techniques by the employed mothers. Employed and nonemployed mothers did not differ in the use of power assertion, but employed mothers tended to use less strong power assertion than nonemployed mothers. There is also a significant difference for permissive action, with lower scores for the single full-time homemakers. The mean scores for homemakers are, in fact, lower than for any other group, suggesting that they are particularly firm in pushing through on their efforts at discipline.

Control (Single Mothers). When the self-report measure was used, employed and nonemployed single mothers did not differ in their endorsement of permissiveness (Table 6.3). However, full-time homemaker mothers report more use of the authoritarian style than do employed mothers. When the subcomponents of the authoritarian style are considered, full-time homemakers place more emphasis on obedience and respect than do employed mothers. Consistent with this pattern, the homemakers also report *less* use of authoritative discipline and both of the subcomponents, promoting child influence and encouraging child to think for him or herself.

Summary of Results for Discipline and Control. The clearest pattern of differences emerged for the single mothers. The full-time single homemakers showed a pattern of strong authoritarian control. They reported more authoritarian and less authoritative discipline, and specifically indicated an expectation for obedience and respect from their children, as well as a lack of interest in encouraging the child's influence. With the discipline measures coded from descriptions of behavioral scenarios, results indicated that they were less likely to give in to the child in a discipline situation, and trend-level results showed that they used more power assertion and less induction (i.e., less use of explanation and reasoning).

The married, full-time homemakers also reported more authoritarian control, and were significantly higher both in their demand for obedience and in their reporting of control styles that seemed hostile. They also, however, indicated more permissiveness, particularly in the working class. The instrument coded from their accounts of behavior scenarios, however, revealed no significant main effects of employment status. There was a trend-level relationship for power assertion that indicated that the middle-class, employed mothers used more power assertion than did full-time homemakers. Inspection of the means suggested that this relationship held mainly for mothers of daughters (i.e., middle-class homemakers used power-based techniques with sons but rarely with daughters, but the gender of the child did not affect the employed mothers' scores).

Links Between Maternal Employment and Independence, Achievement, and Maturity Demands

Married Mothers. Table 6.4 presents the results of the 2 (child gender) by 2 (social class) by 2 (maternal employment) ANOVAs for the independence, achievement, and maturity dependent variables, for married mothers. Means on each of these dependent variables for each employment group are also included in Table 6.4. Table 6.5 presents means on each of these dependent variables, separately for working-class boys, working-class girls, middle-class boys, and middle-class girls with employed versus nonemployed mothers.

Goals (Married Mothers). As shown in Table 6.4, there was only one significant main effect of maternal employment on the goals of married mothers. The full-time homemakers stressed obedience as a goal more than the employed mothers did, a pattern also indicated by the previous set of results. However, in addition, there is a significant interaction effect with child gender and social class, and the means reported in Table 6.5, as well as post-hoc tests, reveal that this difference is carried by the middle-class mothers of boys ($t(42) = -3.60$, $p < .001$). The middle-class homemakers with sons obtain the highest score of any group in their rating of obedience as a goal, while the middle-class, employed mothers of boys give obedience the lowest rating. Post-hoc t-tests do not indicate strong differences between employed and nonemployed mothers for working-class boys ($t(51) = .80$, n.s.), working-class girls ($t(41) = -1.66$, n.s.), or middle-class girls ($t(57) = -.35$, n.s.) in their emphasis on the goal of obedience.

However, although there are few main effects of employment, there are several interaction effects with gender, as predicted. Thus, one expectation was that employed mothers of daughters would indicate that independence was a more important goal for their daughters than would homemaker mothers of daughters. This is supported by the results. The difference between the means for employed mothers of girls and homemaker mothers of girls (14.62 versus 12.82) is statistically significant ($F[1,99] = 5.09$, $p < .05$). For mothers of boys, however, the difference between means is not significant ($F[1,94] = 1.24$, n.s.). The results also indicate that employed mothers value independence more for their daughters than for their sons ($M = 14.62$ versus $M = 13.28$, $F[1,138] = 4.42$, $p < .05$). For homemakers, the pattern of means for boys and girls was reversed, but the difference did not reach statistical significance ($F[1,55] = 1.62$, n.s.).

Table 6.4. *Effects of Child Gender, Social Class, and Maternal Employment on Independence, Achievement, and Maturity Measures, for Married Mothers*

	Means		F-Values from ANOVAs						
	EMP	NE	G	SC	ME	G×SC	G×ME	SC×ME	G×SC×ME[a]
Goals									
Independence	13.99	13.53	1.04	.09	.50	.20	4.21*[b]	1.32	.30
Achievement	16.22	16.81	1.04	7.27**	.39	.28	2.45	.07	1.84
Obedience	3.48	4.05	7.47**	5.08*	4.76*	3.78#	.64	4.16*	12.20***
Kind and good	19.91	18.69	.65	4.65*	1.85	.22	8.34***[c]	.42	.06
Femininity (for girls)	8.51	9.68	Girls only	5.74#	3.90#	Girls only	Girls only	.47	Girls only
Educational Expectations	6.76	5.98	.01	17.69***	5.42*	1.46	.05	.40	1.34
Maturity Expectations	63.87	66.02	.33	5.92*	.84	1.42	.00	.03	1.01
Household Tasks	4.88	4.34	4.75*	.24	2.82#	.15	.22	.55	.15

Notes. EMP = employed; NE = nonemployed; G = child gender; SC = social class; ME = maternal employment.

[a] Means for G × SC × ME interactions are listed in Table 6.5.

[b] Means: Boys EMP = 13.28; Boys NE = 14.20; Girls EMP = 14.62; Girls NE = 12.82.

[c] Means: Boys EMP = 20.19; Boys NE = 16.93; Girls EMP = 19.66; Girls NE = 20.57.

# $p < .10$; * $p < .05$; ** $p < .01$; *** $p < .001$.

Table 6.5. *Means on Independence, Achievement, and Maturity Measures for Employed versus Nonemployed Married Mothers, for Working-class Boys, Working-class Girls, Middle-class Boys, and Middle-class Girls*

| | Working Class | | | | Middle Class | | | |
| | Boys | | Girls | | Boys | | Girls | |
	EMP	NE	EMP	NE	EMP	NE	EMP	NE
Goals								
Independence	12.97	14.59	14.20	12.85	13.56	13.12	14.91	12.80
Achievement	17.35	17.86	16.60	16.69	15.31	17.75	15.91	14.87
Obedience	4.55	4.18	3.20	3.85	3.03	5.25	3.30	3.40
Kind and good	19.52	16.95	18.67	20.00	20.78	16.88	20.34	21.07
Femininity (for girls)	N/A	N/A	9.10	10.62	N/A	N/A	8.11	8.87
Educational Expectations	6.23	5.23	6.27	5.92	7.25	7.25	7.05	6.47
Maturity Expectations	65.23	65.50	66.93	70.15	62.25	66.88	62.16	62.73
Household Tasks	4.35	4.14	5.07	4.77	4.67	4.25	5.30	4.33

Notes. EMP = employed; NE = nonemployed.

Interesting gender of child effects are also found for the goal of being "kind and good." This is a goal parents traditionally hold for daughters more than for sons, a pattern found here only for the full-time homemakers ($F[1,55] = 10.65$, $p < .01$). The gender of the child does not affect the ratings of the employed mother, however ($F[1,138] = .61$, n.s.). Similarly, the goal of *femininity,* obtained only from mothers of girls, is rated more highly by homemakers than employed mothers ($p < .10$).

Achievement does not show a relationship to employment nor an interaction with gender. There is a social class difference, however, that shows that working-class parents ($M = 17.15$) ranked achievement higher as a goal they hold for their children than did middle-class parents ($M = 15.69$).

Educational Expectations (Married Mothers). Employed mothers indicated higher educational expectations for their children. There is also a significant effect of social class, with middle-class mothers ($M = 7.05$) indicating higher expectations than working-class mothers ($M = 5.97$). Although the statistics indicate no interaction effect, it is interesting to note that the higher expectation scores of employed mothers is evident for boys and girls in the working class, but only for girls in the middle class.

Maturity Expectations (Married Mothers). No differences were found between employed and nonemployed mothers in their maturity expectations for the child, as shown in Table 6.4. However, there was a significant effect of social class. Scores for middle-class mothers ($M = 62.64$) were lower than scores for working-class mothers ($M = 66.49$), indicating that they hold earlier expectations concerning their child's maturity.

Household Tasks (Married Mothers). The data reported in Table 6.4 show, as in previous research, that the children of employed mothers help more in the house. However, this is only at the trend-level of significance ($p < .10$). They also show a significant gender difference: across class and employment status, daughters ($M = 5.02$) help more than sons ($M = 4.41$, see also Table 6.5).

Monitoring (Married Mothers). To assess the relationship between parental supervision and maternal employment, a series of 2 (maternal employment) by 3 (supervision and monitoring) chi-square tests was performed (not tabled). Chi-square tests were performed separately for working-class boys, middle-class boys, working-class girls, and middle-class girls. No significant association between maternal employment and super-

Table 6.6. *Effects of Child Gender and Maternal Employment on Independence, Achievement, and Maturity Measures, for Single, Working-class Mothers*

	Means		F-values from ANOVAs		
	EMP	NE	G	ME	G × ME
Goals					
Independence	14.10	13.52	.07	.36	1.09
Achievement	17.03	16.56	3.37[#]	.50	.00
Obedience	4.07	4.56	.26	1.01	.81
Kind and good	17.41	16.04	.54	1.42	3.34[#b]
Femininity (for girls)	9.64	10.83	Girls only	−1.20[a]	Girls only
Educational Expectations	5.69	5.38	4.82*	.63	.14
Maturity Expectations	63.21	66.48	.02	.77	1.86
Household Tasks	5.24	3.52	.48	9.93**	.03

Notes. EMP = employed; NE = nonemployed; G = child gender; ME = maternal employment.
[a] *t*-value.
[b] Means: Boys EMP = 17.89; Boys NE = 14.46; Girls EMP = 16.64; Girls NE = 17.75.
[#] $p < .10$; * $p < .05$; ** $p < .01$; *** $p < .001$.

vision was found for middle-class boys ($\chi^2[2, N = 44] = .65$, n.s.), middle-class girls ($\chi^2[2, N = 59] = 4.33$, n.s.), or working-class girls ($\chi^2[2, N = 43] = .46$, n.s.). However, for working-class boys, a significant association between maternal employment and supervision was indicated ($\chi^2[2, N = 53] = 7.72$, $p < .05$). Full-time homemakers were more likely to supervise their sons, while employed mothers were more likely to leave their sons unsupervised and unmonitored.

Single Mothers. Table 6.6 presents the results of the 2 (child gender) by 2 (maternal employment) ANOVAs for the independence, achievement, and maturity dependent variables for single, working-class mothers. Table 6.6 also includes means on each dependent variable for each of the two employment groups.

Goals (Single Mothers). Although the directions of the relationships for the goal variables were the same for single mothers as married, none of the differences was significant. The trend-level interaction for the goal of being "kind and good" suggested the same lack of gender stereotyping by employed mothers as was found in the married group and in Chapter 4. Post-hoc tests revealed that the full-time homemakers tended to be more likely to indicate they wanted daughters to be "kind and good" than sons ($t(23) = -1.80$, $p < .10$), but gender of child differences were not significant for employed mothers ($t(27) = .74$, n.s.). Compared to homemakers, employed mothers place significantly more emphasis on the goal of being "kind and good" for sons ($t(29) = 2.10$, $p < .05$); but for daughters, this difference is not significant ($t(21) = -.59$, n.s.).

Educational Expectations (Single Mothers). Employed and nonemployed mothers did not differ significantly in the educational expectations they held for their children. However, there was a significant gender difference in mothers' educational expectations. Single mothers expect their daughters ($M = 6.26$) to complete more years of formal schooling than their sons ($M = 5.00$).

Maturity Expectations (Single Mothers). Employed and nonemployed mothers also did not differ in their expectations regarding their children's maturity, as shown in Table 6.6.

Household Tasks (Single Mothers). Among single mothers, employed mothers report their children do more household tasks (Table 6.6). This pattern is consistent with previous research and with the trend-level relationship found here for married mothers.

Monitoring (Single Mothers). To assess the relationship between parental supervision and maternal employment, a pair of 2 (maternal employment) by 3 (supervision and monitoring) chi-square tests were performed. Chi-square tests were done separately for boys and girls. No significant association between maternal employment and supervision was found for either boys ($\chi^2[2, N = 31] = 4.07$, n.s.) or girls ($\chi^2[1, N = 23] = .01$, n.s.).

Summary of Results for Independence, Achievement, and Maturity Demands. Parents were asked about their goals for their children. There was only one significant main effect of the mother's employment status: the married, full-time homemakers stressed obedience as a goal more than employed married mothers. This result was particularly noted for middle-class mothers of boys. Among the married group, middle-class homemakers with sons obtained the highest scores and middle-class employed mothers of sons obtained the lowest scores.

There were, in addition, interaction effects with gender. Thus, consistent with previous hypotheses, married mothers with daughters placed a higher value on independence if they were employed than if they were homemakers. This difference was not found for mothers of sons nor for the single working-class mothers. For both the married and single mothers, however, there was some evidence of less gender stereotyping among those who were employed. The qualities "kind and good" were valued more for daughters by the homemakers, but the rankings given by employed mothers were not affected by the child's gender. Similarly, homemakers were more likely to hold "femininity" as a goal for their daughters than were employed mothers.

Although achievement per se did not show significant differences between employment groups as a goal, educational expectations did. For married mothers, the employed expected their children to obtain more education than the full-time homemakers did.

The participation of children in household tasks has been seen as a maturity demand and has been shown by previous research to be associated with indices of responsibility in children (Bartko & McHale, 1991; Medrich, Roizen, Rubin, & Buckley, 1982). As in prior studies, this analysis found higher participation among employed mothers, significant in one-parent families and at the trend-level in two-parent families.

Examination of the extent to which the mother's employment status affected child monitoring revealed one significant difference: sons in two-parent, working-class families were more likely to be left unsupervised and unmonitored if the mother was employed than if she was a full-time homemaker.

Links Between Maternal Employment and Interaction and Affection

Married Mothers. Table 6.7 presents the results of the 2 (child gender) by 2 (social class) by 2 (maternal employment) ANOVAs for the interaction and affection dependent variables, for married mothers. Means on each dependent variable for each employment group are also included in Table 6.7. Means on each of the dependent variables, for working-class boys, working-class girls, middle-class boys, and middle-class girls, with employed versus nonemployed mothers, are presented in Table 6.8

Mothers' Reports of Mother–Child Activities (Married Mothers). It can be seen in Table 6.7 that there are no main effects of the mother's employment status on the frequencies of mother–child interaction as reported by the mother. There are, however, several interaction effects. For fun, educational, nurturant, and total positive activities, the pattern in working-class families is that employed mothers interact more with daughters than full-

Table 6.7. *Effects of Child Gender, Social Class, and Maternal Employment on Interaction and Affection Measures for Married Mothers*

	Means		F-Values from ANOVAs						
	EMP	NE	G	SC	ME	G×SC	G×ME	SC×ME	G×SC×ME[a]
Mother Report of Activities									
Fun	20.40	20.43	1.39	2.68	.03	.42	.23	2.97#	2.85#
Talk	9.18	9.32	.05	4.57*	1.09	2.21	.58	.64	.32
Educational	16.54	16.81	.11	1.18	.46	3.43#	10.40***	10.89***	4.33*
Nurturance	12.87	13.03	.94	.02	.22	.75	6.81**	6.01*	3.79#
Total positive	57.30	58.12	.73	.50	.31	1.10	.92	5.16*	3.17#
Overt Display of Affection	.64	–.40	.04	6.81**	10.08**	.33	.61	3.29#	3.25#
Commitment to Parenting	73.69	74.17	3.33#	2.50	.07	.05	.00	8.05**b	1.28
Child Report of Interactions									
Fun	4.42	3.91	.59	.02	2.34	1.08	.11	1.72	.01
Talk	4.77	4.24	3.05#	3.87*	3.81#	8.10**	.99	1.35	5.89*
Educational	7.22	6.63	.68	.38	2.60	3.84#	.63	1.83	5.62*
Nurturance	9.27	8.54	.92	13.89***	1.78	3.72#	1.28	.00	.19
Total positive	22.47	20.48	1.69	4.21*	3.35#	4.40*	.37	1.11	.57
Negative affect	4.21	4.69	.15	.13	1.27	.48	.24	1.61	1.45

Notes. EMP = employed; NE = nonemployed; G = child gender; SC = social class; ME = maternal employment.

[a] Means for G × SC × ME interactions are listed in Table 6.8.

[b] Means: Working class EMP = 75.56; Working class NE = 72.80; Middle class EMP = 72.26; Middle class NE = 76.26.

# $p < .10$; * $p < .05$; ** $p < .01$; *** $p < .001$

time homemakers do. Employed mothers engaged in more educational ($t[41] = 3.16$, $p < .01$) and nurturant ($t[41] = 3.56$, $p < .001$) activities with daughters, and they tended ($p < .10$) to engage in more fun ($t[41] = 1.69$, $p < .10$) and total ($t[41] = 1.95$, $p < .10$) activities as well. For sons, the direction of the relationship was in the opposite direction, but none of the differences between employed and nonemployed mothers was significant.

This pattern is not found in the middle class. That is, there is no evidence there of an advantage of maternal employment for daughters. The general picture is one of higher mother–child interaction for full-time homemakers. Full-time homemakers report more educational activities with their children ($M = 18.30$ for homemakers; $M = 16.41$ for employed; $F[1,99] = 6.87$, $p < .01$), and more total positive activities ($M = 60.13$ for homemakers; $M = 56.30$ for employed; $F[1,99] = 4.84$, $p < .05$). However, none of the other relationships within the middle class was significant.

Display of Affection (Married Mothers). The composite measure of showing affection yields a significant difference with employed mothers indicating higher levels than nonemployed. The difference extends across social class and child gender.

Commitment to Parenting (Married Mothers). Among working-class married mothers, the employed and nonemployed do not differ significantly in their commitment to parenting ($F[1,93] = 2.61$, n.s.). For middle-class mothers, however, full-time homemaker mothers report more commitment to parenting than employed mothers ($F[1,100] = 6.63$, $p < .05$). (See the means at bottom of Table 6.7).

Child Report of Mother–Child Interaction (Married Mothers). The children's reports of their interactions with their mothers yielded no significant main effects of employment, but "talk" and "total positive affect" showed trend levels of significance. For each of these two variables, children with employed mothers reported higher levels of interaction ($p < .10$). In addition, for talk and educational interaction, there were significant interactions with social class and gender. The means in Table 6.8, as well as post-hoc tests, indicate that higher levels of interaction on both variables are reported for employed mothers by middle-class boys in particular ($t(41) = 3.19$, $p < .01$ for talk; $t(41) = 2.33$, $p < .05$ for educational).

Single Mothers. Table 6.9 presents the results of the 2 (child gender) by 2 (maternal employment) ANOVAs for the interaction and affection depen-

Table 6.8. *Means on Interaction and Affection Measures for Employed versus Nonemployed Married Mothers, for Working-class Boys, Working-class Girls, Middle-class Boys, and Middle-class Girls*

	Working Class				Middle Class			
	Boys		Girls		Boys		Girls	
	EMP	NE	EMP	NE	EMP	NE	EMP	NE
Mother Report of Activities								
Fun	20.35	20.41	22.83	19.38	19.61	19.50	19.43	21.87
Talk	8.94	8.95	9.13	9.25	9.53	9.62	9.09	9.73
Educational	15.58	17.00	17.87	13.85	16.81	19.38	16.09	17.73
Nurturance	12.26	13.23	13.93	11.38	12.61	13.88	12.80	13.73
Total positive	56.58	57.73	60.73	55.23	56.78	58.88	55.91	60.80
Overt Display of Affection	.15	-.63	.67	-1.57	1.03	.19	.65	.56
Commitment to Parenting	74.55	72.86	76.60	72.69	71.64	73.62	72.77	77.67
Child Report of Interactions								
Fun	4.50	4.45	4.03	3.82	4.45	3.60	4.65	3.50
Talk	4.85	4.82	4.08	3.47	5.12	3.20	4.93	4.83
Educational	7.24	7.45	6.73	6.00	7.52	4.90	7.33	7.17
Nurturance	9.29	8.05	7.81	7.82	9.79	8.90	9.96	9.61
Total positive	22.65	21.64	19.84	18.71	23.48	18.80	23.52	21.67
Negative affect	4.47	4.64	4.19	3.82	4.29	4.40	3.96	5.72

Notes. EMP = employed; NE = nonemployed.

Table 6.9. *Effects of Child Gender and Maternal Employment on Interaction and Affection Measures, for Single, Working-class Mothers*

	Means		F-Values from ANOVAs		
	EMP	NE	G	ME	G × ME
Mother Report of Activities					
Fun	19.93	18.32	.74	1.22	.02
Talk	8.97	8.00	.00	4.31*	2.84#a
Educational	15.97	14.04	1.18	5.05*	.16
Nurturance	12.55	11.64	3.02#	1.92	.68
Total positive	56.17	51.88	2.17	3.62#	.23
Overt Display of Affection	−.31	−2.74	4.05*	10.55**	.36
Commitment to Parenting	73.31	69.16	.05	3.67#	.93
Child Report of Interactions					
Fun	4.71	3.68	2.68	2.62	1.00
Talk	4.91	4.43	.62	1.32	1.35
Educational	7.54	6.79	1.20	1.31	1.36
Nurturance	8.51	7.89	.17	.61	.26
Total positive	22.40	19.82	1.35	1.98	1.32
Negative affect	4.60	5.71	.02	2.43	.02

Notes. EMP = employed; NE = nonemployed; G = child gender; ME = maternal employment.
[a] Means: Boys EMP = 8.67; Boys NE = 8.38; Girls EMP = 9.45; Girls NE = 7.58.
# $p < .10$; * $p < .05$; ** $p < .01$; *** $p < .001$.

dent variables, for single, working-class mothers. Table 6.9 also lists the means for each dependent variable, separately by employment group.

Mother's Reports of Mother–Child Activities (Single Mothers). The results in Table 6.9 indicate that employed mothers report significantly more talk and educational activities with their children than do full-time homemakers in this sample of working-class single mothers. In addition, there is a trend-level relationship for total positive activities.

Display of Affection (Single Mothers). The employed mothers also report that they display more overt affection to their children than nonemployed mothers do, as shown in Table 6.9.

Commitment to Parenting (Single Mothers). At the trend-level, employed mothers in the group report more commitment to parenting than do the full-time homemakers.

Child Report of Mother–Child Interaction (Single Mothers). The children's reports of mother–child interaction indicated no differences between the two employment status groups.

Summary of Results for Interaction and Affection. The mothers reported the frequency of their interactions during the previous week with their third- or fourth-grade child. Among the single, working-class mothers, those who were employed reported more interaction with respect to educational activities and talking. Among married mothers, there were no significant main effects of the mother's employment status. For working-class married mothers, however, the data indicated that employed mothers interact more with daughters, compared to homemakers. This was true for fun and educational activities, nurturance, and the total positive activity score. For middle-class mothers, however, full-time homemakers reported more educational activities with both sons and daughters and more total positive activities as well.

The children's reports of their interactions with their mothers yielded few significant relationships with the mother's employment status, but there were some trend-level relationships in the married sample, with "talk" and "total positive" interactions showing employed mothers higher. For middle-class boys, in particular, higher levels of talking and educational activities are reported by those with employed mothers. Thus, the children's reports showed different effects in the middle class than the mother's reports did.

A composite measure of overt affection toward the child was constructed from the mother's interview. For both the single and the married mothers, the employed indicated a higher level of affection than the homemakers.

Finally, the commitment to parenting measure indicated higher commitment for full-time homemakers in the middle class, but not in the working class. In the working class, for both the married and single mothers, the direction of the relationship was reversed but not statistically significant (although it reached trend-level for single mothers).

Moderating Effects of Ethnicity on Links Between Maternal Employment and Parenting

Analyses were undertaken to determine whether any of the observed links between maternal employment and the mother's parenting style were moderated by ethnicity. Small cell sizes precluded an examination of ethnicity effects for married, middle-class mothers. However, for married, working-class mothers, as well as for single, working-class mothers, a series of 2 (child gender) by 2 (ethnicity) by 2 (maternal employment) ANOVAs was performed, in order to test for significant interactions of ethnicity and maternal employment. Interpretation of significant interactions was, again, aided by post-hoc tests. In addition, for the one categorical variable (monitoring), chi-square tests were performed to determine whether there were any significant associations between ethnicity and parental supervision, for each maternal employment group.

Ethnicity moderated the results only for the single, working-class mothers. For single mothers, the effects of maternal employment were significantly modified for two of the dependent measures, child influence ($F[1,47] = 8.26$, $p < .01$) and mothers' reports of fun activities ($F[1,47] = 4.25$, $p < .05$). The finding reported in Table 6.3 that single employed mothers allowed the child more influence than single homemakers was carried by the African Americans [($M = 14.82$ for employed mothers; $M = 11.89$ for nonemployed mothers), $F[1,26] = 8.04$, $p < .01$]. Differences were not significant among whites [($M = 14.22$ for employed mothers; $M = 15.29$ for nonemployed mothers), $F[1,22] = 1.86$, n.s.]. Finally, although no significant difference was reported in Table 6.9 for mother's participation in fun activities with the child, the moderating analysis revealed that among African Americans, employed mothers reported more engagement in fun activities [($M = 22.18$ versus $M = 17.39$), $F[1,26] = 3.82$, $p < .10$], but among Whites the full-time homemakers reported more ($M = 20.71$ versus $M = 18.56$), although not significantly so ($F[1,22] = .94$, n.s.).

Summary and Discussion

In this chapter we have examined the relationships between the mother's employment status and her childrearing orientations. Three domains of childrearing have been examined: (1) styles of discipline and control; (2) goals emphasized for children with particular attention to the importance of achievement, independence, and maturity; and (3) the quantity and nature of the mother's interaction with the child. A variety of measures and different perspectives have been used to provide a more complete picture, and an effort has been made to identify different patterns in different subgroups.

Discipline, Control, and Goals

Two measures of parental control were used, one based on the mother's descriptions of a set of recent discipline interactions and the other based on the mother's reports of her style of discipline and control. In general, the data indicated that the full-time homemakers were more likely than employed mothers to use authoritarian, power-based control and to demand obedience. This was particularly marked for single mothers, but also characterized the pattern for married mothers. For the latter, however, homemakers also used more permissiveness.

An interesting gender difference was revealed in the middle class. The behavior-based measure of power assertion showed a tendency for more power assertion by employed mothers, a pattern inconsistent with the results just described. However, careful examination revealed that this result was carried by the middle-class daughters. Middle-class homemakers use relatively high levels of power assertion with boys, but almost none with girls. Employed mothers in the middle class show similar levels for boys and girls, lower than the homemakers use with boys but higher than the homemakers use with girls. This pattern of less gender differentiation by employed mothers occurred also in other domains.

For example, in response to the questions about their goals for their children, the full-time homemakers were more likely than the employed mothers to conform to traditional gender stereotypes. Thus, the homemakers with daughters were more likely to give a high rating to the goal of being kind and good than were homemakers with sons, but this difference was not found for employed mothers. Similarly, homemakers rated the goal of femininity higher for their daughters than employed mothers did. And, consistent with previous hypotheses, for mothers of daughters, employed mothers hold independence as a goal more than do homemakers, but employment status was not related to the rating of independence for mothers of sons.

Consistent also with the results for the discipline and control variables, full-time homemakers were more likely to cite obedience as a major goal. This was particularly marked for middle-class mothers of boys where homemakers gave obedience the highest rating of any other group and employed mothers gave it the lowest.

The importance of high achievement for children was not significantly different for employed and nonemployed mothers, but educational expectations were. Among married mothers, the employed expected their children to obtain more education.

There were three additional indices of independence granting and maturity demands. One measure asked mothers to indicate the age at which a child should be expected to handle a range of developmental tasks. This measure was unrelated to maternal employment. A second measure tapped the child's role in household tasks. As in previous research, the children of employed mothers were more active (significantly so in single-mother families and at the trend-level in two-parent families). The third measure tapped patterns of monitoring. The mother's employment status was not related to monitoring in the middle class, for working-class girls, or for single-parent families. However, for two-parent working-class families, sons of employed mothers were more likely to be left unmonitored and unsupervised than were sons of full-time homemakers.

These findings pertaining to styles of discipline and control and to parental goals show some differences between subgroups, but they also show some general consistencies. Two themes seem to come through. First, full-time homemakers, in contrast to employed mothers, seem to stress obedience and to use more power-assertive controls. The employed mothers, on the other hand, rely more on authoritative styles, giving the child more influence. Second, employed mothers seem to show more similarity toward sons and daughters in their control styles and goals than the full-time homemakers do. This includes the goal of independence, which is valued less by homemakers for daughters than for sons.

Interaction, Affection, and Commitment

When we turn to the third domain of childrearing examined here, that dealing with interaction and the affective component, there seems to be less consistency across measures. There were four sets of measures used to examine the effects of mothers' employment status on mother–child interaction and affection: the mother's report of the frequency of parent–child activities, the child's report of interactions, a composite measure of the mother's overt expression of affection, and the mother's score on a scale of parental commitment.

Interaction. The mother's reports of interactions showed different patterns for different groups. Among the single mothers, the employed reported more educational interactions with children and more talking. For married mothers in the working class, the employed mothers also reported more interaction than the homemakers but only for daughters. For married, middle-class mothers, however, the direction of the relationship was reversed, and full-time homemakers reported more educational activities with their children and more positive interactions overall.

However, when the children's reports were used, a different pattern emerged. Children in two-parent families reported more talking and total positive interaction with employed mothers at the trend-level of significance. This finding was across social class, and, contrary to the findings with mothers' reports, seemed even stronger in the middle class (Table 6.8). Furthermore, middle-class boys reported significantly more educational activities with employed mothers and more talk.

Thus, in the middle class, there is a discrepancy between the children's reports and the mothers' reports, with the employed mothers indicating less frequent parent–child interactions and their children indicating a higher level of interaction. This discrepancy may reflect both the difference in measures and the difference in perspectives. The mothers' reports are based on the frequency of interactions, but the child is giving a more qualitative judgment of who does this the most, or the saliency of the mother in this connection. That is, the child was asked questions like, "Who plays with you?" He or she could indicate a sibling, either parent, other household members, or nobody, but the point here is that the child's reply is not really telling us how often this play occurs, but who he or she thinks of as doing it.

To understand how these different frameworks might lead to divergent results, we need to consider findings reported in Chapter 4 on the role of the father. The same measure given to mothers was also given to fathers and discussed in Chapter 4; fathers were also asked to indicate how frequently they interacted with the child during the previous week. As reported in Chapter 4, middle-class fathers in the dual-wage families reported the lowest levels of father–child interaction, despite the fact that they took on a less traditional division of labor in household tasks. It was suggested there that the demands of many middle-class jobs, in combination with the accommodation to the mother's employment, may make inroads into the time available for these "extracurricular" activities with children. Thus, it is possible that middle-class mothers are accurately reporting and that the employed mothers do spend less time in these interactions, but their husbands spend even less time and thus, to the employed mother's child, it is mother who does it. Although this is speculative, it is consistent with the data, and it is a result that is specific to the middle class.

Affection and Commitment. The measure of parental commitment indicated higher commitment for full-time homemakers than employed mothers in the middle class. This measure was designed to tap the centrality of parenting to the self. Thus, this finding might reflect effects of the dual roles that come with employment; that is, the employed mother has an additional role that may also be an important part of her identity. It might, however, also be a result of self-selection; that is, very high commitment to the parental role might operate as a deterrent to employment. In connection with the latter possibility, it is important to note that some of the items in the scale reflect anxiety about nonmaternal care (e.g., "When away from my children, I worry about whether or not the person caring for them would handle it okay if something happened."). Because concern about nonmaternal care is counted as high commitment, these views would operate against entering the labor force.

The possibility that self-selection factors can affect outcomes will be taken up more fully in Chapter 12 because it is a pervasive issue. It is interesting, however, to note that the relationship between the mother's employment status and the measure of parental commitment was not significant in the working class, and for both married and single mothers, the direction was the opposite from that found in the middle class. That is, the employed mothers showed higher mean scores in the working class. Thus, if parental commitment is a selective factor, it operates differently in the two social class groups.

In contrast to the results for parental commitment, the measure of the extent of mothers' expression of affection showed consistency across social class, marital status, and child gender; the employed indicated significantly more. This result seems to fit with results found with the discipline and control measures and, like those findings, adds a new dimension to the maternal employment literature.

In the next chapter, we will look at the direct relationship between the mother's employment status and child outcomes, and in subsequent chapters we will examine how the father's role, the mother's well-being, and childrearing patterns might explain these employment/child outcome relationships, or suggest new connections. This chapter has indicated that employed mothers tend to use authoritative parenting styles that have previously been seen as promoting child competence, and to rear daughters more similarly to sons. For middle-class mothers, there may also be less mother–child interaction and less parental commitment when they are employed, but for working-class mothers, the direction was the opposite. In Chapter 10, we will follow these patterns to assess their impact on the children.

7   Maternal Employment and Child Outcomes: The Direct Relationships*

In this chapter, we turn our focus to an examination of the links between maternal employment patterns and child outcomes. As discussed in Chapter 1, previous research has demonstrated a few consistent differences between children of employed and nonemployed mothers. Daughters of employed mothers indicated greater academic achievements than daughters of nonemployed mothers; likewise, children in poverty have been shown to report higher academic achievement in employed-mother families. For middle-class boys, however, the findings have been more mixed, with some studies reporting that sons of employed mothers have lower academic achievement than sons of nonemployed mothers. When socioemotional development is examined, daughters of employed mothers appear more independent and better adjusted than daughters of nonemployed mothers. For boys, however, these patterns have not been found. Overall, both sons and daughters of employed mothers report less adherence to traditional sex-role ideologies.

In this chapter, we examine the direct relationships between the mother's employment status and child outcomes. Children with full-time employed mothers, part-time employed mothers, and nonemployed mothers are compared on several measures of cognitive and socioemotional functioning. Measures of cognitive and socioemotional functioning include peer reports of liking and behavioral characteristics; teacher reports of cognitive and social skills; child self-reports of perceived self-competence, locus of control, and adherence to sex-role stereotypical beliefs; and scores on standardized achievement tests. In these analyses, attention is given to gender, social class, ethnicity, and marital status. Wherever permitted by sample sizes, full-time and part-time employment groups were examined separately. However, in cases where few mothers fell in the part-time category,

* This chapter was written by Donna Dumm Kovacs.

152

full-time and part-time employed patterns were combined into one category, and then contrasted with the nonemployed mothers.

In addition to examining the effects of the mother's current employment status, we also examine the effects of the mother's employment status in the child's first year. In these analyses, we consider whether the mother's employment patterns early in the child's life have any effects on the child's cognitive and social functioning in the third and fourth grades, after the effects of current maternal employment are controlled.

Sample

In all analyses in this chapter, only families where the mother has had a stable employment status for the past three years are included. Table 7.1 shows the composition of this select sample by child gender, social class, ethnicity, parental marital status, and current maternal employment. Because there was only one child with a single, middle-class, nonemployed mother, the effects of maternal employment could not be examined for children with single, middle-class mothers. Thus, children with single, middle-class mothers were excluded from all analyses. Additionally, children with

Table 7.1. *Sample Distribution by Gender, Social Class, Ethnicity, Parental Marital Status, and Maternal Employment for Children Whose Mothers Have a Stable Employment History for Last Three Years*

		Children with Married Mothers			Children with Single Mothers		
		FT	PT	NE	FT	PT	NE
Boys							
Working class	African American	5	2	9	8	3	22
	White	16	15	16	14	4	11
Middle class	African American	3	0	0	3	1	1
	White	26	14	11	9	1	0
Girls							
Working class	African American	8	1	6	8	4	19
	White	25	11	13	9	2	6
Middle class	African American	3	1	2	4	4	0
	White	27	17	17	14	3	0
Total		113	61	74	69	22	59

Notes. FT = employed full-time; PT = employed part-time; NE = nonemployed.

married mothers were examined separately from children with single mothers for all analyses in this chapter.

Measures

The child outcome measures include peer ratings, teacher reports, child self-reports, and school-administered academic achievement tests. The child outcome measures are listed in Table 7.2, and a description of these measures can be found in Chapter 2.

Relations Between Current Maternal Employment and Child Outcomes for Children with Married Mothers

In order to examine the effects of maternal employment on child outcomes for children with married mothers, a series of 2 (child gender) by 2 (social class) by 3 (maternal employment) ANOVAs were performed, using each of the child outcome measures listed in Table 7.2 as the dependent variable in a separate ANOVA. The results of these ANOVAs are listed in Table 7.3.

As shown in Table 7.3, there were several main effects for gender and social class. Boys were rated by peers as saying more mean things and as hitting others more than girls; boys were also rated by teachers as showing more acting-out behaviors and learning problems. In contrast, girls were rated by peers as more helpful and shy than boys, and teachers rated girls as higher than boys in frustration tolerance, task orientation, and peer social skills. Boys reported better self-competence in athletics, while girls reported better self-competence in behavioral conduct. Girls tended to report more external locus of control than boys–that is, they felt they had less control over their lives. In addition, girls were less stereotyped about masculine activities – they thought women as well as men could do these activities. Boys scored higher on mathematics achievement tests, while girls scored higher on language achievement tests.

Overall, children with working-class parents were rated by peers as saying more mean things, hitting others more, and being more shy than children with middle-class parents. Teachers rated working-class children as higher in acting out behaviors and learning problems, and as lower in assertiveness, task orientation, and peer social skills. Working-class children tended to report more external locus of control than middle-class children, and working-class children were also more stereotyped about masculine activities than middle-class children. Middle-class children

Table 7.2. *Child Outcome Measures*

Peer ratings	Average rating of liking received from same-sex peers	(Higher scores indicate more liking)
	Proportion of peers who nominated child for saying mean things	
	Proportion of peers who nominated child for hitting others	
	Proportion of peers who nominated child for being helpful	
	Proportion of peers who nominated child for being shy and quiet	
Teacher ratings	Acting out behaviors	(Higher scores indicate more difficulty)
	Shyness and anxiety	(Higher scores indicate more difficulty)
	Learning problems	(Higher scores indicate more difficulty)
	Frustration tolerance	(Higher scores indicate more competence)
	Assertive social skills	(Higher scores indicate more competence)
	Task orientation	(Higher scores indicate more competence)
	Peer social skills	(Higher scores indicate more competence)
Achievement test scores	Reading	
	Mathematics	
	Language	
Child self-reports		
Self-competence	Scholastic competence	(Higher scores indicate more self-competence)
	Social acceptance	(Higher scores indicate more self-competence)
	Athletic competence	(Higher scores indicate more self-competence)
	Physical appearance	(Higher scores indicate more self-competence)
	Behavioral competence	(Higher scores indicate more self-competence)
	Global self-worth	(Higher scores indicate more self-competence)
Locus of control	External locus of control	(Higher scores indicate more external locus of control)
Sex-role stereotypes	Masculine activities	(Higher scores indicate more nonstereotyped)
	Feminine activities	(Higher scores indicate more nonstereotyped)

scored higher than working-class children on academic achievement tests in reading, mathematics, and language.

As shown in Table 7.3, for three of the child outcome variables, there were trends for an interaction of gender and social class. For teacher reports of learning problems and reading achievement tests, social-class differences were greater for boys than for girls. In addition, for nonstereotyped attitudes about feminine activities, working-class and middle-class boys did not differ in their scores, but middle-class girls tended to report more nonstereotyped attitudes than working-class girls.

Turning to the focus of the current study, there were a number of significant main effects of maternal employment on child outcomes, as shown in Table 7.3, as well as a number of significant gender by maternal employment interactions, two significant interactions of social class by maternal employment, and one three-way interaction of gender, social class and maternal employment. For all outcome variables, the means for each of the three maternal employment groups are listed in Table 7.3, and the means for each of the three maternal employment groups are listed separately by gender in Table 7.4.

Interpretation of significant interaction effects was aided by a series of post-hoc analyses. For gender by maternal employment interactions, post-hoc ANOVAs were conducted separately for boys and girls; in these ANOVAs, social class was controlled and maternal employment was used to predict the outcome measure of interest. Similarly, for social class by maternal employment interactions, post-hoc ANOVAs were conducted separately for working-class and middle-class children; gender was controlled and maternal employment was used to predict the outcome measure. For the significant three-way interaction of gender, social class, and maternal employment, maternal employment was used to predict the outcome measure separately for working-class boys, working-class girls, middle-class boys, and middle-class girls.

Peer Ratings

As shown in Table 7.3, for peer ratings of acceptance, there was a trend for a gender by maternal employment interaction. In comparison with other boys, boys with part-time employed mothers were most liked by peers ($F[2,112] = 3.80$, $p < .05$). For girls, differences in peer acceptance between maternal employment groups were not statistically significant ($F[2,127] = .44$, n.s.; see means in Table 7.4.)

Table 7.3. *Effects of Child Gender, Social Class, and Maternal Employment on Child Outcomes for Children with Married Mothers*

	Means			F-Values from ANOVAs						
	FT	PT	NE	G	SC	ME	G×SC	G×ME[a]	SC×ME	G×SC×ME
Peer ratings										
Liked by same-sex	4.05	4.20	4.01	2.31	.51	2.02	.40	2.55#	2.14	1.37
Mean	.40	.32	.36	26.48***	12.43***	2.85#	1.35	4.12*	1.31	.92
Hits	.35	.26	.34	53.01***	15.28***	3.62*	1.27	3.80*	3.43*b	.70
Helpful	.56	.59	.59	57.68***	.00	1.50	.75	.68	.50	.31
Shy	.32	.33	.34	58.30***	7.38**	.33	.41	.30	.81	.32
Teacher ratings										
Acting out	9.85	8.39	10.21	20.01***	7.89**	2.71#	2.11	3.23*	3.54*c	.79
Shy/Anxious	9.85	8.62	9.91	.07	1.57	1.29	.18	.01	.18	.01
Learning problems	10.83	9.89	12.70	10.78***	18.62***	3.28*#	3.17#	.97	.75	1.06
Frustration tolerance	17.11	17.74	15.86	6.29#	2.43	2.78*#	.01	3.16*	1.53	.18
Positive assertiveness	17.08	17.92	15.89	.33	8.59*#	2.01	.45	.65	.14	.84
Task orientation	16.91	17.89	15.88	5.82*	14.15***	1.78	.82	1.93	1.69	.03
Peer social skills	18.17	19.79	17.57	5.79*	7.82*#	4.12*	.90	1.92	.33	.32
Self perceptions										
Scholastic competence	17.76	17.98	16.71	1.20	1.09	1.88	.44	.69	.16	1.81
Social acceptance	17.57	17.84	16.46	.44	.02	2.00	.02	1.78	.69	.22
Athletic competence	16.79	16.38	16.10	10.96***	2.21	.62	1.60	.17	.96	.09
Physical appearance	18.23	18.54	17.90	2.37	.24	.29	.00	.07	.01	.50
Behavioral conduct	18.46	18.33	18.36	19.90***	.03	.00	.07	.22	.81	.41
Global self-worth	19.78	19.54	18.37	.98	.20	2.56#	.00	.26	.28	.93
Locus of control	7.05	7.10	7.57	3.09#	3.68#	.54	.14	4.10*	.01	1.80
Nonstereotyped about										
Masculine activities	7.88	8.11	7.06	8.60**	4.60*	1.53	.55	.72	.79	.96
Feminine activities	7.86	7.92	6.36	.44	2.70	5.68**	3.47#	2.08	1.74	.20
Achievement tests										
Reading	59.76	62.85	50.79	.47	43.95***	5.51**	3.13#	.11	.10	.95
Math	64.58	67.59	55.42	4.58*	34.63***	5.81**	.23	.02	.18	3.52*d
Language	61.53	62.30	53.35	6.51*	27.46***	4.00*	1.93	1.03	.40	.67

Notes. FT = employed full-time; PT = employed part-time; NE = nonemployed; G = child gender; SC = social class; ME = maternal employment.

[a] Means for G × ME interactions are listed in Table 7.4.

[b] Means: Working class FT = .36; Working class NE = .45; Middle class FT = .33; Middle class PT = .22; Middle class NE = .17

[c] Means: Working class FT = 9.92; Working class PT = 9.38; Working class NE = 12.09; Middle class FT = 9.79; Middle class PT = 7.50; Middle class NE = 7.34

[d] Means: Boys, Working class: FT = 63.86; PT = 61.41; NE = 48.12. Boys, Middle class: FT = 71.62; PT = 79.79; NE = 73.18. Girls, Working class: FT = 52.36; PT = 62.00; NE = 50.33. Girls, Middle class: FT = 71.70; PT = 67.67; NE = 59.16.

# p < .10; * p < .05; ** p < .01; *** p < .001.

In predicting peer ratings of behavioral characteristics, significant gender by maternal employment interactions were found for the characteristics of mean and hitting. As shown in Table 7.4, this reflects differences for boys. For boys, the sons of part-time employed mothers have the lowest scores on both measures ($F[2,112] = 6.14$, $p < .01$, for mean; $F[2,112] = 6.53$, $p < .01$, for hitting). The differences between the sons of full-time employed mothers and full-time homemakers are not significant. For girls, differences among the three employment groups were not significant ($F[2,127] = .55$, n.s., for mean; $F[2,127] = .06$, n.s., for hitting). In addition, a significant social class by maternal employment interaction was found in predicting peer ratings of hitting. (These means are presented at the bottom of Table 7.3). For working-class children, those with nonemployed mothers tended to be perceived as hitting more than those with employed mothers ($F[2,122] = 2.71$, $p < .10$). In contrast, among middle-class children, those with nonemployed mothers received the *lowest* ratings for hitting others ($F[2,117] = 4.86$, $p < .01$), and for boys, those with full-time employed mothers were perceived as hitting others most. However, it should be noted that the means on hitting are significantly lower for middle-class children. No significant maternal employment effects were found for peer ratings of helpfulness and shyness.

Teacher Ratings

For teacher ratings of acting out behaviors, significant gender by maternal employment and social class by maternal employment interactions were found. As shown in Table 7.4, boys with part-time employed mothers were rated by teachers as acting out significantly less than other boys ($F[2,110] = 3.21$, $p < .05$). For girls, differences between maternal employment groups in acting out behaviors were not statistically significant ($F[2,126] = 1.69$, n.s.). For working-class children, those with nonemployed mothers tended to act out more than those with employed mothers, according to teachers ($F[2,121] = 2.73$, $p < .10$). In contrast, for middle-class children, those with nonemployed mothers received the *lowest* ratings for acting out ($F[2,115] = 3.31$, $p < .05$), and for boys, those with full-time employed mothers were rated as acting out most ($F[2,49] = 5.18$, $p < .01$).

A significant gender by maternal employment effect was also found for teacher ratings of frustration tolerance. As shown in Table 7.4, boys with part-time employed mothers were higher in frustration tolerance than other boys ($F[2,111] = 3.08$, $p < .05$). However, for girls, those with full-time

Table 7.4. *Means on Child Outcome Variables for Three Maternal Employment Groups (Full-time Employed, Part-time Employed, and Nonemployed) for Boys with Married Mothers, Girls with Married Mothers, Boys with Single Mothers, and Girls with Single Mothers*

	Children with Married Mothers						Children with Single Mothers					
	Boys			Girls			Boys			Girls		
	FT	PT	NE	FT	PT	NE	FT	PT	NE	FT	PT	NE
Peer ratings												
Liked by same-sex	3.89	4.28	3.95	4.17	4.12	4.06	3.99	4.23	3.72	3.88	4.08	3.97
Mean	.52	.33	.47	.30	.31	.26	.52	.52	.57	.35	.46	.40
Hits	.50	.32	.44	.23	.21	.23	.51	.56	.58	.30	.35	.39
Helpful	.44	.53	.50	.66	.66	.69	.43	.45	.52	.55	.53	.62
Shy	.20	.22	.22	.41	.43	.46	.20	.30	.29	.40	.29	.50
Teacher ratings												
Acting out	12.21	9.19	11.26	8.03	7.57	9.24	13.23	13.43	14.42	10.29	12.83	11.56
Shy/Anxious	9.58	8.77	10.11	9.58	8.47	9.72	11.06	8.29	10.75	9.18	8.00	12.08
Learning problems	12.29	10.32	14.71	9.70	9.43	10.84	16.67	14.00	15.97	11.71	14.83	15.36
Frustration tolerance	15.49	17.87	15.38	18.38	17.60	16.32	14.25	16.29	13.73	16.71	17.67	16.00
Positive assertiveness	17.06	18.55	15.83	17.10	17.27	15.93	14.10	16.57	15.07	16.76	16.67	11.88
Task orientation	15.34	17.68	15.11	18.15	18.10	16.61	12.80	15.29	13.00	16.29	16.67	14.16
Peer social skills	16.83	19.65	17.00	19.21	19.93	18.11	16.56	17.71	14.67	18.47	17.67	14.72
Self perceptions												
Scholastic competence	18.04	17.87	17.33	17.54	18.10	16.10	18.02	17.86	16.32	16.73	17.27	16.44
Social acceptance	17.24	18.00	17.39	17.83	17.67	15.56	17.90	17.86	17.24	15.67	18.33	16.01
Athletic competence	17.90	17.39	16.76	15.90	15.33	15.46	19.52	20.71	17.21	13.95	16.43	13.93
Physical appearance	18.76	18.77	18.44	17.80	18.31	17.37	18.92	18.71	16.89	16.53	19.00	17.57
Behavioral conduct	17.34	16.94	17.27	19.34	19.77	19.43	17.57	18.86	16.78	18.27	20.17	19.74
Global self-worth	20.20	19.94	18.33	19.45	19.13	18.41	19.07	19.40	17.76	17.68	20.40	17.44
Locus of control	7.20	6.87	6.51	6.92	7.32	8.61	7.00	6.86	6.84	7.23	5.36	8.49
Non-stereotyped about												
Masculine activities	7.24	6.99	6.69	8.38	9.25	7.40	5.21	5.08	7.01	8.28	7.41	5.97
Feminine activities	7.76	7.61	7.19	7.94	8.25	5.60	6.09	4.80	7.92	6.69	5.58	6.40
Achievement tests												
Reading	60.12	61.55	47.20	59.48	64.20	54.19	45.33	49.57	39.47	54.71	50.80	39.72
Math	68.36	69.71	56.00	61.57	65.40	54.86	51.67	52.43	47.06	56.12	55.67	43.79
Language	58.70	61.48	46.89	63.78	63.13	59.46	48.10	47.29	41.53	55.24	56.33	43.40
N	50	31	36	63	30	38	22	7	33	17	6	25

Notes. FT = employed full-time; PT = employed part-time; NE = nonemployed.

employed mothers tended to receive the highest ratings of frustration tolerance ($F[2,125] = 2.75, p < .10$).

Significant main effects of maternal employment were also found for teacher ratings of learning problems and peer social skills. As shown in Table 7.3, children with part-time employed mothers had fewer learning problems than other children, and also had better peer social skills. In contrast, children with nonemployed mothers received the highest teacher ratings of learning problems and the lowest ratings for peer social skills. No maternal employment effects were found for teacher ratings of shyness and anxiety, positive assertiveness, and task orientation.

Self-perceptions

For the six measures of perceived self-competence, there was only one trend for a main effect for maternal employment, as shown in Table 7.3. Children with employed mothers tend to perceive themselves as higher in global self-worth than children with nonemployed mothers.

In assessing locus of control, a significant gender by maternal employment interaction effect was found. As shown in Table 7.4, girls with nonemployed mothers reported more external locus of control than other girls ($F[2,119] = 3.85, p < .05$). For boys, differences between maternal employment groups in locus of control were not significant ($F[2,108] = .92$, n.s.).

Sex-role Stereotypes

Children with employed mothers were more nonstereotyped about feminine activities (the extent to which men could do things traditionally assigned to women) than children with nonemployed mothers, as shown in Table 7.3. Although no significant differences between maternal employment groups were found for nonstereotyped attitudes about masculine activities for the whole group, there was a significant difference for girls. A separate (post-hoc) analysis was conducted. Full-time and part-time employed mothers were collapsed into one group of employed mothers, and contrasted to the group of nonemployed mothers, for girls only. Results of this 2 (social class) by 2 (maternal employment) ANOVA, for girls only, indicated a significant main effect of maternal employment ($F[1,127] = 4.52, p < .05$); girls with employed mothers were more nonstereotyped about masculine activities ($M = 8.66$) than girls whose mothers were full-time homemakers ($M = 7.40$). This was not found for boys ($F[2,113] = .18$, n.s.).

Achievement Tests

As shown in Table 7.3, children whose mothers were full-time home-makers received the lowest scores on all three achievement tests: reading, mathematics, and language. For math achievement tests only, there was a significant three-way interaction of gender, social class, and maternal employment. Post-hoc analyses indicated that differences between maternal employment groups in mathematics test scores were significant for working-class boys ($F[2,59] = 3.50$, $p < .05$), and there was also a trend for the significance of difference for middle-class girls ($F[2,64] = 2.84$, $p < .10$). Differences between maternal employment groups in math test scores were not significant for middle-class boys ($F[2,51] = 1.14$, n.s.) or working-class girls ($F[2,60] = 1.48$, n.s.). (See means at bottom of Table 7.3).

Relations Between Current Maternal Employment and Child Outcomes for Children with Single, Working-class Mothers

Next, a series of analyses similar to those examining the effects of maternal employment on child outcomes for children with married mothers was conducted for the group of children with single, working-class mothers. In order to examine the effects of maternal employment on child outcomes for children with single mothers, a series of 2 (child gender) by 3 (maternal employment) ANOVAs were performed, using each of the child outcome measures listed in Table 7.2 as the dependent variable in a separate ANOVA. The results of these ANOVAs are listed in Table 7.5.

As shown in Table 7.5, there were several main effects for gender. As was true for children with married mothers, within the group of children with single mothers, boys scored higher than girls on peer ratings of mean and hitting and self-perceptions of athletic competence; boys also tended to score higher than girls on teacher ratings of acting-out behavior. Conversely, girls scored higher than boys on peer ratings of helpfulness and shyness, teacher ratings of frustration tolerance, and self-perceptions of behavioral conduct; girls tended to score higher than boys on teacher ratings of task orientation, as well.

In considering maternal employment effects, there were a number of significant main effects of maternal employment on child outcomes, as shown in Table 7.5, as well as two significant interactions of gender by maternal employment. For all outcome variables, the means for each of the three maternal employment groups are listed in Table 7.5, and the means for each of the three maternal employment groups are listed separately by gender in Table 7.4.

Table 7.5. *Effects of Child Gender and Maternal Employment on Child Outcomes for Children with Working Class, Single Mothers*

	Means			F-Values		
	FT	PT	NE	G	ME	G × ME[a]
Peer ratings						
Liked by same-sex	3.94	4.16	3.83	.29	1.19	.91
Mean	.45	.49	.50	8.54**	.39	.24
Hits	.42	.46	.50	15.04***	1.05	.01
Helpful	.48	.48	.56	7.33**	2.35#	.04
Shy	.29	.29	.38	20.16***	2.63#	1.62
Teacher ratings						
Acting out	11.92	13.15	13.19	3.57#	.37	.15
Shy/Anxious	10.22	8.15	11.32	.00	2.72#	1.41
Learning problems	14.45	14.38	15.71	1.88	.38	1.24
Frustration tolerance	15.38	16.92	14.71	6.67*	1.26	.07
Positive assertiveness	15.32	16.62	13.69	.64	2.46#	3.92*
Task orientation	14.41	15.92	13.50	3.22#	.97	.49
Peer social skills	17.44	17.69	14.69	.64	5.42**	.54
Self perceptions						
Scholastic competence	17.48	17.58	16.37	.26	.89	.28
Social acceptance	16.97	18.08	16.71	2.38	.52	.44
Athletic competence	17.20	18.74	15.79	30.79***	3.88*	.97
Physical appearance	17.93	18.85	17.18	.20	.82	1.25
Behavioral conduct	17.86	19.46	18.06	7.27**	.81	1.02
Global self-worth	18.49	19.86	17.62	.41	1.75	.44
Locus of control	7.09	6.17	7.63	1.26	1.22	1.54
Non-stereotyped about						
Masculine activities	6.54	6.16	6.56	2.11	.14	6.84**
Feminine activities	6.35	5.16	7.27	.65	2.49#	1.45
Achievement tests						
Reading	49.53	50.08	39.58	1.18	4.65*	.84
Math	53.66	53.92	45.66	.01	2.51#	.53
Language	51.29	51.46	42.35	2.00	3.80*	.41

Notes. FT = employed full-time; PT = employed part-time; NE = nonemployed; G = child gender; ME = maternal employment.
[a] Means for G × ME interactions are listed in Table 7.4.
# $p < .10$; * $p < .05$; ** $p < .01$; *** $p < .001$.

Again, interpretation of significant interaction effects was guided by a series of post-hoc analyses. Specifically, for the significant gender by maternal employment interactions, post-hoc oneway ANOVAs were conducted separately for boys and girls; in each of these oneway ANOVAs, maternal employment was used to predict the outcome measure of interest.

Peer Ratings

As shown in Table 7.5, there were no significant effects for maternal employment in predicting peer ratings of liking, meanness, or hitting. However, children with nonemployed mothers tended to be rated by peers as more helpful and more shy than children with employed mothers.

Teacher Ratings

According to teachers, children with nonemployed mothers tended to be more shy and anxious than other children. Teachers also rated children with nonemployed mothers as lower in peer social skills than other children (see Table 7.5).

In predicting positive assertiveness, a significant gender by maternal employment interaction was found. There was no effect of maternal employment in predicting positive assertiveness for boys ($F[2,57] = .71$, n.s.). However, girls whose mothers were full-time homemakers were rated by teachers as showing less assertiveness than other girls ($F[2,45] = 5.34$, $p < .01$; see means in Table 7.4). No significant effects for maternal employment were found for the other teacher ratings of acting out, learning problems, frustration tolerance, and task orientation.

Self-perceptions

Significant effects for maternal employment were found for only one of the six perceived self-competence scales: athletic competence. Children with nonemployed mothers scored lower in athletic competence than children with employed mothers, as shown in Table 7.5. The three maternal employment groups did not differ in locus of control.

Sex-role Stereotypes

As Table 7.5 shows, for the measure of stereotypes about masculine activities there was not a significant main effect of maternal employment. There was, however, a significant maternal employment by gender effect. Post-hoc ANOVAs indicated that girls with employed mothers were less stereotyped about masculine activities than girls whose mothers were full-time homemakers ($F[2,44] = 3.26$, $p < .05$), but for boys, it was reversed: sons of full-time homemakers were the least stereotyped ($F[2,58] = 3.67$, $p < .05$; see means in Table 7.4.)

For gender attitudes toward feminine activities, Table 7.5 shows a trend-level relationship ($p < .10$) indicating that the children of part-time employed mothers were more stereotyped than were the children of the full-time homemakers. There is no clear difference between those with full-time employed mothers and those with nonemployed mothers.

Achievement Tests

Children with nonemployed mothers scored lower than other children on achievement tests in reading and language. Children with nonemployed mothers also tended to score lower than other children on mathematics achievement tests, as shown in Table 7.5.

Ethnicity as a Moderator of Maternal Employment Effects

Additional analyses were undertaken in order to examine whether any of the maternal employment effects were qualified by ethnicity of the child. Due to small cell sizes (i.e., no middle-class, African-American boys had nonemployed, married mothers; see Table 7.1), interaction effects of ethnicity and maternal employment could not be estimated for the sample of married, middle-class mothers. Thus, analyses of ethnicity effects were examined only for working-class, married mothers and for working-class, single mothers, separately. In both of these sets of analyses, full-time and part-time employed mothers were collapsed into one group of working mothers (due to small cell sizes; see Table 7.1), and were contrasted to the nonemployed mothers.

For both working-class, married mothers and working-class, single mothers, a series of 2 (gender) by 2 (ethnicity) by 2 (maternal employment) ANOVAs were conducted, using the same child outcome measures. In these ANOVAs, the terms of interest were the ethnicity by maternal employment interactions, and the three-way gender by ethnicity by maternal employment interactions, as these two terms indicate whether any of the links between maternal employment and child outcomes were significantly modified by ethnicity. Table 7.6 shows only the significant ($p < .05$) interactions involving the ethnicity factor that resulted from these ANOVAs. To aid in the interpretation of significant interactions, post-hoc tests were performed. For significant interactions of ethnicity by maternal employment, post-hoc ANOVAs were conducted separately for each of the two ethnic groups, controlling for child gender and using maternal employment as the predictor of the outcome measure. Similarly, for significant interactions of

Table 7.6. *Significant Interaction Effects[a] of Ethnicity by Maternal Employment, and of Child Gender by Ethnicity by Maternal Employment, on Child Outcomes for Working-class Children*

Mother's Marital Status		F-Values from ANOVAs	
		$E \times ME$	$G \times E \times ME$
Married	Peer ratings		
	Liked by same-sex	—	$F(1,118) = 4.85^*$
	Helpful	—	$F(1,118) = 5.66^*$
	Teacher ratings		
	Frustration tolerance	$F(1,116) = 5.48^*$	—
Single	Teacher ratings		
	Positive assertiveness	—	$F(1,100) = 5.68^*$
	Self-perceptions		
	Locus of control	—	$F(1,83) = 6.03^*$

Notes. G = child gender; E = ethnicity; ME = maternal employment.
[a] Nonsignificant ($p > .05$) interaction effects are not shown in table.
$^* p < .05; ^{**} p < .01; ^{***} p < .001$

gender by ethnicity by maternal employment, post-hoc t-tests were performed separately for African-American boys, African-American girls, White boys, and White girls, using maternal employment as the predictor variable.

For children with working-class, married mothers, for only three of the child outcome measures (liking by same-sex peers, peer ratings of helpfulness, and teacher ratings of frustration tolerance) were the ethnicity by maternal employment or gender by ethnicity by maternal employment interaction terms statistically significant. For peer ratings of liking and helpfulness, significant three-way interactions of gender by ethnicity by maternal employment were found, as shown in Table 7.6. Post-hoc analyses indicated that, among working-class, married mothers, the effects of maternal employment on peer ratings of liking were significant for White girls ($t[47] = 2.68$, $p < .01$), with daughters of employed mothers receiving higher ratings of liking by same-sex peers ($M = 4.28$) than daughters of nonemployed mothers ($M = 3.86$). However, mean differences in peer liking by maternal employment group were not significant for White boys ($t[44] = .03$, n.s.), African-American boys ($t[14] = 1.42$, n.s.), or African-American girls ($t[13] = .73$, n.s.). For peer ratings of helpfulness, the effects of maternal employment tended to be significant for African-American girls ($t[13] = 2.15$, $p < .06$), with daughters of nonemployed mothers receiving higher ratings of helpfulness ($M = .75$) than daughters of employed mothers ($M = .55$). However, the effects of maternal employment on peer ratings of helpfulness were not significant for White girls ($t[47] = 1.35$, n.s.), African-American boys ($t[14] = .52$, n.s.), or White boys ($t[44] = .82$, n.s.). In addition, there was a significant interaction of ethnicity by maternal employment in predicting teacher ratings of frustration tolerance (see Table 7.6). Post-hoc analyses indicated that, for Whites ($F[1,91] = 10.29$, $p < .01$), children of employed mothers had more frustration tolerance ($M = 18.06$) than children with nonemployed mothers ($M = 15.19$). For African Americans, differences between maternal employment groups in frustration tolerance were not significant ($F[1,27] = .64$, n.s.).

For the sample of single, working-class mothers, there were no significant interactions of ethnicity by maternal employment for the outcome measures, but there were significant three-way interactions of gender, ethnicity, and maternal employment for two child outcome measures: teacher ratings of positive assertiveness and self-reports of locus of control (see Table 7.6). Post-hoc analyses indicated that for African-American boys ($t[30] = 2.94$, $p < .01$), boys with nonemployed mothers ($M = 14.73$) showed more positive assertiveness than boys with employed mothers ($M = 10.10$). In contrast, among African-American girls ($t[29] = 3.14$, $p < .01$), girls with employed mothers ($M = 17.00$) showed more positive assertiveness than girls with homemaker mothers ($M = 11.32$). Differences in assertiveness by maternal employment group were not significant for White boys ($t[26] = 1.00$, n.s.) or White girls ($t[15] = .99$, n.s.). On the locus of control measure, differences between maternal employment groups were significant for African-American girls ($t[25] = -2.67$, $p < .05$). For African-American girls, those girls with nonemployed, single mothers reported higher external locus of control ($M = 9.06$) than girls with employed single mothers ($M = 5.70$). Differences in locus of control by maternal employment were not significant for White girls ($t[12] = .57$, n.s.), African-American boys ($t[22] = 1.07$, n.s.), or White boys ($t[24] = .74$, n.s.).

Relations Between Current Maternal Employment and Child Outcomes for Children Living in Poverty

Next, we examined whether the links between maternal employment and child outcomes held for the subsample of children living at poverty level. For purposes of these analyses, families were considered to be living in poverty if they received a score of 19 or less on the Hollingshead Four-factor Index of Social Status (see Chapter 2 for description).

According to this definition of poverty, seventy-eight of the families with stable (three-year) maternal employment status were living in poverty. Of these families in poverty, eighteen had married mothers and sixty had single mothers. Because so few families with married mothers were at the poverty level and cell sizes were small, analyses of maternal employment effects for families in poverty were conducted only for single-mother families.

Of the sixty single-mother families living in poverty, a disproportionate number had nonemployed mothers. Specifically, of the sixty target children in these families, there were seven boys (two African American; five White) with employed mothers and ten girls (four African American; six White) with employed mothers. In comparison, there were twenty-three boys (fifteen African American; eight White) with nonemployed mothers and twenty girls (eighteen African American; two White) with nonemployed mothers.

In order to determine whether the effects of maternal employment on child outcomes held for the subset of children with single, working-class mothers in poverty, as well as for the subset of children with single, working-class mothers *not* in poverty ($n = 50$), additional analyses were undertaken. These analyses addressing the influence of poverty were done in a manner similar to that for the previous set of analyses for all working-class children with single mothers; however, social class (coded as poverty versus not poverty) was introduced as a factor in the analyses, and full-time and part-time employed mothers were combined into a single group of employed mothers (due to small cell sizes). A series of 2 (child gender) by 2 (poverty status) by 2 (maternal employment) ANOVAs were performed for the child outcome measures listed in Table 7.2. In these ANOVAs, the terms of interest were the poverty status by maternal employment interaction, as well as the three-way interaction of gender by poverty status by maternal employment as these two interaction terms indicate whether any of the links between maternal employment and child outcomes were modified by poverty status. Again, post-hoc tests were performed for significant interactions. Specifically, for the significant interactions of gender by poverty status by maternal employment, post-hoc *t*-tests, in which maternal employment was used to predict the child outcome measure, were conducted separately for boys in poverty, boys not in poverty, girls in poverty, and girls not in poverty.

Overall, the pattern of findings linking maternal employment to child outcomes for children with single, working-class mothers seemed to hold for children in poverty, as well as for children not in poverty. There were no significant ($p < .05$) interactions of poverty status by maternal employment in predicting child outcomes, but there was a significant three-way interaction of gender, poverty status, and maternal employment for one of the child outcome measures: self-competence in behavioral conduct ($F[1,99] = 6.08$, $p < .05$). For girls in poverty only, girls with full-time homemaker mothers ($M = 20.00$) had more self-competence about their behavioral conduct ($t[26] = -3.01$, $p < .01$) than girls with employed mothers ($M = 15.63$). Differences in behavioral conduct for children with employed and nonemployed mothers were not significant for boys in poverty ($t[27] = .75$, n.s.), girls not in poverty ($t[16] = 1.10$, n.s.), or boys not in poverty ($t[30] = -.27$, n.s.).

Summary and Discussion of the Relations Between Current Maternal Employment and Child Outcomes

Overall, children with employed mothers score higher on academic achievement tests in reading, mathematics, and language. In general, this finding held true across ethnic groups, for children with married mothers, for children with single mothers, and for the subgroup of children living in poverty. Moreover, among children with married mothers, teachers rated children with employed mothers as having fewer learning problems than children with nonemployed mothers, a finding that seems to support the pattern of results on the standardized achievement tests. In general, this pattern of higher achievement test scores for children with employed mothers fits with findings in past research of higher academic achievement for daughters of employed mothers and of higher cognitive scores for children in poverty (see Chapter 1). However, reports of lower school performance for middle-class sons of employed mothers (see Chapter 1) were not supported in the current study, and in fact, the results were in the opposite direction.

With respect to behavior patterns, on the other hand, middle-class boys with full-time employed, married mothers seem to exhibit more acting-out behaviors. This pattern did *not* hold for middle-class boys whose mothers were employed part-time. Further, the pattern for middle-class boys may need to be considered in the context of the low level of acting out and aggressive behavior in the middle class generally. In the working-class, married group, it is the children whose mothers are full-time homemakers who received the highest peer ratings of hitting and teacher ratings of acting out.

In other respects, and particularly for girls, children with employed mothers seemed to be functioning in a more socially and emotionally skilled manner than children with nonemployed mothers. Teachers rated children with employed mothers as higher in peer social skills than children with nonemployed mothers. Daughters of married, employed mothers had more frustration tolerance than daughters of married, nonemployed mothers. And, for the subgroup of White, working-class girls with married mothers, daughters of employed mothers were better liked by peers than daughters of full-time homemakers.

In addition, the findings of the current study suggest that girls with nonemployed mothers present a pattern characterized by a more external locus of control (for girls with married mothers, and for African-American girls with single mothers) and more shyness and less assertiveness (for girls with single employed mothers). In contrast, and in support of previous research (see Chapter 1), daughters of employed mothers appear more assertive, and have more of a sense of internal control.

Previous research has found that children of employed mothers have less traditional attitudes toward sex-roles than do children of full-time homemakers (see Chapter 1). In this research, we differentiated stereotypes about "female" activities from stereotypes about "male" activities. The stereotype measure about "female" activities tapped whether one thinks men, like women, can cook, clean the house, and take care of children. Thus, it is not surprising that it is only in the married-mother families that we find the children of employed mothers are less stereotyped on this measure, for it is only in the married families that the children see their fathers taking on these roles. In this study, as in previous research, fathers in dual-wage families participate more in child care tasks traditionally assigned to women (see Chapter 4).

The stereotype measure about "male" activities, however, showed a different pattern. For boys, there was no evidence that those with employed mothers were less stereotyped about traditionally male activities. In fact, in single-mother families, boys were more stereotyped about male activities when their mothers were employed than when they were not. The reason for this is not clear. It may be that these boys are called on by their employed mothers to help in the house to fill in for the absent father. That is, single, employed mothers, faced with the dual role of employee and sole parent, may enlist their sons' help by appealing to the idea that they have to take on the man's role.

For girls, on the other hand, less stereotyped views about masculine activities were found in single-mother families, as well as in married-mother families, when mothers were employed. In employed-mother families, children see women filling the role of breadwinner, which has traditionally been considered the man's role. Girls may identify with their mothers and see them as role models; in consequence, girls may become less stereotyped about masculine activities when their mothers work, while boys do not.

Effects of Maternal Employment in the Child's First Year on Child Outcomes in the Third and Fourth Grades

Thus far, this chapter has focused on the effects of the mother's current employment status on child outcomes. Current employment has been defined as the mother's stable employment for the last three years, which covers all or most of the years since the child started full-time school. We now turn to an examination of the mother's employment during the child's preschool years, in order to see whether employment during this early time period shows different or additional effects that are manifested in the third and fourth grades. In this section, we consider specifically whether the mother's employment status in the child's *first year* of life has any lasting effects on her child's functioning. We examine the effects of the mother's early employment status on child outcomes in the third and fourth grades, after controlling for her current employment. Because of sample size problems with single mothers, only married mothers are considered in this analysis.

Of the 248 children with married mothers who had a stable three-year employment status, information on early employment was available for 171, including 48 working-class boys, 37 working-class girls, 34 middle-class boys, and 52 middle-class girls. Of these 171 children with early employment information, 69 of the mothers were employed during the child's first year and 102 were not. Note that mothers who worked fewer than ten hours per week, who worked at home, or who switched between employed and nonemployed patterns in the child's first year were excluded from these analyses.

In order to examine the effects of early employment on child outcomes, a series of 2 (child gender) by 2 (social class) by 2 (early employment status) ANOVAs was conducted. In these ANOVAs, each of the dependent variables listed in Table 7.2 was used as the dependent measure in a separate ANOVA. Early employment was coded as either employed or not employed during the child's first year. The purpose of these ANOVAs was to identify those child outcomes that might be affected by the mother's employment status in the child's first year.

For married mothers, there were significant main effects of early employment in predicting child outcomes for peer ratings of meanness ($F[1, 163] = 10.04$, $p < .01$), peer ratings of hitting ($F[1, 163] = 7.54$, $p < .01$), and teacher ratings of frustration tolerance ($F[1, 162] = 6.06$, $p < .05$), as well as a significant interaction of gender by early employment in predicting teacher ratings of acting out behavior ($F[1, 162] = 4.94$, $p < .05$). In no other instances were the main effects of early maternal employment, or the interactions of child gender by maternal employment, social class by maternal employment, or child gender by social class by maternal employment, statistically significant.

The next step in this analysis, then, was to consider whether the effects of early employment were actually due to the mother's current employment status, or whether the effects of early employment would be sustained even after the mother's current employment status was controlled. In order to conduct these analyses, separate regression equations were formed for each of the child outcome variables where a significant effect of early employment, or a significant interaction of early employment and child gender, had been indicated by the ANOVAs. The variables entered at the first step of each regression equation were: child gender, social class, the interaction of gender and social class, current maternal employment (coded as either working or not working), the interaction of current employment and gender, the interaction of current employment and social class, and the interaction of current employment, gender, and social class. Then, at the second step of each regression equation, the mother's employment status during the child's first year of life (coded as working or not working) was entered. In addition, if the gender by early employment interaction had been the term of interest (as indicated by its statistical significance in the ANOVAs), that term was also entered at the second step of the regression equation. In this manner, the effects of early employment status (or the interaction of gender and early employment), over and above the effects of current maternal employment status, could be determined.

Even when current maternal employment was statistically controlled in this manner, early maternal employment was statistically significant in predicting peer ratings of meanness (beta = $.28$, $p < .001$), peer ratings of hitting (beta = $.23$, $p < .01$), and teacher ratings of frustration tolerance (beta = $-.27$, $p < .01$). Examination of means indicates that children whose mothers were employed during the first year were rated as meaner by peers ($M = .46$ versus $M = .32$), were rated by peers as hitting more ($M = .39$ versus $M = .28$), and were rated by teachers as lower in frustration tolerance ($M = 15.93$ versus $M = 17.98$), when compared with children whose mothers were not employed during their first year. Additionally, even when current maternal employment was controlled, the interaction of child gender and early employment in predicting teacher ratings of acting-out behavior remained significant (beta = .38, $p < .01$). As a post-hoc analysis, separate regression equations were established for boys and girls. In each of these two regression equations, social class, current maternal employment, and the interaction of current employment and social class were entered as the first step of the equation; early maternal employment was entered as the second step. For girls, early employment was not a significant predictor of acting out, after controlling for current maternal employment (beta = .16, n.s.). However, early employment was a significant predictor of acting out for boys (beta = –.46, $p < .001$). Boys whose mothers worked in their first year ($M = 12.78$) were rated by teachers as acting out more than boys whose mothers did not work in their first year ($M = 9.25$).

Summary and Discussion of the Effects of Early Maternal Employment on Child Outcomes

For the group of children with married mothers, these results, based on examining the effects of maternal employment during the child's first year, revealed that children whose mothers were employed in the child's first year appear more aggressive than children whose mothers were not employed during the child's first year. Teachers and peers corroborated these differences in aggressiveness between the employed and nonemployed groups.

These findings are consistent with previous research, which has indicated that children with early day-care experience are more aggressive and noncompliant (Belsky, 1990; Clarke-Stewart, 1989). However, it should be noted as well that these findings are in contrast to data reported by the NICHD Early Child Care Research Network (1998), which show little evidence that early, extensive, and continuous care is related to problematic behavior at twenty-four and thirty-six months. In the NICHD study, both quality of care and greater experience in groups with other children predicted socially competent behavior at ages two and three. It was also the case, though, that more hours in care and less stable care predicted problematic and noncompliant behavior at twenty-four months. On the whole, however, family variables were much stronger predictors of child behavior than any of the child-care variables.

Why might children whose mothers had worked during these preschool years be more aggressive, in the third and fourth grades, than children whose mothers had been full-time homemakers? One possible answer is the different child-care experiences of these two groups. Compared to children whose mothers are full-time homemakers, children with employed mothers are more likely to experience longer hours of nonmaternal care, in multiple settings, during their preschool years. This could account, in part, for the aggressive behavior of these children. A fuller discussion and analysis of the effects of early nonmaternal care is included in Chapter 11.

There are other reasons, however, why we might expect these two groups to differ. For example, mothers who choose to work in the child's first year may be different from mothers who do not choose to work in the child's first year, in personality, parenting philosophies, or other characteristics. It might be, then, that these differing parental qualities actually account for different child outcomes, rather than the fact that the mother worked or did not work in the child's preschool years. The data reported by the NICHD group (1998) showing that family variables were stronger predictors of child outcomes than child care variables lends weight to this notion.

Chapter Summary

In this chapter, links between mother's current employment and child outcomes in the third and fourth grades were examined. Children of employed and nonemployed mothers differed in academic achievement, aggressive and socially skilled behaviors, self-perceptions, and attitudes about sex-role stereotypes. In many cases the pattern of differences between children with employed and nonemployed mothers was moderated by child gender or mother's marital status; in other instances, the pattern of differences was modified by social class or ethnicity.

Links between mother's employment in the child's first year and child outcomes in the third and fourth grades were also examined for children with married mothers. Those whose mothers were employed during the first year seem to differ primarily in aggressiveness. Patterns of differences for other outcomes, such as academic achievement, locus of control, and attitudes about sex-role stereotypes, were not apparent when only early maternal employment patterns were considered. These findings suggest that, for children with married mothers, differences in aggressiveness between children whose mothers are currently employed versus nonemployed may actually be due to the mother's employment history earlier in the child's life. In general, however, most other differences found between children of employed and nonemployed mothers seem to emerge on the basis of the mother's current, stable employment, rather than because of the mother's history of employment when the child was very young.

8   The Father's Role, Gender Attitudes, and Academic Outcomes

This chapter deals with the father's role and gender attitudes as possible links between the mother's employment status and child outcomes. The focus here is on academic outcomes, because previous research has suggested that father involvement may enhance children's cognitive competence (Gottfried, Gottfried, & Bathurst, 1988, 1995), and previous chapters in this volume have shown both that fathers were more active in household tasks and child care when mothers were employed (Chapter 4) and that children of employed mothers obtained higher scores on achievement tests (Chapter 7). There are four routes by which effects of maternal employment on children might be carried by the father's role that are described in Chapter 1. The first three of these routes are depicted in Figure 8.1.

The first route (see Figure 8.1A) is that interaction with a father has special advantages for children, particularly with respect to competence in math. An alternative to this hypothesis was suggested in Chapter 1: fathers' involvement with children may prove cognitively advantageous, not so much because it is different in style from mothers', but because it augments the amount of attention the child receives.

The second route (see Figure 8.1B) is that, to the extent that maternal employment functions to move parental roles in a less traditional direction, daughters will benefit with respect to their achievement patterns and sense of competence. This route has two forms: (1) this will occur because they observe a more equalitarian relationship between their parents; and (2) this will occur because the merging of parental roles that accompanies maternal employment diminishes parents' gender-role stereotypes. In either case, the expected effect is that children will hold less gender-stereotyped views, and that girls will have a greater sense of effectiveness and show cognitive benefits because a nontraditional gender-role orientation is more conducive to these outcomes (Block, 1983; Hoffman, 1972, 1977; Huston, 1985).

174

A. Route 1

B. Route 2

C. Route 3

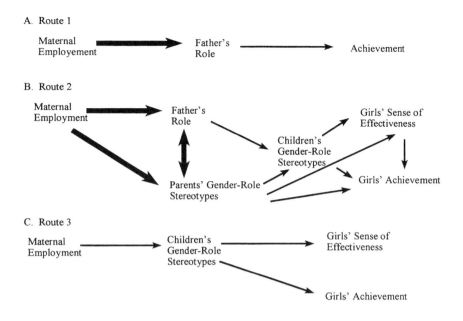

Note. Bold lines indicate relationships discussed in chapter 4.

Figure 8.1. Proposed links between maternal employment and child outcomes relevant to the father's role in the family.

The third route (see Figure 8.1C) that is relevant here does not actually involve the father's role, but posits that children's own gender-role attitudes are affected simply because their mother is employed. That is, when the mother is employed, children see women as more competent and able to do a broader range of activities. As indicated earlier, this less gender-stereotyped view may have benefits for daughters, affecting their sense of effectiveness and their competence. This hypothesis is the same as the second, except that it suggests a direct link between the mother's employment and the child's stereotypes.

The fourth and final hypothesis is that fathers' increased involvement in household tasks and child care can ease the role strain that employed mothers may feel from the dual roles of worker and mother, enabling her to function more effectively in her maternal role. This hypothesis will not be explored here but in Chapter 9.

Because the focus here, as in Chapter 4, is on the role of the father in the household, the analyses include only two-parent families. They also include only those families where the mothers have had a stable employment status for the past three years. It should be noted that the *n* varies: for the first two sets of analyses (i.e., Routes 1 and 2), the *n* is 199. For the last set of analyses, the *n* is 245. The discrepancy is due to the fact that the first two hypotheses involve measures collected only from the interviewed parents; the third route involves only data from the children.

Measures

The measures used in this chapter include various measures of the father's role, measures of parents' gender-based attitudes toward marital roles and childrearing, measures of the children's gender-role attitudes, and measures of the relevant child outcomes. These are described here.

Measures of the Father's Role

The measures of the father's role are the same as those described in Chapter 4. They include the mother's reports of which parent is more active in each of forty-eight household tasks or child-care activities. These items yielded seven composite scores measuring the participation of the father relative to the mother in traditional female household tasks, routine child-care tasks, financial (e.g., pays the family bills), functional-interactive child-care tasks (e.g., takes them to the doctor), plays with the children, school or education-related tasks with children, and nurturance. The child-care items are general and not specific to the child in the study. A higher score indicates the mother is more active; a lower score indicates the father is more active.

A second set of scales measures the frequency of father–child interactions with the target child. These are based on the father's report of how often he had engaged in such activities with the child during the previous week. The eighteen-item measure yielded five composite scores: fun activities, talk, nurturance, school or education related, and total (the sum of the eighteen items.) A higher score indicates more frequent interactions.

In addition, two parallel sets of scales were constructed based on the child's reports. A forty-eight-item instrument called the Day at Home was administered to the children. They were asked to indicate who in the family carried out various household and child-care tasks and who interacted with the child along different dimensions, and to distinguish who did it most of the time, who did it often, who occasionally, and who never did it. From this measure, two sets of scales were constructed that paralleled those derived from the two parent measures. Five scales were constructed that indicated the role of the father relative to the mother. These scales matched the scales from the mother's report: traditional female tasks, child care, financial, school or education-related, and nurturance. A high score indicates the mother is the more active and a low score indicates the father is more active.

In addition, five scales matched to those derived from the fathers' reports were constructed to tap the extent to which the father interacted with the child. These included fun, talk, school or education-related, nurturant, and total positive. More detailed descriptions of these measures are provided in Chapter 4.

Measures of Parents' Gender-Based Attitudes

Two measures of gender-stereotypes about family roles were developed for this study, one having to do with stereotypes about the division of roles and power between husbands and wives and the other having to do with attitudes toward differences in how sons and daughters should be reared. Both measures consisted of statements to which the respondent indicated if he or she strongly agreed, agreed, disagreed, or strongly disagreed.

The scale called Gender-based Attitudes toward Marital Roles (GATMR) is based on six statements such as, "Men should make the really important decisions in the family," and, "A man should help in the house, but housework and child care should mainly be a woman's job." The scale called Gender Attitudes toward Childrearing (GATCR) is based on seven statements, such as, "It is more important to raise a son to be strong and independent than to raise a daughter that way," and, "It's important to raise a son so he will be able to hold down a good job when he's grown, but that's not so major with a daughter." Both of these measures were developed from a larger set of items administered to both mothers and fathers. The factor analyses that led to their development and data supporting their construct validity and inner consistency are reported in Hoffman and Kloska (1995).

Measures of the Child Outcomes

All of the child outcome measures are described in detail in Chapter 2, so only brief descriptions of those used in this chapter are presented here. The hypotheses about the effect of the father's role have to do with the child's gender-role attitudes, cognitive competence, and coping styles, and it is these outcome variables that will be considered.

Children's Gender-role Attitudes. Most measures of gender-role attitudes merge views about men and women, but these are really separate components. For this research, two measures of children's gender-role attitudes were developed: one dealt with whether they thought women could do activities that have been typically seen as things men do, and the other dealt with whether they thought men could do activities that have been seen as activities performed by women. It seemed possible that whereas maternal employment itself might expand children's ideas of women's ability to carry out traditional male tasks, a more liberal view of what men can do might require a change in the father's role. Further, the idea that women can do what men can might be more likely to have a positive effect on daughters' achievement patterns than a more liberal view of what men can do.

The children in the study were given a list of thirty-one activities and were asked to indicate if this was something only men could do, only women could do, or something both could do. Some of the items were stereotypically male (build a house, climb a mountain, collect garbage); some stereotypically female (bake cupcakes, be a nurse); and some neutral (go to the beach). Only the twenty-five gender-typed activities were scored. The stereotyped response was scored 0; "both" or the counter-stereotyped response was scored 1. For both measures – stereotypes about male activities (only men can fix a sink) and stereotypes about female activities (only women can be a nurse) – a high score indicates nonstereotyped attitudes.

Cognitive Competence. The three main measures of cognitive competence were standard achievement test scores in mathematics, language, and reading. These are derived from the Metropolitan Achievement Test, which was administered by the schools in spring of the year that the data were collected. Raw test scores were transformed using national norming tables, and normal-curve-equivalent scores ranging from 1 to 99 were used for each of the three tests.

In addition, a teacher rating of Task Orientation was used. This measure is a subscale of the Teacher-Child Rating Scale (Hightower, et al., 1986) and is based on the teacher's ratings of such behaviors as "functions well even with distractions," "completes work," and "a self-starter." A high score indicates greater competence.

Sense of Effectiveness. To tap the child's sense of effectiveness or competence, the Nowicki and Strickland (1973) measure of "Locus of Control" was used. This is an index of whether the child feels that outcomes are in his or her hands; it is a measure of self-efficacy. A low score indicates an internal locus of control (high efficacy); a high score indicates an external locus of control, the sense that outcomes are in the control of others or depend on luck (see Chapter 2 for a fuller description).

Analyses, Results, and Discussion

In this section, we shall consider each of the hypotheses laid out in Figure 8.1, describing the analyses and results. A final section will provide an overall summary and discussion.

The Father's Role and Children's Academic Outcomes (Route 1)

We first consider whether different aspects of the father's role are linked to indices of the child's academic competence. Correlations between the father's role and the children's achievement test scores were examined, controlling for social class, for the total group, separately for each employment status, and separately for boys and girls. The most interesting results were those conducted separately for each employment status; these are presented in Table 8.1.

The Relative Participation of Mothers and Fathers. Table 8.1A presents the results for parents' relative participation in various tasks and child-rearing functions. A high score for the father-role variables here indicates that the mother is more active than the father; a low score indicates the father is more active. Thus, the top row of correlations shows that when mothers are more active than fathers in those household tasks traditionally considered women's tasks, children whose mothers are full-time homemakers have significantly higher scores on the standard reading tests than do the children of full-time homemakers whose fathers are more active in these tasks. A similar relationship is found for math scores at the trend level of significance ($p < .10$). This pattern is also apparent for financial tasks: the more active the mother relative to the father, the higher are children's test scores on reading ($p < .05$), math ($p < .10$), and language ($p < .05$). For financial tasks, however, higher mother participation is not traditional and, whereas higher mother participation in traditional female tasks was found to characterize homemaker families in Chapter 4, the opposite result was found for financial tasks.

When we look at the results for the children of employed mothers, we find very different results: higher father participation is associated with children's higher test scores. For reading, higher participation by fathers in

Table 8.1. *Correlations Between the Father's Role and Children's Cognitive Outcomes, Controlling for Social Class, and Separately by Employment Category (Homemaker versus Employed)*

	Test Scores					
	Reading		Math		Language	
	HM	EMP	HM	EMP	HM	EMP
A. Relative Participation of Parents in Tasks[a]						
Traditional Female	.28*	−.14	.22#	−.07	.14	−.14#b
Child Care	.00	−.20*	−.08	−.14#	−.07	−.14#
Financial	.29*	−.05	.24#	.00	.32*	−.12
Play	.11	−.17*	.17	−.07	.18	−.05
School/Educational	.08	−.21*	−.15	−.09	−.02	−.07
Nurturance	.10	−.13	.10	−.08	.06	−.12
Functional	.20	−.16#	.04	−.13	.16	−.13b
B. Frequency of Father–Child Interaction[d]						
Fun	−.12	−.05	−.09	−.06	−.08	−.05
Talk	−.34*	−.02	−.23#	−.02	−.26#c	−.09
Educational	−.37**	.02	−.18	.00	−.27#	−.01
Affectionate	−.20	−.03	−.12	−.12	−.13	−.08
Total	−.28#	−.09	−.17	−.14	−.19	−.08

Notes. HM = homemaker; EMP = employed.
[a] Higher scores indicate that mothers perform the task relatively more often than fathers.
[b] Correlation is significant for girls at $p < .05$.
[c] Correlation is significant for boys at $p < .05$.
[d] Higher scores indicate a higher level of activity.
# $p < .10$; * $p < .05$.

Child Care, Play, and School-related activities is significantly associated with children's scores, and higher participation in Functional shows a trend-level relationship. There are three other trend-level results for the children of employed mothers: higher father participation in Traditional Female tasks is associated with higher language scores; higher father participation in Child Care is associated with higher math and language.

The data in Table 8.1A were also examined to see if the results were changed when examined separately by social class and gender of child. Patterns were not notably different when each class was examined separately, but gender of child did slightly modify the results for the children of employed mothers in that they were stronger for daughters than for sons. Thus, the trend-level relationship found for Traditional Female tasks and language achieved statistical significance when examined for daughters of employed mothers, and a significant relationship emerged for Functional tasks and language scores for the daughters of employed mothers. The patterns, however, were basically the same for boys and girls.

Frequency of Father–Child Interaction. Table 8.1B shows the relationships between the father's reports of the frequency of his interactions with the target child and the test scores. As in Table 8.1A, a high level of father–child interaction is associated with lower test scores for the children of full-time homemakers. Reading scores are particularly affected, with significant negative correlations for Talk and Educational activities and trend-level correlations for Total. In addition, there are trend-level correlations between Talk and both math and language scores, and also between Educational activities and language scores. None of the relationships is significant for the children with employed mothers. When the data were examined to see if gender of child modified these results, we found that the negative associations between father–child interaction and test scores for children of homemakers were carried by sons. Examined separately for gender of child, none of the relationships was significant for the girls. For boys, on the other hand, the trend-level relationship between Talk and language scores attained significance, and two new relationships emerged – a significant association between Total interaction and math and a trend-level association between Total and language scores. Thus, for both the role of the father relative to the mother and the sheer frequency of father–child interaction, the more active the father, the lower the scores for homemakers' children, with the latter results carried by the sons. In dual-wage families, however, all the significant associations between father's activity and test scores showed high father activity associated with high test scores, and all were for the father's activity relative to the mother's.

The same analysis that is reported in Table 8.1 for test scores was also conducted for the teacher-ratings of the child's Task Orientation. These results showed the same direction of relationships as were found for the test scores, but fewer results achieved statistical significance.

In view of the differences in the direction of the relationships found in single-wage and dual-wage families, it is not surprising that when these analyses were conducted for the whole sample without differentiating the mother's employment status, there were few significant differences. Even when separate analyses were conducted for boys and girls, but without considering employment status, only a few significant relationships emerged. In Table 8.2, we present these results for the two major father-role variables, the father's relative participation in Traditional Female Tasks and Child Care.

Child Care was one of the few father-role variables that showed significant results. As Table 8.2 indicates, when the father was more active in Child Care tasks, children obtained higher test scores on each of the three tests. The direction of these relationships is the same for both boys and girls. For boys, the correlations are significant for reading and language and for girls they are significant for reading and math. There were no significant relationships for Traditional Female Tasks. The data are not shown here, but when these same analyses were conducted for the fathers' reports of the frequency of their interactions (the variables listed in Table 8.1B), there were no significant results for girls, but for boys, high interaction with fathers on Talk and School/Educational related to lower test scores.

Discussion of Results for the Father's Role and the Child's Test Scores. These data provide support for the expectation that a less traditional division of labor between parents is related to higher cognitive competence for the children in dual-wage families, and that when fathers are more active in Child Care, this advantage is found across employment status. However, there is no indication here that higher levels of interaction with fathers, in itself, is cognitively beneficial to children. This last conclusion is based primarily on the fact that the frequency of father–child interactions reported by

Table 8.2. *Correlations Between the Father's Role and Children's Cognitive Competence for the Total Sample and Separately by Gender, Controlling for Social Class*

	Test Scores		
Relative Participation of Parents in Tasks[a]	Reading	Math	Language
Traditional Female	−.06	−.04	−.08
Boys	.04	.09	.02
Girls	−.15	−.13	−.19[#]
Child Care	−.18**	−.17*	−.16*
Boys	−.21*	−.16[b]	−.23*
Girls	−.19*	−.20*	−.14

[a] Higher scores indicate that mothers perform the task relatively more often than fathers.

[b] When boys' math scores were examined separately by social class, the correlation for working-class boys was −.28 ($p < .05$). For middle-class boys the correlation was .05 (n.s.).

[#] $p < .10$; * $p < .05$; ** $p < .01$.

fathers shows no positive association with the children's test scores. The significant relationships that are found for the frequency of father–child interaction are negative in direction, and they are found only for the homemaker families and mainly for boys. It is possible that in homemaker families, fathers are brought in when there are problems, and particularly when there are problems with boys. The idea that interaction with fathers is beneficial in itself is also inconsistent with the results in Table 8.1, which show that the higher participation of fathers relative to mothers does not seem to benefit the children in single-wage families as it does in dual-wage families.

At the beginning of this chapter, we listed three hypotheses to explain how fathers' roles might affect children's cognitive competence. The first hypothesis listed (Route 1 in Figure 8.1A), drawn from previous research though never directly demonstrated empirically, was that interaction with a father has special advantages, particularly with respect to math. This hypothesis is not supported for the reasons just presented, and also because math is not the academic subject most associated with the father's more active role.

An alternative version of this hypothesis was that fathers' involvement with children might be advantageous not because it differs in style, but because it augments the amount of attention the child receives. The data presented do not rule out this possibility, but suggest that if it is true, it is not sheer augmentation, but compensation. That is, it might be that the reason the higher participation of fathers relative to mothers increases cognitive scores for the employed mothers' children is because the dual-wage fathers are filling in for their wives; that is, in dual-wage families, father's participation is needed.

The second hypothesis (Figure 8.1B), however, is also consistent with the data. This hypothesis holds that what is important is the movement toward less traditional gender roles. This hypothesis would predict that cognitive advantages would be manifested only for the relative scores, for it is these that tap the traditionalism of parents' roles, and it would also predict that effects would be stronger for girls. Both of these patterns were found. In the next section, we pursue this line and examine the relationships between the father's role and the children's gender-role stereotypes, and between the children's gender stereotypes and their cognitive scores.

The Father's Role, Children's Gender-Role Attitudes, and Academic
Outcomes (Route 2)

As indicated in the Measures section of this chapter, there were two measures of children's stereotypes about gender roles. One tapped chil-

dren's attitudes about whether men could perform activities that were traditionally considered women's activities, and the other tapped views about
whether women could perform activities traditionally considered men's
activities. It was our expectation that the sheer fact that the mother was
employed would affect the latter, because employment itself represents an
expansion of the women's sphere into what was traditionally considered a
male domain, but that it was through the father's expanded role in the family that the former would be affected. The analysis reported in Chapter 7,
however, found that the expected direct effect of maternal employment status operated only for daughters: a significant relationship between maternal
employment status and attitudes about who could perform "men's activities" was found only for the girls. However, both sons and daughters of
married, employed mothers were less stereotyped about the activities traditionally assigned to women; that is, they thought that men were also capable of performing these traditionally "female" activities.

Here we examine directly the relationships between the father's role
and children's gender-role attitudes, first separately for each employment
status, and then separately for boys and girls. In Table 8.3, the correlations
between the relative participation of mothers and fathers and each of the
two scales are reported separately for homemaker and employed-mother
families. There were no significant relationships for the frequencies of
activities reported by fathers (the variables listed in Table 8.1B) and these
are not included in the table. For the employed-mother families, each
father-role variable is significantly associated with the children's stereotypes about female activities, with the exception of Financial, which is the
only one that is traditionally in the father's domain. None of these relationships are found for the families with full-time homemakers. The only relationship that is significant is in the opposite direction. Thus, in the
dual-wage families, but not in the single-wage families, higher father participation in traditionally feminine household tasks and child-care significantly related to the child's view that men as well as women can perform
the various activities that have been traditionally associated with women.
In addition, significant relationships to nonstereotyped views about traditionally male activities are found for the children of employed mothers
only, here significant for Child Care, School/Educational activities, and
Nurturance.

Table 8.4 presents these analyses for the two major father-role variables,
Traditional Female Tasks and Child Care, for the total sample and separately by child gender. In Table 8.4A, we have used the mothers' reports of
the father's role. In Table 8.4B, we have used the children's reports.

Table 8.3. *Correlations Between the Father's Role and Children's Gender-role Attitudes, Controlling for Social Class, and Separately by Employment Status (Homemaker versus Employed)*

| | Children's Gender-role Stereotypes[a] | | | |
| | Women Can Do "Male" Activities | | Men Can Do "Female" Activities | |
Relative Participation of Parents in Tasks[b]	HM	EMP	HM	EMP
Traditional female	.17	−.09	−.07	−.19*
Child care	.00	−.21*	.30*	−.28**
Financial	−.09	−.10	.03	−.10
Play	.16	−.13	.12	−.18*
School/Educational	.01	−.23**	.23[#]	−.27**
Nurturance	.14	−.18*	.19	−.22**
Functional	.10	−.13	.09	−.17*

Notes. HM = homemakers; EMP = employed.
[a] Higher scores indicate less stereotyped attitudes.
[b] Higher scores indicate that mothers perform the task relatively more often than fathers.
[#] $p < .10$; * $p < .05$; ** $p < .01$.

Again, there are more significant results with the stereotypes about men's competence to perform female activities, as expected. For the mothers' reports, fathers' roles in both Traditional Female Tasks and Child Care are significantly related to the stereotypes about female activities for the total sample. For Traditional Female Tasks, significant relationships are also found for boys and girls examined separately. For Child Care, however, when examined separately, this relationship is only significant for girls.

When we look at the children's reports, the total sample shows a significant relationship for Traditional Female Tasks and the stereotypes about female activities and a trend-level relationship for Child Care. The separate analyses by gender of child show the same results for girls – significant for Traditional Female Tasks and at the trend level for Child Care. In all cases, the greater the father's participation, the more the child believes that men can function in areas traditionally associated with women.

There are, in addition, some significant relationships to stereotypes about women's ability to carry out male activities: Mothers' reports about Child Care show an association between the father's involvement and the

Table 8.4. *Correlations Between the Father's Role and Children's Gender Stereotypes, Controlling for Social Class: Total Sample and Separately by Gender*

	Children's Gender-Role Stereotypes[a]	
	Women Can Do "Male" Activities	Men Can Do "Female" Activities
A. Relative Participation of Parents in Tasks (Mother's Report)[b]		
Traditional Female	−.06	−.22**
Boys	−.01	−.20*
Girls	−.16	−.27**
Child Care	−.18**	−.17*
Boys	−.15	−.08
Girls	−.22*	−.22*
B. Relative Participation of Parents in Tasks (Child's Report)[b]		
Traditional Female	−.12[#]	−.13*
Boys	.02	.02
Girls	−.23**	−.29**
Child Care	−.08	−.13[#]
Boys	−.14	−.10
Girls	−.02	−.15[#]

[a] Higher scores indicate less stereotyped attitudes.
[b] Higher scores indicate that mothers perform the task relatively more often than fathers.
[#] $p < .10$; * $p < .05$; ** $p < .01$.

view that women can do things traditionally assigned to men – significant for the total sample and for the separate analysis with girls. The children's own reports of the father's role show one significant relationship for girls: high father participation in Traditional Female Tasks is associated with the view that women can perform activities in traditionally male realms.

In general, Tables 8.3 and 8.4 indicate that the higher the relative participation of fathers in family tasks and child care, the less stereotyped are children's views about fathers' capacity to carry out a wide variety of activities that have been traditionally assigned to women. These relationships seem to be stronger in the context of the dual-wage family and slightly stronger for girls than for boys. In addition, some significant relationships were found between fathers' relative participation and children's stereotypes about women's ability to function in traditional male realms.

Academic Outcomes. Table 8.5 shows the results of the analyses examining the relationships between the children's gender stereotypes and their scores on the three achievement tests. It had been our expectation that, for girls, holding a less restricted view of what women were capable of would increase their own confidence and motivation, and thus would have a positive impact on their academic competence. Thus, we expected there would be significant relationships between the gender stereotypes about women's ability to function in male realms and achievement tests scores. This result can be seen in Table 8.5: girls who hold the view that women are capable of doing the activities that have been traditionally assumed to be areas of male competence have significantly higher scores on all three achievement tests – reading, math, and language. We also expected no significant relationships between the measure tapping the view that men can perform activities in the female realm and girls' test scores, and this result is also found.

The results in Table 8.5 also show, however, that the same significant relationships are found for the total sample. Furthermore, even when boys are examined separately, there is a significant relationship between the measure of stereotypes about what women can do and reading and a trend-level relationship between that measure and math.

These data seem to suggest that holding a nonstereotyped view about women's competence may have a positive effect on children's academic performance. With correlational data, there is always the possibility that causality is reversed, that academic competence diminishes stereotypes. However, the fact that there are no significant relationships for the equally nonstereotyped view that men can do those activities traditionally viewed as part of the woman's realm argues against this interpretation.

The Father's Role, Gender Attitudes, Daughters' Test Scores: A Mediation Analysis. A number of connections between the father's role and children's academic competence, as measured by their scores on achievement tests, have been indicated by the results presented. The most directly relevant to the hypothesis depicted as "Route 2" in Figure 8.1 is the link from the father's relative participation in child care to daughters' test scores through the daughters' attitudes toward women's competence (i.e., women are capable of performing the activities traditionally considered in the male domain). Table 8.2 shows that the higher the father's relative participation in child care (as reported by mothers), the higher the daughter's scores on the reading and math tests. Table 8.4A shows that the father's role in child care (mother's report) is also significantly related to these gender-

Table 8.5. *Correlations Between Children's Gender Stereotypes and Achievement Test Scores and Locus of Control: Total Sample and Separately by Child Gender, Controlling for Social Class*

Gender Stereotypes[b]	Achievement Test Scores			Locus of Control[a]
	Reading	Math	Language	
Women Can Do "Male" Activities				
Total	.31***	.21**	.21**	−.20**
Boys	.29**	.18#	.16	−.25*
Girls	.34***	.30**	.20*	−.22*
Men Can Do "Female" Activities				
Total	.10	.07	.01	−.10
Boys	.10	.03	−.04	−.16
Girls	.16	.15	.10	−.03

[a] Higher scores indicate external locus of control; lower scores indicate internal locus of control.
[b] Higher scores indicate less stereotyped attitudes.
# $p < .10$; * $p < .05$; ** $p < .01$.

role attitudes for girls. And, finally, in Table 8.5, we see that daughters who believe "women can do 'male' activities" score higher on reading and math.

Thus, each of the hypothesized connections is significant for the link from the father's role to girls' reading and math scores. As a further step, an analysis was undertaken to see if these gender-role attitudes actually mediate the links between parents' relative participation in child-care tasks and girls' reading and math scores. The analyses, conducted with social class controlled, are presented in Figure 8.2.

Baron and Kenny's (1986) criteria for determining mediation (described in Chapter 4) was used in this analysis. As seen in Figure 8.2, there are direct links from the father's relative participation in child care and girls' math ($F[2,98] = 8.39$, $p[.001]$) and reading ($F[2,98] = 6.98$, $p<.01$) scores. In addition, Child Care directly predicts the mediator, "women can do male activities" ($F[2,98] = 4.85$, $p<.05$). When reading and math scores are regressed on Child Care and the gender stereotype measure, the previous significant relationship between Child Care and the test scores becomes nonsignificant and the relationship between the gender stereotype scores and the test scores is significant (math:$F[3,97] = 8.59$, $p<.001$; reading:$F[3,97] = 8.45$, $p<.001$). Thus, for both reading and math scores, girls' attitudes about women's competence to perform typically male activities mediate the effect of fathers' relative participation in child care.

A. Predicting Girls' Math Scores

   1. Direct Relationship

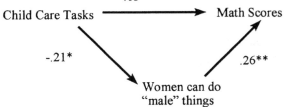

   2. Mediated Relationship

B. Predicting Girls' Reading Scores

   1. Direct Relationship

   2. Mediated Relationship

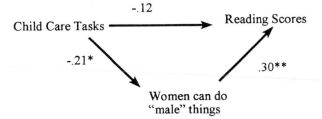

Figure 8.2. Girls' gender-role attitudes as a mediator between the father's role and girls' academic achievement, controlling for social class. $* p < .05$; $** p < .01$.

Locus of Control. As already discussed, a measure of *locus of control* was used in the study to tap the child's sense of *effectiveness,* the extent to which the child feels his or her behavior affects outcomes. It is a feeling of being self-empowered that has been linked to motivation for successful outcomes in a wide range of areas (Kliewer 1991; Nowicki & Strickland 1973). It was our expectation that, for girls, the belief that the capabilities of women extended across a wide area and included activities traditionally labeled as male would increase their sense of empowerment, and this might have a positive effect on academic performance.

As a first step, correlations were run, controlling for social class, between each of the two measures of children's gender-role attitudes and Locus of Control. The results are included in Table 8.5 and are similar to the results found with the test scores. As expected, girls who hold non-stereotyped views about women's competence in traditionally male activities indicate a more internal Locus of Control, and there is no relationship between Locus of Control and their attitudes about men's competence to perform traditionally female activities. Not expected, however, is the finding that these same patterns are found for the total sample and for boys when examined separately.

In addition, correlations were run, controlling on class, between the Locus of Control scores and the three tests scores. For the full sample of children, boys and girls, the more internal the child's sense of control, the higher were his or her scores on each academic test. This was significant for reading ($r = -.28$; $p < .001$) and math ($r = -.22$; $p < .01$), and at the trend level for language ($r = -.13$; $p < .10$). For girls, this relationship was significant for all three: reading ($r = -.36$; $p < .001$), math ($r = -.28$, $p < .01$), and language ($r = -.25$; $p < .05$). For boys, the relationship was significant for reading ($r = -.24$; $p < .05$) but not for math ($r = -.14$; n.s.); for language, the correlation was close to 0.

The results for Locus of Control enabled us to examine the possibility that this variable mediated the relationship between gender role attitudes and reading and math scores. This analysis is shown in Figure 8.3.

As before, Baron and Kenny's (1986) criteria for determining mediation are used, and social class is controlled in these regressions. As seen is Figure 8.3, there are direct links from children's attitudes about women's ability to perform typically male activities and children's math ($F[2,193] = 25.44$, $p = < .001$) and reading ($F[2,193] = 35.41$, $p < .001$) scores. In addition, these attitudes significantly predict children's Locus of Control scores ($F[2,193] = 6.60$, $p < .01$). When math and reading scores are regressed on Locus of Control and children's stereotypes, the previously significant relationships

A. Predicting Math Scores

1. Direct Relationship

2. Mediated Relationship

B. Predicting Reading Scores

1. Direct Relationship

2. Mediated Relationship

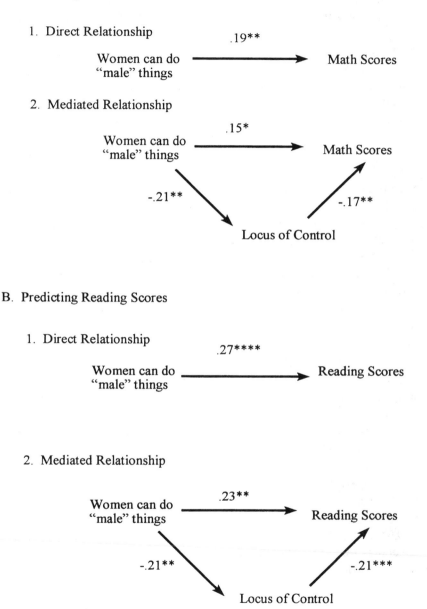

Figure 8.3. Locus of control as a mediator of the link between children's gender-role stereotypes and academic achievement, controlling for social class. * $p < .05$; ** $p < .01$; *** $p < .001$.

between the children's attitudes and math and reading scores are attenuated but still remain significant. And, Locus of Control significantly predicts both math and reading scores (math: $F[3,192] = 19.78$, $p < .001$; reading: $F[3,192] = 28.68$, $p < .001$). These analyses indicate that Locus of Control partially mediates the relationships between children's attitudes about women's competence and both math and reading scores. To test the significance of the partial mediation, Sobel's (1982) t-ratio was calculated. For the partial mediation of math scores $t = 1.96$ and for the partial mediation of reading scores $t = 2.19$, both significant at $p < .05$. Thus, Locus of Control partially mediates the connection from children's attitudes about women's ability to perform typically male activities to both math and reading scores.

Summary of the Results Thus Far Presented Examining Links from the Father's Role to Children's Gender Attitudes to Academic Outcomes. In considering the effects of the father's role on children's gender-role stereotypes and cognitive competence, the data presented thus far suggest that the higher participation of fathers relative to mothers has a major effect on children's attitudes about the ability of men to perform activities that are traditionally part of women's domain, and an additional, though less extensive, effect on children's attitudes about the ability of women to perform activities that are traditionally part of men's domain (Tables 8.3 and 8.4). However, it is the latter that is related to children's test scores, not the former. As a follow-through on these outcomes, a mediation analysis was conducted that indicated that, for girls, the expanded view of women's competence mediates the relationship between the father's child-care involvement and both reading and math scores.

It is also the expanded view of women's competence in male domains that is related to the Locus of Control scores (Table 8.5), and these, in turn, were significantly related to reading and math scores. Thus, a second mediation analysis was conducted, and those results indicated that the connection between the attitudes toward women's competence and the reading and math scores was partially mediated by Locus of Control.

The analyses thus far presented have provided considerable support for Route 2 in Figure 8.1. Not yet examined, however, is the part played by the parents' own gender-role attitudes. This is the focus of the next section.

Parents' Gender-role Attitudes, Children's Gender-role Attitudes, and Academic Outcomes

In this section, we turn our attention to the parents' gender-based attitudes and examine the relationships between these attitudes and the children's academic test scores, both directly and through the children's gender attitudes (see Figure 8.1B).

For each parent, two measures of gender-role attitudes were obtained: Gender-based Attitudes toward Martial Roles (GATMR), which measured the extent to which the parent endorsed traditional views about the division of labor and power between husbands and wives, and Gender-based Attitudes toward Child Rearing (GATCR), which measured the extent to which the parent endorsed traditional views about differences in how sons and daughters should be reared. For both measures, a higher scores indicates a less traditional view.

In Chapter 4, it was reported that in dual-wage families, both parents held less gender-stereotyped views about marital roles (GATMR), but maternal employment status was not related to gender-based views of childrearing (GATCR). It was also reported in Chapter 4 that fathers in dual-wage families were more active in Traditional Female Tasks and Child Care, both of which were related to the two measures of parents' gender-based attitudes (GATMR and GATCR). Thus, there are direct links from maternal employment status to parents' gender-based attitudes toward marital roles and indirect links to both attitude scales. Here we want to see if parents' gender-based attitudes are related to the children's gender attitudes and to their achievement test scores.

Relationship Between the Parents' and the Children's Gender-based Attitudes. In Table 8.6 correlations are presented for the children's scores on the two gender-attitude measures administered to them and the two measures administered to each parent. Social class is controlled and the results are presented for the full sample, just boys, and just girls. Fathers who endorse a more equalitarian division of tasks and power between husbands and wives have daughters who think that women are capable of performing activities that have traditionally been seen as in the male domain. Fathers' equalitarian marital views are also related to children's views that men are capable of performing activities traditionally considered in the women's domain, significant for the total sample and for girls alone. Mothers' views of marital roles are not related to children's attitudes about women's competence in "male" activities. However, equalitarian attitudes did relate significantly to children's more liberal views about men's competence to perform "female" activities, significant for the full sample and for girls alone.

Fathers who held equalitarian childrearing attitudes had daughters who thought that women could be competent in activities stereotypically seen as male. No other relationships between the GATCR and children's gender

Table 8.6. *Correlations Between Parent Sex-role Traditionalism and Children's Gender Stereotypes: Total Sample and Separately by Gender, Controlling for Social Class*

Child Gender Stereotypes	Marital Role Stereotypes[a]		Childrearing Stereotypes	
	Mother's	Father's	Mother's	Father's
Women Can Do "Male" Activities				
Total	.07	.12	.10	.10
Boys	.04	−.01	.08	−.04
Girls	.10	.28**	.07	.23*
Men Can Do "Female" Activities				
Total	.14*	.19**	.14#	.11
Boys	.11	.11	.12	.13
Girls	.21*	.32**	.17#	.13

[a] Higher scores indicate less stereotyped attitudes.
# $p < .10$; * $p < .05$; ** $p < .01$.

stereotypes achieved statistical significance, but there were two trend-level relationships: Mothers' GATCR scores were related to children's views that men could do traditionally female activities for the total group and for the girls alone.

Parents' Attitudes and Children's Test Scores. In Table 8.7, the correlations are presented between each of the parents' scores on the GATMR and the GATCR and the children's scores on the three achievement tests, with class controlled and separate by gender. It was our original expectation that a less gender-based attitude on both scales would benefit daughters' scores more than sons. As Table 8.7 shows, however, only one correlation is significant – the relationship between fathers' GATCR scores and girls' math scores.

The same analysis shown in Table 8.7 was conducted separately for each social class instead of with social class controlled. This approach revealed significant results for middle-class girls that were previously obscured. For middle-class girls, mothers' gender-equalitarian childrearing attitudes were significantly associated with daughters' higher scores in math ($r = .26$; $p < .05$) and language ($r = .33$; $p < .01$), and fathers' were associated with higher scores in language ($r = .35$; $p < .05$). In addition, mothers' equalitarian attitudes toward marital roles were significantly related to higher scores on the language tests ($p = .26$; $p < .05$). In all these cases, there was a sig-

Table 8.7. *Correlations Between Parent Sex-role Traditionalism and Children's Achievement Test Scores: Total Sample and Separately by Gender, Controlling for Social Class*

Achievement Test Scores	Marital Role Stereotypes[a]		Childrearing Stereotypes	
	Mother's	Father's	Mother's	Father's
Reading	.11	.03	.07	.02
Boys	.15	−.08	.10	−.08
Girls	.03	.09	.02	.10
Language	.10	.04	.05	.04
Boys	.08	−.15	.00	−.14
Girls	.09	.16	.10	.14
Math	.03	.07	.11	.08
Boys	.07	−.09	.07	−.03
Girls	−.02	.19[#]	.08	.26*

[a] Higher scores indicate less stereotyped attitudes.
[#] $p < .10$; * $p < .05$.

nificant positive association for middle-class girls, but a nonsignificant negative association for lower-class girls.

As a follow-up to these results for middle-class girls, analyses were conducted to see whether the links between middle-class parents' attitudes and their daughters' math and language scores were mediated by the daughters' attitudes about women's competence to perform stereotypically male activities. The relationship between mothers' childrearing attitudes and daughters' math scores was found to be mediated by the daughters' attitudes (see Figure 8.4). The relationships between parents' attitudes and language scores, however, did not show this mediation.

Summary of the Links from Parents' Gender-role Attitudes to Children's Gender-role Attitudes and Achievement Test. There were only two significant relationships between children's gender-based attitudes about women's competence and parents' attitudes: fathers who held less traditional gender-role attitudes toward marital roles and childrearing had daughters who were less traditional. For children's gender-based attitudes about men's competence to perform "women's activities," there were significant relationships to both parents' marital-role attitudes for the total sample and for girls examined separately; but none to the childrearing attitudes.

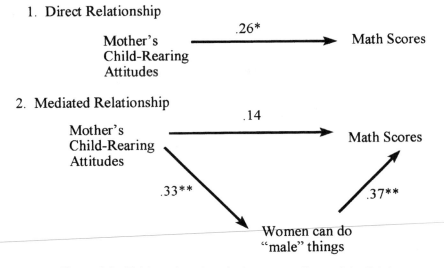

Figure 8.4. Girls' gender-role attitudes as a mediator of the link between mothers' childrearing attitudes and middle-class girls' math scores. *$p <$ .05; **$p < .01$.

When these parental attitudes were related to the children's academic tests scores, the only significant relationship was between fathers' gender-stereotyped childrearing views and girls' math scores: the less stereotyped, the higher the girls' scores. However, when this analysis was conducted separately for each social class, several significant relationships emerged for middle-class girls linking parental attitudes to math and language scores. For mothers, childrearing attitudes were related to both math and language scores and marital-role attitudes were related to language. For fathers, a relationship emerged between childrearing attitudes and language scores. In all cases, less gender-stereotyped attitudes were related to daughters' higher scores. A followup analysis showed that the relationship between mothers' childrearing attitudes and daughters' math scores was mediated by the daughter's views about women's competence.

Two Path Analyses

Considerable support has been provided for Route 2 in Figure 8.1. This hypothesis was originally developed to explain the finding, frequently reported in previous research, that daughters of employed mothers show higher academic performance than daughters of full-time homemakers. In our investigation, the academic advantage of the mother's employment for children was not confined to daughters (see Chapter 7) and some of the hypotheses proposed for daughters here also received some support for sons. Nevertheless, the hypotheses represented in Route 2 received their primary support for the girls, as expected.

Several viable paths were suggested by these results that would link the mother's employment status to daughters' higher achievement test scores. Two of these are presented here as Figures 8.5 and 8.6. They differ in that Figure 8.5 focuses on the father's child-care role and Figure 8.6 focuses on the father's gender-based attitudes toward the marital relationship.

Figure 8.5 is a path analysis tracing the links from maternal employment, to the father's role in child care, to girls' attitudes about the competence of women to perform stereotypically male activities, to girls' scores on the achievement tests and Locus of Control. As seen in the figure, maternal employment significantly predicts the father's child-care role ($F[2,96] = 7.16$, $p < .001$). The father's child-care role significantly predicts the daughters' attitudes about women's competence ($F[2,96] = 5.12$, $p < .01$), which, in turn, predicts the daughters' math ($F[2,96] = 11.24$, $p < .0001$), reading ($F[2,96] = 11.38$, $p < .001$), and language scores ($F[2,96] = 5.18$, $p < .01$), as well as their locus of control ($F[2,96] = 3.52$, $p < .05$).

Figure 8.5 presents, in effect, a diagram of a process by which the mother's employment status can affect girls' academic competence. It illustrates that there is nothing automatic or magical in the connection between maternal employment status and academic outcomes, but rather, that the mother's employment increases the likelihood of the father's becoming more active in child care, and this event (particularly in the context of the mother's employment, as shown in Table 8.3) increases the likelihood that the daughter will adopt a less gender-restricted view of competence. This view includes two components (as shown in Table 8.3) one concerning men's competence to perform "female tasks" and one concerning women's competence to perform "male tasks." The latter view is the more important for girls' own competence and relates to their sense of effectiveness (Locus of Control) and their academic test scores.

This path, however, is not the only path. Figure 8.6 presents another, a variation that traces the links from the mother's employment status to the father's gender-based attitudes about the husband/wife relationship, to girls' attitudes about women's competence, and from there to girls' achievement and Locus of Control scores. The two paths presented can operate as complementary processes or as alternatives, and they do not exhaust the possibilities. In the next section, we consider another path, a

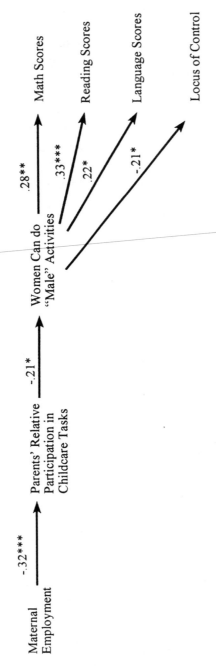

Figure 8.5. Path diagram of the links from maternal employment to girls' academic achievement scores and locus of control through the father's role and daughters' gender-role attitudes, controlling for social class. *p < .05; **p < .01; ***p < .001.

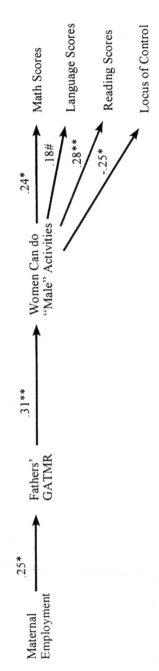

Figure 8.6. Path diagram of the links from maternal employment to girls' academic achievement scores and locus of control through fathers' and daughters' gender-role attitudes controlling for social class. #$p < .10$; *$p < .05$; **$p < .01$.

more direct one in which the mother's employment status itself might affect daughters' views about women's competence.

Maternal Employment, Children's Gender-role Attitudes, and Academic Outcomes (Route 3)

The third route diagramed in Figure 8.1 suggests that when a mother is employed, the child sees the mother as more competent simply because the role of wage earner itself suggests a broader area of competence, and, thus, the relationship between the mother's employment and children's view of women's competence can be a direct one, not necessarily mediated by the father's role or gender-based attitudes. Because of the expanded view of women's competence, the daughter's own sense of competence and effectiveness is increased with positive consequences for her academic performance. This possibility is explored here.

Table 8.8 presents the direct correlations between maternal employment and the two gender-role attitude scales for children and the achievement test scores, for the total sample and for boys and girls separately. Although different statistics are used, these results parallel those reported in Chapter 7. For girls, both their attitudes about whether women can do stereotypically male activities and their attitudes about whether men can do stereotypically female activities are related to maternal employment. In addition, girls with employed mothers obtained higher scores on the math and reading tests. For boys, the mother's employment is associated with higher achievement scores, but neither of the other relationships is significant.

Analyses were undertaken to test whether girls' gender-role attitudes about women's competence mediate the relationship between the mother's employment status and math and reading scores. The results are presented in Figure 8.7. As the figure shows, there are direct links from maternal employment to girls' math ($F[2,119] = 8.95$, $p < .001$) and reading scores ($F[2, 119] = 7.37$, $p < .001$) and from maternal employment to gender attitudes about women's competence ($F[2,119] = 6.40$, $p < .01$). When math and reading scores are regressed on maternal employment and girls' stereotypes, girls' stereotypes are a significant predictor of both math and reading scores (math: $F[3,118] = 11.71$, $p < .0001$; reading: $F[3,118] = 12.58$, $p < .0001$), and the previously significant relationships between maternal employment and the two test scores become nonsignificant. These analyses indicate that girls' attitudes about women's competence to perform typically male activities mediate the link between maternal employment and

Table 8.8. *Correlations Between Maternal Employment and Children's Gender-Role Attitudes, Achievement Test Scores, and Locus of Control for the Total Sample and Separately by Gender, Controlling for Social Class*

	Children's Gender-Role Attitudes[a]		Achievement Test Scores			
Maternal Employment	Women Can Do "Male" Things	Men Can Do "Female" Things	Math	Reading	Language	Locus of Control[b]
Total	.11	.21***	.23***	.22***	.21**	-.07
Boys	.00	.04	.22*	.21*	.26**	.11
Girls	.23**	.39***	.23**	.19*	.14	-.25**

[a] Higher scores indicate less stereotyped attitudes.
[b] Higher scores indicate external locus of control; lower scores indicate internal locus of control.
# $p < .10$; * $p < .05$; ** $p < .01$; $p < .001$.

A. Predicting Girls' Math Scores

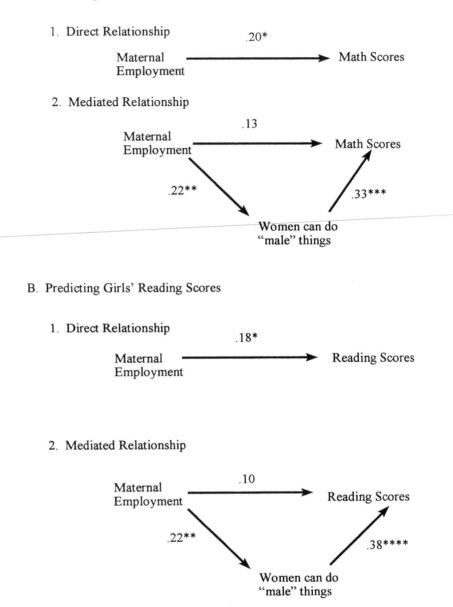

B. Predicting Girls' Reading Scores

Figure 8.7. Girls' stereotypes about women performing "male" tasks as a mediator of the link between maternal employment and academic achievement, controlling for social class. *p < .05; **p < .01; ***p < .001; ****p < .0001.

the two achievement measures. Analyses also were undertaken to see if the gender attitude scale mediated the relationship between maternal employment and Locus of Control, but it did not.

Discussion of Results. The results of this analysis provide some support for the third hypothesis, Route 3, diagrammed in Figure 8.1. That is, they are consistent with the idea that daughters' views about women's competence are directly responsive to having an employed mother and that this view can play an important role in affecting the daughters' academic competence. This does not mean that the father's role is not also important, or even that the father's role and equalitarian attitudes cannot have a positive effect on daughters' achievement scores, even in the absence of the mother's employment. But it does suggest that maternal employment itself may also have this effect.

Relevant to this issue, recall that in Chapter 7 it was reported that daughters of single, employed mothers also held a broader view of women's competence than did the daughters of the single homemakers. Despite the absence of a father in the home, the daughters of the employed mothers obtained less stereotyped scores on this measure. Employment status did not differentiate daughters of single mothers with respect to their attitudes about men's competence to handle typically female activities but it did differentiate them with respect to their attitudes about women's competence to handle typically male activities. This supports the idea that there can be a direct effect of employment status, even in the absence of a father, on gender stereotypes about women's competence, and, as we have seen in this chapter (Table 8.5), it is that aspect of the gender stereotypes that relates to girls' academic test scores. Consistent with this, daughters of employed mothers in single-parent families, like daughters of employed mothers in two-parent families, obtain higher test scores (see Table 7.4).

Summary and Conclusions

In this chapter we have examined three hypotheses about how the increased involvement of fathers in household activities and child care might benefit children academically, and provide a link between maternal employment and children's higher academic performance. The higher participation of fathers in dual-wage families was documented in Chapter 4; the higher academic competence of children with employed mothers was documented in Chapter 7.

Hypothesis 1

The first hypothesis (Figure 8.1A) has two forms. The one derived from previous literature is that interaction with a father has special advantages for children, particularly with respect to competence in math (Gottfried, Gottfried, & Bathurst, 1988; Herzog & Sudia, 1973). There was little support for this hypothesis in our data. There were two different kinds of measures of the father's role. One tapped the relative involvement of the mother and the father, or the father's involvement vis-à-vis the mother's. The other was based on the sheer frequency of the activities as reported by the father. When the father's role in routine child-care tasks was relatively higher than the mother's, children obtained higher scores on achievement tests, but there were no positive outcomes associated with the sheer frequency of father–child interaction. Further, the benefits of the father's involvement relative to the mother, across activities, were more apparent for children in dual-wage than single-wage families. And there were not indications that math test scores were more positively affected than reading or language.

An alternative version of this hypothesis was that the father's involvement with children might be cognitively advantageous, not because of its special style, but because it augments the amount of attention the child receives. The absence of positive outcomes associated with the frequency of father–child interaction, however, also argues against this.

It is possible that the negative relationships found between the frequency of father–child interaction and test scores in the single-wage families is because, in single-wage families, fathers, and particularly fathers of boys, are enlisted to help out only when there is an existing problem. However, it is also true that, even in the dual-wage families, there were no significant positive relations between frequency and test scores (Table 8.1).

Hypothesis 2

The second hypothesis (Figure 8.1B) includes two interrelated processes. The basic idea is that to the extent that maternal employment operates to diminish gender-role traditionalism, the academic achievement of daughters will be enhanced. The first process focuses on the division of roles between the parents; the second focuses on the parents' gender-role stereotypes. The greater the father's involvement in the traditional female household tasks and child care, and/or the less the parents hold traditional gender-based attitudes, the more likely it is that the children will also hold less stereotyped attitudes. Daughters who think that women's competence includes activities in the male domain will have a higher sense of their own effectiveness and show higher academic competence.

The data presented have provided considerable support for both processes. There were two measures of children's gender-role attitudes. One focused on the extent to which the child thought that women were competent to carry out activities in what has traditionally been the male domain; the other focused on the extent to which the child thought men were competent to carry out activities traditionally in the female domain. The results indicated that the higher the involvement of the father in household tasks and child care, the less stereotyped were the children about men's competence in women's domain. These results were stronger when the mother was employed and somewhat stronger for girls than boys but quite robust generally. In addition, the higher participation of fathers in child care was also related to the view that women could be competent in men's domain. However, only the view that women could be competent was related to the academic achievement test scores and the measure of personal effectiveness, Locus of Control.

Two mediation analyses were conducted: One indicated that the significant relationships between the father's participation in child care and daughters' scores on reading and math achievement tests were fully mediated by the daughters' attitudes about women's competence. The other indicated that the relationships between children's attitudes about women's competence and reading and math scores were partially mediated by Locus of Control. In addition, a path analysis was conducted demonstrating the linkage from maternal employment to the father's role in child care, to the daughter's attitudes about women's competence, and from there to Locus of Control and the three academic test scores.

Support was also found for the importance of parents' gender-role stereotypes in explaining the maternal employment/child outcome link. There were two different measures of parent's gender-based attitudes. One had to do with attitudes about the marital role, the other with childrearing attitudes. The scale, Gender-based Attitudes toward Marital Roles, was directly related to the mother's employment status, but Gender-based Attitudes toward Childrearing was indirectly related through the father's role.

When the father held equalitarian attitudes, either about marital roles or about childrearing, daughters believed that women were competent in "male" activities. These relationships were not found for sons, nor for mothers and daughters, although there were significant relationships between parents' marital role stereotypes and children's views that men can be competent in "female" activities. Fathers' equalitarian childrearing views also predicted girls' math scores. For the sample as a whole, though, parents' gender-role attitudes showed few relationships to children's test scores.

However, a separate analysis by class and gender showed stronger effects of parents' gender attitudes for middle-class girls. Both mothers' and fathers' attitudes were related to the daughters' stereotypes and to their test scores. A mediation analysis showed that, for middle-class girls, the relationship between the mother's gender-based attitudes toward childrearing and her daughter's math scores was carried by the daughter's attitudes toward women's competence. If the mother held gender-stereotyped childrearing views, the daughter felt that women could not perform male-typed activities, and that view statistically "explained" the lower math scores.

Hypothesis 3

The third hypothesis (Figure 8.1C) is simple and direct. Like the second, it is intended to explain higher achievement patterns for daughters of employed mothers. This hypothesis posits that the sheer fact that the mother is employed presents a model of competence in a traditionally male domain. Thus, it is predicted that daughters of employed mothers will reject the traditional stereotype about women's competence and feel that women can carry out a range of activities considered part of men's domain. This view, in turn, will affect their own sense of effectiveness and academic competence.

The analyses also provided some support for this hypothesis. Daughters with employed mothers were less stereotyped on both gender-attitude measures, obtained higher scores on the math and reading tests, and their scores on the Locus of Control measure indicated a higher sense of internal control. A mediation analysis was conducted which indicated that the relationships between maternal employment, and both the reading and math scores were mediated by the nonstereotyped view that women were competent in traditional male arenas.

Additional support for the hypothesis that the effect of maternal employment on daughters' attitudes about women's competence may be a direct one and not necessarily dependent on the father's role was provided in Chapter 7. In fatherless families, daughters of employed mothers also saw women as more competent than did daughters of full-time homemakers and they also obtained higher test scores.

It is important to note that the three hypotheses examined in this chapter are not mutually exclusive. They could all be true. In fact, it seems likely that there are several different routes connecting these two distal variables, the mother's employment status and the child's academic competence. Even between closer variables, different routes are possible. Thus, the father's active role and equalitarian attitudes may increase the likelihood that a daughter will see women as competent, but it is also possible that the effect will occur as a result of the mother's employment itself. What we may have is a chain of often mutually reinforcing variables, and the accumulation of influences pushing in the same direction may increase the likelihood of the outcome. Nevertheless, for the second and third hypotheses, both of which were seeking to explain the higher achievement patterns of girls with employed mothers, a pivotal variable was the girls' conceptions of women's competence and, for girls, this may be a particularly important link in the chain.

In the next chapter, we will consider the fourth hypothesis, that the increased involvement of the father benefits children through the support it provides for the mother.

9 The Mother's Well-being and Child Outcomes

In this chapter we extend the analyses from Chapter 5 to consider the links from maternal employment to parenting styles and child outcomes, through the mother's sense of well-being. In Chapter 5, we found that working-class employed mothers were less depressed and had higher morale than nonemployed mothers, but that there was no relation between maternal employment and mothers' mood among married, middle-class women. Here, we consider the possibility that the greater advantage of maternal employment for working-class children often found in the literature is mediated by the positive effect of employment on the mother's sense of well-being. This possibility is bolstered by a large body of research that demonstrates a positive relationship between maternal mental health and both more effective parenting and children's cognitive and emotional adjustment (see Chapter 1). However, with one possible exception (McLoyd, Jayaratne, Ceballo, & Borquez, 1994), there has not yet been an adequate study that investigates whether maternal mood mediates the relationship between a mother's employment status and her childrearing orientation, or between maternal employment and children's outcomes. In a study of working-class, single, African-American mothers of adolescents, McLoyd and her colleagues (1994) found that the mother's current employment status was significantly related to depressive mood, with nonemployed mothers significantly more depressed than employed. They also found that depressive mood was significantly related to both a negative perception of the maternal role and the mother's use of power-assertive discipline. Current employment status, however, was not directly related to the mother's negative perception or to discipline, so no statistical test for depressive mood as a mediator was made.

These are the issues we pursue here. Specifically, we explore the mother's morale as a mediator between maternal employment and childrearing patterns, and between maternal employment and child outcomes. As in Chapter 5, particular attention is given to social-class differences. Differences based on child gender, marital status, and ethnicity are explored as well.

Moderators of the Relationship Between Depressive Mood and Parenting Styles

In addition to investigating whether maternal mood mediates associations between maternal employment and parenting orientations or child outcomes, four moderators of the relationships between depressive mood and parenting orientations will be considered: commitment to parenting, education, the father's help with household tasks, and the father's help with child care. A strong commitment to parenting might operate to buffer negative effects of depressive mood on parenting. Similarly, more educated parents might monitor their childrearing orientations toward the more widely advocated authoritative style, even when depressed. Finally, we explore the hypothesis raised in Chapter 8, that fathers' increased involvement in household tasks and child care can ease the role strain that employed mothers may feel from the dual roles of worker and mother, enabling mothers to function more effectively in the maternal role.

Sample

For these analyses, we use the same sample that is described in Chapter 5. Briefly, we selected only those interviewed mothers who had either been employed or nonemployed for the preceding three consecutive years. The working-class sample was comprised of 150 mothers (54 single mothers; 96 married mothers). The middle-class group had 103 married mothers.[1]

Measures

Maternal Well-being. The two measures of maternal well-being were depressive mood and morale (see Chapter 5). Depressive mood was assessed using the Center for Epidemiologic Studies Depression Scale (CES-D; Radloff, 1977). Participants are asked to indicate how frequently they experienced the listed symptoms within the past week. Each frequency level is translated into a numerical score ranging from 0 (rarely or none of the time) to 3 (most or all of the time). Answers are summed into a total score, with higher scores indicating a higher frequency of depressive symptomatology.

Morale is a three-point variable based on the mothers' answers to two items asking (1) if she is satisfied with how her life is going these days and (2) if this is a particulary happy time in her life. If the mother was satisfied and happy, morale was scored as a *2;* if the mother was satisfied and not happy or not satisfied and happy, morale was scored as a *1*; and if the mother's was not satisfied and not happy, morale was scored as a *0*.

Demographic information. The demographic data described in Chapter 5 are also used in this analysis. In addition, a measure of the mother's education is used based on her report of how much schooling she had completed. Education was scored on a Seven-point scale ranging from sixth-grade or less at the low end to graduate or professional degree at the high end.

Parenting. To assess mothers' overall parenting styles, we selected the three main scales from the parent control measure (see Chapters 2 and 6). These three dimensions of parenting are similar to those of Baumrind (1971): authoritarian, authoritative, and permissive. These dimensions have been linked to children's social and cognitive competence, with authoritative parenting styles associated with higher competence than the other two (Baumrind, 1971; Dornbusch, Ritter, Leiderman, Roberts, & Fraleigh, 1987). Briefly, *authoritative* reflects disciplinary attitudes that respect the rights of the child but still maintain parental control. *Permissive* attitudes toward discipline are beliefs about letting children rear themselves. *Authoritarian* reflects discipline attitudes that are power-based (e.g., setting rules without discussion).[2]

Parent–Child Interaction. Mothers' reports of the frequency of eighteen parent–child activities (e.g., fun activities, talk, educational activities, nurturance) were used as a global index of parent–child interaction (see Chapter 6 for description). A higher score indicates more mother–child interaction.

Commitment to Parenting. Parental commitment was assessed with an age-appropriate adaptation of Greenberger's (1988) scale (see Chapter 6). The scale measures the centrality of parenting to the self, the psychological salience of parenting relative to other activities, and the level of aspirations for performance as a parent (e.g., "Being a parent allows me to express some of the traits and values I most prize in myself"). Respondents answered on a six-point scale, ranging from "agree very strongly" to "disagree very strongly." A total score was derived by summing the twenty-two items; the higher the score, the higher the parental commitment.

Father's Help with Household Chores and Child Care. These two measures are described in Chapters 4 and 5. Married mothers were asked to indicate whether they or their husbands typically perform a series of ten traditionally female household chores and seven child-care chores. Mothers' answers for each chore were scored on a five-point scale: 4 = mother, not father; 3 = mother mostly, but father sometimes; 2 = both equally or neither does it; 1 = father mostly, but mother sometimes; 0 = father, not mother. The scores for each household chore were summed to create a composite index of who performs traditionally female household chores more often. Likewise, the scores for each child-care chore were summed to create a composite index of who performs the child-care chores in the household more often.

Higher scores indicate that the mother performs the activity *relatively* more often than the father does, whereas lower scores indicate that the mother performs the activity *relatively* less often than the father does. For the analyses to follow, a median split was created on each of these two variables to represent mothers who received less help from their husbands and mothers who received more help from their husbands with these chores.

Child Outcomes. The child outcome measures are described in Chapters 2 and 7. In this chapter, we use the three standard achievement test scores in mathematics, language, and reading, derived from the Metropolitan Achievement Test. The test was administered by the schools in the spring of the year that the data were collected. Raw test scores were transformed using national norming tables, and normal-curve-equivalent scores ranging from 1 to 99 were used for each of the three tests.

In addition, teacher ratings of task orientation, learning problems, frustration tolerance, acting out, shy/anxious behavior, peer social skills, and positive assertiveness were used. These ratings are subscales of the Teacher–Child Rating Scale (Hightower et al., 1986). Higher scores indicate more of the behavior.

Peer ratings were also utilized. The peer measures include same-sex likability ratings, as well as nomination scores of meanness, hitting, helpfulness, and shyness (see Chapter 2 and 7).

Finally, two self-perception measures were used. The first is the global self-worth scale of the Harter Perceived Competence Scale for Children (Harter, 1982, 1983); higher scores indicate higher self-esteem. The second is the Nowicki and Strickland (1973) measure of Locus of Control. On this scale, a low score indicates an internal locus of control (high efficacy); a high score indicates an external locus of control (low efficacy).

Does the Mother's Mood Mediate Maternal Employment and Parenting?

Analyses to answer this question are presented in three sections, which address the criteria proposed by Baron and Kenny (1986; see Chapter 4). Recall from Chapter 5 that maternal employment is significantly related to depression and morale (the proposed mediators) in the working class but not in the married, middle class. In this chapter, then, we first explore the direct relations between maternal employment and parenting. Second, we look at the relations from depression and morale to parenting. In this section, we also consider gender, marital status, and ethnic differences in the relations between mood and parenting. Third, regression analyses are undertaken to test for mediation.

Maternal Employment and Parenting. Our first analysis concerns the direct relations between maternal employment and the mother's parenting orientations. To examine these associations, a series of regression analyses were run, separately by social class, regressing each parenting variable on maternal employment. These analyses are presented in Table 9.1.

As seen in Table 9.1, in the working class, employed mothers were less authoritarian, more authoritative, and less permissive than nonemployed

Table 9.1. *Regression of Parenting Variables on Maternal Employment: Standardized Regression Weights and F-values*

	Working Class		Married, Middle Class	
	ME	$F(1,148)$	ME	$F(1,98)$
Parent Control				
Authoritarian	−.33****	18.48****	−.25**	6.35**
Authoritative	.26***	10.40***	−.08	.71
Permissive	−.16*	3.99*	−.06	.38
Mother–Child Interaction				
Total Positive Interaction	.17*	4.20*	−.21*	4.87*

Notes. ME = maternal employment.
* $p < .05$; ** $p < .01$; *** $p < .001$; **** $p < .0001$.

mothers. Employed mothers also reported having more positive interactions with their children than did full-time homemakers.

In the married, middle-class sample, employed mothers were less authoritarian toward their children than homemakers. In terms of mother–child interaction, employed mothers reported having fewer positive interactions with their children than nonemployed mothers.

Mother's Mood and Parenting. We next consider the relations between the mother's mood and her parenting. Correlations between depression and morale and the parenting variables are in Table 9.2.

As seen in Table 9.2, in the working class, more depressed mothers were more authoritarian and permissive, and less authoritative. Working-class mothers with higher morale used more authoritative discipline and had more positive interactions with their child. In the married, middle class, more depressed mothers were less authoritative. And, married, middle-class mothers with higher morale were less permissive ($p < .10$), and had more positive interactions with their child.

These relations were also examined separately by gender, marital status, and ethnicity. Because there were too few single homemaker mothers in the middle-class sample, and too few middle-class African Americans, marital status and ethnicity were explored only for the working class.

In general, there were few differences by gender. For mothers of boys in the working class, higher depressive mood was significantly associated with less authoritative parenting, and lower morale was significantly associated with less positive mother–child interaction. For mothers of working-class girls, greater depressive mood was significantly correlated with more

Table 9.2. *Correlations Between the Mother's Mood and Parenting*

| | Working Class | | Married, Middle Class | |
	Depression	Morale	Depression	Morale
Parent Control				
Authoritarian	.29***	−.07	−.03	−.01
Authoritative	−.22**	.20*	−.20*	.15
Permissive	.21**	−.10	.12	−.17#
Mother–Child Interaction				
Total Positive Interaction	−.09	.20*	−.10	.20*

# $p < .10$; * $p < .05$; ** $p < .01$; *** $p < .001$.

permissive parenting. In the married, middle-class sample, greater depressive mood was significantly correlated with less positive mother–child interaction for mothers of boys. For mothers of girls, higher depressive mood was significantly associated with less authoritative parenting.

In terms of marital status, among married mothers in the working class, maternal depression was significantly related to more authoritarian, more permissive, and less authoritative parenting. Higher morale was significantly associated with less permissive parenting. Single mothers with higher morale were more authoritative, and reported having more positive interactions with their child than single mothers with lower morale.

In terms of ethnicity, a recent study by Harnish, Dodge, and Valente (1995) found that depressive mood was significantly related to parenting behavior for Whites but not for African Americans. In contrast to Harnish et al. (1995), however, we found that African-American mothers with higher morale were more authoritative and reported more positive interactions with their child than those with lower morale; there were no significant relations between morale and parenting for Whites. Moreover, there were no significant relations between depressive mood, as measured by the CES-D, and parenting for either African-American or White mothers.

Does the Mother's Mood Mediate the Links Between Maternal Employment and Parenting?

In order to test for mediation, we followed Baron and Kenny's (1986) four criteria (see Chapter 4 for description). First, we demonstrated significant relations between maternal employment and parenting. Second (see Chapter 5), we demonstrated significant associations between maternal employment and maternal depression and morale in the working class. However, because there were no associations between maternal employment and the mother's mood in the married, middle-class sample, the mother's mood cannot mediate the relationships between maternal employment and parenting.

Baron and Kenny's third and fourth criteria were tested in the working class via a third set of regression analyses. Separate regressions were run regressing each parenting variable that had been significantly linked to maternal employment simultaneously on maternal employment and either depression or morale. Here, we tested (1) whether the mediator (i.e., depression or morale) was significant when entered simultaneously with the predictor (maternal employment) and (2) whether the original direct relationship between the predictor and criterion (parenting variable) was attenuated with the addition of the mediator.

A. Authoritarian

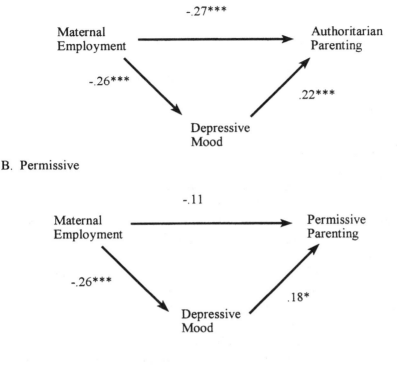

B. Permissive

C. Authoritative

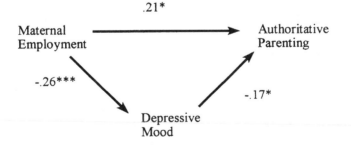

Figure 9.1. Mediated model of the effect of maternal employment on parenting orientations: working-class patterns. * $p < .05$; ** $p < .01$; *** $p < .001$. (*continues*)

D. Mother-Child Positive Interaction

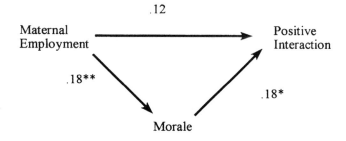

Figure 9.1 *(continued)*.

The analyses revealed that the mother's depressive mood mediated the link between maternal employment and parent control. And, the mother's morale mediated the association between maternal employment and her report of positive interaction with her child. These analyses are presented in Figure 9.1.

As seen in Figure 9.1, when controlling for maternal employment, depressive mood was significantly associated with authoritarian, permissive, and authoritative parenting orientations; and morale was significantly associated with positive mother–child interaction. In terms of the attenuation of the original direct relation between maternal employment and each of the parenting variables, note that in the case of permissive parenting and positive interaction, the regression coefficients are nonsignificant. This indicates that depression mediates the relation between maternal employment and permissive parenting, and morale mediates the relation between maternal employment and positive mother–child interactions. In the cases of authoritarian and authoritative parenting, however, the relationship is attenuated but not reduced to zero. To test whether this partial reduction is significant, Sobel's (1982) t-test was calculated for these two models. For the model predicting authoritarian parenting, Sobel's t-ratio was 2.13 ($p < .05$), which indicates that the partial mediation is significant. For the model predicting authoritative parenting orientation, Sobel's t-ratio was marginally significant ($p < .10$) at 1.65. However, when the models were run separately by child gender, the model predicting authoritative parenting was significant for mothers of boys (see Figure 9.2). In other words, depressive mood mediated the link between maternal employment and authoritative parenting, but only for mothers of boys. No other models were significant by gender, nor by ethnicity or marital status.

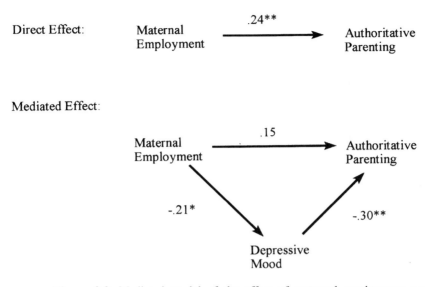

Figure 9.2. Mediated model of the effect of maternal employment on authoritative parenting for mothers of boys in the working class. * $p < .05$; ** $p < .01$.

Thus, to summarize, in the working class, the analyses are consistent with the hypothesis that the mother's mood mediates the link between maternal employment and parenting. Specifically, the data revealed that maternal depressive mood as measured by the CES-D mediates the association between maternal employment and permissive parenting, and partially mediates the association between maternal employment and authoritarian parenting. The mother's morale, or current satisfaction with life, mediates the association between maternal employment and positive mother–child interactions. And, for mothers of boys, maternal depression mediates the link between maternal employment and authoritative parenting. For the married, middle-class sample, although maternal employment was linked to parenting, it was not associated with maternal mood. Therefore, maternal mood cannot mediate the relationship between maternal employment and parenting for married, middle-class mothers.

*Does the Mother's Mood Mediate Maternal Employment
and Child Outcomes?*

We now consider the possibility that the mother's mood directly mediates a relationship between maternal employment and child outcomes.

Here, we follow the same strategy as in the preceding section. Because the direct relations between maternal employment and child outcomes are reported in Chapter 7, we start here by examining the relations from depression and morale to child outcomes. For those child outcome variables that are related both to maternal employment status and to the mood measures, regression analyses will be undertaken to test for mediation.

The Mother's Mood and Child Outcomes. The correlations between the mother's mood and child outcomes are presented in Table 9.3.

As seen in Table 9.3, there were no significant ($p < .05$) correlations between the mother's mood and child outcomes. In the working class, a few trends ($p < .10$) emerged which indicated that children of more depressed mothers had poorer peer social skills than children of less depressed mothers, and children of mothers with higher morale had higher math scores, more frustration tolerance, and better peer social skills than children of mothers with lower morale. In the married, middle-class sample, there was only an anomalous trend indicating that children of more depressed mothers had a more internal locus of control.

These correlations were run separately by gender and, in the working class, by marital status and ethnicity. In terms of gender, in the working class none of the correlations between depression, morale, and child outcomes was significant for girls. For boys, mother's greater depression was significantly associated with poorer peer social skills, and mothers' higher morale was significantly associated with more frustration tolerance, less acting out, being liked by same-sex peers, and being rated by peers as hitting less and being less mean. In the married, middle-class sample, the correlations by gender were more mixed. For boys, mothers' higher morale was significantly correlated with less task orientation and less positive assertiveness. For girls, mothers' higher morale was significantly associated with less shy/anxious behavior. However, mothers' higher depressive mood and lower morale were both correlated with girls' more internal locus of control.

The correlations between the mother's mood and child outcomes were also run separately by marital status in the working class. There were no significant correlations ($p < .05$) between depression and any of the child outcomes for children in two-parent families. In single-parent families, mothers' higher depressive mood was significantly associated with their children's more shy/anxious behavior, poorer peer social skills, and less positive assertiveness, and mothers' higher morale was significantly associated with their children's less peer-rated meanness.

In terms of ethnicity, the only significant correlations emerged for African Americans. African-American mothers' higher morale was signifi-

Table 9.3. *Correlations Between the Mother's Mood and Child Outcomes*

	Working Class		Married, Middle Class	
	Depression	Morale	Depression	Morale
Academic Test Scores				
Reading	−.09	.08	.08	−.06
Language	−.11	.12	.01	−.06
Math	−.11	.14#	−.12	.03
Teacher Ratings				
Learning problems	−.03	−.04	−.02	.05
Task orientation	−.02	.11	.05	−.16
Frustration tolerance	−.03	.14#	−.04	−.08
Acting out	.06	−.13	.07	.02
Shy/anxious	.05	−.02	.04	−.09
Peer social skills	−.14#	.13#	.03	−.04
Positive assertiveness	−.08	.06	.02	−.08
Peer Ratings				
Liked by peers	−.05	.02	.11	−.03
Mean	.04	−.01	−.13	−.01
Hits	.02	.01	−.12	.15
Helps	.07	.02	−.01	.04
Shy	.03	−.06	−.06	.05
Global Self Worth	−.04	.09	.11	−.10
Locus of Control	−.02	−.06	−.18#	−.09

# $p < .10$; * $p < .05$; ** $p < .01$; *** $p < .001$.

cantly associated with more frustration tolerance, less acting out, less shy/anxious behavior, better peer social skills, more positive assertiveness, and less hitting in their children.

Follow-up analyses were conducted to see whether parenting mediated the association between the mother's mood and child outcomes for various subgroups. (Recall from Table 9.3 that there were no significant correlations between the mother's mood and child outcomes for the total sample, so parenting cannot mediate mood and child outcomes for the total sample). That is, where there were significant associations between mood and child outcome for mothers of boys or girls, married or single mothers, or African-American or White mothers, mediation analyses were undertaken. For the most part, these proved nonsignificant. However, for African-American mothers, the relation between higher morale and children's better peer skills was mediated by authoritative parenting. That is, African-American mothers who had higher morale used more authoritative discipline and this, in turn, accounted for their children's better skills with peers.

Does the Mother's Mood Mediate the Links Between Maternal Employment and Child Outcomes?

Again, Baron and Kenny's (1986) criteria were followed. First, significant relations between maternal employment and child outcomes were demonstrated in Chapter 7. Second, in Chapter 5 we demonstrated significant associations between maternal employment and maternal depression and morale in the working class. However, because of the nonsignificant associations between maternal employment and the mother's mood in the married, middle-class sample, the mother's mood cannot mediate the relationships between maternal employment and child outcomes.

To test for mediation, separate regressions were run regressing each child outcome variable that had been significantly linked to maternal employment (see Chapter 7) simultaneously on maternal employment and either depression or morale. These analyses revealed no evidence that the mother's mood mediates the associations between maternal employment and child outcomes. To further explore the mediation possibility, we ran the mediation models separately by gender, marital status, and ethnicity. None of these mediation models proved significant.

Because the results thus far revealed that mood accounted for associations between maternal employment and parenting, but did not mediate maternal employment and child outcomes, we undertook a final set of path analyses that involved tracing the paths from maternal employment, via mood and parenting, to child outcomes. These analyses were conducted for working-class mothers only, given the nonsignificant association between employment and well-being in the married, middle-class sample. Figure 9.3 illustrates the results of these analyses.

The figure depicts findings discussed earlier in the chapter. That is, depressive mood partially mediates the link between maternal employment and authoritarian and authoritative ($p < .10$) parenting, and mediates the association between employment and permissive parenting, and morale mediates the connection between maternal employment and positive mother–child interaction. In the case of permissive parenting, more depressed homemaker mothers used more permissive discipline. The only effects of permissive parenting on children, however, were evident for sons of married mothers, where permissive parenting increased the likelihood of acting out, hitting, and being mean. In the case of authoritarian parenting, more depressed homemaker mothers used more authoritarian discipline, which, in turn, increased the likelihood that their children would have more learning problems, less task orientation and frustration tolerance, poorer test scores, more acting-out behavior, and poorer peer skills, and would hit more and be meaner. The pattern for authoritative parenting was inverse, such that employed mothers, who were less depressed, were more authoritative, and their children, in turn, evinced more positive academic and social outcomes. The pattern for authoritative parenting, however, is qualified somewhat by child gender. Recall from earlier that depressive mood completely mediated the effect of maternal employment on authoritative parenting only for mothers of boys. For boys, then, regression analyses revealed that authoritative parenting predicted higher math scores and higher global self-worth. Finally, working mothers, who had higher morale than full-time homemakers, engaged in more positive mother–child interaction, and their children subsequently displayed less acting-out behavior, although teachers also rated them as being more shy.

Summary and Discussion

Previous research on work and mental health suggests that employment has a positive effect on the mother's emotional well-being (Kessler & McRae, 1982; Repetti, Mathews, & Waldron, 1989), and considerable research by developmental psychologists indicates that a mother's emotional well-being enhances her parenting style (Harnish, Dodge & Valente, 1995; Zahn-Waxler, 1995). However, no previous study has examined whether relationships between maternal employment and parenting style or between maternal employment and child outcomes exist that are mediated by the mother's well-being or mood state. Furthermore, the previous data supporting the hypothesis that employed mothers have higher morale than full-time homemakers have been more consistent for research conducted with working-class than with middle-class samples (Warr & Parry, 1982).

Our results showed that, in the lower socioeconomic groups, as would be expected, depressive mood and morale mediated the relationship between employment status and parenting orientations. The same analyses were carried out in the middle class, but with very different results. In the middle class, although there were connections between maternal employment and parenting, there were no significant relationships between employment status and depressive mood or morale, thus ruling out the mediational role of the mother's mood between employment status and parenting orientations.

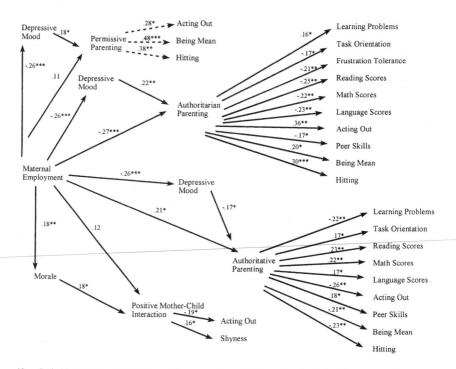

Note. Dashed lines refer to working-class sons of married mothers. Solid lines refer to the total working-class sample.

Figure 9.3. Path analyses of the associations between maternal employment, mood, parenting and child outcomes in the working class. * $p < .05$; ** $p < .01$; *** $p < .001$.

Additional analyses were undertaken to see if the mother's mood itself mediates the link between employment and child outcome, but there was no support for this hypothesis in either class. Path analyses suggested the following scenario in the working class: the mother's well-being accounts, at least in part, for the effect of employment on parenting, and parenting subsequently predicts child outcome. Thus, the relation between mood and child outcome is indirect. The higher morale of employed mothers increases the likelihood of more positive parenting, which, in turn, increases the probability of more positive academic and social outcomes for children. The extent to which parenting, itself, may mediate the links between employment and child outcomes will be explored in the next chapter.

Moderators of the Effect of the Mother's Mood on Parenting

The last set of analyses involved evaluating four potential moderators of the effect of maternal mood on parenting. These moderators included parental commitment, the mother's education, and, for married mothers only, the father's help with household chores and child care.

The analyses were run separately by social class. To examine the effect of each potential moderator, regressions were run in the following way. Each parenting variable was regressed on depression, the moderator (e.g., parental commitment), and the interaction between depression and the moderator. Each regression was also repeated using the morale variable in place of the depression variable. Following Baron and Kenny (1986), a significant interaction term reveals moderation, whether or not main effects also occur. Thus, in each regression, the term of interest was the interaction term.

Working-class Patterns. No significant interaction terms emerged in any of the analyses involving parental commitment, the mother's education, the father's help with household tasks, or the father's help with child care. Thus, the effects of depressive mood and morale on parenting in the working class are not moderated by commitment to parenting, mothers' education, or fathers' help.

Married, Middle-class Patterns. Regressions were run again for the married, middle-class mothers to examine the moderating effect of commitment to parenting, education, and the father's help with household chores and child care. Analyses with significant interaction terms are in Table 9.4. Post-hoc analyses to interpret the interactions are in Table 9.5.

To examine the nature of the interaction effects, median splits on each moderating variable (i.e., parental commitment, education, the father's help with household chores, the father's help with child care) and on depression and morale were created. Then, for each analysis, four groups were formed based on these results (e.g., high parental commitment/low depression; high parental commitment/high depression; low parental commitment/low depression; low parental commitment/high depression), and means on the parenting variables were compared. The use of groups based on median splits is intended to descriptively tease apart the interaction.

A mother's commitment to parenting significantly modified the effects of both depression and morale on authoritative parenting (see Table 9.4). In general, for those mothers with higher depressive mood and lower morale scores, parental commitment served as a buffer: mothers with higher

Table 9.4. *Regression of Selected Parenting Measures on Depression, Morale and Moderators for Married, Middle-Class Mothers: Standardized Regression Weights and* F-*Values*

A. Parental Commitment

	Depression	Par. Comm.	D × PC	$F(3,96)$
Authoritative	−.12	.20*	.27**	6.09***
	Morale	Par. Comm.	M×PC	$F(3,96)$
Authoritative	.02	.29**	−.34***	6.78***

B. Education

	Depression	Education	D × ED	$F(3,96)$
Authoritative	−.20*	.14	.26**	4.45**
	Morale	Education	M × ED	$F(3,96)$
Authoritative	.05	.15	−.32**	4.59**
Permissive	−.05	−.25**	.26**	4.81**

C. Father's Help with Child Care

	Morale	Father's Help	M × CC	$F(3,98)$
Authoritative	.02	.13	.21*	2.30#

Notes. D = depression; PC = parental commitment; M = morale; ED = education; CC = father's help in child care.

# $p < .10$; * $p < .05$; ** $p < .01$; *** $p < .001$.

parental commitment evinced higher authoritative scores than mothers lower parental commitment (see Table 9.5).

We next examined the moderating role of mothers' education. Regression analyses revealed that mother's education modified the effects of depression on authoritative parenting. Education also modified the links between morale and authoritative and permissive parenting (see Table 9.4). For those mothers with higher depressive mood scores, mothers with more education were more authoritative than mothers with less education. For those mothers with lower morale, mothers with more education were more authoritative and less permissive than less educated mothers (see Table 9.5).

Finally, we examined the moderating role of father's help. Father's help with household chores did not moderate any connections between mood and parenting. However, fathers' help with child care moderated the effect of morale on authoritative parenting (see Table 9.4). Mothers with lower morale whose husbands helped more with child care were more authoritative than mothers with lower morale whose husbands helped less.

Summary and Discussion. Analyses were conducted to see if parental commitment, education, and father's help moderated the relationship

Table 9.5. *Means for Selected Parenting Measures by Moderated Effect: Married, Middle Class*

A. Parental Commitment

	Low Depression		High Depression	
	Low PC	High PC	Low PC	High PC
Authoritative	39.43	40.74	38.20	40.00
	Low Morale		High Morale	
	Low PC	High PC	Low PC	High PC
Authoritative	38.00	41.00	39.09	40.14

B. Education

	Low Depression		High Depression	
	Low ED	High ED	Low ED	High ED
Authoritative	40.84	39.35	38.39	40.65
	Low Morale		High Morale	
	Low ED	High ED	Low ED	High ED
Authoritative	38.45	40.50	39.57	39.83
Permissive	11.50	8.67	9.29	9.54

C. Father's Help with Child Care

	Low Morale		High Morale	
	More Help	Less Help	More Help	Less Help
Authoritative	39.83	38.14	39.29	40.03

Notes. PC = parental commitment; ED = education.

between depressive mood and parenting orientations. No moderating effects were revealed in the working class. In the middle class, however, education, parental commitment and father's help with child care moderated the effect of depressive mood on authoritative parenting. In the face of higher depressive mood and lower morale, more commitment to parenting, higher education, and more help from the father raised the level of positive parenting and lowered the level of negative parenting, relative to those depressed mothers with less parental commitment, less education, and less help from their spouse. It is not clear whether this social class difference resulted from the higher educational level of the middle class generally and their greater exposure to the advice of childrearing experts, or whether it reflects the fact that the depressive mood level is lower in the middle class.[3] It may be that parental commitment, father's help, and education lead mothers to overcome their mood states in dealing with children, but only when the mood is just slightly depressed. These competing explanations deserve further attention. They would, for example, have different implications for intervention programs: Is education for parenting sufficient, or is attention to the mother's emotional state necessary? Although the CES-D is intended for use in normal populations, scores of 16 are viewed as marking more serious pathology. In the working class, the nonemployed mothers obtained a mean of 14.98 and the single mothers in that group obtained a mean of 16.72, suggesting that education alone may not be sufficient.[4] Finally, in terms of the father's help, the analyses are congruent with the suggestion that father's increased involvement in child care may temper the stress that employed mothers may feel from the dual roles of worker and mother, enabling mothers to function more effectively in the maternal role.

Chapter Summary

The purpose of this chapter was to consider the interrelationships of maternal employment, the mother's well-being, parenting, and child outcomes. Analyses were conducted separately by social class. In addition, attention was paid to gender, marital status, and ethnicity.

We investigated two hypotheses. The first hypothesis was that the relation between maternal employment and parenting is mediated by the mother's mood. Our analyses supported this hypothesis, but only in the working class. In the working class, employed mothers were less permissive and authoritarian, were more authoritative, and had more positive interactions with their child than full-time homemakers. Mediation analyses revealed that these connections were due to the employed mother's higher morale and lower depressive mood. In the married, middle-class sample, employed mothers were less authoritarian but also reported having fewer positive interactions with their child. However, although maternal employment was linked to parenting, employment was not significantly associated with the mother's well-being. Therefore, for married, middle-class mothers, mood did not mediate employment and parenting.

The second hypothesis was that the relation between maternal employment and child outcomes is mediated by the mother's mood. Although a number of significant relations between employment and child functioning emerged in this study (see Chapter 7), the mother's mood did not mediate these relations in either class. Path analyses suggested that, in the working class, the mother's mood mediates the associations between maternal employment and parenting, and that parenting subsequently leads to child outcomes. Mood thereby has an indirect effect on child outcomes. In other words, the higher morale of employed mothers increases the likelihood of positive parenting techniques, which lead, in turn, to more positive social and academic child outcomes.

Finally, four moderators of the relations between the mother's well-being and parenting were considered. No moderating effects of parental commitment, the mother's education, or the father's help with household chores or child care were revealed in the working class. Among middle-class, married mothers, parental commitment, education and the father's help with child care mitigated the effect of depression and lower morale on parenting.

Notes

1. Recall from Chapter 5 that, because there were no middle-class, single, nonemployed mothers, causing empty cells in the analyses to follow, the final middle-class sample contains only married mothers.

2. The analyses involving authoritarian were run a second time, dropping the physical punishment items and retaining only those items relevant to demanding obedience. The pattern of results was identical, so the authoritarian analyses presented in this chapter include the physical punishment items.

3. The CES-D mean for employed, married, middle-class mothers was 8.23 ($sd = 7.88$). The mean for nonemployed, married, middle-class mothers was 6.04 ($sd = 5.24$). The mean for employed, working-class mothers was 10.20 ($sd = 8.12$). The mean for nonemployed, working-class mothers was 14.98 ($sd = 9.27$).

4. These scores may involve slight underestimations because of the deleted item (see Chapter 5).

10   Childrearing Patterns and Child Outcomes*

In this chapter, childrearing patterns are examined as links between maternal employment and child outcomes. In Chapter 6, differences in the childrearing styles of employed and nonemployed mothers were reported. This chapter extends these findings by examining the relationships between the parenting styles already tied to the mother's employment status and child outcomes.

Thus, we begin this chapter with a review of the results presented in Chapter 6. These findings showed that, across marital status, employed mothers were less likely to use an authoritarian style of control, and they showed less differentiation between sons and daughters in their discipline style and in their goals for children. In the one-parent sample, all of whom are working class, employed mothers also indicated more use of authoritative discipline, a style of control tempered by explanations and allowing input from the child. In the two-parent families, consistent with the general pattern, the full-time homemakers stressed obedience as their goal for children, but, particularly in the working class, they also indicated more permissiveness than the employed mothers. In addition, the homemakers held lower educational expectations for their children. With respect to child monitoring, there was only one significant difference: sons in dual-wage working-class families were more likely to be left unsupervised and unmonitored.

Mothers reported the frequency of their interactions with their child over the previous week. For middle-class, married mothers, the full-time homemakers indicated more frequent positive and educational interactions with their children; for working-class, married mothers, more frequent positive and educational activities with daughters were reported by the employed

* This chapter was written by Lois W. Hoffman and Donna Dumm Kovacs.

228

mothers and there was no difference for sons. Single employed mothers reported more interaction with respect to educational activities and "talking." The data also indicated that children of employed mothers helped more in household tasks, but the difference was significant only in single-mother families.

Finally, across marital status, employed mothers indicated more frequent expression of overt affection, but on a measure of "commitment to parenting", higher scores were obtained in the middle class by the full-time homemakers.

All of the childrearing variables that showed a significant relationship to the mother's employment status in Chapter 6, as well as those that showed a trend-level relationship ($p < .10$), are included in this chapter. We examine the relationships between them and the child outcome variables tapping three domains of competence: social adjustment, cognitive competence, and independence and assertiveness. Because discipline and control styles have in past research been linked to all three domains (Baumrind, 1967; M. Hoffman, 1988), these variables were used throughout the analysis, but other parenting variables were more domain specific. For the social adjustment variables, relationships with maternal expression of affection and parental commitment were also examined. For the cognitive competence variables, relationships with educational expectations and mother/child activities were added. For independence and assertiveness, we also examined the parents' goals for the child and the child's participation in tasks. The latter is added because children's task participation has been linked to maturity and responsibility in previous research (Medrich, Roizen, Rubin, & Buckley, 1982). Table 10.1 lists the parenting measures examined for each outcome domain. All the analyses are conducted separately for the married and single mothers, as they were in Chapter 6. The criterion of using only those parenting variables that were related to the mother's employment status means, therefore, that the specific measures used for each group are different, as indicated in Table 10.1.

Method

Sample

The sample is the same as that used in Chapter 6. As in Chapter 6, only mothers who had a stable history of employment over the preceding three years were included, and single, middle-class mothers were excluded from all analyses. For measures drawn from mother interviews, the sample size

Table 10.1. *List of Parenting Measures Examined for Each of Three Child Outcome Domains (Social Adjustment, Cognitive Competence, and Independence and Assertiveness) for Married Mothers and for Single Mothers*

Child Outcome Domain	Parenting Measures Examined	
	Married Mothers	Single Mothers
All (social, cognitive, independence)	Discipline: Power assertion Strong power assertion Parental Control: Authoritarian Obedience and respect Physical punishment Hostile Child influence	Discipline: Induction Strong power assertion Parental Control: Authoritarian Obedience and respect Authoritative Child influence Child thinking for self
Social adjustment	Parental Control: Permissive Overt Display of Affection Commitment to Parenting Supervision and Monitoring	Overt Display of Affection Commitment to Parenting
Cognitive competence	Educational Expectations Mother Report of Activities: Educational Total Positive	Mother Report of Activities: Talk Educational Total positive
Independence and assertiveness	Goals: Independence Obedience Kind and good Femininity (for girls only)	Goals: Kind and good
	Household Tasks	Household Tasks

was 199 married mothers and 54 single, working-class mothers. For measures obtained from children, the sample size was 226 for children with married mothers and 63 for children with single mothers.

Measures

A description of the parenting measures can be found in Chapter 6. Only those parenting measures that showed a significant or trend-level relationship with maternal employment in Chapter 6 were retained for the current analyses.

A description of the child outcome measures can be found in Chapter 2. Included in the child outcome measures are peer ratings, teacher reports, child self-reports, and school-administered academic achievement tests. For purposes of the current analyses, child outcome variables were categorized into three domains, as follows:

1. *Social adjustment.* Measures of child social adjustment included three peer-rating measures and two teacher-report measures. Peer ratings of meanness and hitting, as well as liking by same-sex peers, were considered social adjustment measures, as were teacher reports of acting out and peer social skills.

2. *Cognitive competence.* Measures of child cognitive competence included two teacher-report measures: learning problems and frustration tolerance. In addition, children's standardized test scores on the three tests of reading, mathematics, and language were used.

3. *Independence and assertiveness.* To assess child independence and assertiveness, four measures were used: peer ratings of shyness; teacher reports of shyness and anxiety; teacher ratings of positive assertiveness; and children's self-reports of external locus of control.

Analysis Plan

As a first step, the direct links between each of the parenting measures and the child outcome measures were explored. Specifically, correlations between each set of parenting measures (with the exception of the categorical variable of monitoring) and the corresponding child outcomes were calculated. Correlations were computed in multiple ways in order to determine whether there were differences between subgroups based on social class and gender. To test links between child social adjustment and the categorical variable of parental monitoring and supervision, 2 (child gender) by 2 (social class) by 3 (supervision and monitoring) ANOVAs were conducted for married mothers.

As a second step in the analysis plan, for selected variables, mediation analyses were undertaken using a regression approach, following Baron and Kenny's (1986) criteria (see Chapter 4).

Results

Links Between Parenting and Child Social Adjustment

Married Mothers. Table 10.2 presents the results of the correlations between social adjustment and the parenting variables for children in the two-parent families. These analyses are presented separately for social class and gender.

The only significant effects found for boys are for maternal permissiveness. In the working class, higher maternal permissiveness is associated with boys' low scores on the peer ratings of how much the child is liked, and with high scores on acting mean and hitting. It is also associated with the teacher rating of acting out; high scores on permissiveness are related to high acting-out scores. The pattern for middle-class boys is an interesting contrast. Although it is not significant, the direction of the relationship to peer liking is similar: maternal permissiveness is associated with low scores. However, in the middle class, high permissiveness is associated with low scores on the teacher rating of acting out. This class discrepancy ties into a pattern reported in Chapter 7. It was noted there that in the working class, higher acting-out scores were obtained by the homemakers' sons, but in the middle class, higher scores were obtained by the sons of full-time employed mothers. Further, a social-class difference was also indicated in the levels of acting out, such that the higher acting out scores of the middle-class sons of employed mothers were still lower than any of the scores in the working class, but the scores of the middle-class sons of homemakers were extremely low ($M = 7.00$), lower than the scores of the middle-class girls ($M = 7.70$). Thus, the full pattern suggests that the two social classes represent such different levels of acting out that the "higher" level in each class represents a very different point on the continuum. In the middle class, the relationship between permissiveness and acting out may involve a reverse causality: the child's high level of conformity may induce the mother's permissiveness. Consistent with this, the same relationship found for middle-class boys is also found for middle-class girls; high maternal permissiveness goes with low levels of acting out. Further, it was only in the working class that the mother's employment status was significantly related to permissiveness; the full-time homemakers were more permissive.

Turning now to the girls, the middle-class girls show two significant results besides the permissiveness–acting-out link. Strong power assertion is associated with high acting-out scores. In addition, high parental commitment scores are related to lower peer ratings of saying mean things. For

Table 10.2. *Correlations Between Parenting Measures and Child Social Adjustment, Separate by Social Class and by Child Gender, for Married Mothers*

Parenting Measures	Peer Ratings						Teacher Ratings			
	Liked by same-sex		Mean		Hits		Acting out		Peer social skills	
	Boys	Girls	Boys	Girls	Boys	Girls	Boys	Girls	Boys	Girls
For Working Class:										
Authoritarian style										
Power assertion	-.12	-.17	-.04	.21	-.06	.12	-.00	.34*	-.01	.15
Strong power assertion	.08	-.21	-.00	.15	.01	.03	.08	.31*	.01	-.12
Authoritarian	.12	-.24	-.01	.19	.04	.29#	.10	.51***	.18	-.25
Obedience and respect	.10	-.20	-.06	.25	-.02	.26#	.04	.47**	.16	-.36*
Physical punishment	.00	-.37*	.03	.19	.03	.28#	.14	.42**	.05	-.15
Hostile	.22	-.11	.04	.14	.13	.20	.08	.37*	.24#	-.11
Authoritative style										
Child influence	-.12	.38*	-.00	-.19	.00	-.41**	-.06	-.36*	-.11	-.01
Permissive style										
Permissive	-.38**	-.10	.51***	-.10	.42**	-.07	.34*	-.07	-.12	.12
Overt display of affection	-.03	.15	.02	-.27#	.05	-.40**	.06	-.43**	-.14	.30#
Commitment to parenting	.08	.19	.03	-.10	.02	-.15	-.10	-.18	-.01	-.00
For Middle Class:										
Authoritarian style										
Power assertion	-.08	-.01	.23	.07	.12	-.18	-.08	-.08	.10	.03
Strong power assertion	-.27#	-.02	.10	-.12	-.11	.08	-.15	.34**	.02	-.03
Authoritarian	.05	.05	.03	-.11	.01	-.11	.07	-.06	-.03	-.10
Obedience and respect	.13	.02	-.00	-.08	-.03	-.11	.13	-.07	-.08	-.11
Physical punishment	-.28#	.02	.15	-.14	-.01	.03	-.15	.00	.02	-.03
Hostile	.07	.01	-.22	-.09	-.07	-.04	.04	-.05	.03	-.19
Authoritative style										
Child influence	-.17	-.02	-.04	-.02	-.11	.08	-.01	.00	-.07	.06
Permissive style										
Permissive	-.22	.01	.04	.00	.04	-.06	-.31*	-.26*	.10	.17
Overt display of affection	-.12	-.17	.17	-.01	.16	.12	.16	.19	-.11	-.06
Commitment to parenting	.14	.06	.10	-.35**	.11	-.21	.22	-.09	-.08	.01

# *p* < .10; * *p* < .05; ** *p* < .01; *** *p* < .001.

working-class girls, high acting out is associated with power assertion, strong power assertion, hostile control, and authoritarian control and both of its subparts: demand for obedience and respect, and the use of physical punishment. In addition, high child influence and a high level of maternal affection are associated with low acting-out scores. Additional relationships for working-class girls are consistent with this general pattern of parental coerciveness being associated with lower social competence. The use of physical punishment is associated with lower peer ratings of liking; the demand for obedience is associated with lower scores on the teacher rating of peer skills. Further, the data indicate that mothers who allow the child more influence have daughters who are well-liked and do not hit their peers. Maternal affection is also associated with lower hitting scores. In addition, the five trend-level relationships for working-class girls are all consistent with the picture of poor social adjustment associated with authoritarian parenting and positive social adjustment associated with maternal affection.

For the categorical variable of supervision and monitoring, there were no significant main effects in predicting the child social adjustment outcomes in the ANOVAs. There were also no significant interaction effects of supervision and monitoring with child gender or social class in these ANOVAs.

Single Mothers. Correlations between parenting measures and child adjustment for the overall sample of children with single, working-class mothers are shown in Table 10.3. Because patterns were similar for boys and girls, they are shown here combined. For both boys and girls, the use of authoritative parenting styles related to increased child social competence. Specifically, mothers' use of authoritative control, as well as both subcomponents (allowing child influence and encouraging child to think for self), were negatively correlated with peer ratings of meanness, peer ratings of hitting, and teacher ratings of acting out, and positively correlated with teacher ratings of social skills. When mothers used more induction, children also hit less (according to peers) and were more socially skilled (according to teachers).

Consistent with these results, the findings indicate that, whereas authoritative discipline is associated with higher levels of social adjustment, authoritarian discipline is associated with lower levels. Specifically, strong power assertion is associated with more hitting, as reported by peers, and to poorer peer skills, as reported by teachers. In addition, higher maternal affection is related to better peer skills, and commitment to parenting sig-

Table 10.3. *Correlations Between Parenting Measures and Child Social Adjustment, for Single, Working-class Mothers*

Parenting Measures	Peer Ratings			Teacher Ratings	
	Liked by same sex	Mean	Hits	Acting out	Peer social skills
Authoritarian style					
Strong power assertion	−.09	.21	.33*	.23#	−.34*
Authoritarian	−.05	.10	.18	.23	−.22
Obedience and respect	−.04	.05	.10	.16	−.20
Authoritative style					
Induction	.14	−.18	−.29*	−.23	.35**
Authoritative	.10	−.28*	−.23#	−.37**	.43***
Child influence	.19	−.31*	−.25#	−.46***	.36**
Child thinking for self	.05	−.27#	−.26#	−.24#	.45***
Overt display of affection	.15	−.17	−.22	−.24#	.35*
Commitment to parenting	.22	−.35*	−.40**	−.24#	.16

# $p < .10$; * $p < .05$; ** $p < .01$; *** $p < .001$.

nificantly predicted lower scores on the peer ratings of who hits and who says mean things.

Summary of the Links Connecting the Mother's Employment Status, Parenting, and Children's Social Adjustment. The findings reported in Chapter 6 indicated that, across marital status, full-time homemakers use more authoritarian parenting styles. The results presented here examining the relationships between the various indices of authoritarian parenting and children's social competence also found consistencies across marital status, but there were gender differences within the married sample. For girls in two-parent families and both boys and girls in one-parent families, significant relationships were found between authoritarian parenting and social adjustment problems. None of these relationships, however, were significant for boys in two-parent families.

The married homemakers in the working class used more permissiveness. This was linked to adjustment problems for working-class boys, but permissiveness was not related for the girls. Thus, the parenting patterns of working-class homemakers were associated with lower social adjustment for children, but for boys it was their permissiveness and for girls, it was their authoritarian style.

Only in the one-parent families was there a significant effect of the mother's employment status on the use of authoritative discipline; it was used more by the employed mothers than by the full-time homemakers. The findings here revealed that this discipline style was associated with more positive social adjustment for both boys and girls. Thus, both control patterns associated with employment in one-parent families, low authoritarian and high authoritative, were related to the children's more positive social adjustment.

Overt affection was expressed more by employed mothers and, in one-parent families, it was significantly related to better peer skills. For working-class girls in two-parent families, it was significantly related to less hitting and acting out. Parental commitment, on the other hand, was significantly higher for homemakers in the middle class, but showed a trend-level relationship indicating higher commitment in the working class for the employed, single mothers. It was related to lower scores on "mean" for middle-class girls and to lower scores on mean and hits for the children of single mothers.

Links Between Parenting and Child Cognitive Competence

Married Mothers. The correlations between the selected parenting variables and children's cognitive competence are presented in Table 10.4 separately by child gender. The table shows that for girls, maternal demands for obedience and respect are significantly associated with lower frustration tolerance. A hostile style of parenting is also significantly associated with lower frustration tolerance and with lower scores on the language achievement test. There is also a trend-level association with learning problems, as indicated by the teacher ratings. For boys, mothers' use of strong power assertion is significantly associated with lower scores on the math test. In addition, strong power assertion shows trend-level relationships to reading and language scores.

Although the number of significant associations between parenting styles and cognitive outcomes is modest, most are in the expected direction showing an association between authoritarian discipline and lower cognitive competence. The one exception is a trend-level relationship between the mother's hostile style and boys' language scores. When examined separately for each social-class group, the data indicated that this reversed relationship held only for working-class boys. There was no significant relationship for middle-class boys.

Table 10.4. *Correlations Between Parenting Measures and Child Cognitive Competence, Controlling for Social Class and Separate by Child Gender, for Married Mothers*

| | Teacher Ratings | | | | Achievement Tests | | | | | |
| | Learning problems | | Frustration tolerance | | Reading | | Math | | Language | |
Parenting Measures	Boys	Girls	Boys	Girls	Boys	Girls	Boys	Girls	Boys	Girls
Authoritarian style										
Power assertion	-.03	-.05	.04	.01	.15	.02	.09	-.05	.11	-.02
Strong power assertion	.09	-.02	.07	-.13	-.20#	.05	-.23*	-.14	-.20#	.04
Authoritarian	-.10	.02	-.03	-.16	-.04	.05	-.06	-.06	-.06	-.10
Obedience and respect	-.05	.08	.02	-.24*	-.02	-.02	-.04	-.11	-.09	-.13
Physical punishment	-.07	-.06	-.05	-.07	-.05	.11	-.09	-.06	-.03	-.05
Hostile	-.05	.17#	-.06	-.21*	.11	-.07	.13	-.06	.20#a	-.21*
Authoritative style										
Child influence	.04	-.07	-.08	.06	.08	-.03	.04	.04	-.03	.14
Educational expectations	-.08	-.15	-.04	.07	.30**	.17#	.19#	.31**	.24*	.16
Mother report of activities										
Educational	.05	.14	-.02	-.10	-.01	-.19#	-.04	-.19#	-.13	-.12
Total positive	.07	.16	-.10	-.12	-.03	-.14	-.10	-.22*b	-.14	-.12

[a] Working-class boys: $r = .29*$; Middle-class boys: $r = -.04$.
[b] Working-class girls: $r = -.29\#$; Middle-class girls: $r = -.08$.
# $p < .10$; * $p < .05$; ** $p < .01$.

The relationships between mothers' educational expectations and children's test scores show consistency in direction across class and gender: the higher the expectations, the higher the test scores. The relationships are significant for reading and language for boys and at the trend level for math. For girls, they are significant for math and at the trend-level for reading. When the sample is combined, and gender and class are controlled, all three relationships are significant ($r[193] = .25$, $p < .001$, for reading; $r[193] = .25$, $p < .001$, for mathematics; and $r[193] = .20$, $p < .01$, for language).

The only other significant relationship reported in Table 10.4 is a negative one between mothers' reports of the frequency of positive interactions with daughters and math scores. This relationship, however, when examined separately for each social-class group, showed a trend-level relationship for the working class only.

None of the relationships between the frequency of educational interactions and test scores are significant, but there are two trend-level negative relationships for girls. The negative direction here is because the educational interactions consist primarily of helping the child with homework. In this study, as well as in others, negative relationships are found because parental help is often a response to signaled academic difficulty, particularly in the working class (Fuligni 1995).

Single Mothers. Table 10.5 lists correlations between parenting and child cognitive competence for the overall sample of single, working-class mothers. In general, both boys and girls exhibit more cognitive competence when their mothers rely more on the authoritative discipline style and less on the authoritarian discipline style. Specifically, children with single mothers had fewer learning problems, according to classroom teachers, when mothers used more authoritative control, and more of the subcomponent of allowing child influence. Also, when mothers used more authoritative control, including both subcomponents (allowing child influence and encouraging child to think for self), and when mothers used more induction, children had more frustration tolerance and scored higher on achievement tests in reading and math. For language achievement tests, test scores were significantly correlated with allowing the child influence, and tended to be correlated with mothers' use of induction as well.

In contrast, mothers' use of strong power assertion was related to less frustration tolerance, and to lower test scores in reading and math. Similarly, the use of authoritarian control and its subcomponent, obedience and respect, related to lower scores on tests of reading, math, and language.

Table 10.5. *Correlations Between Parenting Measures and Child Cognitive Competence, for Single, Working-class Mothers*

	Teacher Ratings		Achievement Tests		
Parenting Measures	Learning problems	Frustration tolerance	Reading	Math	Language
Authoritarian style					
Strong power assertion	.20	−.32*	−.36**	−.31*	−.21
Authoritarian	.13	−.14	−.35*	−.40**	−.29*
Obedience and respect	.09	−.12	−.36**	−.43***	−.29*
Authoritative style					
Induction	−.06	.32*	.32*	.45***	.25#
Authoritative	−.30*	.31*	.34*	.33*	.23
Child influence	−.34*	.32*	.32*	.38**	.37**
Child thinking for self	−.16	.24#	.37**	.34*	.21
Mother report of activities					
Talk	−.38**	.22	.46***	.33*	.12
Educational	−.03	.10	.28*	.19	.01
Total positive	−.12	.15	.30*	.15	.14

# $p < .10$; * $p < .05$; ** $p < .01$; *** $p < .001$.

For children with single mothers, the data also indicate more cognitive competence when mothers report more mother–child interaction. Specifically, children had significantly higher reading test scores when mothers reported more talk, educational, and total positive activities. Children also scored higher on math tests and had fewer learning problems, as rated by teachers, when mothers reported more frequent talking with children.

Summary of the Links Connecting the Mother's Employment Status, Parenting, and Children's Cognitive Competence. For the authoritarian parenting styles that were used more by the full-time homemakers, the general picture showed an association with lower scores on the achievement tests and with lower skills as measured by teacher ratings of learning problems and frustration tolerance. Higher levels of interaction between the mother and child, a pattern found for the working-class, single, employed mothers, across child gender, and for working-class, married, employed mothers of girls, were associated with cognitive competence in single-mother families but not in the two-parent families. Finally, mothers' higher educational expectations, which characterized the employed mothers but only in two-parent families, were associated with higher academic test scores.

Links Between Parenting and Child Independence and Assertiveness

Married Mothers. One of the most pervasive hypotheses in the maternal employment literature is that employed mothers, in contrast to full-time homemakers, encourage independence in their daughters, and that this has positive consequences for the daughters' competence and higher achievement (Hoffman, 1974, 1989). However, as indicated in Chapter 1, very little empirical evidence has previously been presented for the view that the parenting orientations of employed mothers really are more conducive to the development of independence in daughters. The data presented in this section pertain to this issue.

Table 10.6 shows the relationships between parenting variables and each of four indices of assertiveness and independence: peer ratings of shyness, teacher ratings of shy and anxious behavior, teacher ratings of positive assertiveness, and the children's "locus of control" scores, which indicate the extent to which they feel capable of affecting personal outcomes, or believe them to be externally determined. As presented in the table, only one of the relationships for the authoritarian discipline group is significant for girls: the emphasis on obedience and respect is associated with lower positive assertiveness. However, there are, in addition, four trend-level relationships: an external sense of control is associated with authoritarian discipline, demand for obedience and respect, and hostile style; and high scores on the teacher rating of shy and anxious behavior are also associated with a hostile parenting orientation. Further, there are several class-specific significant results: middle-class girls who are rated by peers as shy have mothers who are authoritarian and use physical punishment; teacher ratings of shy/anxious are related to hostile style; and for working-class girls, the relationship between hostile style and external sense of control is significant. For boys, there are two significant relationships: both power assertion and the subpart, strong power assertion, are related to external sense of control.

The particular aspect of authoritative parenting, allowing the child to have some influence or to present his or her side, is also negatively associated with shy/anxious behavior in daughters. This held across social class in its tie to the child outcome.

Table 10.6. *Correlations Between Parenting Measures and Child Independence and Assertiveness, Controlling for Social Class Separate by Child Gender, for Married Mothers*

| | Peer Ratings | | Teacher Ratings | | | | Self-Perceptions | |
| | Shy | | Shy/Anxious | | Positive assertiveness | | Locus of control[a] | |
Parenting Measures	Boys	Girl	Boys	Girls	Boys	Girls	Boys	Girls
Authoritarian style								
Power assertion	.02	-.07	.03	-.08	.11	.16	.21*	.03
Strong power assertion	.09	.03	.11	-.00	-.15	-.01	.22*	.14
Authoritarian	-.04	.15[b]	-.10	.08	.13	-.10	.02	.18[#]
Obedience and respect	-.02	.16	-.07	.08	.08	-.22*	.00	.17[#]
Physical punishment	-.10	.16[c]	-.10	.01	.07	.03	.00	.16
Hostile	-.15	-.01	-.10	.16[#d]	.19[#]	-.11	.09	.19[#e]
Authoritative style								
Child influence	.01	.04	.00	-.29**	-.06	-.01	-.06	-.02
Goals								
Independence	-.02	-.24*	-.03	-.16[f]	-.01	.08	-.17	-.04
Obedience	.06	.22*	.03	.20*	-.07	-.22*	-.12	.18[#]
Kind and good	.09	.05	.11	.00	-.07	-.03	-.07	-.17[#]
Femininity	N/A	.15	N/A	.10	N/A	-.27**	N/A	.11
Household tasks	-.11	-.07[g]	-.17[#]	.02	.13	-.07	-.10	-.05

[a] High scores indicate external control; low scores indicate internal control.
[b] Working-class girls: r = -.04; Middle-class girls: r = .30*.
[c] Working-class girls: r = -.14; Middle-class girls: r = .37**.
[d] Working-class girls: r = .01; Middle-class girls: r = .29*.
[e] Working-class girls: r = .30*; Middle-class girls: r = .15.
[f] Working-class girls: r = -.34*; Middle-class girls: r = -.05.
[g] Working-class girls: r = -.37*; Middle-class girls: r = .17.
# p < .10; * p < .05; ** p < .01.

Turning to the parental goals presented in Table 10.6, it can be seen that parents who hold independence as a goal for their daughters have daughters who are less likely to be rated shy by their peers. A comparable relationship is found for the teacher rating of shy, but this obtained statistical significance only for the working class. Mothers who hold the contrasting goal of obedience, on the other hand, have daughters who are rated as shy by both peers and teachers; and there is an additional significant relationship to low scores on positive assertiveness and a trend-level relationship to a sense of external control. Since employed mothers were more likely to cite independence as their goal for their daughters and to shun the goal of obedience, a link between maternal employment and daughters' independence is suggested here.

For the two other goals that were related to the mother's employment status, being "kind and good" and "femininity," we find an expected relationship for femininity: daughters whose mothers set femininity as a goal are rated low in assertiveness. Kind and good shows no significant relationship, but the trend-level relationship to locus of control is in the opposite direction.

Single Mothers. The correlations between the parenting variables that were related to single mothers' employment status and their children's scores on the indices of independence and assertiveness are presented in Table 10.7. For girls, the data indicate that strong power assertion is significantly related to daughters' sense that they have little control over outcomes, i.e., an external "locus of control". In addition, mothers who use inductive controls, providing reasons rather than coercion, have daughters rated low on shy/anxious behavior by their teachers. This outcome is also significantly associated with mothers' encouraging their daughters to "think for themselves". Encouraging the child to think for herself also shows a trend-level relationship with positive assertiveness. For boys also, there are trend-level relationships showing low authoritarianism and high reliance on authoritative discipline associated with positive assertiveness. In fact, the relationships for the discipline patterns and child outcomes are similar for boys and girls. For boys and girls combined (not shown in the table), it was found that when mothers used more authoritative control (r [51] = .29, $p <$ .05), and the subcomponent of encouraging the child to think for him- or herself (r [51] = .29, $p < .05$), children were rated as more assertive. Moreover, the relationship between "think for self" and lower scores on the teacher ratings of shy and anxious were also significant for the two groups combined (r [51] = −.41, $p < .01$).

Table 10.7. *Correlations Between Parenting Measures and Child Independence and Assertiveness, Separately by Child Gender, for Single, Working-class Mothers*

	Peer Ratings		Teacher Ratings				Self Perceptions	
	Shy		Shy/Anxious		Positive assertiveness		Locus of control[a]	
Parenting Measures	Boys	Girls	Boys	Girls	Boys	Girls	Boys	Girls
Authoritarian style								
Strong power assertion	.13	-.08	.12	-.02	-.33#	.14	.02	.48*
Authoritarian	.10	.13	-.08	.07	-.33#	-.10	.04	.33
Obedience and respect	.17	.26	-.13	.19	-.29	-.22	.04	.29
Authoritative style								
Induction	.24	-.03	.01	-.43*	.08	.23	.10	.02
Authoritative	-.12	.18	.03	-.33	.31#	.27	.04	-.13
Child influence	.03	.22	.15	-.14	.13	.24	.19	-.18
Child thinking for self	-.17	-.09	-.26	-.56**	.15	.41#	-.05	-.19
Goals								
Kind and good	-.11	.35	.02	.06	.36*	-.07	-.37*	.08
Household tasks	-.08	-.24	-.06	-.05	-.09	.20	.11	-.14

[a] High scores indicate external control; low scores indicate internal control.

# p < .10; * p < .05; ** p < .01.

It is interesting, also, to note that the maternal goal of *kind and good* was significantly related for boys to both positive assertiveness and internal sense of control. Kind and good was a goal selected more by the employed mothers for boys.

Summary of the Links Connecting the Mother's Employment Status, Parenting, and Children's Independence and Assertiveness. The data presented here lend support to the idea that the control techniques favored by employed mothers – less use of authoritarian controls and more use of authoritative techniques – are associated with less shy and more assertive behaviors in children and to a more internal sense of personal control. In two-parent families, employed mothers also stressed the goal of independence for their daughters, and this was associated with less shyness in daughters. In addition, they were less likely to hold obedience as a goal, and obedience was associated with shyness, less assertiveness, and, at the trend level, with a less internal sense of personal control for daughters. Finally, the goal of femininity for daughters, also shunned by the married, employed mothers, was related to less positive assertiveness. The goal of rearing children to be "kind and good" was chosen more by full-time homemakers for daughters but less than employed mothers for sons in both one-parent and two-parent families. The only significant relationships to child outcomes, however, were for boys in single-mother families where it related to more positive assertiveness and a more internal sense of personal control.

Mediated Relationships From Maternal Employment, Through Childrearing, To Child Outcomes

Overall, the style of authoritative parenting, used more by employed mothers, was found to relate to children's social and cognitive competence. In contrast, the authoritarian style of parenting, which was more often used by nonemployed mothers, was found to relate to decreased child social and cognitive competence. These findings are suggestive of a pathway whereby childrearing practices are the link connecting maternal employment to child outcomes. This model is shown in Figure 10.1.

In order to test this mediational model, instances were selected where there existed (1) a significant relationship between maternal employment and child outcomes, as suggested in Chapter 7 (and as replicated with the smaller sample of interviewed mothers, using a two-category code of employed/not employed); and (2) a significant relationship between mater-

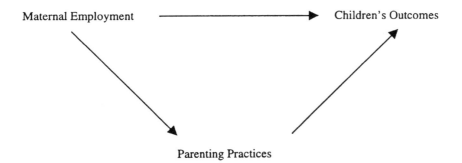

Figure 10.1. Mediated model of the effect of maternal employment on child outcomes.

nal employment and childrearing, as shown in Chapter 6. These first two criteria were required in order to test for mediation, according to Baron and Kenny's (1986) criteria (see Chapter 4). Mediations which were successful are described in this section. All variables that met these criteria were examined to see if the parenting variable mediated the relationship between the mother's employment status and the child outcome.

Maternal Employment, Educational Expectations, and Language Scores. The first mediation is shown in Figure 10.2. Specifically, for married mothers, direct links were found between maternal employment and children's language test scores, and between maternal employment and mothers' educational expectations. Children with employed mothers in two-parent families scored higher on language tests ($M = 63.59$) than children with nonemployed mothers ($M = 55.39$), and employed mothers had higher educational expectations for children. When language test scores were regressed simultaneously on both maternal employment and educational expectations, with child gender and social class controlled, the previous significant link between maternal employment and language scores became nonsignificant, and educational expectations emerged as a significant predictor ($F[4, 192] = 12.68$, $p < .001$), indicating mediation. The interpretation of this mediation is that the higher educational expectations held by employed mothers leads to children's higher test scores.

However, an alternate interpretation of this mediation is possible. Specifically, it could be the case that when children perform better academically, mothers' educational expectations are raised. Mothers may be more likely to work if they expect to pay for children's college education than if they do not. In order to test the viability of this alternative explanation, a

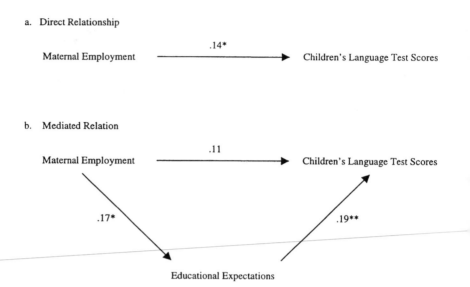

a. Direct Relationship

Maternal Employment   ——— .14* ———>   Children's Language Test Scores

b. Mediated Relation

Maternal Employment   ——— .11 ———>   Children's Language Test Scores

.17*   .19**

Educational Expectations

Figure 10.2. Mediation of the link between maternal employment, parental educational expectations, and children's language test scores, for children with married mothers, with social class and child gender controlled. * $p < .05$; ** $p < .01$.

separate regression equation was tested, in which mothers' educational expectations were regressed simultaneously on both maternal employment and language test scores, controlling for child gender and social class. In this equation, both maternal employment (beta = .14, $p < .05$) and language test scores (beta = .20, $p < .01$) emerged as significant predictors of educational expectations ($F[4,192] = 9.42$, $p < .001$). Although the link from maternal employment to educational expectations was attenuated, partial mediation was not evident, according to Sobel's t-test ($t = 1.61$, n.s.). Therefore, maternal employment seems to account for variation in educational expectations that is *not* explained by variation in language test scores. These results are, overall, consistent with the earlier interpretation: higher educational expectations, held by employed mothers, lead to higher language test scores.

Maternal Employment, Authoritarian Control, and Acting-out Behavior. For girls with married, working-class mothers, a significant relationship was found between maternal employment and teacher ratings of acting-out behaviors, with daughters of employed mothers acting out less ($M = 7.73$) than daughters of full-time homemakers ($M = 10.46$).

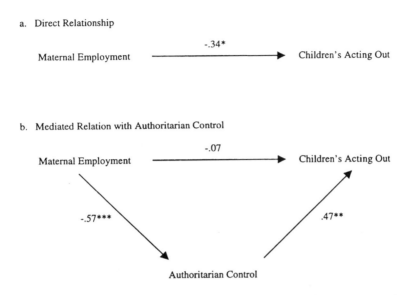

Figure 10.3. Mediation of the link between maternal employment, parental use of authoritarian control, and teacher ratings of acting-out behaviors, for working-class girls with married mothers. * $p < .05$; ** $p < .01$; *** $p < .001$.

Employed mothers were also found to use less authoritarian discipline styles, and authoritarian control was tested as a potential mediator of this link between maternal employment and acting out, as shown in Figure 10.3. When children's acting-out behavior was regressed simultaneously on maternal employment and authoritarian control, authoritarian control emerged as a significant predictor ($F[2,40] = 7.19$, $p < .01$), but maternal employment did not, suggesting a mediated relationship. The results support the hypothesis that less use of the authoritarian discipline style by employed mothers mediates the relationship between maternal employment and lower acting-out scores by daughters in the working class. This mediated pattern of relationships was also found to hold when the subcomponents of authoritarian control, demanding obedience and respect ($F[2,40] = 6.01$, $p < .01$) and using physical punishment ($F[2,40] = 5.04$, $p < .05$) were tested in separate equations, as shown in Figure 10.4.

Maternal Employment, Overt Affection, and Acting-out Behavior. In addition, for girls with married, working-class mothers, employed mothers showed more overt affection than nonemployed mothers, and so maternal displays of affection were tested as an additional mediator of the link from

A. Mediation of the Link Between Maternal Employment, Parental Use of Demanding Obedience and Respect, and Teacher Ratings of Acting Out Behaviors, for Working-Class Girls with Married Mothers

a. Direct Relationship

b. Mediated Relation with Obedience and Respect

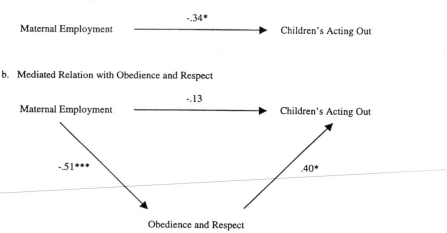

B. Mediation of the Link Between Maternal Employment, Parental Use of Physical Punishment, and Teacher Ratings of Acting Out Behaviors, for Working-Class Girls with Married Mothers

a. Direct Relationship

b. Mediated Relation with Physical Punishment

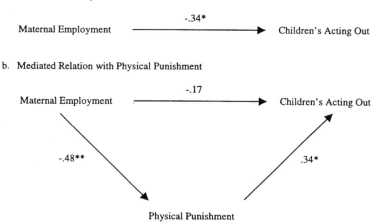

Figure 10.4. Mediation of link between maternal employment and children's acting-out behaviors by obedience and respect and physical punishment. * $p < .05$; ** $p < .01$; *** $p < .001$.

maternal employment to acting-out behaviors. As shown in Figure 10.5, when children's acting-out behavior was regressed on both maternal employment and maternal displays of affection, displays of affection emerged as a significant predictor ($F[2,39] = 5.76$, $p < .01$), but maternal employment did not, again suggesting a mediated relationship. More overt displays of affection by employed mothers might, thus, also lead to decreased acting-out behaviors for working-class girls with married mothers.

Maternal Employment, Control Styles, Talking, and Reading Scores in Single-Mother Families. For single mothers, a significant relationship existed between maternal employment and children's reading test scores, with employed mothers' children scoring higher ($M = 48.29$ versus $M = 40.84$). Employed, single mothers were also found to use less authoritarian control, to demand obedience and respect less, to encourage the child to think for self more, and to engage in more talk interactions with the child. Each of these four childrearing variables was tested as a potential mediator of the link from maternal employment to children's reading test scores, in separate equations, with child gender controlled. All four of these child-

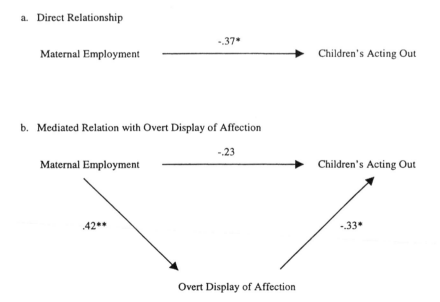

Figure 10.5. Mediation of the link between maternal employment, maternal display of affection, and teacher ratings of acting-out behaviors, for working-class girls with married mothers. * $p < .05$; ** $p < .01$.

rearing variables: authoritarian control, shown in Figure 10.6A ($F[3,49] = 4.67$, $p < .01$), obedience and respect, shown in Figure 10.6B ($F[3,49] = 4.84$, $p < .01$), encouraging child to think for self, depicted in Figure 10.7A ($F[3,49] = 4.85$, $p < .01$), and mother–child talk activities, shown in Figure 10.7B ($F[3,49] = 6.94$, $p < .001$), emerged as viable mediators. These results are consistent with the interpretation that employed mothers use a style of discipline characterized as low in authoritarian control and demands for obedience and respect, but high in encouraging children's thinking for themselves and in mother–child talk, and this discipline style leads to children's increased academic achievement, as shown on reading tests.

Summary of the Mediation Analyses. The results reported in this chapter indicated a considerable number of chains by which the mother's employment status was linked to parenting styles and these styles were, in turn, linked to child outcomes. Such linkages suggest that the parenting effect at least increases the likelihood of the child outcome. In this section, we have tried to identify instances of direct mediation where the relationship between the mother's employment status and the child outcome is carried by the particular parenting variable and would not exist without it. Several such mediations were demonstrated.

The tests for mediation provided support for the following:

1. The relationship between maternal employment and higher scores on language tests in two-parent families is mediated by the higher educational expectations of the employed mothers.
2. The relationship between maternal employment and less acting-out behavior by daughters in two-parent, working-class families is mediated by less use of authoritarian control by employed mothers.
3. The relationship between maternal employment and less acting out by daughters in two-parent, working-class families is also mediated by the higher level of overt affection expressed by employed mothers.
4. The relationship between maternal employment and children's reading test scores in single-mother families is mediated by the employed mothers' lower use of authoritarian control, their greater encouragement of children's "thinking for themselves," and their more frequent engagement in conversations with their children.

A. Mediation of the Link Between Maternal Employment, Parental Use of Authoritarian Control, and Children's Reading Test Scores, for Children with Single Mothers, with Child Gender Controlled

a. Direct Relationship

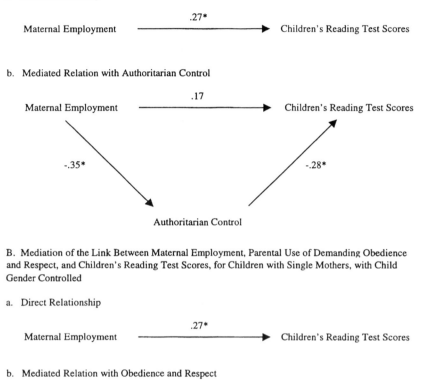

b. Mediated Relation with Authoritarian Control

B. Mediation of the Link Between Maternal Employment, Parental Use of Demanding Obedience and Respect, and Children's Reading Test Scores, for Children with Single Mothers, with Child Gender Controlled

a. Direct Relationship

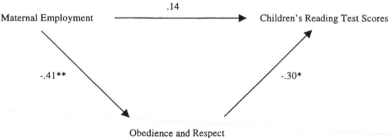

b. Mediated Relation with Obedience and Respect

Figure 10.6. Mediation of link between maternal employment and children's reading test scores by authoritarian control and obedience and respect. $* p < .05; ** p < .01$.

A. Mediation of the Link Between Maternal Employment, Parental Use of Encouraging Child to Think for Self, and Children's Reading Test Scores, for Children with Single Mothers, with Child Gender Controlled

a. Direct Relationship

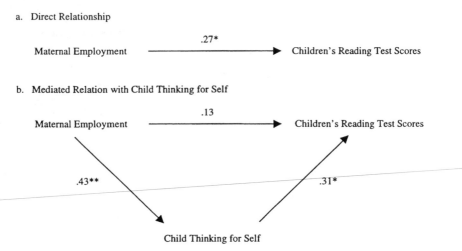

b. Mediated Relation with Child Thinking for Self

B. Mediation of the Link Between Maternal Employment, Mother's Report of Mother-Child Talk Activities, and Children's Reading Test Scores, for Children with Single Mothers, with Child Gender Controlled

a. Direct Relationship

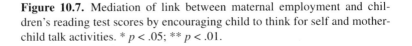

b. Mediated Relation with Mother's Report of Talking with Child

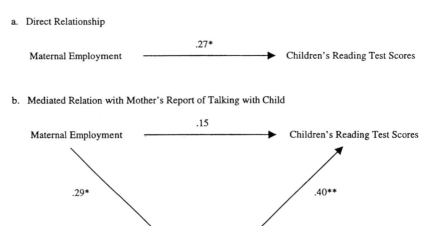

Figure 10.7. Mediation of link between maternal employment and children's reading test scores by encouraging child to think for self and mother-child talk activities. * $p < .05$; ** $p < .01$.

Chapter Summary

In this chapter, the parenting variables that were found to be related to the mother's employment status in the analyses reported in Chapter 6 were examined for their relationship to child outcome measures. Selected child outcome variables were used to tap the child's social adjustment, cognitive competence, and independence and assertiveness. Measures of the mother's discipline and control styles were used for each of the three child outcome domains, but the other parenting measures were examined only for the particularly relevant domain.

Social Adjustment

In general, full-time homemakers indicated a more authoritarian style of control, and this pattern was associated with various social adjustment problems, such as acting-out behavior, being disliked by peers, and less adequate social skills. However, whereas the authoritarian style of homemakers held across marital status and child gender, these child outcomes were found for both boys and girls in one-parent families and girls in two-parent families, but not for boys in two-parent families. In married, working-class families, higher permissiveness was also used by full-time homemakers, and this predicted social adjustment problems for their sons. Only in single-mother families was authoritative discipline related to mothers' employment status. It was used more by the employed mothers and was positively related to social adjustment for both boys and girls. On the whole, the discipline and control styles used by employed mothers were the ones associated with a higher level of social adjustment and competence. However, the pattern of advantages seemed more pronounced in the working class, in both one-parent and two-parent families, than in the married, middle-class families.

Employed mothers also indicated a higher level of overt affection across social class and marital status. This was related to less acting out by working-class girls in two-parent families and to better peer skills for children in one-parent families.

The results of this analysis suggested a number of paths by which maternal employment is linked to more positive social adjustment through less coercive control styles and higher levels of overt affection, particularly in working-class families. This was specifically demonstrated in mediational analyses, which found that the lower level of acting-out behavior by the daughters of employed mothers in two-parent, working-class families was mediated by less reliance on authoritarian controls and the higher level of overt affection manifested by the employed mothers.

Cognitive Competence

The results of the analyses focused on cognitive competence yielded a fairly consistent picture, linking the employed mother's lesser reliance on authoritarian discipline to higher scores on the achievement tests, and to more effective learning patterns as rated by teachers. However, these relationships are notably stronger in one-parent families.

In addition, other paths emerged that were specific for one-parent or two-parent families. Thus, although higher levels of interaction between the working-class, employed mother and her child were found across marital status, this was significantly tied to children's academic competence only in the single-mother families. It may be that interaction with mothers is more crucial when there is no father in the household to fill in. On the other hand, only in two-parent families did the employed mothers hold higher educational expectations for their children than the full-time homemakers, possibly reflecting the particular advantage of the dual incomes. Higher educational expectations, in turn, were related to higher scores on the achievement tests. For the language tests in particular, the mediational analyses indicated that the higher educational expectations mediated the relationship between maternal employment and children's higher test scores. However, the higher reading scores obtained by children in single employed-mother families were found to be mediated by their mothers' lesser reliance on authoritarian controls, stronger support for children's "thinking for themselves", and their more frequently spending time "just talking" with their children.

Independence and Assertiveness

Four measures were used to tap the child's independence and positive assertiveness. These included two measures of shyness, a peer rating of who is shy and a teacher rating of shy and anxious behavior; a teacher rating of positive assertiveness (e.g., defends own views, comfortable as a leader, expresses ideas, questions rules that seem unfair or unclear); and a measure based on children's reports of whether they feel their own behavior affects what happens to them or whether personal outcomes are out of their control. Prevailing hypotheses in the literature have suggested that the mother's employment encourages independence and assertiveness, particularly in daughters.

The results of the analyses indicated that the control styles used by employed mothers, less use of authoritarian methods and more use of authoritative patterns, were associated with less shy and more positive assertive behaviors in children and a more internal sense of control. In addition, employed, married mothers were less likely to indicate that obedience was an important goal for them in childrearing, and, for daughters, obedience as a goal was associated with both measures of shyness, less positive assertiveness, and, at the trend level, with a sense of external, rather than internal, control. In addition, the goal of independence was more often cited by the married, employed mothers of girls and this was also related to less shyness. Finally, the goal of femininity, which was less often cited by the married, employed mothers, was associated with less positive assertiveness.

This chapter, in combination with Chapter 6, has provided considerable evidence for a link between maternal employment and parenting styles which, in turn, are related to children's social and cognitive competence and to more positive assertiveness and a stronger sense of independence. In some cases, results were stronger for some subgroups than others, but the positive direction of the paths from maternal employment through parenting to children's social and academic competence was consistent. There was little evidence here for a link between employment and negative outcomes.

11   Nonmaternal Care and Supervision: Prevalence and Effects of Child-care Arrangements on Child Well-being*

In this chapter, we turn from our concentration on maternal employment in the study sample to consider the related issues of child care and child supervision, with a focus both on national trends and findings of large, nationally representative studies and on results from our sample of families.

As outside employment becomes the norm for mothers of children of all ages in the United States, more and more families must find alternative care for their children. Considering that the majority of children will receive substantial care by adults other than their parents during their formative years before beginning elementary school, it is rather surprising how relatively little attention is given in our society to child care. Not only is research on the prevalence and effects of child care on children not as extensive as many other areas of literature on child development, but in the United States, government support for children of working parents lags far behind that of most other industrialized nations (Chilman, 1993). Very little financial help is available for families above the poverty line, either in the form of family subsidies or government-sponsored child-care centers, and regulations regarding child-care quality vary greatly between states and overall are much less stringent than both regulations in other areas of public health in the United States and child-care regulations in other countries (Chilman, 1993).

In this chapter we focus on three main issues related to child care and maternal employment: the prevalence of families' use of various types of nonmaternal care; the effects of such care on child functioning within emotional, social, and cognitive realms; and the related issue of supervision and monitoring of school-age children. We describe the variety of nonmaternal care choices, which include care by fathers or other relatives, by babysitters or friends, or care in home day cares or professional day-care centers, and

* This chapter was written by Rebekah Levine Coley.

256

consider whether child and family characteristics influence parents' choice of type of care. We then consider how nonmaternal care influences children; whether infant day-care is as detrimental as many people believe, and whether there are consistent findings regarding effects of different types of care on child development. Finally, as we consider child-care issues for school-age children, we turn our focus from various types of adult care to self care, addressing the issue of children who are left unsupervised by adults. In each of these areas, we first summarize existing literature, and then detail how our sample of families fits into the national trends and how our data can add to the growing information regarding this important aspect of child and family functioning.

Children's Experiences with Nonmaternal Care in the United States

Patterns of Nonmaternal Care in the United States

As more mothers of young children in the United States go to work, their children are in greater need of nonmaternal care. Estimates vary, but concur that the majority of American children will experience regular and substantial nonparental care before they reach school age (West, Wright, & Hausken, 1995). The greatest recent change in the use of nonmaternal child care has been among infants under 1 year of age. National data indicate that in 1995, 1.87 million infants under age 1 were in need of alternate care while their mothers worked (U.S. Department of Education, 1995). National studies of child care conducted in the early 1990s found that about half of infants receive regular nonparental care in their first year of life (Hofferth, Brayfield, Deich, & Holcomb, 1991; U.S. Department of Education, 1995).

Another major study, the National Institute of Child Health and Human Development Early Child Care Study, found even higher rates of infant child care. This extensive project has followed more than 1200 infants in ten sites across the nation from birth to age three to generate detailed information on the use, quality, and effects of nonmaternal care on children in the first years of life (NICHD Early Child Care Network, 1994). The NICHD Early Child Care Study sample is not nationally representative. It includes a higher proportion of employed mothers (66 percent in the first year after birth, compared with 59 percent nationally), and higher socioeconomic status than the country as a whole. Nevertheless, this work contributes substantially to the rather sparse base of knowledge concerning child-care trends among American children, presenting an unprecedented detailed look at infant and toddler care.

All told, this project has found a substantial amount of nonmaternal care (NICHD, 1997d). In this sample, 82 percent of the infants experienced regular care by someone other than their mothers during their first year, 72 percent by a nonparent. These children began nonmaternal care at an early age and experienced substantial time in these care situations: almost three out of four infants (72 percent) entered nonmaternal care before the age of four months, for an average of almost thirty hours per week. Finally, the instability of care was also substantial, especially for children of mothers with variable or nondaytime work hours: more than one-third of infants in nonmaternal care experienced three or more different care arrangements in their first year of life. Although public rhetoric often claims that parents, especially mothers, should provide the majority of care for their infants during the first year of life, these data show this to be a relatively rare occurrence.

Who is caring for these young children? In the NICHD study (1997a), at the initiation of nonmaternal care about one-fifth of infants were cared for by fathers or partners of the mother (21 percent), one-fifth by other relatives (19 percent), and one-fifth in a child-care home (20 percent). One in ten children received care in a child-care center (10 percent) or by a nonrelative babysitter (10 percent). Other data indicate that the use of professional day-care centers tends to increase with age, while reliance on child-care homes and relative care decreases (U.S. Bureau of the Census, 1987). For example, the National Child Care Survey found that 20 percent of infants and toddlers of employed mothers were cared for in child-care centers, 22 percent in child-care homes, and 21percent by nonparental relatives (comparable figures were 5 percent, 3 percent, and 13 percent respectively, for children of nonemployed mothers). During the preschool years, the use of centers doubled to 43 percent, while the use of child-care homes and relatives both fell to 17 percent and 16 percent, respectively (30 percent, 1 percent, and 8 percent for children of nonemployed mothers; Willer, Hofferth, Kisker, Divine-Hawkins, Farquhar, & Glantz, 1991).

For school-age children, patterns of care again change. The majority of school-age children either receive no nonparental care (44 percent of children of employed mothers and 72 percent of children of nonemployed mothers) or are cared for by relatives during nonschool hours when their parents are not available (25 percent and 15 percent of children of employed and nonemployed mothers, respectively). Relatively few attend child-care centers (14 percent and 6 percent), child-care homes (7 percent and 1 percent), or have regular in-home care (3 percent and 2 percent; Willer et al., 1991).

Predictors of Use of Nonmaternal Care. Numerous family and structural characteristics have been found to affect families' choices concerning their children's care. Maternal employment is possibly the greatest contributing factor, with children of employed mothers twice as likely to receive non-parental or nonmaternal care as children of nonemployed mothers (70 percent versus 35 percent for children under age five in the National Child Care Study, and 99 percent versus 58 percent for children in the NICHD Early Child Care Study; Hofferth et al., 1991; NICHD, 1997a). The amount and schedule of mothers' work hours also matter. For example, children of full-time employed mothers are almost twice as likely to be cared for in out-of-home settings as children of part-time employed mothers (49 percent versus 24 percent for infants in the NICHD study; 42 percent versus 24 percent for preschoolers in national data; Hayes, Palmer, & Zaslow, 1990; NICHD, 1997a). Conversely, father care is more than twice as prevalent for children of part-time employed mothers than for full-time (35 percent versus 17 percent in NICHD study; 24 percent versus 11 percent in national data; Hayes et al., 1990; NICHD, 1997a).

Family income also plays a large role in determining access to, and type of, nonmaternal care, although this relationship is not simple and linear. Rising government subsidies of child-care centers for poor children have led to a curvilinear relationship, with poor parents who have access to subsidies, and wealthier parents with financial resources, showing higher use of the more costly center-based care, while middle-income families more often access less formal and more affordable situations such as day-care homes and relatives (Hofferth, West, & Henke, 1994; Phillips, Voran, Kisker, Howes, & Whitebrook, 1994).

In addition to employment and income, other family characteristics have been shown to influence child-care choices. Maternal education shows effects separate from the influence of income, although at the high levels these two variables function similarly, with more educated mothers with greater financial resources more likely to choose in-home, nonrelative care for infants and center-based care for preschoolers (NICHD, 1997a). The availability of fathers and other relatives either in the home or close by largely determines their use as alternate caregivers. For example, only 2 percent of preschool children of unmarried mothers are cared for by fathers while mothers work, as compared to 19 percent of children of married mothers. The former group, however, are much more likely to receive care from grandparents (16 percent versus 3 percent; Bureau of the Census, 1987). Race and ethnicity are also influential, although like socioeconomic status, not in a simple manner. Numerous hypotheses have been suggested to explain racial and ethnic differences in parental choices of child-care settings, including income and maternal employment differences, parenting practices, and language issues (Fuller, Holloway & Liang, 1996). Parents' childrearing beliefs and attitudes also seem influential, with parents who place greater emphasis on educational activities more likely to choose center-based care than other types for preschool-age children. Finally, as already noted, child age is important, with center care much more prevalent among preschoolers than infants and toddlers (Hofferth et al., 1991).

Effects of Nonmaternal Care on Children

Effects of Care During Infancy, Toddlerhood, and Preschool Years

Due to the great prevalence of nonmaternal care experiences for young children, a pressing question concerns what effects such experiences have on children's emotional, social, and cognitive development. Some studies from the 1980s found links between early and extensive nonmaternal child care and attachment security. If the child had 20 or more hours of care per week during the first year, there was a greater likelihood of insecure attachment between baby and mother as measured by the Ainsworth Strange Situation task (Ainsworth & Wittig, 1969; Belsky & Rovine, 1988; Clarke-Stewart, 1989; Lamb & Sternberg, 1990). These findings were taken as support for the claims that regular and substantial separations between mothers and babies led to feelings of rejection by babies, lowered abilities of mothers to respond sensitively to their infants, and caused emotional difficulties in children (Barglow, Vaughn, & Molitor, 1987; Brazelton, 1985; Owen & Cox, 1988). However, numerous arguments have called into question the validity of these results for current cohorts of infants and mothers. For example, Clarke-Stewart (1989) suggests that the Strange Situation task might not be appropriate for children used to being left in day care by their mothers each day. In addition, as the proportion of working mothers of infants has increased, both maternal, societal, and day-care provider attitudes and behaviors surrounding infant care may have changed, thus affecting the influence of day-care experience on mother–child attachment (NICHD, 1997b).

The NICHD Early Child Care Study provides an up-to-date look at this issue. This study found no direct effects of child care, either time of entry, amount of care, quality, stability or type of care, on infant–mother attachment (NICHD, 1997b). Rather, maternal sensitivity and psychological adjustment were significant predictors of infant attachment. Child care did play a role in interacting with maternal behaviors, however, since poor quality care, significant amounts of care, and unstable care situations all appeared to increase the negative effects of low maternal responsiveness on child attachment. Finally, the Strange Situation procedure, as used in this study, did appear to produce valid and reliable attachment ratings for children with substantial child-care experience (NICHD, 1997b).

Findings regarding other measures of socioemotional adjustment also provide a complicated story of the effects of day care on children. Although some studies have indicated that children who begin day care as infants tend to be more aggressive with peers and less compliant with parents than at-home babies, as great a number of other studies fail to find this difference (see Clarke-Stewart, 1989, for a review). In addition, these same children, those with early day-care experience, also tend to be more independent, persistent, and self-confident than comparison children; thus, Clarke-Stewart (1989) argues that day-care babies are more experienced in peer group interactions than children reared at home who have few competitors for toys and attention.

With respect to children's cognitive development, much of the data in this area come from studies on the effects of early enrichment programs for disadvantaged children. Such programs, like Head Start, have consistently been found to predict higher IQ scores and better cognitive functioning for poor and minority children exposed during infancy, toddler, or preschool years (see Bryant & Ramey, 1987; Haskins, 1989, for reviews). However, less attention has been given to more typical child-care settings, especially to home-based child care and care in children's own homes. As the intervention research implies, the socioeconomic status of the child appears to be an important moderator of the influence of child care on cognitive development. In general, it is thought that for children from impoverished families, high-quality child care might provide stimulation and learning opportunities superior to those available at home, thus leading to improvements in cognitive functioning (Desai, Chase-Lansdale, & Michael, 1989). Research has generally born out this assumption, finding improved cognitive scores for low-income children in alternate care situations versus those in home care (e.g., Caughy, DiPietro, & Strobino, 1994), especially for those beginning care early, during infancy and toddlerhood, and for children accessing center-based care. For children from more advantaged home environments, however, results are less consistent, although the most recent and extensive data, from the new NICHD study, find no differences in cognitive outcomes related to early nonmaternal care (NICHD Early Child Care Research Network, 1997c; also see Hayes et al., 1990, for a review).

In addition to a greater focus on moderators of the effects of day care on child development, recent research is also assessing the influence of the stability and general quality of care. The stability and type of care are important in determining its effects, with high stability, low child–adult ratios, smaller group sizes, and safe, child-friendly environments all linked to higher quality care (NICHD Early Child Care Research Network, 1996). Quality of care, in turn, has shown relationships to children's social, emotional, and cognitive development, both concurrently and longitudinally, although the effect sizes are quite small (Hayes et al., 1990; NICHD Early Child Care Research Network, 1997c).

Effects of Nonmaternal Care for School-age Children

Once children begin formal schooling, their needs for alternative care tend to shift. Most often, school-age children need nonmaternal or nonparental care only a few hours a day, after and possibly before school. Consideration of the effects of different types of nonmaternal care on school-age children has received much less attention than consideration of effects for younger children. In general, studies in this area have compared the functioning of children in different types of after-school care, including formal after-school programs, informal care, mother care, and self care (Galambos & Maggs, 1991; Posner & Vandell, 1994; Rodman, Pratto, & Nelson, 1985; Vandell & Corasaniti, 1988). Like the influences of infant and preschool care, effects of different types of after-school care on school-age children appear to be moderated by the social class of the child. For example, participation in formal after-school programs has been linked to better academic and behavioral functioning for urban, low-income children (Posner & Vandell, 1994), but to worse academic functioning and more negative peer nominations for suburban, middle-class children (Vandell & Corasaniti, 1988). Little attention has been paid to the effects of the amount or quality of care, although one study indicates that the positive effects of formal programs on low-income children's cognitive and behavioral functioning may stem from increased opportunities to participate in academic activities, more time with adults and peers, and less time watching television (Posner & Vandell, 1994). A substantial body of research has focused more directly on latchkey children; that is, children unsupervised by adults (Coley & Hoffman, 1996; Rodman, Pratto, & Nelson, 1985; Vandell & Ramanan, 1991; Woods, 1972). This work will be discussed in detail in this chapter. Overall, many questions remain concerning the effects of nonmaternal care experiences on school-age children.

Use and Influence of Nonmaternal Care in the Current Sample

We now turn to a consideration of early nonmaternal child-care experiences among our sample of children.

Children's Experiences with Nonmaternal Care

Patterns of Nonmaternal Care Among the Study Sample. How do the patterns of child care in the study sample compare to the national trends already presented? Mothers in the home interview reported information on study children's nonmaternal care experiences throughout their lifetimes. To analyze these data, we used four child-age groups and five types of care. Table 11.1 presents the percent of children in each type of care at each age. The four age groups are: infants, which include children from birth to their first birthday; toddlers, children between 1 and 3 years; preschoolers, children 3 to 5 years, and school-age children, age 5 years and older. For each of these age periods, mothers reported their child's most frequent nonmaternal care experience, as well as additional nonmaternal care situations used during that period. It is important to note that only mothers who were employed in each time period reported on nonmaternal care. These care situations were then compressed into five types of care. Mother care includes children who go to work with their mothers, or whose mothers work at home. Father care includes mainly biological fathers, but during the later years includes stepfathers as well. Relative care includes all other relatives who care for the children, either in the child's home or in the home of the

Table 11.1. *Patterns of Nonmaternal Care Among the Employed Mothers in the Study Sample*

Type of Child Care	Infancy (Birth to Age 1)	Toddlerhood (Ages 1 to 3)	Preschool (Ages 3 to 5)	School-age (Ages 5 and up)
Mother	3	3	5	7
Father	25	22	19	26
Relative	33	28	24	27
Friend/Sitter	29	26	18	19
Day Care	10	22	35	22
N	167	205	233	274

Note. Numbers represent the percentage of children in each type of care for each age group. Columns may not add to 100 percent due to rounding error.

relative. Similarly, friends (who in later years also include a few maternal partners who are not biological fathers of the children) and babysitters may also provide care either in their own homes or the home of the child. Finally, day-care centers include professional centers, home-based day-care centers, and, for school-age children, before-and after-school programs.

When considering these statistics, it is important to keep in mind the proportion of the mothers who were employed in each of these time periods, and thus, the proportion of the sample from which these statistics are drawn. As expected, this proportion increased substantially with the age of the child. During infancy, just under half of the interviewed mothers (46 percent) were employed and thus reported about alternate care. This rose to over half (55 percent) during toddlerhood, almost two-thirds (63 percent) during preschool, and three-quarters (75 percent) during school years. Table 11.1 shows that, as expected, during all time periods, the vast majority of children of employed mothers experienced regular nonmaternal care. The use of different types of care changes only slightly over the development of the child. More specifically, during infancy relative care is the most popular choice, used by one-third of children, followed by friend/sitter and father care, about one-quarter each, and finally, day-care centers, attended by only one in ten children. The use of day-care centers increases after infancy, so that in both the toddler and school age periods, fathers, relatives, friends/sitters, and day-care centers are all chosen in relatively equal amounts. During the preschool period, however, when children still need extensive care and parents are often concerned about their children's preparation for formal schooling, the use of day care increases to over one-third of the group. These results parallel those found in the NICHD child-care study, indicating that mothers seem to choose relatively equally among other individuals such as fathers, other relatives, and babysitters to provide care for their children, while the choice of more formal settings peaks during the preschool years.

Predictors of Use of Nonmaternal Care Among the Current Sample

The previous description implies that child age and developmental level affects mothers' choices of child-care setting and type. What other factors might influence this choice? Here we consider the influence of mothers' hours of employment, child gender, and ethnicity.

First, we address whether mothers' work hours, or more specifically part-time versus full-time work, influences child-care decisions. Table 11.2 presents the results of a cross tabulation between children's primary-care

Table 11.2. *Relations Between Maternal Work Patterns and Use of Nonmaternal Care Among the Employed Mothers in the Study Sample*

Type of Child Care	Infancy Maternal Employment		Toddlerhood Maternal Employment		Preschool Maternal Employment		School-age Maternal Employment	
	Part-Time	Full-Time	Part-Time	Full-Time	Part-Time	Full-Time	Part-Time	Full-Time
Mother	5	1	6	0	9	2	12	2
Father	29	21	27	17	27	13	36	16
Relative	37	29	32	24	25	23	21	32
Friend/Sitter	25	34	20	31	16	20	16	22
Day Care	5	16	15	28	24	44	15	29
Chi-square	$9.65(4)\ p < .05$		$16.19(4)\ p < .005$		$19.20(4)\ p < .005$		$28.87(4)\ p < .001$	
N	167		205		233		274	

Note. Numbers represent the percentage of children in each type of care by maternal employment type and age group. Columns may not add to 100 percent due to rounding error.

situation and mothers' employment, coded as part-time for 1 to 34 hours per week and full-time for 35 hours or more. The chi-square statistics are significant for every age period. In general, these results indicate that mothers who work part-time are more likely than expected to manage to care for their children themselves at all times or to employ the more informal care settings of father or relative care, while full-time working mothers are more likely to use friends/sitters or day-care centers. These patterns hold for all age groups with one exception: relative care is utilized more frequently by full-time than part-time employed mothers of school-age children.

Fewer links are seen between children's gender and child-care choices. Only during infancy is this relationship significant (chi-square [4] = 9.90, *p* < .05; data not shown), with boys more likely to be in day care, while girls are more often cared for by mothers or friends/sitters. Few studies have looked for links between child gender and child-care decisions, and the meaning of this new result is unclear. It is possible that families are more likely to see infant boys as active enough to sustain the stresses of day-care centers, whereas they are more likely to want their infant girls in quieter, more one-on-one situations of personal or in-home care. This result underscores the different environmental influences affecting boys and girls from the very beginning of their development.

Families' ethnic background also appears to influence maternal day-care decisions (results shown in Table 11.3). Although results of chi-square statistics with type of child care and ethnicity were not significant during the infancy or preschool periods, for toddlers and school-age children, African-American and White mothers chose different child-care options. Children of African-American mothers were more likely to receive care by relatives, whereas children of White mothers were more frequently cared for by fathers and, for toddlers, in day care. The use of friend/sitter care did not differ substantially by ethnicity. These patterns are consistent with the view that extended family ties are stronger in African-American families (Stack, 1974), and may also reflect the higher marriage rates among Whites.

Effects of Nonmaternal Care Among the Study Sample

As noted, the vast majority of research that has considered effects of child care on child functioning has focused on the infant and preschool years. Relatively little work has considered influences of child care on school-age children, and the work that is available is correlational, considering relations between the type of care and functioning at a single point in time, without taking into account previous experiences. In this study, we

Table 11.3. *Relations between Child Ethnicty and Use of Nonmaternal Care Among the Employed Mothers in the Study Sample*

Type of Child care	Infancy		Toddlerhood		Preschool		School-age	
	White	African American	White	African American	White	African American	White	African American
Mother	4	0	4	0	5	4	8	3
Father	25	23	24	12	20	15	29	13
Relative	30	43	23	49	20	35	22	45
Friend/Sitter	30	29	26	27	17	20	20	17
Day Care	11	6	24	12	37	26	22	22
Chi-square	3.58 (4) n.s.		13.90 (4) $p < .01$		6.56 (4) n.s.		15.66 (4) $p < .005$	
N	167		205		233		274	

Note. Numbers represent the percentage of children in each type of care by race and age group.

are able to assess effects of type of care on school-age children in a more comprehensive and longitudinal nature than most previous research. We do this by using mothers' reports of the predominant type of care their children have been in since the age of five, thus capturing a longer view of children's experiences than a single snapshot in time, and relating this to functioning at ages 8 and 9. Although this measure may not agree with the type of care the child is in at the time of the interview, due to its longitudinal nature it may show effects of type of care that take some time to appear.

To address the relationship between type of care and child functioning, a series of Analyses of Variance (ANOVAs) were run using the predominant type of care the child had been in outside of school hours since the age of 5, including the previously described categories of mother care only, father, relative, friend/sitter, and formal day care, which during school age typically refers to before- and after-school programs. Outcome variables cover a broad range of child functioning, including teacher reports of children's behavioral and academic functioning, peer ratings of children's behaviors, children's reports of their self-efficacy (locus of control), and children's academic achievement scores (see Chapter 2 for descriptions of the child outcome measures). These analyses control for the child's gender, maternal ethnicity and current marital status, and the current socioeconomic status of the family.

Results of these analyses indicate significant links between children's early elementary nonmaternal care experiences and their behavioral and academic functioning in the third and fourth grades. Table 11.4 presents these results for the outcomes in which type of care relates to children's functioning at the $p < .10$ level or better. Classmates rated children who received care from relatives or in formal centers as showing the most aggressive behaviors, and children cared for solely by mothers the least. Conversely, formal center and mother-care children received the lowest ratings for shy behavior by their peers. With respect to academic achievement, children cared for by father and in formal centers scored the highest in reading and math skills, while children cared for by relatives scored the lowest.

Overall, these results do not show extremely strong or wide-ranging effects of out-of-school care experiences on children's classroom and emotional functioning. Numerous measures of children's classroom behavior as rated by teachers, as well as their self-efficacy, were not affected by the type of child care they experienced during the early elementary years. However, the results do point to significant influences of

Table 11.4. *Relations Between Predominant Type of Child Care Since Age 5 and Child Functioning at Ages 8 to 9*

Types of Child Care	Child Functioning Measure			
	Nominations of Hitting	Nominations of Shyness	Reading Skills	Math Skills
Mother	.21	.28	61.06	64.22
Father	.30	.35	63.44	67.80
Relative	.38	.33	52.93	58.45
Friend/Sitter	.30	.35	60.43	60.88
Day Care	.36	.25	64.10	66.49
F	2.57*	2.39#	3.57**	2.65*

Note. Numbers in columns 2–5 represent mean scores for each child-care group.
# $p < .10$, * $p < .05$, ** $p < .01$. All ANOVA models control for children's gender, and maternal ethnicity, marital status, and socioeconomic status.

care experiences, most notably of formal child care and relative care, on children's peer-rated behaviors and academic functioning. Children who have attended formal day care or before-or after-school programs perform very well academically and are socially active, receiving low shyness but high hitting ratings. Children cared for by nonparental relatives, on the other hand, perform poorly in all these areas. The outcomes related to formal day care might be due to such programs' emphasis on group activities and social interactions, and also might reflect many school-age child-care centers' emphasis on academic work with specific time set aside for homework completion. In contrast, the poor functioning of children cared for by relatives may reflect a lack of structured and social activities. Other research has found that children who spend all their nonschool time at home watch substantially more television and take part in fewer peer interactions, outside activities, and academically related activities than children in center-based or other group-based care (Posner & Vandell, 1994). Further research is required to more specifically determine which aspects of such child-care situations are driving these results and to bolster the hypothesized explanations given. In addition, other characteristics of the children's homes and families may be important. Although these analyses controlled for maternal marital and socioeconomic status, these controls may not be adequate for determining the possible influences of other maternal or household characteristics.

Supervision and the Lack of Care

Supervision and Monitoring Research

So far, we have discussed the prevalence and correlates of various types of nonmaternal care from birth through school age, covering both previous research and findings from our sample of children. Now we turn to the related, but distinct, issue of supervision and monitoring of school-age children. Once children reach mid-elementary-school age, concerns with characteristics of child care such as type and quality are largely replaced by another dimension of care: that is, whether any direct supervision is provided or whether children care for themselves, unsupervised by an adult. By elementary school, significant proportions of children are regularly left unsupervised by adults. Data from the mid 1980s indicate that almost one-fifth of school-age children of employed mothers were in self care on a regular basis. Regular self care was far more common for older than younger children, with rates ranging from 25 percent for eleven- to thirteen-year-olds to 5 percent of five- to seven-year-olds (Hayes et al., 1990). The topic of self care has received substantial public attention, with the rather emotional term *latchkey children* used to refer to those who return home from school with a key to let themselves into an empty house to await the return of their parents. Concern has been expressed over the loneliness of such children, over the opportunities a lack of supervision presents for aberrant behaviors such as minor delinquency, and over how inadequate structure and aid surrounding academic pursuits (e.g., too much television and too little homework) might lead to poor academic outcomes.

However, empirical results have failed to provide strong or consistent support for the public concern over latchkey children. More than two decades of research have to date led to inconclusive results regarding the effects of a lack of supervision and monitoring on school-age children or adolescents. No studies have found across-the-board direct negative effects of self-care on child functioning for representative samples of children (e.g., Galambos & Maggs, 1991; Rodman, Pratto & Nelson, 1985; Vandell & Corasaniti, 1988). So is public concern on this issue misguided? Not necessarily. Like the effects of other types of child care, influences of self care appear to be moderated by child and family characteristics. For example, poor children seem more negatively affected by a lack of supervision than children from working- or middle-class homes. One of the earliest published studies on supervision found that poor, urban African-American girls who were regularly unsupervised showed lower cognitive scores than their supervised peers, although there were no differences between the groups in teacher ratings or delinquency records (Woods, 1972). A more recent study found more antisocial behavior among poor, urban self-care children than among either their peers cared for in out-of-home settings, or self-care children from more advantaged families. However, the disadvantage of self care was not apparent for working- and middle-class children in this or other studies (Rodman, Pratto, & Nelson, 1985; Vandell & Ramanan, 1991).

Other research has broadened the view of adult supervision, considering both the location of the child (whether the child is home unsupervised or in a nonhome setting) and monitoring: that is, whether parents actively check up on the child, such as through phone contact, or at least know details of the child's activities during the unsupervised time. Such research has found that children and adolescents who are unsupervised and outside of their own homes tend to spend time with more deviant peers, be more susceptible to negative peer influences, and show higher rates of problem behaviors than children who remain at home in self care or are directly supervised (Galambos & Maggs, 1991; Steinberg, 1986). A lack of parental monitoring has also been linked to lower achievement and higher behavior problems, especially among boys (Crouter, MacDermid, McHale, & Perry-Jenkins, 1990).

Study Children's Experiences of Supervision and Monitoring and Links to Child Functioning

Here we draw the implications from this previous research and develop a model of the effects of supervision and monitoring (considered together in one comprehensive measure) on the behavioral, emotional, and cognitive functioning of children in the study sample, with considerations of moderating effects of child gender, ethnicity, socioeconomic status, and maternal employment status. Based on previous research, it was expected that supervision would not show direct effects on children's functioning, but that a lack of both supervision and distal monitoring would be linked to lower cognitive achievement and higher behavioral problems among children from disadvantaged populations.

For these analyses, we created a new measure of child supervision and monitoring, distinct from the previously discussed measures of child care. Whereas the retrospective data from the maternal interviews reported on children's primary child-care providers, questions about current care focused instead on issues of supervision and monitoring from both mother and child reports. These reports were not parallel, however. Rather, mothers were asked direct questions concerning whether their children were ever left unsupervised, and if so, for how long and whether any distal monitoring practices (such as phone contact) were regularly used. Children, on the other hand, provided information through an extensive narrative time diary format (see Chapter 2), which was coded to provide indices of the level of supervision and monitoring reported by the child. Each maternal and child report was scored on a three-point rating: Supervised, with children who were not regularly left unsupervised; Unsupervised/Monitored, including children who were regularly (once a week or more) unsupervised but were left alone for times of less than one hour or were monitored through phone contact; and Unsupervised/Unmonitored, those who received neither supervision nor monitoring. These ratings from mothers and children were then combined, with the score indicating the least amount of supervision and monitoring used in cases of discrepancy between child and mother reports (29 percent of the cases).

These data indicate that within this sample of third and fourth graders, 62 percent of children are always supervised, 26 percent are regularly unsupervised but monitored, and 12 percent are both unsupervised and unmonitored on a regular basis. Comparisons between subgroups of children reveal that White children are marginally more likely than expected to be unsupervised but monitored and less likely to be supervised; the opposite is true of African-American children. No differences are apparent in supervision status related to child gender, socioeconomic status, or maternal employment, except for the one reported in Chapter 6: In two-parent, working-class families, sons of employed mothers were more likely to be left unsupervised and unmonitored.

In these analyses, socioeconomic status is used as a three-level variable (poor, working class, middle class, as described in Chapter 7) in order to compare these results with previous findings related to supervision among poor children. ANOVAs were run with children's level of supervision and the teacher ratings, peer ratings, self efficacy, and achievement scores, controlling for child gender, race, socioeconomic status, and maternal employment status. Interaction effects between supervision and each of the covariates were also considered. Results are presented in Tables 11.5 through 11.7.

Main Effects of Supervision and Monitoring. Table 11.5 presents results of the main effects of the supervision and monitoring variable on children's behavioral, emotional, and academic functioning. (Only significant findings are presented.) As expected, very few main effects are found. Unsupervised

Table 11.5. *Main Effects of Supervision on Child Functioning*

Children Functioning Measure	Supervision Level			
	Supervised	Unsupervised/ Monitored	Unsupervised/ Unmonitored	F-Value
Learning problems	11.73	10.10	12.05	3.01[#]
Shy and anxious behaviors	9.56	8.34	9.37	2.76[#]
Math achievement	61.28	60.27	68.15	3.15*

Note. Numbers in columns 2–4 represent mean scores for each supervision group.
[#] $p < .10$, * $p < .05$.

but monitored children show marginally lower learning problems and less shy/anxious behaviors as rated by teachers, while the unsupervised and unmonitored group scores the highest in math achievement.

Interaction Effects Between Supervision and Monitoring and Socioeconomic Status. In contrast, when one considers differential influences of supervision and monitoring among subgroups of children, significant patterns emerge. Several significant interaction effects were found between supervision and children's socioeconomic status, shown in Table 11.6. For behavioral outcomes, these results indicate that unsupervised and unmonitored time is especially deleterious for poor children, whereas monitoring is advantageous, and continual supervision falls in the middle. In contrast, for lower-class children supervision and monitoring show a generally linear relation to behavioral functioning, with unsupervised and unmonitored children receiving more negative teacher and peer ratings than their monitored peers, who, in turn, are rated more poorly than the supervised low-income children. For middle-class children, however, a lack of both supervision and monitoring appears to pose no negative influences on behavioral functioning. Cognitive achievement shows similar patterns for poor children, with unsupervised and unmonitored children performing poorly on standardized tests as compared to their peers who are supervised or monitored. For lower-and middle-class children, a lack of supervision and monitoring is not detrimental for school achievement scores. These findings reinforce the claim that a lack of supervision and monitoring is detrimental for poor children, relating to both higher antisocial and lower prosocial behaviors and to lower academic achievement.

Table 11.6. *Interaction Effects Between Supervision and Socioeconomic Status on Child Functioning*

Child Functioning Measure	SES	Supervised	Unsupervised/ Monitored	Unsupervised/ Unmonitored	F-Value
		Supervision Level			
Acting-out behaviors	Poor	14.81	10.80	18.75	3.49**
	Low SES	10.28	11.09	11.47	
	Mid SES	9.18	8.64	8.14	
Peer hitting rating	Poor	.49	.51	.66	2.63*
	Low SES	.38	.38	.43	
	Mid SES	.28	.27	.20	
Peer meanness rating	Poor	.49	.51	.67	2.16#
	Low SES	.42	.40	.41	
	Mid SES	.34	.32	.25	
Overall peer liking	Poor	3.84	4.14	3.56	2.72*
	Low SES	4.10	4.00	3.93	
	Mid SES	3.98	4.18	4.13	
Language achievement	Poor	46.30	50.20	31.00	2.34#
	Low SES	53.70	53.48	65.36	
	Mid SES	67.52	67.54	64.39	
Math achievement	Poor	47.30	42.00	28.25	4.10**
	Low SES	55.42	53.00	69.71	
	Mid SES	71.07	70.72	74.13	

Note. Numbers in columns 3–5 represent mean scores for each supervision × SES group
# $p < .10$; * $p < .05$; ** $p < .01$.

Interaction Effects Between Supervision and Monitoring and Child Gender, Child Ethnicity, and Maternal Employment Status. The results of interactions between supervision and monitoring and the other correlates in the model are much less prevalent and are reported together in Table 11.7. Results differentiated by gender indicate that girls with greater freedom from supervision and monitoring by adults obtain higher math scores, whereas boys show little difference related to supervision level. Regarding ethnicity, White children show the lowest acting out behaviors when they are unsupervised but monitored distally, whereas African-American children in this situation show the highest level of behavior problems. Finally, teacher-rated learning problems are highest for children with employed mothers when they are neither monitored nor supervised, and for children of full-time homemakers when they are continually supervised.

Table 11.7. *Interaction Effects Between Supervision and Child Gender, Child Ethnicity, and Maternal Employment on Child Functioning*

Child Functioning Measure	Child Gender/ Ethnicity/Maternal Employment	Supervision Level			
		Supervised	Unsupervised/ Monitored	Unsupervised/ Unmonitored	*F*-value
Language achievement	Male	52.69	58.22	54.74	3.26*
	Female	64.79	60.94	70.06	
Math achievement	Male	60.74	61.31	63.13	3.34*
	Female	61.79	59.35	74.56	
Acting-out behaviors	White	9.31	8.97	9.73	3.48*
	Af. Am.	13.05	14.00	12.18	
Learning problems	Not Emp.	13.37	10.50	9.00	2.09#
	PT Emp.	10.54	10.28	11.38	
	FT Emp.	11.60	9.77	13.70	

Note. Numbers in columns 3–5 represent mean scores for each supervision × gender group. Af. Am. = African American; PT Emp. = part time employment; FT Emp. = full time employment.
# $p < .10$, * $p < .05$.

Overall, the results concerning supervision and monitoring are complex and intriguing. The socioeconomic interaction findings suggest that mid-elementary-aged children in more enriched environments are not negatively influenced by, and actually may benefit from, freedom from constant adult supervision, while those in less-enriched or impoverished environments show greater behavioral problems and fewer behavioral skills when they lack consistent adult monitoring and feedback. Academic achievement results show similar findings: girls and children from working-and middle-class homes appear to perform very well academically when they are free from direct monitoring and supervision after school, whereas children in poor families once again fare poorly in this scenario. Although the apparent advantage of a lack of supervision and monitoring could simply reflect the parent's judgment of the child's maturity, the findings, nevertheless, highlight concerns over the home environments of children in poor households. They suggest that the lack of safe and stimulating environments and possible low access to prosocial activities such as after-school clubs and sports and academically enriching experiences, present developmental challenges when combined with a lack of a consistent adult presence for impoverished children.

Clearly, these findings point to the need for more attention to be given to disentangling the complex relationships between children's broader family environments and their experiences of adult supervision and care. Future work should focus both on the decision-making processes used by parents in deciding the level of supervision and monitoring to provide for their children (including child maturity, environmental dangers and supports, and work and other demands), as well as on a broader array of characteristics of the children's home and outside environments, which might both influence and be influenced by children's supervisory experiences.

Conclusions

Recent research from both this sample and other studies continues to explore the complex relationships between maternal employment, child-care choices, and child development. The most recent and comprehensive evidence goes against older claims that infant day care is detrimental for children's emotional health and development, although early and extensive care, especially in poor-quality settings, has been found to exacerbate difficulties in the mother–child relationship initiated by less-than-optimal parenting skills (NICHD, 1997b). Recent findings on social and cognitive development also appear reassuring for the most part, with day-care infants and preschoolers showing high levels of independence and social skills, and equal or superior cognitive functioning for most children.

However, families' access to high-quality and affordable infant and preschool care remains a substantial problem in this country, one that is likely to grow with the ever-increasing numbers of mothers seeking employment. This concern is especially relevant regarding more informal child-care arrangements such as relative care and unlicensed home centers, the types of care that show links to poor child functioning in social and cognitive realms. It is expected that the use of these more informal care arrangements will grow substantially in the coming years as large numbers of welfare mothers begin training or employment, raising the need for child care much more quickly than the supply. Overall, much remains to be learned concerning indices of quality of child care, relations among different types of care and child well-being, and interactions between various child and family characteristics and the influence of nonmaternal care on children.

Similarly, research concerning school-age children's supervisory experiences continues to grow and expand, yet much remains unknown. Although recent evidence regarding effects of self care on middle-class children is reassuring, with such children showing no negative influences of a lack of supervision and monitoring, the data regarding poor and lower-class children is cause for significant concern. Children from disadvantaged families, families that typically cannot afford to purchase prosocial and cognitively enriching experiences for their children such as lessons and after-school activities, and who are likely to reside in households and neighborhoods with few child resources, safe places, or supportive role models, are the same children who are negatively affected by a lack of supervision and monitoring. And as more and more impoverished mothers join the work force, the number of poor school-age children in self care is likely to rise. The findings reported here and elsewhere regarding links between self care and behavioral problems and low school achievement for poor children reinforce the need for expanded attention to providing enriching programs and experiences for children outside of school hours.

Together, these findings help expand our understanding of how maternal employment influences families and children through numerous pathways. These data, recounting in statistical terms the real-life challenges that families face providing appropriate care and supervision to children, provide a strong argument for enhancing our society's resources for child-focused centers and programs, for both preschool and school-age children.

12 Summary and Overview

In the first chapter, we presented a broad review of the literature on the effects of maternal employment on families and children. From this we drew several conclusions. First, the link between maternal employment and child outcomes is a distal one. To understand its effects on children, we need to investigate the steps in between. We need to know how maternal employment affects family interaction and the attitudes of the parents and children. We need to understand the process by which effects take place. Further, we concluded that there were three major paths to explore: (1) the role of the father; (2) the mother's sense of well-being; and (3) the patterns of parenting in the family.

To examine these issues, a research project was launched. The sample covered a broad socioeconomic range of families living in an industrialized city in the Midwest. The focus of the investigation was a child in the third or fourth grade of the public schools. The sample size was modest but an extensive volume of data was collected from parents, children, teachers, peers, and school records. The results of this investigation have been reported in the preceding chapters.

Throughout the book, our aim has been to understand how the employment *status* of the mother, whether she is employed or a full-time home-maker, affects the family and children. There is another body of research that investigates effects of different aspects of work – the number of hours of employment, the stress on the job, or specific aspects of the work such as the degree of autonomy or whether the work requires cooperation with others rather than individual initiative (Kohn, 1963; Miller & Swanson, 1958; Hoffman, 1986; Repetti, 1985; Greenberger, O'Neil, & Nagel, 1994). This research is an important part of the full picture, but it is a different focus than the one here. Here we are trying to understand how the simple fact that the mother is in the labor force affects family life and the socialization

278

process. Whether the mother is a plastic surgeon or a worker in a plastics factory is very different in its effects in many ways, but there are also commonalities. The status of being a wage-earner itself, for example, changes the woman's role in the family. It increases her power, alters the gender roles, provides her with an additional role that may buffer or augment family-centered anxieties, increases her social contacts, influences her goals for her children, and changes the way she is perceived. Although the importance of parenting may not be diminished, it seems likely that its centrality in her life is. This does not mean that she is a lesser parent. It may be that the full-time role of homemaker/mother, given our current state of technology and the tendency toward smaller family size, is not sufficient for many mothers' sense of well-being or for effective parenting once the children are school age (Hoffman, 1979).

It is, then, this more general question that has guided our inquiry: How does the fact that the mother is employed or not employed affect families and children? With this approach, we have been attuned to socioeconomic status, marital status, and ethnicity as context variables that may moderate effects, but not to characteristics of the job. We have also avoided the effects of transitional employment and concentrated on the roles themselves by selecting, for most of our analyses, only those women whose employment status has been stable for at least three years.

In the first chapter, we presented a picture of today's social context. We live in a world where most mothers work. It is the norm. It is important to realize that the present social setting is different from what existed in the recent past. The demands of homemaking have lessened, the number of children in families has decreased, gender-role attitudes have changed, individuals' expectations for a satisfying life have altered, marital stability has declined, there are fewer full-time homemakers in the neighborhoods, and the adult goals for which children are being socialized are not the same. These interactive changes have operated to increase the rate of maternal employment and they have also been augmented by the increase in the employment rate. Interactive influences are intrinsic to social change in society and they are intrinsic to changes in the family. In Chapter 4, analyses indicated that a less traditional attitude toward gender-roles may facilitate the entry of the woman into the labor force, but employment itself moves the family toward less traditional gender-role attitudes. Similarly, in society, the very changes that operate to increase the employment rates are also increased by them.

These changes in the social climate are important to keep in mind in considering the effects of maternal employment today. We cannot expect to replicate some of the results of previous studies. For example, previous research has sometimes found a strain in the father–son relationship when lower-class mothers were employed. This was interpreted as a reflection of the idea that in the working class, where gender-role attitudes were more traditional, the mother's employment was seen as a sign of the father's failure as a breadwinner (Hoffman, 1979). There was no indication of this in our study and, in fact, working-class fathers with full-time employed wives reported a slightly higher rate of engagement in father–child "fun" activities, a pattern not replicated in the middle class. This difference in results across the two time periods may reflect a shift in working-class gender attitudes and the greater acceptance of maternal employment as a normative pattern. We also failed to find lower cognitive scores for sons of middle-class, employed mothers, a much-cited result from earlier research. In fact, the most robust result from the examination of direct relationships between employment status and child outcomes was the higher scores on cognitive tests obtained by children of employed mothers, across class, gender, and marital status.

The change in social climate and the switch from the norm of full-time homemaker to the norm of maternal employment also affects what selective factors are operating. Whereas previous research had to consider the special qualities of mothers who entered employment to be certain that the results were not carried by these factors rather than reflecting effects of employment per se; today's research needs to consider the special qualities of the mothers who have elected to stay home. We will return to this point later in this chapter.

Summary of Results

The major results of the analyses are presented in Chapters 4 through 10. In Chapters 4, 5, and 6, we report our findings on the link between maternal employment and the family. Chapter 7 provides a detailed report on the more distal relationships between employment status and child outcomes, and Chapters 8, 9, and 10 trace the connections from the family patterns that are linked to employment status to the child outcomes. A summary of our results follows.

The Father's Role

Previous research has provided considerable evidence that when mothers are employed, fathers become more active in household tasks and child care. This has been suggested as the link between maternal employment and both the less traditional gender-role attitudes of children and indices of higher academic performance, particularly for daughters. Three different routes by which this effect occurs have been suggested:

1. The higher involvement with fathers is cognitively beneficial for children either because of special advantages from interacting with fathers, particularly in math, or because it augments the amount of attention the child receives.

2. A less gender-stereotyped division of roles will lead to more equalitarian attitudes in children either because they observe more equality between their parents or because the parents' own attitudes are affected and this is transmitted to the children. The less stereotyped attitudes will lead to a higher sense of effectiveness in daughters, higher motivation for achievement, and more academic competence for girls.

3. The third hypothesis is related to the second, but it is an alternative or a complementary one and does not involve the father's role. This hypothesis posits that children will have less stereotyped gender roles simply because employed mothers represent a less stereotyped role and a higher level of competence.

Consistent with previous research, our investigation found that fathers in dual-wage families played a more active role than fathers in single-wage families in traditional female household tasks, routine child care, and functional interactive tasks with children, such as taking them to the doctor or on errands. That is, dual-wage fathers took on a higher proportion of the household tasks and child care than did fathers in the single-wage families. They did not, however, report more frequent playful, educational, or affectionate interactions. Thus, there was clear indication of a less traditional role in the dual-wage families, but there was not more father–child interaction in general. Although there was no indication that fathers' involvement increases the overall amount of attention children receive, there was a child-gender effect: single-wage fathers reported fewer interactions with daughters than sons, but the gender of the child was not a factor for the dual-wage fathers.

The data also indicated that in dual-wage families, parents held less gender-based attitudes about the roles of men and women, but gender-based attitudes about expectations and goals for children were not related to mothers' employment status. However, when fathers were more active in household tasks and child care, they also held less gender-based attitudes toward children, and this effect was particularly robust when the mothers were employed.

To tap children's gender-role stereotypes, two measures were used. One measured the extent to which the child thought that women were capable of carrying out activities that are traditionally considered part of men's domain; the other measured the extent to which the child thought men were capable of carrying out activities that are traditionally assigned to women. In two-parent families, both boys and girls with employed mothers were less stereotyped on the latter; but only girls with employed mothers were less stereotyped on the former, the measure of women's competence.

The analyses of the relationship between the father's role and child outcomes provided little support for the first hypothesis. The sheer frequency with which fathers engaged in interaction with their children was not positively related to children's achievement test scores. However, the relative frequency of the father's involvement in child-care activities, that is, the extent to which he shared child care with the mother, was related. When fathers had a larger share of the child care, children's test scores were higher for the whole group, but particularly in the dual-wage families. And there was no indication that father-interaction was more relevant for math scores than for reading and language.

For the second hypothesis, however, there was considerable support. The data indicated that the higher the involvement of the father in household tasks and child care, the less stereotyped were the children about men's competence in the woman's domain. In addition, the higher participation of fathers in child care was also related to the view that women could be competent in men's domain. It was expected that the measure of women's competence in men's domain would be related to test scores and to the child's sense of efficacy for girls, but, in fact, this was the case for both boys and girls.

Two mediation analyses were conducted. One indicated that the significant relationships between the father's participation in child care and daughters' scores on reading and math achievement tests were mediated by the daughters' attitudes about women's competence. The other indicated that the relationships between these attitudes and reading and math scores were partially mediated by the children's sense of efficacy. A path analysis demonstrated the linkage from the mother's employment to the father's greater help with child care, to the daughter's less stereotyped attitudes about women's competence, and from there to a higher sense of efficacy and higher scores on the three academic tests.

Support was also found for the importance of the parents' gender-role attitudes in explaining the employment/child outcome link. When fathers held equalitarian attitudes, either about marital roles or about childrearing, daughters believed that women could be competent in "male" activities. The relationship between parents' attitudes and children's academic test scores, however, held only for middle-class girls. For middle-class girls, both mothers' and fathers' attitudes were related to daughters' stereotypes and test scores. A mediation analysis showed that the relationship between the mother's gender-based childrearing attitudes and daughters' math scores was carried by the daughters' attitudes toward women's competence.

The third hypothesis – that the sheer fact of having an employed mother affects the daughter's view of women's competence and thus enhances her cognitive performance – also received empirical support. A mediation analysis showed that the relationships between maternal employment and both reading and math scores were mediated by the daughters' nonstereotyped view of women's competence.

Additional support for this last hypothesis that the effect of maternal employment on daughters' views of women's competence may be a direct one, and not necessarily dependent on the father's role, was provided by data from the single-parent families. In fatherless families, daughters of employed mothers also saw women as competent in the male domain, and they also obtained higher test scores than did the daughters of full-time homemakers.

The three hypotheses examined are not mutually exclusive. There can be more than one route between employment and the outcome variables. For the last two hypotheses, it is possible that having a mother employed may often be sufficient to make the daughter feel that women are competent, but the father's active role and parents' equalitarian attitudes may increase the likelihood. For both, a pivotal variable was the girls' conceptions of women's competence, and, for girls, the data suggest that may be a particularly important link in the chain.

The Mother's Well-being

The second path by which maternal employment was expected to affect child outcomes was through the mother's sense of well-being. Several previous studies have shown that the mother's satisfaction with her employment status was related to the mother's sense of well-being, to more positive parenting, or to better child outcomes, whether she was employed or a full-time homemaker. This research, however, is confounded by the fact that the mother's role satisfaction can be a function, or expression of her happier state, her attitude toward her child, or the child's level of functioning. The predictor and the outcome may not be independent. Further, in studies that have examined the relationship more thoroughly, the data indicated that these results were carried by the dissatisfied homemakers, suggesting that the mother who is home full-time with her children and indicates a preference for employment is expressing dissatisfaction with her mother role, while the employed mother's dissatisfaction may indicate a preference for more time with her children. The consequences for mother–child interaction might be different in each case.

Our approach was to trace the path from the mother's employment status to her sense of well-being and from there to her parenting style and on to child outcomes, with measures of each step in the path. We also examined the possible moderating effects of social class, marital status, ethnicity, the number and ages of the children, social support, and the father's role.

In Chapter 4, the relationship between mothers' employment status and parents' marital satisfaction was reported and, in Chapter 5, the relationships between employment and two measures of the mother's morale, a measure of depressive mood and a measure of the mother's current life satisfaction and happiness, were examined. Maternal employment was not related to the marital satisfaction of either parent, and there was no moderating effect of social class. In dual-wage families, fathers' involvement in child care predicted higher marital satisfaction for both parents, but especially so for the mother. The pattern of findings was less extensive for the single-wage families but generally in the same direction.

The results reported in Chapter 5, however, indicated that social class was an important moderator of the relationship between mothers' employment status and mothers' well being for both measures, depressive mood and positive morale. Because of this, all of the analyses dealing with maternal well-being were conducted separately for each socioeconomic group. The working-class analysis included both married and single mothers with marital status examined for moderating effects, but the middle-class analysis included only married mothers because there were very few single mothers in the middle class who were not employed.

In the working-class, employment showed a positive mental health advantage; employed mothers were less depressed and had higher morale than full-time homemakers. No relationship between employment and either measure was found in the middle class. Although several possible moderators of these relationships were examined, none changed the basic finding of a mental health advantage of employment for working-class mothers, married and single, and the absence of such a relationship in the middle class.

For the working class, where a relationship was found between employment status and the mood measures, three possible mediators of this relationship were examined – financial concerns, a sense of loneliness, and a sense of control. As in two previous studies (McLoyd, Jayaratne, Ceballo, & Borquez, 1994; Waldron & Jacobs, 1989), this analysis did not find that financial concerns operated as a mediator. Rather, it was the sense of control or efficacy that mediated it.

Subsequent analyses, reported in Chapter 9, indicated that, in the working class, employed mothers were less likely than full-time homemakers to use authoritarian or permissive parenting styles and more likely to use authoritative styles. They also indicated more positive interactions with their children. The mothers' mood states were also related to these four parenting variables; a greater sense of well-being predicted less authoritarianism, less permissiveness, more reliance on authoritative controls, and more frequent positive interactions. Although there were some variations in patterns by marital status, ethnicity, and child gender, these basic relationships remained intact.

A mediation analysis was conducted which showed that the mother's depressive mood mediated the link between maternal employment and permissive parenting and partially mediated the link to authoritarian parenting. For mothers of boys, maternal depression also mediated the link between maternal employment and authoritative parenting. The mother's morale, or current satisfaction with life, mediated the relationship between maternal employment and positive mother–child interactions. Thus, the data supported the hypothesis that the more positive parenting styles used by working-class employed mothers were due to their greater sense of well-being.

In the married, middle-class group, employed mothers used less authoritarian controls, but also reported fewer positive interactions with their children. Depressive mood was related to less use of authoritative discipline and positive morale was related to more positive interactions. However, since maternal employment was not related to the mood variables, the relationship between employment and parenting cannot be mediated by mood.

Additional analyses were undertaken to see if mood itself mediated relationships between the mother's employment status and child outcomes. However, this was not the case. There were few direct relationships between either measure of mother's mood and child outcome measures. Path analyses were conducted which suggested that, in the working class, maternal well-being accounts, at least in part, for the effects of employment on parenting, and parenting affects child outcomes, but the relationship between mood and child outcomes is indirect. Higher morale increases the likelihood of more positive parenting, which, in turn, increases the probability of more positive academic and social outcomes for children.

Analyses were also conducted to see if parental commitment, mother's education, and father's help moderated the relationships between depressive mood and parenting orientations. No moderating effects were revealed in the working class. In the middle class, however, education, parental commitment, and father's help with child care moderated the effect of depressive mood on authoritative parenting. In the face of higher depressive mood and lower morale, more commitment to parenting, higher education, and help from the father raised the level of positive parenting, relative to the mothers with higher depression and lower morale with less parental commitment, less education, and less help from their husband. The difference found here between the two classes might reflect the higher educational level of the middle class generally and their greater exposure to the advice of experts, but it may also reflect the different levels of depression in each group. It may be that commitment, education, and fathers' support enables mothers to overcome their mood states, but only when the mood is moderately depressed. The higher levels of depression indicated for the working-class homemakers, and particularly the single mothers in that group, may require intervention programs that deal with their mental health. Parent education programs and facilitated entry into the labor force may not be sufficient.

Patterns of Parenting

In Chapter 6, the relationship between the mother's employment status and various aspects of her parenting were examined. The findings indicated that, although there were specific differences for subgroups based on social class, marital status, and child gender, in general, employed mothers used less authoritarian patterns of control, less permissiveness, and more authoritative styles. They also showed less differentiation between sons and daughters in their styles of control and their goals for their children. Married mothers who were employed held higher educational expectations for their children. In the married middle class, full-time homemakers indicated more frequent positive interactions with their child, but in the married working class, more frequent interactions with daughters were reported by the employed mothers and there was no difference for sons. Single, employed mothers reported more educational interactions with their children and more frequent talks. Across class and marital status, employed mothers indicated expressing overt affection to their children more often.

For those parenting variables that were related to the mother's employment status, the relationships to child outcomes were examined and reported in Chapter 10. They were organized around three domains: social adjustment, cognitive competence, and indications of independence and positive assertiveness. Only the parenting variables that seemed relevant to the outcomes in each domain were examined.

Social Adjustment. The authoritarian style of control, used more by full-time homemakers, was associated with various adjustment problems such as acting-out behaviors, less adequate social skills, and being less well-liked by peers. These effects, however, were somewhat stronger in the working class, across marital status, than in the middle class. Higher permissiveness, which was used particularly by married homemakers in the working class, showed similar negative effects, but only for boys.

The higher level of overt affection used by employed mothers also predicted social adjustment. This was related to better peers skills in one-parent families and to lower acting-out scores for working-class girls in two-parent families.

Cognitive Competence. There was a consistent picture across social class, marital status, and child gender indicating that the employed mother's lesser reliance on authoritarian discipline related to higher scores on the achievement tests and to more effective learning patterns as rated by teachers. Other results were found only for specific groups. For example, only in two-parent families did the employed mothers hold higher educational expectations for their children than the full-time homemakers, possibly reflecting the advantage of the dual incomes. This expectation was related to children's higher scores on the achievement tests. As another example, the higher levels of mother/child interaction found for employed mothers were related to children's academic competence only in the single-mother families.

Independence and Assertiveness. Four measures were used to tap independence and assertiveness: peer ratings of who is shy, teacher ratings of shy/anxious behavior, teacher ratings of positive assertiveness, and a measure of the child's sense of efficacy, a belief that he or she affects outcomes and they are not determined by luck or by others. Again, less use by mothers of authoritarian controls and more use of authoritative controls proved important; they were associated with less shy and more positive assertive behaviors in children and a higher sense of efficacy. In addition, employed, married mothers were less likely to indicate that obedience was an important goal for them in childrearing, and for daughters, obedience as a goal was associated with both measures of shyness, less positive assertiveness, and a lower sense of efficacy. Employed, married mothers were also more likely to cite independence as a goal for daughters and to reject the goal of femininity; the first pattern was associated with less shyness and the second patterns was associated with positive assertiveness.

Supervision and Monitoring. A measure was developed based on both children's and mothers' reports to distinguish three types of child supervision and monitoring: Supervised children were rarely left unsupervised, Unsupervised/Monitored children were regularly unsupervised but were monitored – usually by phone – and Unsupervised/Unmonitored children were left neither monitored nor supervised. In Chapter 6, the relationship between this variable and the mother's employment status was considered. The only significant relationship that emerged was that sons in dual-wage working-class families were more likely to be left unsupervised and unmonitored. Chapter 11, which focused on issues of nonmaternal care generally, reports the relationships between the supervision/monitoring variable and child outcomes. In general, these data indicate that among children in poverty circumstances, those who are unsupervised and unmonitored obtain lower scores on various indices of social and academic competence; among children in nonpoverty, working-class circumstances, the unsupervised/unmonitored obtain lower scores on social, but not academic, competence; and in the middle class, being unsupervised and unmonitored is not related to either social or academic outcomes.

Do These Paths Explain Differences Between Children in Each Employment Group?

How do the results obtained here explain the differences we found between the children of full-time homemakers and those who are employed? We have traced three paths from maternal employment to child outcomes. In doing this, we have shown how family patterns can be affected by the mother's employment status and thus increase the likelihood of certain child outcomes. Child outcomes, however, depend on multiple influences, and there may be effects in the family that contribute to outcomes but are not so potent or pervasive that they show up in the simple comparison between children with employed mothers and those with full-time homemakers. Nevertheless, if our hypothesized paths are adequate, they should be able to explain the differences that *are* found between the two groups. In this section, we will start with the outcomes and see how well they are explained by the three paths.

Daughters. The comparison of girls with employed mothers and those with mothers who are full-time homemakers indicated that those with employed mothers obtained higher scores on the three achievement tests, were rated by their teachers as showing fewer learning problems, more frustration tolerance, better social skills, and, in the working class, less acting out. They also showed more positive assertiveness, particularly in single-mother families. Daughters of employed mothers also indicated a greater sense of efficacy, a view that their own actions are important determinants of what happens to them. There were some differences across social class and marital status (e.g, for single mothers, they were also less shy), but all of the differences were in the direction of better social and academic competence for daughters with employed mothers (see Table 7.4). The route by which these outcomes occur has been illuminated in this research.

One important link would seem to lie in whether the child believes that women can function in the areas where only men were traditionally seen as capable. This view was directly related to maternal employment status for girls in both single and married families, and it was augmented by the less-traditional division of labor in two-parent families and by parents' more liberal gender-role attitudes. This view mediated daughters' higher academic scores and sense of efficacy. In addition, the data indicated that the parenting practices of employed mothers include less reliance on authoritarian methods, and these were found to be particularly deleterious for girls' social and academic adjustment. The mother's state of well-being is relevant for working-class daughters because, in both one-parent and two-parent families, the higher morale of the employed mothers was shown to mediate their lesser reliance on authoritarian controls. Furthermore, employed mothers were less likely than homemakers to indicate that obedience and femininity were goals they held for their daughters, and holding these goals was associated with less positive assertiveness for girls. Finally, the higher educational expectations of the married employed mothers were specifically related to higher test scores.

Sons. Sons of employed mothers, like daughters, obtained higher scores on the achievement tests, and were rated by teachers as having fewer learning problems. With respect to behavior patterns, in the working class, higher acting-out scores were obtained by the homemaker's sons, but in the middle class, the sons of *full-time* employed mothers (though not the sons of part-time employed mothers) obtained higher acting out scores. In the single-mother families, the employed mothers' sons showed the same higher achievement scores, as well as more frustration tolerance and better peer skills, but there were no effects of employment status on acting out.

The benefits for boys' academic competence that accrue from the mother's employment come also from the father's role in the family and from the parenting variables. Thus, boys as well as girls, in two-parent families, obtained higher scores on the three achievement tests when their fathers played a more active role in child care (Table 8.2). In addition, they also had higher scores when they believed that women were competent in male areas, although there was no relationship to the parents' gender attitudes nor to their own nonstereotyped view about men's competence in female areas. In addition, the employed mother's lesser reliance on authoritarian control was associated with higher test scores, as was the mother's higher educational expectations. In the one-parent families, the lesser use of authoritarian controls, the higher reliance on authoritative controls, and the higher level of interaction with mothers were all more characteristic of the employed mothers and were related to higher test scores, fewer learning problems, and more tolerance of frustration.

With respect to the behavior patterns, although authoritarian parenting was negatively related to children's social adjustment for girls across marital status and for boys in one-parent families, this pattern not found for boys in two-parent families. Rather, it was the permissiveness of mothers that was related to social adjustment problems, particularly aggressiveness and acting out, for boys in working-class, two-parent families (Table 10.2). The higher use of permissiveness by full-time homemakers, moreover, was only found in the working-class. Thus, the higher level of acting out found for sons of working-class, married homemakers may be explained by this pattern. Further, the higher depressive mood scores for these women was found to mediate their higher use of permissiveness. Thus, maternal depression and permissiveness may be the link between the mother's employment status and the aggressive/acting-out behavior of the married homemakers' sons.

The higher social skills of sons of employed mothers in one-parent families also benefited from their mothers' higher use of authoritative discipline, a result noted only in the one-parent families, and also by their mothers' more overt expression of affection.

None of the parenting data provides insight as to why sons of full-time employed mothers in the middle class might show higher acting-out scores.

However, as indicated in Chapter 10, it is important to realize that these "higher" acting-out scores are not very high. What might be carrying the difference is the very low scores obtained by the sons of full-time home-makers in the middle class. Their mean score of 7.0 is lower than any other group, including even their female counterparts, the middle-class daughters of full-time homemakers. At this level of acting-out, the differences in scores may take on another meaning; it may be these very low scores that need to be explained.

On the whole, however, the differences in the child outcomes associated with the mother's employment seem to be well-explained by the three paths considered here and the results of our analysis.

Effects of Ethnicity

Throughout the analyses, effects of ethnicity were examined for the working-class sample. As in previous research (Alessandri, 1992; Parcel & Menaghan, 1994), ethnicity was rarely a significant moderating variable. The directions of relationships were basically the same for African Americans as for Whites. For example, when the relationship between employment status and the two maternal mood variables were examined for the working-class sample, ethnicity showed no moderating role. For both groups, employed mothers obtained lower scores on the measure of depression and higher scores on the measure of positive morale.

Nevertheless, there are a few scattered differences found between African Americans and Whites that are reported in the chapters. For example, for African Americans, mothers' higher morale was significantly associated with several of the child outcome variables: more frustration tolerance, less acting out, less shy/anxious behavior, better peer skills, more positive assertiveness, and less hitting. None of these relationships between morale and child outcomes were found for Whites. Further, mediation analyses indicated that, for the African-American mothers, the relationship between their higher morale and their children's peer skills was mediated by their higher use of more authoritative discipline.

Another example is reported in Chapter 7. In examining the relationships between the mother's employment status and child outcome variables, a three-way interaction was found for employment status, gender, and ethnicity. Among African Americans, sons of full-time homemakers obtained higher scores on positive assertiveness than sons of employed mothers, but for girls, the opposite pattern was found; it was the daughters of the employed mothers who showed more positive assertiveness. And, as a last example, in Chapter 6, only for African Americans did the data show that employed mothers engaged in more "fun" activities than did full-time homemakers. On the whole, however, the few differences in the relationships found for the two ethnic groups seem to be isolated findings. No pattern emerged.

There did not seem to be general support for the hypothesis in the literature that because of their longer history of maternal employment, African-American families will show more positive effects (Woods, 1972; McLoyd, 1993). The data did indicate more positive effects in the working class than in the middle class, but within the working class the few ethnic differences that were found did not, on the whole, indicate a greater advantage for African Americans.

Discussion of the Study

Twenty years ago, it would have seemed strange to do a study of maternal employment and not focus on it as a social problem, but there is little in these data to suggest that it is. The bulk of what we have found is that most families accommodate to the mother's employment and in doing so provide a family environment that works well. In two-parent families, the fathers take on a larger share of the household tasks and child care, and this seems to be beneficial for their children. In the working class, employed mothers indicate a higher level of well-being than the full-time homemakers and this, in turn, has benefits for their children. Even in the middle class, where employed mothers did not show a higher level of well-being, neither did they show a lower one. Nor have we detected many examples of employed mothers engaged in less-effective parenting styles. These results are not unusual; they are, in fact, consistent with what most of the recent research on maternal employment has found (Gottfried, Bathurst, & Gottfried, 1994).

This study is also different from earlier ones in that we have not concentrated so much on child effects as on the process by which effects occur. This approach has a number of advantages. First, it has made the findings more valuable for understanding the socialization process itself, quite apart from the issue of maternal employment. We have gained insights into the role of fathers, for example, and the part they play in children's socialization. Their involvement in child care, apart from the mothers' employment status, has positive effects on their children's academic competence in a way that extra time with them, per se, does not. In our examination of the mothers' sense of well-being, we identified factors that influence it and that modify its effects on children. For example, we found that when middle-class mothers are depressed, but not pathologically so, their commitment to parenting and the fathers' help with child care can avert a negative effect on their parenting behavior. In the examination of the effects of parenting styles on children, the results indicated that outcomes were sometimes moderated by social class, marital status, or children's gender. For example, evidence was presented suggesting that permissiveness may have more negative effects on boys' social competence than authoritarian control, but, for girls, authoritarian control is more deleterious.

In addition, however, concentrating on the process involved reveals action implications that simply concentrating on the child outcomes associated with employment cannot. If negative outcomes are found to be associated with either employment status, the only implication is to change one's employment status. But this is not always possible, and, if possible, could produce other negative effects by increasing maternal stress or depressed mood. A process-oriented approach, however, suggests behavior changes that can be made without a change in the mother's employment status. For example, the data here have indicated that the belief that women are competent affects girls' sense of efficacy and improves their academic performance. Armed with this knowledge, a full-time homemaker who wanted these outcomes for her daughter could help her believe in women's competence without seeking employment.

There are implications for social policy also that are informed by this approach. The negative effects found for the children of full-time, single homemakers in the lower class would seem to support a policy geared toward getting these mothers into the labor force. However, our analysis revealed a subgroup among them whose state of depression is severe, despite their having high levels of help with their children. Moving such women into employment would need to be accompanied by programs geared toward improving their mental health if they are to be successful as employees and as mothers.

Strengths and Weaknesses of the Research

Self-selection and the Direction of Causality

In any field study, there are two major limitations: self-selection and the direction of causality. The researcher studying effects of maternal employment needs to cope with the possibility that characteristics that led some mothers into employment and some mothers to remain in the home are carrying the results, rather than employment status itself. This was handled here by a combination of control variables supplemented by moderation analyses. For example, mothers' education was viewed as a possible selective factor. It was, therefore, used here as a control and examined as a moderating variable. The Hollingshead Four-factor Index of Social Class (1970) was used as a control throughout these analyses. This measure is based on both parents' occupations and education, and it is one of the only validated social-class measures that incorporates the mother's education. However, since there can still be some educational variation within class groups, the mother's education was also used to see if it had moderating effects on relationships. The potential selective factors examined for moderation effects throughout these analyses included mother's education, ethnicity, number of children, age of children, marital status, and poverty status. In addition, the search for self-selection variables was extended for specific analyses. For example, we were concerned that the higher depression scores of lower-class, single homemakers were carried by the presence of a chronically ill child, which affected their employment status as well as their mood state, so this was examined but found not to be the case. Thus, our efforts to deal with the problem of self-selection were extensive, but it is an issue that is never completely solved. The analyses did find, for example, that among the lower-class single homemakers there is a small group whose state of depression might indeed operate to keep them out of the labor force. Although employment might benefit them, it could also exacerbate their situation.

In addition to the problem of self-selection which raises issues of what is really driving the relationship, field research faces other questions about the direction of causality. For example, does the mother use authoritarian control because the child is aggressive, or is the child aggressive because the mother uses authoritarian control? To some extent, such problems are unsolvable because there is usually an interactive effect in which authoritarian parenting may increase the child's level of aggression, but the child's aggression may then, in turn, augment the mother's authoritarianism. However, in a study of maternal employment status such as the present one, which has shown a chain from employment status to parenting to child outcomes, it confounds logic to assume that children's behavior drove mothers three or more years earlier into the labor force. The fact that the parenting variables are associated with the mother's employment status makes it unlikely that the mother's behavior is child-driven.

Nevertheless, the direction of causality has had to be addressed at several points in this research. For example, in Chapter 10, the relationship between mothers' higher expectations for children's education and the children's test scores was examined by testing for mediation in both directions. In this case, the data supported the hypothesis that the mother's employment status and not the test scores was the predictor. A similar test in Chapter 4, however, supported the hypothesis of two-way causality: there is an interaction between gender attitudes and the father's role, such that each is affected by the mother's employment status and each also affects the other. Further, in this case, it seems likely that both the role and the attitudes also affect employment status. Thus, there are issues of causal direction, and in many cases these are because the variables do interact, but we have tried to address them where they are salient.

Sample Size

A strength of this research is the breadth and quality of the measures. Multiple sources were used in measurement. For the family variables, we obtained reports from the mothers, fathers, and children. Outcome variables were based on teacher ratings, peer ratings, test scores, and the children's self-reports. (Mothers' reports of child outcomes were not used because these can involve contamination between predictor and outcome variables.) In addition, a wide range of family variables and child outcomes were examined. Not only were questionnaires administered to parents, children, teachers, and peers, but personal interviews were also conducted with mothers and children. However, this effort was expensive and time-consuming, and thus, our sample-size, though not small, was limited. Furthermore, because we were interested in effects of employment status itself, we avoided involuntary unemployment and shifts in employment status by limiting analyses to families where the mother's employment had been stable for at least three years, and this further reduced the sample.

Most studies of maternal employment have used homogeneous samples, and generalizations about social-class differences have been based on generalizations drawn from different investigations that used different measures and different methodologies. Others are based on large preexisting data sets that facilitate subgroup comparisons, but where the quality of the measures is limited and pertinent variables may not be measured at all. This study was specifically designed to include a wide socioeconomic range and both African-American families and White families. The fact that we did was a strength of this research, but it was also a strain on the sample size. Our ability to conduct subsample analyses was taxed.

In two cases, our failure to find enough subjects for analysis was unavoidable and reflects the demography of America. Specifically, the sample included an insufficient number of single, middle-class homemakers and middle-class African Americans for analyses. For both groups, this reflects their shortage in the larger population. As an endnote in Chapter 5 indicates, in the United States, only 15 percent of single mothers with school-aged children and at least some college were not in the labor force (U.S. Bureau of the Census, 1996). Even a much larger sample would not have filled this void. Similarly, African Americans are still underrepresented in the middle class, and our efforts to find an adequate sample of middle-class African American children in the third and fourth grades were unsuccessful.

Social Change

This book began with a discussion of social change in the United States and we will end it on the same theme. The results of this research support the idea that the prevalence of maternal employment is itself a force for social change. This is particularly apparent with respect to gender roles. Evidence has been presented which suggests that the mother's employment tends to diminish gender distinctions in family roles, in childrearing goals, in the rearing of children, and in the attitudes of parents and children. And although these changes may take place first in the families with employed mothers, the prevalence of maternal employment generally – particularly among professional women whose voice is heard in the media and in the pediatrician's office – extends them to all of society. It is possible, then, that the parenting patterns and childrearing goals that now characterize employed mothers, will also become more general. Thus, the focus here has been only on within-family effects, but these may also portend broader social changes that are already apparent and likely to increase.

Appendix: Measures Developed for this Study

Measures of the Father's Role

A. Division of Labor Between Parents: The "Who Does It More" Measure

The same measure was administered to mothers and fathers, but mothers were administered it in a personal interview and the fathers' form was self-administered. The format used with mothers is presented here.

We are interested in how parents divide household tasks and activities. I'm going to read some family activities and I'd like you to tell me if you do it, your husband does it, or, if both, who does it more. Here is a card with the possible answers. (Interviewer hands card to mother.)

1. Mother–not father
2. Mother mostly but father sometimes
3. Both pretty equally
4. Father mostly but mother sometimes
5. Father–not mother
6. Neither does it

Here are the questions:

1. Gets breakfast–*Who gets breakfast in your family–you and not your husband, you mostly, pretty equally, your husband more, only your husband?*
2. Mows the lawn and shovels the snow?
3. Cleans and dusts?
4. Cooks the evening meal?
5. Washes and cleans the car?
6. Fixes things when they go wrong like stopped-up sinks and blown-out fuses?

7. Cleans the basement and the garage?
8. Does the dishes?
9. Sets the table?
10. Makes the beds?
11. Gets the children to eat the foods they should?
12. Gets the children to help around the house?
13. Gets the children to go to bed?
14. Takes care of the children?
15. Makes sure the children get to school on time?
16. Gets the children to behave right at the table?
17. Gets the groceries?
18. Puts out the garbage or the trash?
19. Does the family laundry?
20. Washes the kitchen floor?
21. Vacuums the rugs?
22. Gives spending money or allowance to the children?
23. Pays the monthly bills?
24. Buys big new things for the family like a car, refrigerator, or stove?
25. Plays games in the house with the children?
26. Plays outside with the children?
27. Talks with the children about school?
28. Helps the children with school work?
29. Teaches them different things?
30. Reads to them or listens to them read?
31. Punishes them?
32. Praises them?
33. Explains things to the children?
34. Answers their questions?
35. Buys the children's clothes?
36. Watches television with the children?
37. Spends time talking with them?
38. Roughhouses with the children?
39. Takes them shopping?
40. Takes them to the doctor?
41. Takes them to places just for fun?
42. Takes them to the library or museum?
43. Expresses affection to the children?
44. Takes care of them when they're sick?
45. Jokes with them?

46. Goes for walks with the children?
47. Does household tasks with (name of child)?
48. Drives the children to school, lessons, or places they need a ride to?

Scoring. Scales were formed from these items by assigning numerical values to each response as follows: $1 = 4$; $2 = 3$; 3 or $6 = 2$; $4 = 1$; $5 = 0$. For each scale, numerical values were summed. If more than half of the items were answered, any unanswered item was given the value of the mean of the others in that scale.

Scale	Items
Traditional female tasks	1, 3, 4, 8, 9, 10, 17, 19, 20, 21
Child care tasks	11, 12, 13, 14, 15, 16, 40
Functional interactions	39, 40, 47, 48
Financial	22, 23, 24
Play	25, 26, 36, 37, 38, 41, 45, 46
School/educational	27, 28, 29, 30, 33, 42
Nurturance	32, 34, 43, 44, 45

B. Father-Child Interactions with Target Child: Parents' Self-Reports

The same measure was administered to fathers and mothers, each asking the parent to report about his or her own behavior. The mothers' questions were administered in a personal interview; the fathers' in a self-report questionnaire. The format used with fathers is presented here.

The next set of questions is about what activities you and the child in the study did together last week. Please think about how many times you and the child did each of the following activities over the last seven days and check the answer that fits best.

1. Watched television together?
   1. Not at all
   2. Once
   3. Twice
   4. Three or four times
   5. More than four times
   6. Not at all this past week, but we usually do.

2. Read a book or something together?
3. Played a game in the house?
4. Played outside?
5. Did work together – like dishes or fixing something?
6. Showed affection – hugged or kissed?
7. Talked about what happened at school?
8. Had a talk about other things?
9. Helped the child with homework?
10. Helped the child with something else he or she wanted help with?
11. Went on errands together – shopping or to the grocery store or something like that?
12. Went somewhere just for fun – like movies or a park?
13. Drove the child somewhere – for lessons or scouts or something like that?
14. Ate dinner together?
15. Visited relatives with the child?
16. Went with child to church or religious services?
17. Went for a walk together?
18. Went out to eat or for ice cream?

Scoring. Scales were formed from these items by assigning numerical values to each response as follows: 1 = 1; 2 = 2; 3 = 3; 4 = 4; 5 = 5; 6 = modal score for items in scale. The following items were summed for each scale:

Scale	Items
Fun activities	3, 4, 12, 17, 18
Talk	7, 8
Affectionate	2, 6, 10, 17
Educational	2, 7, 9, 10, 13
Total	all 18 items

Measures of Parents' Gender-based Attitudes

This twenty-two item measure, developed by Hoffman and Kloska (1995), was administered to both mothers and fathers. The mothers' questions were administered in a personal interview; the fathers' in a self-report questionnaire. The format used with mothers is presented here. The following items are not included in either measure of parents' gender-based attitudes: 4, 5, 9, 11. They are measures of locus of control, which were interspersed to break the set. Three items, 8, 15, and 22, do not deal with family roles and were not expected to be part of the final scales. They were included, however, in the factor analyses to see if they did fall into one of two possible husband–wife role factors. They did not and are not included in the final scales. Higher scores indicate less stereotyped attitudes.

I am going to read some statements and I would like you to tell me whether or not you agree with them. Tell me if you strongly agree, agree, disagree, or strongly disagree.

1. Nowadays men and women should share household tasks and parenting equally.
   1. Strongly agree
   2. Agree
   3. Disagree
   4. Strongly disagree
2. Education is important for both sons and daughters, but it is more important for a son.
3. Some equality in marriage is OK, but by and large, the man should have the main say-so.
4. Many times you feel that you have little influence over the things that happen to you.
5. Getting ahead in life is mostly a matter of luck.
6. A husband's job is more important than a wife's.
7. It isn't always possible, but ideally the wife should do the cooking and housekeeping and the husband should provide the family with money.
8. It doesn't seem right to have a woman supervising men on the job.
9. It is not always wise to plan too far ahead because many things turn out to be a matter of good or bad luck anyway.
10. It is as important to steer a daughter toward a good job as it is with a son.
11. If a person plans ahead things are pretty likely to work out.
12. For a woman, taking care of the children is the main thing, but for a man, his job is.
13. I would give a daughter as much encouragement and help in getting an education as I would a son.
14. Men should make the really important decisions in the family.

15. If a company has to lay off workers, they should lay off women before men.
16. It may be necessary for mothers to be working because the family needs the money, but it would be better if she could stay home and just take care of the house and kids.
17. It is more important to raise a son to be strong and independent than to raise a daughter that way.
18. It's important to raise a son so he will be able to hold down a good job when he's grown, but that's not so major with a daughter.
19. A man should help in the house, but housework and child care should mainly be a woman's job.
20. I see nothing wrong with giving a little boy a doll to play with.
21. It's okay for children to help around the house, but I would not ask a son to dust or set the table.
22. I would not vote for a woman for president of this country.

Scoring. Two scales were created by summing the following items. For items 10, 13, and 20, answer values are reverse scaled (1 = 4, 2 = 3, 3 = 2, 4 = 1) prior to summing.

Scale	Items
Gender-based attitudes toward marital roles	3, 6, 7, 12, 14, 19
Gender-based attitudes toward child rearing	2, 10 (reversed), 13 (reversed), 17, 18, 20 (reversed), 21

Measures of Children's Gender-role Attitudes

This thirty-one item questionnaire was administered to children in the classroom. The child was asked to indicate if each item was something only men could do, something only women could do, or something both could do.

People have different ideas about what they think men and women can do. We're interested in what you think. Some people think that only men can do certain things, and some think that there are things that only women can do, and some think that there are things that both men and women can do.

"Who can fix a sink?" Is that something only men can do and women can't, or is that something only women can do and men can't, or is that something both men and women can do? If you think only men can fix a sink, put an `X' in the column named "Men." If you think only women can fix a sink, put an `X' in the column named "Women." Or if you think both men and women can fix a sink, put an `X' in the "Both" column. Remember, mark only 1 column.

1. Fix a sink?
2. Ride a bike?
3. Set the table?
4. Build a house?
5. Shovel snow?
6. Go grocery shopping?
7. Work in an office?
8. Go to the beach?
9. Wash dishes?
10. Bake cupcakes?
11. Be a doctor?
12. Fly a plane?
13. Use a sewing machine?
14. Take care of children?
15. Fix a car?
16. Mow the lawn?
17. Play football?
18. Go to the movies?
19. Be a secretary?
20. Cook a meal?
21. Be a lawyer?
22. Wash the family clothes?
23. Collect garbage?
24. Teach school?
25. Climb a mountain?
26. Race a car?
27. Be a nurse?
28. Clean house?
29. Write a book?
30. Change a baby's diapers?
31. Tell jokes?

Scoring. Only the twenty-five gender-typed activities (see below) were scored. Each item was given a score of 0 if the answer indicated that only men could do the male activities or only women could do the female activities (i.e., the stereotyped response); each item was given a score of 1 if the answer indicated "both" or the counter-stereotyped choice. For this study, scores were summed to yield two scores: a score for the activities stereotyped as male, and a score for the activities stereotyped as female. Higher scores indicate less stereotyped attitudes. (No item was considered stereotyped unless 40% or more gave the stereotyped response. Item 30 was not included because the children found it humorous.)

Scale	Items
Women Can Do "Male" Things	1, 4, 5, 11, 12, 15, 16, 17, 21, 23, 25, 26, 31
Men Can Do "Female" Things	3, 6, 9, 10, 13, 14, 19, 20, 22, 24, 27, 28

Measures of Discipline and Parental Control

A. Behavior-Based Discipline

The behavior-based discipline measures were coded from the following set of questions from the mother's interview:

We're interested in how parents get their children to do things when the child doesn't want to. For example:

1. Think about the last time you wanted (name of child) to stop watching television and he/she didn't want to stop. What did you do? Which of these fits most closely what you did? (The interviewer hands the mother a card with the possible responses and reads them. The mother's first choice is marked 1 and any other responses selected are circled. The cards used are specific for the child's gender.)
   a. Just turned off the set.
   b. Pulled him/her from the set.
   c. Told him/her loud and clear what he/she was to do.
   d. Explained why I wanted him/her to stop.
   e. Hit him/her.
   f. Threatened to hit but didn't.

    g. Promised him/her something nice if he/she would.

    h. Let him/her keep watching. It wasn't important.

    i. Told him/her he/she could watch for a little while longer but then off.

    j. Just showed him/her I didn't like it.

    k. Told him/her if he/she didn't stop, he/she would be punished.

2. How about the last time (name of child) didn't want to go to bed and you wanted him/her to? What did you do?

    a. Turned things off – the lights or TV – so he/she had to go.

    b. Just took him/her to bed.

    c. Made a kind of game of it so he/she went.

    d. Hit him/her.

    e. Threatened to hit, but didn't.

    f. Explained why he/she had to go to bed then.

    g. Said very sternly, "Go to bed."

    h. Let him/her stay up, but he/she knew I was angry.

    i. Gave him/her a few more minutes.

    j. Promised him/her something nice if he/she would.

    k. Let him/her stay up. It was OK.

    l. Told him/her he/she could stay up some other night – like on a weekend.

    m. Told him/her that if he/she didn't go, he/she would not be able to do something else he/she wanted to do.

3. Now think about another time when (name of child) was doing something – like playing Nintendo, or playing with friends – and you wanted him/her to stop – maybe to eat dinner or to go somewhere, but he/she didn't want to stop. What did you do?

    a. Yelled at him/her.

    b. Told him/her loud and clear he/she was to stop.

    c. Explained why he/she had to stop.

    d. Just let it go.

    e. Threatened to punish him/her.

    f. Told him/her he/she could have a few more minutes but then he/she had to stop.

    g. Asked him/her a few more times and then he/she stopped.

    h. Told him/her to stop now and he/she could go back to it later.

4. Now think about the last time (name of child) talked back to you. What did you do?
   a. Nothing. It was OK.
   b. Hit him/her.
   c. Threatened to hit but didn't.
   d. Told him/her loud and clear there would be none of that.
   e. Sent him/her to his/her room.
   f. Deprived him/her of something he/she wanted.
   g. Explained why he/she was wrong.
   h. Just showed that I felt bad; looked sad.
   i. Told him/her that I was hurt.
   j. Stopped talking to him/her.
   k. Walked away.
   l. Told him/her that his/her father would hear about it.

5. Think about the last time you wanted (name of child) to clean his/her room and he/she didn't want to. What did you do?
   a. Let it go.
   b. Told him/her to stay in his/her room until it was cleaned.
   c. Told him/her he/she would not be able to do something he/she wanted to do if the room wasn't cleaned.
   d. Told him/her he'd/she'd get a whipping if he/she didn't.
   e. Explained that it was his/her job and he/she had to do it.
   f. Explained why the room had to be cleaned and why he/she was the one who had to do it.

6. How do you get (name of child) to do his/her homework?
   a. He/she always does it on his/her own.
   b. We have a set rule that he/she always follows.
   c. Tell him/her about why it is important.
   d. Promise a reward for doing his/her homework.
   e. Tell him/her the teacher will be mad if he/she doesn't.
   f. I have to nag him/her.
   g. Tell him/her he/she won't have some privilege if he/she doesn't.
   h. Tell him/her we'll do something nice when he/she finishes.
   i. I leave it up to him/her.
   j. I don't think homework is very important at this age.

7. How do you get (name of child) to help around the house?
   a. Pay him/her for chores.
   b. Tell him/her he/she can't do something else until the chores are finished.
   c. Tell him/her that everyone in the family has to do his part.

    d. Tell him/her I need his/her help.

    e. Just keep at him/her til he/she does it.

    f. Tell him/her how good he/she is at doing things.

    g. Tell him/her how helpful he/she is.

    h. Just let it go if he/she doesn't want to.

    i. He/she doesn't do chores.

8. If (name of child) has fights with another child or a brother or sister, what do you do?

    a. Let them work it out for themselves.

    b. Tell him/her there is to be no fighting.

    c. Talk to him/her about what happened.

    d. Tell him/her to keep away from the other child.

    e. Punish him/her.

    f. Tell him/her to tell the teacher.

    g. Call the other parent or the teacher.

    h. Comfort him/her if he/she is upset.

    i. Child never has fights.

9. If your child clearly disobeyed you or did something you really thought was wrong, what would you do?

    a. Punish him/her by taking away some privilege.

    b. Send him/her to his/her room.

    c. Hit him/her.

    d. Have his/her father handle it.

    e. Threaten to punish but probably not do it.

    f. Tell him/her that I was very disappointed in him/her.

    g. Ignore him/her for a time.

    h. Talk with him/her about what happened.

    i. Make him/her say he/she was sorry.

    j. Nothing probably. That's the way kids are.

10. Now for this question, the last in this set, I'd like you to pick what you usually do and then two or more others. In general, how do you get (name of child) to do what you want?

    a. I just tell him/her firmly.

    b. I usually make a game of it.

    c. I often have to hit him/her.

    d. Just threaten to hit him or say he/she will get a whipping.

    e. Tell him/her I'll tell his/her father.

    f. If I explain the reason, he/she will usually go along.

    g. I point out why it's important, but that often isn't enough.

    h. If I just suggest it, he/she will do it.

    j. Stop talking to him/her.

    k. I just look hurt or sad or disappointed.

    l. Tell him/her he/she can't have something or do something he/she wants.

    m. Promise an extra something if he/she'll go along.

    n. Tell him/her I'll leave.

    o. Tell him/her we'll send him to live elsewhere.

    p. Remind him/her of how lucky he/she is.

    q. I set very firm rules and he/she knows they are to be followed.

Indices of discipline styles. These questions were used to derive several indices of mother's discipline styles. Four of these were used in this analysis: induction, power assertion, strong power assertion, and permissive action. The scoring for each is indicated as follows:

Induction: 1 point is given for each of questions 1–9 if an inductive response is given as a primary or secondary response. If an inductive response is given as a first choice to question 10, two points are added. If an inductive response is given as a secondary response to question 10, 1 point is added (range: 0–12). The inductive responses for each question are: 1: d; 2: f; 3: c; 4: g; 5: e or f; 6: c; 7: c or d; 8: c; 9: h; 10: f and g.

Power Assertion: 1 point is given for each of questions 1–9 if a power assertive response is given as a primary or secondary response. If a power assertive response is given as a first choice to question 10, two points are added. If one power assertive response is given as a secondary response to question 10, 1 point is added, but if more than one response is given as a secondary response, 2 points are added (range: 0–13). The power assertive responses for each question are: 1: a,b,c,e,f, or k; 2: a,b,d,e,g, or m; 3: a,b, or e; 4: b,c,d,e,f, or l; 5: b,c, or d; 6: g; 7: b; 8: b or e; 9: a,b,c,e, or i; 10: a,c,d,e or l.

Strong Power Assertion: 1 point is given for each strong power assertive response chosen in questions 1–9. There are nine possible strong power assertive answers across the nine items, so the range of possible scores for the 9 items is 0–9. In addition, if c (hits) is chosen for question 10 as the primary response, 3 points are added and if c is chosen as a secondary response, 2 points are added. For the other strong power assertive response (d), 2 points are added if it is the primary response, and 1 point if it is the secondary response (range: 0–13). The strong power assertive responses for each question are: 1: b,e,f; 2: d,e; 3: none; 4: b,c; 5: d; 6: none; 7: none; 8: none; 9: c; 10: c,d.

Permissive Action: 2 points are given for each of questions 1–9 if a permissive response is given as the primary response. 1 point is given for each secondary permissive response chosen across the 9 question. Question 10 includes no permissive response (range: 0–22). The permissive responses for each question are: 1: h; 2: k; 3: d; 4: a; 5: a; 6: i,j; 7: h,i; 8: a,d, h; 9:j.

B. Parental Control

This measure was adapted from Greenberger (1988). The parental control measures were coded from the following set of questions from the mother's interview. Respondents were asked to rate the degree to which they agreed or disagreed with each statement on a scale of 1 (disagree a lot) to 6 (agree a lot).

1. It is very important for children to respect authority.
   1. Disagree a lot
   2. Disagree
   3. Disagree a little
   4. Agree a little
   5. Agree
   6. Agree a lot
2. Third or fourth-grade children should be allowed to take part in family decisions.
3. I give my child a lot of freedom to express anger.
4. I "play it by ear" with my child, rather than keeping to any schedule.
5. Before punishing my child, I always listen to his/her side of the story.

6. The most important thing I want to teach my child is to think for himself/herself.

7. I show my child love, but I don't go in for a lot of hugging and kissing.

8. I often try to point out to my child how things might seem from another person's point of view.

9. When my child asks questions, I try to answer with a simple "yes" or "no" rather than going into a full explanation.

10. If child can give me a good reason for getting out of a rule, I'll usually go along.

11. If I have a disagreement with child, we generally talk things out until we reach an understanding.

12. It's impossible to bring up a child properly without occasionally hitting or spanking them.

13. I have no particular rules about bed time – I leave it up to the child.

14. A child in the third or fourth grade should never argue with his/her parents.

15. A well-raised child is one who doesn't have to be told twice to do something.

16. When my child needs discipline, I try not to dilute it with sympathy or affection.

17. I don't give my child a lot of praise when he/she does something well, so as not to spoil him/her.

18. I expect my child to accept what I say as a fact and not question it.

19. I let child pretty much watch what he/she wants on television so long as it doesn't interfere with the rest of the family.

20. If the family is having money problems, children should know about it.

21. If I enforce a rule or say no to the child, I think it's important to explain the reason.

22. If you give children love, the rest will take care of itself.

23. The less rules, regulations, and discipline children get, the better off they will be.

24. A child in the third or fourth grade should be encouraged to think for himself.

25. When I give my child responsibility for tasks around the house, I expect him/her to carry them out without my guidance or company.

26. I let my child decide when to go to bed.
27. I always praise my child when he/she does something well.
28. It is very important for child to be obedient.
29. I think it is OK for a child in third or fourth grade to be home without an adult or babysitter sometimes.
30. I expect my child to tell me exactly where he/she is when he/she is not home or in school.
31. I find explanations work best in getting my child to listen to me.
32. I do not have rules about where my child can go on his/her own.
33. When my child has done something really wrong, I show my disappointment by spanking him/her.
34. When I make a rule, I just make it; I don't go into explanations.
35. I don't lay out a lot of rules but just deal with things as they come up.
36. A major goal for me is to teach my child to show concern for the rights of others.
37. Rearing a happy child is more important to me than rearing a respectful or obedient child.
38. I do not let my child show anger toward me.

Indices of Parental Control. Three main scales (authoritarian, authoritative, permissive) and five sub-scales (hostility, obedience and respect, physical punishment, child influence, and child thinking for self) were used in this study. These parental control composites were made by summing the following items. Several items are reverse scaled (1=6, 2=5, 3=4, 4=3, 5=2, 6=1) before being summed.

Main Scales	Items
Authoritarian	1, 12, 14, 15, 16, 18, 28, 33, 34, 37 (reversed), 38
Authoritative	2, 5, 6, 8, 10, 11, 17 (reversed), 21, 24, 27, 31
Permissive	4, 13, 19, 22, 23, 26, 30 (reversed), 32, 35, 38 (reversed)

Sub-Scales	Items
Hostility	9, 17, 25
Obedience and respect	1, 14, 15, 18, 28, 37 (reversed), 38
Physical punishment	12, 33
Child influence	2, 5, 11, 25
Child thinking for self	6, 24

References

Ainsworth, M., Blehar, M., Waters, E., & Wall, S. (1978). *Patterns of attachment.* Hillsdale, NJ: Erlbaum.

Ainsworth, M. D., & Witting, B. (1969). Attachment and exploratory behavior of one-year-olds in a strange situation. In B. M. Foss (ed.), *Determinants of infant behavior* (pp. 129–173). London; Methuen.

Alessandri, S. M. (1992). Effects of maternal work status in single-parent families on children's perceptions of self and family and school achievement. *Journal of Experimental Child Psychology, 54,* 417–433.

Baker, C. P., & Mott, F. L. (1989). *NLSY child handbook, 1989: A guide and resource document for the National Longitudinal Survey of Youth 1986 child data.* Columbus: Ohio State University.

Baldwin, A. L., Baldwin, C., & Cole, R. E. (1990). Stress-resistant families and stress-resistant children. In J. Rolf, A. S. Masten, D. Cicchette, K. Neuchterlein, & S. Weintraub (eds.), *Risk and protective factors in the development of psychopathology.* Cambridge, England: Cambridge University Press.

Barber, B. L., & Eccles, J. S. (1992). Long-term influence of divorce and single parenting on adolescent family and work-related values, behaviors, and aspirations. *Psychological Bulletin, 111,* 108–126.

Barglow, P., Vaughn, B., & Molitor, N. (1987). Effects of maternal absence due to employment on the quality of infant-mother attachment in a low-risk sample. *Child Development, 58,* 945–954.

Barnett, R. C., & Baruch, G. K. (1987). Determinants of fathers' participation in family work. *Journal of Marriage and the Family, 49,* 29–40.

Baron, R. M., & Kenny, D. A. (1986). The moderator-mediator variable distinction in social-psychological research: Conceptual, strategic and statistical considerations. *Journal of Personality and Social Psychology, 51,* 1173–1182.

Bartko, T., & McHale, S. M. (1991). The household labor of children from dual-versus single-earner families. In J. V. Lerner & N. L. Galambos (eds.), *Employed mothers and their children* (pp. 159–180). New York: Garland Press.

Baruch, G. K., & Barnett, R. C. (1986a). Consequences of fathers' participation in family work: Parents' role strain and well-being. *Journal of Personality and Social Psychology, 51,* 983–992.

Baruch, G. K., & Barnett, R. C. (1986b). Fathers' participation in family work and children's sex-role attitudes. *Child Development, 57,* 1210–1223.

Baruch, G. K., & Barnett, R. C. (1986c). Role quality, multiple role involvement, and psychological well-being in midlife women. *Journal of Personality and Social Psychology, 49,* 135–145.

Baruch, G. K., & Barnett, R. C. (1987). Role quality and psychological well-being. In F. Crosby (ed.), *Spouse, parent, worker* (pp. 63–84). New Haven, CT: Yale University Press.

Baumrind, D. (1967). Childcare practices anteceding 3 patterns of preschool behavior. *Genetic Psychology Monographs, 4* (1, Pt. 2).

Baumrind, D. (1971). Current patterns of parental authority. *Developmental Psychology Monograph, 4* (No. 1, Part 2), 1–103.

Baydar, N., & Brooks-Gunn, J. (1991). Effects of maternal employment and child-care arrangements on preschoolers' cognitive and behavioral outcomes: Evidence from the children of the National Longitudinal Survey of Youth. *Developmental Psychology, 27,* 932–945.

Beck, A. T., & Beck, R. W. (1972). Screening depressed patients in family practice: A rapid technique. *Journal of Postgraduate Medicine, 52,* 81–85.

Belsky, J. (1988). The "effects" of infant daycare reconsidered. *Early Childhood Research Quarterly, 3,* 235–272.

Belsky, J. (1990). Developmental risks associated with infant day care: Attachment insecurity, noncompliance, and aggression? In S. Chehrazi (ed.), *Psycholocial issues in day care* (pp. 37–68). Washington, DC: American Psychiatric Press.

Belsky, J., & Eggebeen, D. (1991). Early and extensive maternal employment and young children's socioemotional development: Children of the National Longitudinal Survey of Youth. *Journal of Marriage and the Family, 53,* 1083–1110.

Belsky, J., & Rovine, M. (1988). Nonmaternal care in the first year of life and the security of infant–parent attachment. *Child Development, 59,* 157–167.

Birnbaum, J. A. (1975). Life patterns and self-esteem in gifted family-oriented and career-committed women. In M. S. Mederick, S. S. Tangri, & L. W. Hoffman (eds.), *Women and achievement* (pp. 396–410). Washington, DC: Hemisphere.

Block, J. H. (1983). Differential premises arising from differential socialization of the sexes: Some conjectures. *Child Development, 54,* 1335–1354.

Blood, R. O. (1963). The husband–wife relationship. In F. I. Nye & L. W. Hoffman (eds.), *The employed mother in America.* Chicago: Rand McNally.

Bond, J. T., Galinsky, E., & Swanberg, J. E. (1998). *The 1997 national study of the changing workforce.* New York: Families and Work Institute.

Brazelton, T. B. (1985). *Working and caring.* New York: Basic Books.

Bronfenbrenner, U., Alvarez, W. F., & Henderson, C. R. (1984). Working and watching: Maternal employment status and parents' perceptions of their three-year-old children. *Child Development, 55,* 1362–1378.

Bronfenbrenner, U., & Crouter, A. (1982). Work and family through time and space. In S. B. Kamerman & C. D. Hayes (eds.), *Families that work: Children in a changing world* (pp. 39–83). Washington, DC: National Academy Press.

Bryant, D. M. & Ramey, C. T. (1987). An analysis of the effectiveness of early intervention programs for high-risk children. In M. Guralnick and C. Bennett (eds.), *The effectiveness of early intervention for at-risk and handicapped children.* (pp. 33–78). New York: Academic Press.

Burchinal, L. G. (1963). Personality characteristics of children. In F. I. Nye & L. W. Hoffman (eds.), *The employed mother in America*. Westport, CT: Greenwood Press.

Bureau of the Census (1987). *Who's minding the kids?* Current Population Reports, Series P-60, No. 160. Washington, DC: U.S. Department of Commerce.

Burke, R. J., & Weir, T. (1976). Relationship of wives' employment status to husband, wife, and pair satisfaction and performance. *Journal of Marriage and the Family, 38,* 279–287.

Caldwell, B. M., & Bradley, R. H. (1987). *Home observation for measurement of the environment*. Homewood, IL: Dorsey Press.

Caughy, M. O., DiPietro, J. A., Strobino, D. M. (1994). Day-care participation as a protective factor in the cognitive development of low-income children. *Child Development, 65,* 457–471.

Chase-Lansdale, P. L., Michael, R. T., & Desai, S. Maternal employment during infancy: An analysis of "Children of the National Longitudinal Survey of Youth (NLSY)." In J. V. Lerner & N. L. Galambos, *Employed mothers and their children* (pp. 37–62). New York: Garland.

Chase-Lansdale, P. L., & Owen, M. T. (1987). Maternal employment in a family context: Effects on infant-mother and infant-father attachments. *Child Development, 58,* 1505–1512.

Cherry, F. F., & Eaton, E. L. (1977). Physical and cognitive development in children of low-income mothers working in the child's early years. *Child Development, 48,* 158–166.

Chilman, C. S. (1993). Parental employment and child care trends: Some critical issues and suggested policies. *Social Work, 38,* 451–460.

Clarke-Stewart, K. A. (1989). Infant day care: Maligned or malignant? *American Psychologist, 44,* 266–273.

Cleary, P. D., & Mechanic, D. (1983). Sex differences in psychological distress among married people. *Journal of Health and Social Behavior, 24,* 111–121.

Coleman, L. M., Antonucci, T. C., Adelman, P. K., & Crohan, S. E. (1987). Social roles in the lives of middle-aged and older black women. *Journal of Marriage and the Family, 49,* 761–771.

Coley, R. L. (1998). Children's socialization experiences and functioning in single-mother households: The importance of fathers and other men. *Child Development, 69,* 219–230.

Coley, R. L., & Hoffman, L. W. (1996). Relations of parental supervision and monitoring to children's functioning in various contexts: Moderating effects of families and neighborhoods. *Journal of Applied Developmental Psychology, 17,* 51–68.

Crouter, A. C., & Crowley, M. S. (1990). School-age children's time alone with fathers in single- and dual-earner families: Implications for the father-child relationship. *Journal of Early Adolescence, 10,* 296–312.

Crouter, A. C., & Huston, T. (1985, April). *Social psychological and contextual antecedents of fathering in dual-earner families.* Paper presented at the biennial meeting of the Society for Research in Child Development, Toronto, Ontario.

Crouter, A. C., MacDermid, S. M., McHale, S. M., & Perry-Jenkins, M. (1990). Parental monitoring and perceptions of children's school performance and conduct in dual-and single-earner families. *Developmental Psychology, 26,* 649–657.

Crouter, A. C., Perry-Jenkins, M., Huston, T. L., & McHale, S. M. (1987). Processes underlying father involvement in dual-earner and single-earner families. *Developmental Psychology, 23,* 431–440.

D'Amico, R. J., Haurin, J., & Mott, F. L. (1983). The effects of mother's employment on adolescent and early adult outcomes of young men and women. In C. D. Hayes & S. B. Kamerman (eds.), *Children of working parents* (pp. 130–219). Washington, DC: National Academy Press.

Desai, S., Chase-Lansdale, P. L., & Michael, R. T. (1989). Mother or market? Effects of maternal employment on four-year-olds' intellectual abilities. *Demography, 26,* 545–561.

Dienstag, E. L. (1986, August). *The transition to parenthood in working and non-working pariparous mothers.* Paper presented at the meeting of the American Psychological Association, Washington, DC.

Dornbusch, S. M., & Gray, K. D. (1988). Single-parent families. In S. M. Dornbusch & M. H. Stroker (eds.), *Feminism, children, and the new families* (pp. 274–296). New York: Guilford Press.

Dornbusch, S. M., Carlsmith, J. M., Bushwall, S. J., Ritter, P. L., Leiderman, H., Hastorf, A. H. & Gross, R. T. (1985). Single parents, extended households, and the control of adolescents. *Child Development, 56,* 326–341.

Dornbusch, S. M., Ritter, P. L., Leiderman, P. H., Roberts, D. F., & Fraleigh, M. J. (1987). The relations of parenting style to adolescent school performance. *Child Development, 58,* 1244–1257.

Downey, G., & Coyne, J. C. (1990). Children of depressed parents: An integrative review. *Psychological Bulletin, 108,* 50–76.

Duckett, E., & Richards, M. H. (1989, April). *Maternal employment and young adolescents' daily experience in single-mother families.* Paper presented at the biennial meeting of the Society for Research in Child Development, Kansas City, MO.

Easterbrooks, M. A., & Goldberg, W. A. (1985). Effects of early maternal employment on toddlers, mothers, and fathers. *Developmental Psychology, 4,* 774–783.

Easterbrooks, M. A., & Goldberg, W. A. (1988). Security of toddler-parent attachment: Relation to children's socio-personality functioning during kindergarten. In M. Greenberg, D. Cicchetti, & M. Cummings (eds.), *Attachment in the preschool years: Theory, research, and intervention.* Chicago: University of Chicago Press.

Eccles, J. P., & Hoffman, L. W. (1984). Sex roles, socialization, and occupational behavior. In H. Stevenson & A. Siegal (eds.), *Child development research and social policy* (pp. 367–420). Chicago: Chicago University Press.

Elder, G. H. Jr. (1974). *Children of the great depression.* Chicago: Chicago University Press.

Emmons, C. A., Biernat, M., Tiedje, L. B., Lang, E. L. & Wortman, C. B. (1987). *Stress, support, and coping among women professionals with preschool children.* Unpublished manuscript, Institute for Social Research. University of Michigan.

Farel, A. N. (1980). Effects of preferred maternal roles, maternal employment, and sociographic status on school adjustment and competence. *Child Development, 50,* 1179–1186.

Ferree, M. M. (1976). Working class jobs, housework, and paid work as sources of satisfaction. *Social Problems, 22,* 431–441.

Fuligni, A. S. (1995). *Effects of parental involvement and family context on academic achievement of third and fourth grade children.* Unpublished doctoral dissertation, University of Michigan, Ann Arbor, MI.

Fuller, B., Holloway, S. D., & Liang, X. (1995). *Which families use nonparental child care and centers? The influence of family structure, ethnicity, and parental practices.* Cambridge, MA: Department of Human Development and Psychology, Harvard University.

Galambos, N. L., & Maggs, J. L. (1991). Out-of-school care of young adolescents and self-reported behavior. *Development Psychology, 27,* 644–655.

Gilbert, L. A. (1985). *Men in dual-career families.* Hillside, NJ: Erlbaum.

Gold, D., & Andres, D. (1978a). Developmental comparisons between adolescent children with employed and nonemployed mothers. *Merrill-Palmer Quarterly, 24,* 243–254.

Gold, D., & Andres, D. (1978b). Developmental comparisons between 10-year-old children with employed and nonemployed mothers. *Child Development, 39,* 75–84.

Gold, D., & Andres, D. (1978c). Relations between maternal employment and development of nursery school children. *Canadian Journal of Behavioral Science, 10,* 116–129.

Goldberg, W. A., & Easterbrooks, M. A. (1988). Maternal employment when children are toddlers and kindergartners. In A. E. Gottfried & A. W. Gottfried (eds.), *Maternal employment and children's development: Longitudinal research* (pp. 121–154). New York: Plenum.

Goodnow, J. J. (1988). Children's household work: Its nature and functions. *Psychological Bulletin, 103,* 5–26.

Gottfried, A. E., Bathurst, K., & Gottfried, A. W. (1994). Role of maternal and dual-earner employment status in children's development. In A. E. Gottfried & A. W. Gottfried (eds.), *Redefining families* (pp. 55–97). New York: Plenum.

Gottfried, A. E., Gottfried, A. W., & Bathurst, K. (1995). Maternal and dual-earner employment status and parenting. In M. Bornstein (ed.), *Handbook of parenting, Vol. 2* (139–160). Mahwah, N. J.: Erlbaum.

Gottfried, A. E., Gottfried, A. W., & Bathurst, K. (1988). Maternal employment, family environment and children's development: Infancy through the school years. In A. E. Gottfried & A. W. Gottfried (eds.), *Maternal employment and children's development: Longitudinal research* (pp. 11–58). New York: Plenum.

Gove, W. R., & Zeiss, C. (1987). Multiple roles and happiness. In F. Crosby (ed.), *Spouse. parent, worker* (pp. 125–137). New Haven, CT: Yale University Press.

Greenberger, E. (1988). *New measures for research on work, parenting, and the socialization of children.* Unpublished manuscript, University of California, Program in Social Ecology. Irvine, CA.

Greenberger, E., & Goldberg, W. A. (1989). Work, parenting, and the socialization of children. *Development Psychology, 25.* 22–35.

Greenberger, E., & O'Neil, R. (1992). Maternal employment and perceptions of young children: Bronfenbrenner et al. revisited. *Child Development, 63.* 431–448.

Greenberger, E., O'Neil, R., & Nagel, S. K. (1994). Linking workplace and homeplace: Relations between the nature of adults' work and their parenting behaviors. *Developmental Psychology, 30.* 990–1002.

Guidubaldi, J., & Nastasi, B. K. (1987, April). *Home environment factors as predictors of child adjustment in mother-employed households: Results of a nationwide study.* Paper presented at the biennial meeting of the Society for Research in Child Development, Baltimore, MD.

Harnish, J. D., Dodge, K. A., & Valente, E. (1995). Mother-child interaction quality as a partial mediator of the roles of maternal depressive symptomatology and sociometric status in the development of child behavior problems. *Child Development, 66,* 739–753.

Harter, S. (1982). The perceived competence scale for children. *Child Development, 53,* 87–97.

Harter, S. (1983). *Revision of the perceived competence scale for children.* Unpublished manuscript, University of Denver.

Haskins, R. (1989). Beyond metaphor: The efficacy of early childhood education. *American Psychologist, 44,* 274–282.

Hayes, D. D., Palmer, J. L., & Zaslow, M. J. (1990). *Who cares for America's children? Child care policy for the 1990s.* Washington, D C: National Academy Press.

Herbst, P. G. (1952). The measurement of family relationships. *Human Relations, 5,* 3–30.

Herzog, E., & Sudia, C. E. (1973). Children in fatherless families. In B. M. Caldwell & H. N. Ricciuti (eds.), *Review of child development research, Vol. 3.* Chicago: University of Chicago Press.

Hetherington, E. M. (1979). Divorce: A child's perspective. *American Psychologist, 34,* 851–858.

Hetherington, E. M., Cox, M., & Cox, R. (1982). Effects of divorce on parents and children. In M. Lamb (ed.), *Nontraditional families* (pp. 233–288). Hillsdale, NJ: Erlbaum.

Heynes, B. (1978). *Summer learning and the effects of schooling.* New York: Academy Press.

Heynes, B. (1982). *The influence of parents' work on children's school achievement.* In S. B. Kamerman & D. C. Hayes (eds.), *Families that work: Children in a changing world* (pp. 229–267). Washington, DC: National Academy Press.

Heynes, B., & Catsambis, S. (1986). Mother's employment and children's achievement: A critique. *Sociology of Education, 59,* 140–151.

Hightower, A. D., Work, W. C., Cowen, E. L., Lotyczewski, B. S., Spinell, A. P., Guare, J. C., & Rohrbeck, C. A. (1986). The teacher-child rating scale: A brief objective measure of elementary children's school problem behaviors and competence. *School Psychology Review, 15,* 393–409.

Hill, C. R., & Stafford, F. P. (1980). Parental care of children: Time diary estimates of quantity, predictability, and variety. *Journal of Human Resources, 15,* 219–289.

Hock, E. (1980). Working and nonworking mothers and their infants: A comparative study of maternal care-giving characteristics and infant social behavior. *Merrill-Palmer Quarterly, 26,* 79–101.

Hock, E., & DeMeis, D. (1990). Depression in mothers of infants: The role of maternal employment. *Developmental Psychology, 26,* 285–291.

Hoepfner, R., J. Wellisch, and H. Zagorski (1977). *The sample for the sustaining effects study and projections of its characteristics to the national population.* Santa Monica: System Development Corp.

Hofferth, S., Brayfield, A., Deich, S., & Holcomb, P. (1991). *National child care survey. 1990.* Washington, DC: Urban Institute.

Hofferth, S., West, J., & Henke, R. (1994). *Access to early childhood programs for children at* risk. Washington, DC: National Center for Educational Statistics.

Hoffman, L. W. (1961). Effects of maternal employment on the child. *Child Development, 32,* 187–197.

Hoffman, L. W. (1972). Early childhood experiences and women's achievement motives. *Journal of Social Issues, 28,* 129–156.

Hoffman, L. W. (1974). Effects of maternal employment on the child – a review of the research. *Developmental Psychology, 10,* 204–228.

Hoffman, L. W. (1977). Changes in family roles, socialization, and sex differences. *American Psychologist, 32,* 644–657.

Hoffman, L. W. (1979). Maternal employment: 1979. *American Psychologist, 34,* 859–865.

Hoffman, L. W. (1980). Effects of maternal employment on children's academic motivation and performance. *School Psychology Review, (Special issue), 9,* 319–335.

Hoffman, L. W. (1983). Increased fathering: Effects on the mother. In M. Lamb & A. Sagi (eds.), *Fatherhood and family policy* (pp. 167–190). Hillside, NJ: Erlbaum Press.

Hoffman, L. W. (1984a). Maternal employment and the young child. In M. Perlmutter (ed.), *Parent-child interaction and child development. The Minnesota Symposia on Child Psychology* (Vol. 17, pp. 101–127). Hillsdale, NJ: Erlbaum.

Hoffman, L. W. (1984b). The study of employed mothers over half a century. In M. Lewin (ed.), *In the shadow of the past: Psychology portrays the sexes* (pp. 295–320) New York: Columbia University Press.

Hoffman, L. W. (1984c). Work, family, and the socialization of the child. In R. D. Parke (ed.), *The family: Review of child development research* (Vol. 7, pp. 223–282). Chicago: University of Chicago Press.

Hoffman, L. W. (1986). Work, family and the child. In M. S. Pallak & R. O. Perloff (eds.), *Psychology and work* (pp. 169–220). Washington, DC: American Psychological Association.

Hoffman, L. W. (1989). Effects of maternal employment in the two-parent family: A review of the recent research. *American Psychologist, 44,* 283–292.

Hoffman, L. W. (1991). Afterword. In J. Lerner & M. Galambos (eds.), *The employment of mothers during the childrearing years* (pp. 283–290). New York: Garland.

Hoffman, L. W., & Kloska, D. D. (1995). Parents' gender-based attitudes toward marital roles and child rearing: Development and validation of new measures. *Sex Roles, 32,* 273–295.

Hoffman, L. W., & Lippitt, R. (1960). The measurement of family life variables. In P. Mussen (ed.), *Handbook of research methods in child development.* New York: Wiley, 945–1013.

Hoffman, L. W., & Nye, F. I. (1974). *Working mothers.* San Francisco: Jossey-Bass.

Hoffman, M. L. (1988). Moral development. In M. H. Bornstein & M. E. Lamb (eds.), *Developmental Psychology.* Hillsdale, NJ: Erlbaum.

Hollingshead, A. B. (1970). *Four-factor index of social status.* Unpublished manuscript, Department of Sociology, Yale University, New Haven, Conn.

Holtzman, E. H., & Gilbert, L. A. (1987). Social support networks for parenting and psychological well-being among dual-earner Mexican-American families. *Journal of Community Psychology, 15,* 176–186.

Huston, A. C. (1985). The development of sex typing. *Developmental Review, 5,* 1–17.

Hymel, S., & Rubin, K. (1985). Children with peer relationship and social skills problems: Conceptual, methodological, and developmental issues. In G. J. Whitehurst (ed.), *Annals of child development* (Vol. 2, pp. 251–297). Greenwich, CT: JAI.

Kessler, R. C., & McRae, J. A., Jr. (1982). The effects of wives' employment on the mental health of married men and women. *American Sociological Review, 47,* 216–227.

Kessler, R. C., Turner, J. B., & House, J. S. (1989). Unemployment, reemployment, and emotional functioning in a community sample. *American Sociological Review, 54,* 648–657.

Kinard, E. M., & Reinherz, H. (1984). Marital disruption: Effects of behavioral and emotional functioning in children. *Journal of Family Issues, 5,* 90–115.

Kliewer, W. (1991). Coping in middle childhood: Relations to competence, Type A behavior, monitoring, blunting, and locus of control. *Developmental Psychology, 27,* 689–697.

Kliewer, W., & Sandler, I. N. (1992). Locus of control and self-esteem as moderators of stressor-symptom relations in children and adolescents. *Journal of Abnormal Child Psychology, 20,* 393–413.

Kohn, M. L. (1963). Social class and parent-child relationships: An interpretation. *American Journal of Sociology, 68,* 471–480.

Kovacs, D. M. (1996). Ethnicity and socioeconomic status in elementary school: a compatison of children's peer relationships in three socioculturally diverse classroom settings. Unpublished doctoral dissertation, University of Michigan, Ann Arbor.

Kovacs, D. M., Parker, J. G., & Hoffman, L. W. (1996). Behavioral, affective, and social correlates of involvement in cross-sex friendship in elementary school. *Child Development, 67,* 2269–2286.

Kriesberg, L. (1970). *Mothers in poverty: A study of fatherless families.* Chicago: Aldine.

Lamb, M. E. (1981). Fathers and child development: An integrative overview. In M. E. Lamb (ed.), *The father's role in child development* (rev. ed., pp. 1–90). New York: Wiley.

Lamb, M. & Sternberg, K. (1990). Do we really know how day-care affects children? *Journal of Applied Developmental Psychology, 11,* 351–379.

Locke, H. J., & Wallace, K. M. (1959). Short marital-adjustment and prediction tests: Their reliability and validity. *Marriage and Family Living, 21,* 251–255.

Lyons-Ruth, K. (1995). Broadening our conceptual frameworks: Can we reintroduce relational strategies and implicit representational systems to the study of psychopathology? *Developmental Psychology, 31,* 432–436.

MacKinnon, C. E., Brody, G. H., & Stoneman, Z. (1982). The effects of divorce and maternal employment on the home environments of pre-school children. *Child Development, 53,* 1392–1399.

McCartney, K., & Rosenthal, S. (1991). Maternal employment should be studied within social ecologies. *Journal of Marriage and the Family, 53,* 1103–1107.

McCord, J., McCord, W., & Thurber, E. (1963). Effects of maternal employment on lower-class boys. *Journal of Abnormal and Social Psychology, 67,* 177–182.

McLoyd, V. C. (1990). The impact of economic hardship on black families and children: Psychological distress, parenting, and socioemotional development. *Child Development, 61,* 311–346.

McLoyd, V. C. (1993). Employment among African American mothers in dual-earner families: Antecedents and consequences for family life and child development. In S. Frankel (ed.), *The employed mother and the family context* (pp. 180–226). New York: Springer Publishing Co.

McLoyd, V. C., Jayaratne, T. E., Ceballo, R., & Borquez, J. (1994). Unemployment and work interruption among African American single mothers: Effects on parenting and adolescent socioemotional functioning. *Child Development, 65,* 562–589.

Medrich, E. A., Roizen, J. A., Rubin, V., & Buckley, S. (1982). *The serious business of growing up.* Berkeley: University of California Press.

Menaghan, E. G., & Parcel, T. L. (1990). Parental employment and family life: Research in the 1980's. *Journal of Marriage and the Family, 57,* 69–84.

Menaghan, E. G., & Parcel, T. L. (1995). Social sources of change in children's home environments: The effects of parental occupational experiences and family conditions. *Journal of Marriage and the Family, 57,* 69–84.

Messaris, P., & Hornik, R. C. (1983). In C. D. Hayes & S. B. Kamerman (eds.), *Children of working parents* (pp. 44–72). Washington, DC: National Academy Press.

Miller, S. M. (1975). Effects of maternal employment in sex-role perception, interests, and self-esteem in kindergarten girls. *Developmental Psychology, 11,* 405–406.

Miller, D. R., & Swanson, G. E. (1958). *The changing American parent.* New York: Wiley.

Milne, A. M., Myers, D. E., Rosenthal, A. S., & Ginsburg, A. (1986). Single parents, working mothers, and the educational achievement of school children. *Sociology of Education, 59,* 125–139.

Model, S. (1981). Housework by husbands. *Journal of Family Issues, 2,* 225–237.

Moore, T. W. (1975). Exclusive early mothering and its alternatives: The outcome to adolescence. *Scandanavian Journal of Psychology, 16,* 255–272.

Moorehouse, M. J. (1991). Linking maternal employment patterns to mother–child activities and children's school competence. *Developmental Psychology, 27,* 295–303.

Moos, R. H., & Moos, B. S. (1981). *Family Environment Scale Manual.* Palo Alto, CA: Consulting Psychologists Press.

National Opinion Research Center (1980). *High school and beyond information for users, base year (1980) data. Report to the National Center for Education Statistics.* Chicago: National Opinion Research Center.

NICHD Early Child Care Research Network (1994). Child care and child development: The NICHD Study of Early Child Care. In S. L. Friendman & H. C. Haywood (eds.), *Developmental follow-up: Concepts, domains, and methods* (pp. 377–396). San Diego, CA: Academic Press.

NICHD Early Child Care Research Network (1996a). Characteristics of infant child care: Factors contributing to positive caregiving. *Early Childhood Research Quarterly, 11,* 269–306.

NICHD Early Child Care Research Network (1996b, April). Infant child care and attachment security: Results of the NICHD Study of early child care. Symposium presented at the International Conference on Infant Studies, Providence, RI.

NICHD Early Child Care Research Network (1997a). Familial factors associated with the characteristics of nonmaternal care for infants. *Journal of Marriage and the Family, 59,* 389–408.

NICHD Early Child Care Research Network (1997b). The effects of infant child care on infant-mother attachment security: Results of the NICHD Study of Early Child Care. *Child Development, 68,* 860–879.

NICHD Early Child Care Research Network (1997c). *Mother–child interaction and cognitive outcomes associated with early child care: Results of the NICHD study.* Posters presented at the biennial meetings of the Society for Research on Child Development, Washington, DC: April 1997.

NICHD Early Child Care Research Network. (1997d). Child care in the first year of life. *Merrill-Palmer Quarterly, 43,* 340–360.

NICHD Early Child Care Research Network. (1998). Early child care and self-control, compliance, and problem behavior at 24 and 36 months. *Child Development, 69,* 1145–1170.

Nowicki, S., & Barnes, J. (1973). Effects of a structured camp experience on locus of control orientation. *Journal of Genetic Psychology, 122,* 247–252.

Nowicki, S., & Strickland, B. R. (1973). A locus of control scale for children. *Journal of Consulting and Clinical Psychology, 40,* 148–154.

Nye, F. I., & Hoffman, L. W. (1963). *The employed mother in America.* Chicago: Rand

Owen, M. T., & Cox, M. J. (1988). Maternal employment and the transition to parenthood: family functioning and child development. In A. E. Gottfried & A. W. Gottfried (eds.), *Maternal employment and children's development: Longitudinal research* (pp. 85–119). New York: Plenum.

Parcel, T. L., & Menaghan, E. G. (1994). *Parents' jobs and children's lives.* New York: Walter de Gruyter, Inc.

Pedersen, F. A., Cain, R., Zaslow, M., Anderson, B. (1982). Variation in infant experience associated with alternative family role organization. In L. Laosa & I. Sigel (eds.), *Families as learning environments for children* (pp. 87–95). New York: Plenum.

Phillips, D. A., Voran, M., Kisker, E., Howes, C., & Whitebrook, M. (1994). Child care for children in poverty: Opportunity or inequity? *Child Development, 65,* 472–492.

Pleck, J. H. (1983). Husbands' paid work and family roles: Current research issues. In H. Z. Lopata & J. H. Pleck (eds.), *Research in the interweave of social roles: Families and jobs* (pp. 251–333). Greenwich, CT: JAI press.

Posner, J. K., & Vandell, D. L. (1994). Low-income children's after-school care: Are there effects of after-school programs? *Child Development, 65,* 440–456.

Radloff, L. (1977). The CES-D scale: A self-report depression scale for research in the general population. *Applied Psychological Measurement, 1,* 385–401.

Radloff, L. S. (1980). Depression and the empty nest. *Sex Roles, 6,* 775–782.

Repetti, R. L. (1985). *The social environment at work and psychological well-being.* Unpublished doctoral dissertation. Yale University, New Haven, CT.

Repetti, R. L., & Crosby, F. (1984). Gender and depression: Exploring the adult role explanation. *Journal of Social and Clinical Psychology, 2,* 57–70.

Repetti, R. L., Mathews, K. A., Waldron, I. (1989). Employment and women's health: Effects of paid employment on women's mental and physical health. *American Psychologist, 44,* 1394–1401.

Richards, M. H., & Duckett, E. (1991). Maternal Employment and adolescents. In J. V. Lerner, & N. L. Galambos (eds.), *Employed mothers and their children* (pp. 85–130). New York: Garland Press.

Rieber, M., & Womach, M. (1967). The intelligence of preschool children as related to ethnic and demographic variables. *Exceptional Children, 34,* 609–614.

Robinson, J. P., & Shaver, P. R. (1973). *Measures of psychological attitudes.* Ann Arbor, MI: Survey Research Center, Institute for Social Research.

Rodman, H., Pratto, D. J., & Nelson, R. S. (1985). Child care arrangements and children's functioning: A comparison of self-care and adult-care children. *Developmental Psychology, 21,* 413–418.

Rosen, E. I. (1987). *Bitter choices: Blue collar women in and out of work.* Chicago: University of Chicago Press.

Rosenfeld, S. (1989). The effects of women's employment: Personal control and sex differences in mental health. *Journal of Health and Social Behavior, 30,* 77–91.

Ross, C. E., Mirowsky, J., & Huber, J. (1983). Dividing work, sharing work, and in-between: Marriage patterns and depression. *American Sociological Review, 48,* 809–823.

Rutter, M. (1990). Commentary: Some focus and process considerations regarding effects of parental depression on children. *Developmental Psychology, 26,* 60–67.

Scanzoni, J. H. (1978). *Sex roles, women's work, and marital conflict.* Lexington, MA: Heath.

Schachter, F. (1981). Toddlers with employed mothers. *Child Development, 52,* 958–964.

Schubert, J. B., Bradley-Johnson, S., & Nuttal, J. (1980). Mother-infant communication and maternal employment. *Child Development, 51,* 246–249.

Schwartz, P. (1983). Length of day care attendance and attachment behavior in 18-month-old infants. *Child Development, 54,* 1073–1078.

Siegel, A. E., Stolz, L., Hitchcock, E., & Adamson, J. (1963). Dependence and independence in children. In F. I. Nye & L. W. Hoffman (eds.), *The employed mother in America,* Westport, CT: Greenwood Press.

Signorella, M. L., & Liben, L. S. (1985). Assessing children's gender-stereotyped attitudes. *Psychological Documents, 15,* 7.

Smith, D. S. (1985). Wife employment and marital adjustment: Accumulation of results. *Family Relations, 34,* 483–490.

Sobel, M. E. (1982). Asymptotic confidence intervals for indirect effects in structural equation models. In S. Leinhard (ed.), *Sociological methodology, 1982* (pp. 290–312). San Francisco: Jossey-Bass.

Sroufe, A., & Waters, E. (1977). Heart rate as a convergent measure in clinical and developmental research. *Merrill-Palmer Quarterly, 23,* 5–25.

Stack, C. B. (1974). *All our kin: Strategies for survival in a Black community.* New York: Harper & Row.

Staines, G. L., Pleck, J. H., Shepard, L. J., & O'Connor, P. (1978). Wives' employment status and marital adjustment: Yet another look. *Psychology of Women Quarterly, 3,* 90–120.

Steinberg, L. (1986). Latchkey children and susceptibility to peer pressure: An ecological analysis. *Developmental Psychology, 22,* 433–439.

Stevenson, N. G. (1982). *The role of maternal employment and satisfaction level in children's cognitive performance.* Unpublished doctoral dissertation, University of Michigan, Ann Arbor.

Stewart, A. J., & Malley, J. E. (1987). Role combination in women: Mitigating agency and communion. In F. Crosby (ed.), *Spouse, parent, worker* (pp. 44–62). New Haven, CT: Yale University Press.

Stewart, A. J., & Salt, P. (1981). Life stress, life styles, depression and illness in adult women. *Journal of Personality and Social Psychology, 40,* 1063–1069.

Stuckey, M. R., McGhee, P. E., & Bell, N. J. (1982). Parent-child interaction: The influence of maternal employment. *Developmental Psychology, 18,* 635–644.

Thompson, R. A. (1981). *Continuity and change in socioemotional development during the second year.* Unpublished doctoral dissertation, University of Michigan, Ann Arbor.

Thompson, M. S., & Ensminger, M. E. (1989). Psychological well-being among mothers with school age children: Evolving family structures. *Social Forces, 67,* 715–730.

U. S. Bureau of the Census (1995). Current population survey, March, 1995. (Special tabulation request).

U. S. Bureau of the Census (1997). *Statistical abstract of the United States (112th ed.).* Washington, DC: U. S. Government Printing Office.

U. S. Department of Education (October, 1995). *Statistics in brief: Child care and early education program participation of infants, toddlers and preschoolers* (NCES 95-824). Washington DC: U.S. Department of Education.

Valdez, E. O., & Coltrane, S. (1993). Work, family, and the Chicana: Power, perception, and equity. In J. Frankel (ed.), *The employed mother and the family context* (pp. 153–179). New York: Springer.

Vandell, D. L. (1991). Belsky and Eggebeen's analysis of the NLSY: Meaningful results or statistical illusions? *Journal of Marriage and the Family, 53,* 1100–1103.

Vandell, D. L. & Corasaniti, M. A. (1988). The relation between third graders' after-school care and social, academic, and emotional functioning. *Child Development, 59,* 868–875.

Vandell, D. L., & Corasaniti, M. A. (1990). Child care and the family: Complex contributors to child development. In K. McCartney (ed.), *New directions in child development research* (pp. 23–37). San Francisco: Jossey-Bass.

Vandell, D. L., & Ramanan, J. (1990). *Effects of early and concurrent maternal employment on children from economically disadvantaged families.* Paper presented at the International Conference on Infant Studies, Montreal, Canada.

Vandell, D. L., & Ramanan, J. (1991). Children of the national longitudinal survey of youth: Choices in after-school care and child development. *Developmental Psychology, 27,* 637–643.

Vandell, D. L., & Ramanan, J. (1992). Effects of early and recent maternal employment on children from low-income families. *Child Development, 63,* 938–949.

Vaughn, B. E., Deane, K. E., & Waters, E. (1985). The impact of out-of-home care on child-mother attachment quality: Another look at some enduring questions. In I.

Bretherton & E. Waters (eds.), *Growing points of attachment theory and research.* Monographs of the Society for Research in Child Development, 55 (1–2, Serial No. 209).

Vaughn, B. E., Gove, F. I. & Egelund, B. (1980). The relationship between out-of-home-care and the quality of infant-mother attachment in an economically disadvantaged population. *Child Development, 51,* 1203–1214.

Verbugge, L. (1987). Role burdens and physical health of women and men. In F. Crosby (ed.), *Spouse, parent, worker.* New Haven, CT: Yale University Press.

Veroff, J., Douvan, E., Kukla, R. (1981). *The inner American: A self-portrait from 1957 to 1976.* New York: Basic Books.

Waldron, I., & Jacobs, J. A. (1989). Effects of labor force participation on women's health – New evidence from a longitudinal study. *Journal of Occupational Medicine, 30,* 977–983.

Warr, P., & Parry, G. (1982a). Depressed mood in working-class mothers with and without paid employment. *Social Psychiatry, 17,* 161–165.

Warr, P., & Parry, G. (1982b). Paid employment and women's psychological well-being. *Psychological Bulletin, 91,* 498–516.

Weinraub, M., & Jaeger, E. (1990). The timing of mothers' return to the workplace: Effects on the developing mother–child relationship. In J. S. Hyde & M. J. Essex (eds.), *Parental leave and child care: Setting a research and policy agenda.* Philadelphia: Temple University Press.

Weinraub, M., Jaeger, E., & Hoffman, L. W. (1988). Predicting infant outcome in families of employed and non-employed mothers. *Early Childhood Research Quarterly, 3,* 361–378.

Weinraub, M., & Wolf, B. M (1983). Effects of stress and social supports on mother-child interactions in single- and two-parent families, *Child Development, 54,* 1297–1311.

West, J., Wright, D., & Hausken, E. G. (1995). *Child care and early education program participation of infants, toddlers, and preschoolers.* Washington, DC: National Center for Educational Statistics.

Willer, B., Hofferth, S. L., Kisker, E. E., Divine-Hawkins, P., Farquhar, E., & Glantz, F. B. (1991). *The demand and supply of child care in 1990.* Washington, DC: National Association for the Education of Young Children.

Woods, M. B. (1972). The unsupervised child of the working mother. *Developmental Psychology, 6,* 14–25.

Yarrow, L. (1964). Separation from parents during early childhood. In M. L. Hoffman & L. W. Hoffman (eds.), *Review of child development research* (Vol. 1, pp. 89–136). New York: Russell Sage Foundation.

Yarrow, L. (1979). Emotional development. *American Psychologist, 34,* 951–957.

Yarrow, M. R., Scott, P., Deleeuw, L., and Heinig, C. (1962). Child-rearing in families of working and nonworking mothers. *Sociometry, 25,* 122–140.

Zahn-Waxler, C. (1995). Introduction to special section: Parental depression and distress: Implications for development in infancy, childhood, and adolescence. *Developmental Psychology, 31,* 347–348.

Zaslow, M. (1987). *Sex differences in children's response to maternal employment.* Unpublished manuscript, prepared for the Committee on Child Development Research and Public Policy, National Research Council, Washington, DC.

Zaslow, M., Pederson, F. A., Suwalsky, J. T. D., Cain, R. L., & Fivel, M. (1985). The early resumption of employment by mothers: Implications for parent–infant interaction. *Journal of Applied Developmental Pcychology, 6,* 1–16.

Zaslow, M., Pedersen, F. A., Suwalsky, J. T. D., and Rabinovich, B. (1983, April). *Maternal employment and parent-infant interaction at one year.* Paper presented at the biennial meetings of the Society for Research in Child Development, Detroit, MI.

Author Index

Subject Index

academic achievement, 5, 16–8, 89, 152, 154, 156, 161, 164, 168, 173, 174, 179–92, 194–207, 218, 221–3, 227, 236, 238–9, 239–40, 245–6, 249–50, 254, 268, 270, 273, 274–5, 281–3, 286, 289, 290
   daughter-specific hypothesis, 5, 7, 8–9, 19–20, 26, 88–90, 101, 174, 175, 183, 187, 197–204, 205–7, 240
   measure of, 38, 43, 154, 211, 231
   motivation for, 7, 13, 16–9, 23
   parent's expectations for, 122, 138–41, 147–9, 228, 229, 238, 240, 245–6, 250, 286, 289, 290
   (*see also* cognitive competence; school performance)
acting-out, 158, 168, 171–2, 218, 220, 221, 232, 234, 247–9, 250, 253, 287, 289, 290–1
   (*see also* aggression)
after-school care, 5, 23, 28, 47, 58, 258, 262, 266, 267–9
   effects on children, 262, 267–9
age, children's, 29–30, 257–8, 260, 264–6
aggressiveness, 154, 158, 163, 168, 173, 218, 219, 220, 232, 234–5, 268, 269, 273
   and early employment, 170–3, 261–2
assertiveness, positive, 160, 163, 166, 169, 218, 219, 240, 242, 244, 254, 255, 287–8, 289, 291
   (*see also* independence)

autonomy-granting (*see* maturity demands)

behavior, teacher ratings of, 154, 156, 158–60, 163, 166, 168, 171–2, 173, 181, 218–21, 222, 232–5, 236, 238, 239, 240, 242, 246–9, 250, 254, 268–9, 273, 274–5, 287–8, 289, 290–1
   measure of, 42–3, 211

child care, 10, 46, 58, 59, 60, 172, 173, 256
   and child's age, 257–8, 260, 264–6
   and variations in work patterns, 63–4
   child-care centers 58, 256, 258, 259, 261, 264–6, 268–9
   (*see also* after-school care; daycare; nonmaternal care; self care)
child gender, 1, 4, 5, 8–9, 13, 19–20, 70–1, 84–5, 88, 89, 101, 129, 132–4, 135, 138–43, 146, 147, 148–9, 150, 152–3, 154–66, 173, 174–5, 180–3, 184–7, 193–207, 209, 212, 213–4, 216–8, 221, 226, 229, 232–4, 235–6, 236–8, 239, 240–2, 244, 245, 246–9, 250, 253–5, 264–6, 272, 274–5, 281–3, 285, 286–8
   explanation of study results for daughters, 289
   explanation of study results for sons, 289–91